Holistic Anthropology

Methodology and History in Anthropology

General Editor: David Parkin, Institute of Social and Cultural Anthropology, University of Oxford

HOLISTIC ANTHROPOLOGY

EMERGENCE AND CONVERGENCE

Edited by

David Parkin and Stanley Ulijaszek

Berghahn Books
New York • Oxford

First published in 2007 by
Berghahn Books
www.berghahnbooks.com

©2007, 2011 David Parkin and Stanley Ulijaszek
First paperback edition published in 2011

Library of Congress Cataloging-in-Publication Data

Holistic anthropology : emergence and convergence / edited by David
Parkin and Stanley Ulijaszek.
    p. cm. -- Methodology and history in anthropology ; v. 16
Includes bibliographical references and index.
ISBN 978-1-84545-354-1 (hbk) -- ISBN 978-0-85745-152-1 (pbk)
1. Anthropology. 2. Holism. I. Parkin, David J. II. Ulijaszek, Stanley J.

GN25 .H63 2007
301--dc22
                                                    2007039216

British Library Cataloguing in Publication Data

A catalogue record for this book is available from the British Library

Printed in United States on acid-free paper

ISBN 978-1-84545-354-1 (hardback)
ISBN 978-0-85745-152-1 (paperback)
ISBN 978-0-85745-319-8 (ebook)

CONTENTS

LIST OF FIGURES AND TABLES

Figures

Tables

LIST OF CONTRIBUTORS

Robin Dunbar, British Academy Centenary Research Project, School of Biological Sciences, University of Liverpool, Crown Street, Liverpool L69 7ZB. From October 2007, Professor of Evolutionary Anthropology, School of Anthropology, University of Oxford.

Chris Gosden, Institute of Archaeology, University of Oxford, 34–36 Beaumont Street, Oxford OX1 2PH.

Elisabeth Hsu, Institute of Social and Cultural Anthropology, University of Oxford, 51 Banbury Road, Oxford OX2 6PF.

Tim Ingold, Department of Anthropology, School of Social Science, University of Aberdeen, Aberdeen AB25 2DA, Scotland.

Howard Morphy, Centre for Cross-Cultural Research, College of Arts and Social Sciences, Australian National University, Canberra ACT 0200, Australia.

David Parkin, Institute of Social and Cultural Anthropology, University of Oxford, 51 Banbury Road, Oxford OX2 6PF.

Laura Peers, Institute of Social and Cultural Anthropology, University of Oxford, 51 Banbury Road, Oxford OX2 6PF, and Pitt Rivers Museum, University of Oxford, South Parks Road, Oxford OX1 3PP.

Laura Rival, Department of International Development, Queen Elizabeth House, University of Oxford, 3 Mansfield Road, Oxford OX1 3TB.

Stanley Ulijaszek, Institute of Social and Cultural Anthropology, University of Oxford, 51 Banbury Road, Oxford OX2 6PF.

Harvey Whitehouse, Institute of Social and Cultural Anthropology, University of Oxford, 51 Banbury Road, Oxford OX2 6PF.

PREFACE

The broad reach of anthropology as the science of humankind has inevitably meant that there are times when the subject fragments into specialisms and times when there is rapprochement. Rather than just seeing them as reactions to each other, it is perhaps better to say that both tendencies co-exist and that it is very much a matter of perspective as to which is dominant at any moment. The perspective adopted by the contributors to this volume is that some anthropologists have, over the last decade or so, been paying considerable attention to developments in the study of social and biological evolution and of material culture, and that this has brought social, material cultural and biological anthropologists closer to each other and closer to allied disciplines such as archaeology and psychology. It is thereafter a matter of debate as to whether anthropology in the broader sense appropriates and incorporates findings from these other subjects and then moves on more richly endowed or whether it transacts its ideas piecemeal, so to speak, with other disciplines, each of which retains its distinctive boundaries. The difference is itself one of methodological standpoint. We could say that a more eclectic anthropology once characteristic of an earlier age is re-emerging, which has something in common with the so-called four-fields approach associated with the United States. The long-established American version has, by popular report, often been at the basis of departmental factionalism, as a result of different funding demands and allocations, with the biological, material and museological allegedly more costly than the social. If that is in fact what has happened, then it is possible that a similar fate awaits those British and other European departments that try to broaden their range of anthropology. On the other hand, it has not evidently happened in, say, the very few universities in the United Kingdom where anthropology of this wide reach is well established. Distinctive funding and recruitment practices encouraging cross-disciplinary collaboration may partly account for the resilience. But it is difficult also not to recognise the sheer enthusiasm among a number of anthropologists who wish to see, for example, social organisation as fundamentally a problem of human ecology and, from that, of human biology and, further, of co-evolution.

This second sense is not just of anthropology picking up its fragmented and dispersed pieces, some of them accredited to other disciplines, and putting them together again. It is of social anthropology itself widening its scope and understanding of the social to include all these other aspects. The key word in this volume taken to depict this process, is holism which, as no more than an odd-job word, can enjoy a short moment of interrogation and revelation before it is returned to the banality of meaning too many things. What it describes, however, is not banal. It is an attempt to understand human activities, claims and beliefs as part of a much wider intellectual interest within and beyond anthropology. This sometimes shades from the academic to the popular, and sometimes draws on inferential reasoning and on speculative as well as 'hard' evidence. We can say that some social anthropologists have expanded their methodological remit to include what was previously regarded as non-social, and that some biological anthropologists have gone in the other direction. Or we can simply call them all anthropologists *tout court*. It is however prolonged, intensive and linguistically-informed fieldwork and comparison that in the end give anthropology its primary data for theoretical use in all its branches, and so provide a special handle on how a new, holistic study of humankind may develop.

Thanks are due to Exeter College, University of Oxford for permission to allow the annual Marret Lecture to be presented as part of the Oxford Anthropology Centenary Conference in September 2005, on which this volume is based. The editors also thank the Royal Anthropological Institute, the British Academy and the Oxford University Life and Environmental Studies Division for contributing to the funds needed for the conference. Thanks are also due to Rohan Jackson for his considerable organisational skills.

Gina Burrows is owed an enormous debt of gratitude both by the four hundred or so who attended the Oxford Anthropology Centenary Conference at St Hughes College, Oxford, and by the editors and contributors to this volume and its companion, on the history of anthropology at Oxford University, edited by Peter Rivière. Over the months beforehand, and during the conference itself, she ensured that the event ran smoothly, certainly carrying out tasks and spending time well beyond the call of duty. This commitment then extended to the volume itself, whose bibliography she collated and checked with the editors.

David Parkin and Stanley Ulijaszek

EMERGENCE AND CONVERGENCE

David Parkin

To argue for holism is to state the obvious in anthropology. With its inductive method as starting-point, and its attempt to explain an encountered pattern, it has after all to take account of all that it observes and hears in fieldwork, while gradually honing its field data to address a recognisable problem in the discipline. Yet, as it is used in the literature, holism has many senses. There is, to begin with, conceptual divergence arising from the Greek term *hólos*, whole or entire. The Greek term denotes wholeness, or synonyms such as entirety, all-inclusiveness or completeness primarily as a matter of fact. There is no particular moral or judgemental loading, except in the limited sense that things which are complete and undivided are presumed to be the normal, natural or virtuous state. The Germanic form, holy, extends the notion of virtuous completeness or all-inclusiveness and imputes characteristics of divine omniscience, omnipotence and judgement, so setting up morality. It is thus intrinsically concerned with judgement.

The modern sense of holism (i.e. wholism) in philosophy and the social and human sciences flirts with both connotations of factual description and moral judgement. Confining discussion to some well-known tenets of anthropology, Durkheim's sociological legacy to Radcliffe-Brown was to see early or pre-industrial society as deified totality, by which fundamental moral and social rules were followed more by their ritual and religiously prescribed nature than by whether or not they satisfied the canons of rational calculation. Yet another legacy was the analysis of social solidarity as either organic or mechanical. The ascription of purpose to social institutions carried the image away from society as premised on God to that of a mechanically or organically functioning whole made possible by the workings of its constituent parts. The metaphorical duality of mechanism-organism and morality has characterised holism ever since in anthropology. This division itself echoes that occurring somewhat earlier between two approaches to the study of society, with so-called natural science concerned with mechanical and organic or anatomical order, and the humanities addressing moral and religious order. The persistence of such epistemological dualism made it inevitable that Radcliffe-Brown's scientific claim that social are also natural laws should in due course be followed by Evans-Pritchard's contrary claim that social anthropology be regarded as one of the humanities.

The dualism extends as well as persists. Of the two senses of holism, that of society as a whole being made up of functioning parts parallels a wider idea of the discipline of anthropology itself. As is well known, in early twentieth-century America, the four-fields approach in anthropology comprised the complementary study of social and material culture, physical anthropology, archaeology and linguistics, with Boas the principal architect, noted for his advocacy of cultural relativism and his criticism of orthogenetic evolutionism (Silverman 2005: 261–65). Earlier, there had been in nineteenth-century Europe the seamless holism of natural history and natural philosophy that had not yet been divided into sharply separated, named disciplines. In Britain, Tylor's similarly comprehensive view of culture included the material, ideational, social, and, in some respects and indirectly, biology. Nevertheless, with other scholars, he distinguished anthropology from psychology and biology, though anthropology at Oxford was at one point located in the Department of Anatomy. The later British view, still prevalent today, derived from Durkheim and Radcliffe-Brown. It refused to incorporate other disciplines within a wider remit of the subject and to draw sharp boundaries between them. Concessions were made, as in Gluckman's edited volume of 1964, allowing the abridgement and incorporation of individual conclusions from other disciplines but not analysis of them as such, the intention of which was to reaffirm social anthropology as a coherent, rigorously rule-based, and methodologically distinctive discipline. This remains today for many anthropologists a methodological basis of the subject. While partly originating in the functional social holism of Durkheim and Radcliffe-Brown, it has run alongside Marxist and Weberian paradigms and, more specifically, the structuralist and interpretive holism of Lévi-Strauss and Geertz respectively, the first decoding and the second creating webs of social meaning, both now rarely distinguished as such and yet implicit in modern studies to varying degrees.

The holism of structuralism and that of interpretivism has in each case more in common with the idea of society as God than as machine or organism. Any attention paid to internally functioning parts perpetuating the whole is secondary rather than primary. Rather, it is the seamlessness of matter making up the whole that is emphasised, an expression of the universal human mind in structuralism and boundless meaning-making emanating from a general human creativity in interpretivism. Socio-cultural practices, beliefs and institutions are subsumed in the *fons et origo* of mind and creativity, which thus take the place of God. Extending the analogy further, seamless holism also sometimes describes religious cosmologies allegedly different from western explanation (Cooper 1996: 206–11).

At this point, we may be forgiven for thinking that holism seems to refer to any approach that embraces an undivided view of society and humanity, and so has little analytical worth. It may even seem at times to make comparison difficult. After all, if a society, or society generally, or humanity, or religion, are internally seamless but externally marked wholes, then you might think that it is only by placing boundaries between them that they can be compared. And yet hardly anyone nowadays subscribes to this view of the consistently demarcated society or culture, preferring the analysis of human activity clusters and movements across shifting, situational and imagined or temporarily traced distinctions and frontiers. To the idiom of 'pick and mix' are joined 'flow and flux' as prevalent glosses on human and social variation. Nevertheless, the invitation to the contributors to this volume to consider holism in anthropology has resulted in not only a diversity of claims for its value, but some critical thinking about it as a viable concept. Ingold, for instance, states strongly that he is against a traditional concept of holism that seeks to bring together discrete parts into a coherent whole. This for him is a form of totalisation. By contrast, his thesis is to describe social and personal life as on-going, organically open, expanding in different, criss-crossing and unpredictable directions, which are interconnected but not constrained by the configuration of a totalising whole. An early idea of the 'moving-together' of knowledge and action, which we in effect 'make up as we go along' (Parkin 1984), was undoubtedly influenced by the post-modernist, anti-essentialist distrust in the 1970s and 1980s of the idea that socio-cultural phenomena could be regarded as analytically isolable, bounded and cordoned off from each other. Such phenomena were rather seen as currents of discourse that inevitably flowed into each other. In his developing exploration of 'lines', however, Ingold takes the organic analogy further, seeing the world as one of 'movement and becoming, in which any thing, caught at a particular moment, enfolds within its own constitution the history of relations that brought it there'. He sees the life-course as converging and diverging bundles of lines, and constantly travelling 'along the paths of its relations'. Indeed, life and line as open-ended, developing organisms is no less metaphorical than much description in biology itself, his preferred primary image for biology being that of the fungal mycelium (rather than cellular construction) which echoes that of social life as an ever-ramifying web of lines of growth.

While this idea of holism as a process of enfoldment and, at the same time, exploration, is an attempt to describe what actually happens in life-courses, there is another 'linear' sense in which we can think of holism as process. This is in fact the method by which socio-cultural anthropologists trace connections between ethnographic phenomena and build up a larger picture. Take for instance Morphy's use of painting as his starting-point for an analysis of Australian Yolngu society. In observing a Yolngu painter's cross-hatched lines, he focuses on the *marwat*, the brush of human hair used for painting. It is seen by Yolngu as connecting in turn to the head, the fontanelle, the fountainhead of wisdom, a bodily manifestation of the clan, and hence knowledge of brother–sister avoidance, and thence to concepts of anger and shame counterposed by rules of marriage and intimate association, which in turn connect to ideas of gender relations, the division of labour and violence. One of the distinctive features of anthropological field analysis is this capacity to take almost any cultural practice or statement and to fan out web-like into others, a process partially captured in Geertz's idea of thick description and in fact the holistic method which long-term fieldwork in the local language is most likely to invoke.

An even more comprehensive methodological use of linear development is that proposed by Hsu in her study of what she calls the body ecologic in Chinese medicine. For Hsu the genealogical method is not to be taken in the sense of a trajectory from a point of origin to a known destiny and controlled by regulative mechanisms, as when descent or kinship are recalled and reckoned. She sees genealogy instead in Foucault's sense as being able to uncover different layers of unknown history marked by responses to haphazard conflicts. For instance, a modern view is of Traditional Chinese Medicine as having always used the five agents or elements of wood, fire, earth, metal and water, in explaining illness. But Hsu shows, through linguistic examination of Chinese medical texts at critical points in past dynasties, that there was an earlier ecological view of illness as being associated with particular seasons but that this was superseded by the theory of illnesses as correlating with distinctive agents. The biology of the body ecologic (illness resulting from the body's interaction with seasonal climate and environment) has thus been subsumed within a cultural system of illness explanation which is seen by modern observers as reaching back into history, as having always been there, and therefore as 'natural'. This use of genealogical method is therefore able over time to re-collect different strands in the development of a medical tradition. In comparison, Morphy's thick description is also linear, not however, over time but across the whole canvas of society at present time. Holistic connectedness is evident in both cases, the one through layers of buried concepts and the other through the interconnections of current, customary inference.

Gosden's holistic project starts not from thick description but from western epistemology. Beginning, like Hsu, with the long-established critique of what used to be called the Cartesian dualism of mind and body as each proceeding independently according to its own laws, he dissolves not only this but also such related dichotomies as the social and material, emphasising instead the body as an active and agentive being-in-the-world made up of experience, practice and varying degrees of consciousness, and fused with and expressed through physical as well as social extensions. As an anthropological archaeologist he witnesses a division between those who regard the subject of archaeology as affiliated to classical art and ancient history and those such as himself who straddle anthropology, social reconstruction, biology, and human evolution. The dramatic intellectual developments occurring in this branch of archaeology have blunted the neatness of such disciplinary boundaries. This has happened less out of a self-conscious will on the part of archaeologists to demolish them in the pursuit of the assumed benefits of so-called interdisciplinarity, and more because the questions demanded by discoveries, aided by new technological props, have forced such merging. In this respect, archaeology and anthropology have come home to each other, united by a common interest in life as lines, to use Ingold's metaphor. More generally, there has also been the excitement of what Whitehouse calls 'a veritable explosion of powerful new theories and methods in such fields as neuroscience, genetics, cognitive, developmental, and evolutionary psychology, and linguistics'. To this we may add Dunbar's observation that the intellectual richness of Darwinian evolutionary theory has increasingly in recent times provided the overarching unifying framework for biosciences which were formerly taught separately in university departments. Biochemistry, physiology, botany, zoology and genetics are nowadays often brought together as a single school. The complaints that some of these subjects individually do not attract enough students is counterbalanced by the widespread enthusiasm for Darwinian ideas outside as well as within universities. It has indeed been difficult if not impossible not to be affected by such excitement, much of it communicated to non-specialists in the first instance by the media, sometimes with millennial overtones and undesirable results, as in the probably false expectations raised by the discovery in

Indonesia of the 'Hobbit' (*Homo floresiensis*). And yet it is important that academics do disseminate their ideas through the media, despite such risks. It is, moreover, also from the media that raw ideas sometimes percolate to other academics across disciplines, providing if not precisely usable information then at least an atmosphere in which cross-disciplinary thinking becomes feasible.

Notwithstanding Ingold's idea of holism – inspired by Bohm's *Wholeness and the implicate order* (1980) – as the world of movement and becoming rather than that of disciplines being brought together, it is nevertheless important for the history of ideas for us to dwell on the significant rapprochement of the disciplines that has occurred in recent years, including those of anthropology, archaeology, biology and, as discussed below, ecology and evolutionary psychology. It is significant in that it represents the first major theoretical development in the social sciences and humanities since the post-modern renunciation of the so-called meta-narratives of theory during the 1980s. They were deemed narratives in view of their tendency to act as self-verifying paradigms acting each within their own individual closure, repeatedly telling a story of how they came to be and why they could be justified as bounded. As I have indicated above, the new holism of complementing disciplines has come about not as a result of conscious attempts to meet hollow exhortations for inter- or multi-disciplinarity but in order to tackle cognate problems genuinely requiring the input of other methodologies. It is in fact a case for each discipline of the 'other' coming to its rescue, with (in this case) the other constituting alternative interpretative techniques.[1] Archaeology needs anthropology and biology, biology needs, for example, ecology and political economy (see Goodman and Leatherman 1996), and anthropology needs ecology, and, I would argue, psychology and biology if it is to avoid repeating, admittedly in new language, earlier generalisations and claims for society and culture.

Rival has for some years focused on what she identifies as 'historical ecology' (Rival 2006a) and in this volume argues also for the need to view ecology and culture holistically as interdependent variables which take into account not just the outside analyst's view but also those of Amazonian peoples, whose own conceptualisations of nature and society reframe our own. As her bibliographical references indicate, this focus is shared by other Amazonianists and suggests a case of regional leading to theoretical specialisation (see Fardon 1990). The bringing together of ecology and culture, understood indigenously as well as by outsiders, is then not a simple case of reconciling two previously separate disciplinary areas. It is the idea that culture and ecology are already part of each other. The natural environment affects cultural creativity and vice versa, just as the study of Amazonian hunter–gatherers cannot but help extend to that of agriculturalists. Both have to be seen historically and ecologically as transformations of each other, especially in the way they have each domesticated and thus genetically changed plants and converted forests into and from plantations or gardens. This is holism practised and indigenously taken for granted, so to speak, which we analytically call the mutual involvement of ecology and culture.

The use of holism is therefore broad but deserves acknowledgement as a development that transcends the mechanical sense of different disciplines simply coming together and acting on each other. In fact, it is rather the other way round. Particular problems set up investigations of overlapping concern to other disciplines. Gosden questions how the body–mind operates as an intelligence, and so reaches out to whatever methods are available; Morphy's unbounded aesthetics carries him on a journey from paint brush to whole society, from art to kinship, which has no legitimate stages or stopping point; Hsu finds that relating current practice to ancient medical texts takes her into linguistic, semantic, historical, medical and social analysis; Parkin discovers that the concept of 'crowd' is not contained by Durkheim's notion of effervescence but spills out into visceral or biological and psychological issues; Whitehouse invokes psychology to ask how much intuitive and counterintuitive presuppositions underlying religious belief are humanly universal; Rival asks how indigenous subsistence knowledge and practices comprise what we translate as nature, culture and ecology and shows their inextricable relationship; while diversity may be at the basis of ecology, it is also at the basis of Dunbar's emphasis on evolutionary transmission as arising not just from variation at the level of a species but variation at the level of individuals within that species, without which evolution could not take place. We thus start with not, say, ecology or genetics, but with diversity as the matrix of method. Malinowski's demand for *Problemstellung* now starts out as a trans-disciplinary project and seems destined to set the course of future research, notwithstanding the attempts of government funding bodies to encourage internecine competition and demarcation among disciplines and university departments through such flawed audits as the Research Assessment Exercise.

So, while holism may be *inter alia* about either 'totalising' integration or open-ended comprehensiveness, it is also clearly about method, or how to go about posing and answering problems. In an exploration of how sago came to be used as a staple food in various parts of the world, Ulijaszek cites Townsend's appeal to a biocultural approach which requires a 'willingeness to try to bridge ... disparate specialisms' such as agronomy, botany, geography, archaeology, food chemistry, nutrition, plant physiology, hydrogeology, and toxicology.

Of course one cannot be a specialist in all these areas and perhaps it might seem to be no more than an appeal to Gluckman's exhortation in 1964 to abridge and incorporate concepts from other disciplines within a faithfully patrolled framework of social anthropology. But what happens to such a framework if it is so altered by methodological experiment that it loses the shape by which it was previously known? The case of sago is instructive, though by no means the sole example. In the evolution of its cuisine, it has through poor or incomplete cooking methods provided over time some genetic resistance to malaria, owing to its inherent toxicity if not finely processed as a food. People who grow and harvest the sago palm know that badly prepared sago causes illness even if they are unaware of its long-derived protection against malaria. Knowing the one fact – that incompletely prepared sago causes illness – is part of cultural memory which when investigated by the anthropologist and so-called specialists, also tells the story of malaria resistance of relevance today to health workers and inevitably passed on in turn to people who eat sago. Such discoveries are after all part of a widening field of knowledge transmission imparted to the people on the ground, so to speak, as well as to the investigator. If, as anthropologists, we study only the production, preparation and distribution of sago, and not also consumers' bodily responses to the food over time, we miss this fuller story. A conclusion might then be to say that anthropologists studying nutrition should also be aware of the genetic history of a staple food plant and the peoples who eat it. This methodological innovation then alters the discipline's framework, and points to a concern with what has been called social and biological co-evolution, but which could simply be regarded as a now standard anthropological approach to a problem of long-term nutrition and consequences. Rappaport's pioneering study of ritual feasts as occasioned by a periodic need for protein (1968) (especially as later qualified, 1984), fits this approach, but was much criticised in its time for false inferences and inadequate socio-cultural explanation.

Nevertheless, we have to recognise that there are limits to a rapprochement with biology. Or at least the nature of collaboration will depend on whether the biological anthropologist adopts a strictly deductive or inductive method. The first is that of so-called 'hard science' which mainly proceeds from hypotheses and laboratory experimentation. The second, like the social anthropologist, sees a pattern and then wishes to explore, compare and explain it. Collaboration with 'hard scientists' may amount to little more than accepting certain conclusions and using these as a background factor in the analysis of social and cultural organisation. But, as Dunbar and Ulijaszek show in their work and in their chapters of this book, collaboration with biological anthropologists prepared to use the inductive method (sometimes in addition to their other uses of the deductive) is potentially closer and more involved and extends the holistic venture to include, for example, the socio-cultural dimensions of human energetics in the case of Ulijaszek (1995), and, in the case of Dunbar, the social brain hypothesis and influence of social group size on language acquisition (Dunbar (2003 [1998]). The various, overlapping senses in which holism is understood in anthropology may therefore indicate it as being little more than an odd-job word, but its application to particular problems raises questions about the boundaries not just of what it is anthropologists study but also of other, encroaching disciplines.

It is in this respect that there appears to be what one can only call a sense of occasion in the current state of anthropology in the early twenty-first century, especially in the United Kingdom, for which the term holism seems the most appropriate epithet. It appears that more social anthropologists are putting aside an earlier generation's distrust of collaboration with biologists, biological anthropologists, psychologists, neuro-scientists, and to a lesser extent archaeologists, and wish to explore human and cultural evolution in new ways. It is taken further in the adoption of evolutionary psychology and cognitive science in the explanation of, especially, religious conviction and development, and social reasoning (Boyer 1994b; 2000; 2003; Whitehouse 2000; Deeley 2004). The criss-crossing of disciplinary influences is evident also in more emphasis on ecology as concerned not just with human interaction generally with its environment, but, more specifically with the evolution of all life forms through studies of human nutrition, growth, energetics, and infectious diseases, and of human domestic creation of plant and animal genetic diversity, as apparent in Ulijaszek's discussion of the sago palm and in Rival's chapter. Acting as a kind of pivot in this new holism of evolving life forms has been the life-like and life-enhancing role of artefacts, objects and performances of material culture, and their dwelling places and movements between museum and other collections.

From abstracts to objects

An apt illustration of this intercalary role is the chapter by Peers, which addresses the issue of human remains collected generations ago and now resting in museum collections. They are regarded by some scientists as objects of value to humans everywhere for the information they may provide on human biological diversity and evolution, and by others, usually non-scientists including many anthropologists, as potentially identifiable persons and so as providing the opportunity to repair the history of colonial predation by returning the remains to the families and communities of alleged descendants claiming them.

This ethical dilemma goes beyond being a question of moral judgement. It also sets up the problem of how to go about filling the gap in possible scientific knowledge and at the same time trying to meet new knowledge claims. Put simply, the challenge is how to return the objects and continue studying them, a possibility, by no means easy, that in fact opens up an opportunity to link up places, people and domains of study not previously connected. The negative alternative is to preserve the boundaries that first gave rise to the events resulting in restitution claims. We have long since known that, having become institutionally set and resourced, disciplinary divisions are perpetuated by choosing problems that are regarded by funding councils and professional hierarchies as falling within them, notwithstanding the pleas for so-called cross-/multi- and inter-disciplinarity. But the problem of human remains and their location in and removal from museums straddles many possible issues that do not fall within existing subject parameters. Are museums equivalent to a university department based on a single discipline? It hardly seems so. Brought together and sustained by mixed and complex motives and histories, they stand apart as providing interactive learning (schoolchildren on scheduled visits) as well as the formulaic kind. Museums produce research that often results in the loss of the very resources being researched (ancient collections being returned to places of origin; or biological specimens being sampled for analysis sometimes to destruction). They sometimes and perhaps increasingly dilute the ethos of preservation, conservation and non-cumulative knowledge in favour of radical reinterpretation and the collection, display and subsequent disposal of 'non-traditional' objects. In fact, it can be argued that, despite their cultural embeddedness in classical knowledge, museology and museum ethnography bring together for the first time a number of interests that have formerly flourished in separate provinces. The society of the spectacle, exhibitions as political display, debates on intellectual and communal copyright, the deconstruction of object-based ethnic creations, the redefinitions of public and private gaze, representation as only possible in context and the impossibility of providing full contexts, are all issues that nowadays variously ride through departments of literature, sociology, politics, law, international relations, and media and cultural studies, and yet find the easiest home in a broadening concept of anthropology. The anthropological preference for seeing human remains as belonging to their alleged communities of provenance rather than as scientific objects alone paradoxically makes the latter kind of investigation more feasible. Think of them as partial embodiments of genealogy and so as susceptible to methods of kinship analysis, and the challenge to scientists seems less formidable and more agreeable. The hope here is that the investigation of human remains can go beyond aiming only at genotypical classification for use in broader scientific contexts such as human migration and origins. It can also be used to indicate elements of kinship continuity and so be more acceptable to the families of origin, who may be prepared to collaborate in this attempt at re-personalising the remains.

Although not normally presented as such, human remains can be seen as occupying central ground in the question of how much life or biology we ascribe to things, and hence how much they are part of social interaction. No longer living, arguments are made in support of the dignified treatment of human remains, either through home return or sanctified burial, which confers on them rights normally accorded to recently living humans. Some might say that this view of human things as having the rights of the living could not be applied to material things which were never alive in the first place. But it is clear cross-culturally that what some regard as never-living objects are treated by others as having life, or in some cases as having had life. Wooden table and wooden fetish were both once tree but only the latter is normally regarded as having life. But the line is not always easily drawn, for it depends on how wooden objects are treated. Do the Chinese five agents in Chinese medicine have life, as described by Hsu, namely wood, fire, earth, metal and water? What about elements important in other ontologies? Consider how Galen integrates human psychology with cosmology. He equates the humours of being sanguine, choleric, phlegmatic and melancholic, with, respectively, the elements of air, fire, water and earth, and with the planets of Jupiter, Mars, Moon and Saturn (N.J. Allen 2000–9). These elements and cosmic entities clearly have inter-relational efficacy. But such efficacy is not necessarily equivalent to life. The term, agency, has entered anthropological vocabulary to an enormous extent. It variously means self-determination, means of determination, intended activity, animation and even personhood. The range thus covers things as well as people and reflects anthropologists' concern to demonstrate different ontologies.

Sometimes efficacy is enough to set up the presumption of life. Medicinal herbs are known to have the capacity to cure but, like living beings, have in some societies to be persuaded to agree to become curative, and will harm the practitioner who ill-uses them, this being their punishment for the equivalent of breaking the Hippocratic oath (Parkin 1991: 173–81). So-called holistic medicine therefore depends not only on mind and body being treated as one, but on a particular patient drawing life or sustenance from phenomena drawn from many sources seen as interconnected. The list of such sources of succour is endless, spanning things which have conscious life (creatures and plants which think and respond) to those which simply have non-conscious effect (hot and cold foods prescribed as remedy through rebalance). People's emotional regard for such things varies enormously. Deep gratitude may be felt for the successful medicine as well as the healer. This is part of what Mithen calls the human propensity to develop 'social relationships' with plants and animals, which he sees as resulting from the human ability to integrate social and natural history intelligence (Mithen 1996: 256), so providing the socio-cognitive 'fluidity' and holism necessary to adapt to different environmental and other circumstances. Regarding plants, animals and people in terms of each other provides the cognitive 'fluidity', metaphors and analogies to expand understanding of and adaptation to changing environments and circumstances. In this sense, theoretical holism turns on the use of metaphor to compare and so link different domains of experience. Linking different experiences in this way is not normally arrived at through some kind of dispassionate rational calculation but rather through unintended consequences: the same plant can poison as well as cure according to correct or incorrect dosage, a discovery which can be as much a cause of fear and anxiety as of satisfaction and which requires that the plant be entreated with respect and care.

This takes us into the question of how to assess human emotion for intuitively non-human objects, and how much this bridges human and inanimate forms as part of each other. It has not been recognised that Mauss's insight that donors give part of themselves in their gifts is a claim for holism, though it can be gleaned from Strathern's partible person-objects (1988) and Gell's dispersed agency (1998), in which fragments connect back to the person as well to other persons. But what is not emphasised in these accounts is the role of emotion in the participation in each other of person and object. It is true that for most of us the emotional association of gifts or personal possessions with loved ones is normally weak, and regarded as metaphorical in most western circles, with little expectation that the objects really have agency. But sometimes objects instil stronger sentiments of affection or fear and even have to be avoided or specially treated. We can acknowledge Tylor's 'primitive' animism (object or body activated by a vital principle or soul separate from the body) as emitting such stronger sentiment but as being also part of a shading rather than sharp separation from the feelings all of us have in varying degrees for any number of material objects around us. The counter-intuitive, as discussed here by Whitehouse, possibly gets some of its religious strength precisely from its apparent denial of one rationality in favour of another: that objects are not always inertly constituted as environment but sometimes seek us out, whether as vengeful objects and poltergeists or as invisible but materially manifest and sometimes benign spirits constituting a pantheon. The holistic openness of many cosmologies entails the so-called inanimate being regarded as, and sometimes becoming, part of the animate: all is a chain of being. Some popular versions of modern science, like much right-wing political ideology, reverse this and see the animate as reducible to the inanimate (e.g. people regarded as objects), a view reversed again by scientific research on the origins of life as constituted by cosmic 'dust'.

This alternation of views on the relationship between people and objects is part of their *longue durée*, for, as Gosden reminds us, some objects and material settings pre-exist and outlast individuals who use them and who are thus, in a sense, socialised by them. A potter can start again when a pot s/he is making goes wrong, for the plasticity of the unfired clay allows him or her a second chance, whereas sculpting with stone does not. One learns through such experiences over time to personalise 'nature' as sometimes unforgiving as well as forgiving, to understand society as its objects as well as its people in on-going interrelationship and mutual effect, and to appreciate the distinctive interpretive and practical skills and intelligence needed in any society for objects to become part of people's lives. Gosden's concern with the temporal dimension of socialised and socialising materiality extends to showing how the different substances people use to make objects each have distinctive steps and stages in the production process. Clay and stone are respectively flexible and inflexible, metals must be heated to change shape but can many years later be melted down into some other object, flexibility in the use of wood endures much longer than that of hardened clay; while raffia, textiles, bone, glass, and so on, also tread different routes in the transformation of material into utility or treasure. We can imagine society therefore as peopled by risky production materials each known, loved or hated by distinctive characteristics: can the person choose to make the object out of stone, clay, metal or wood, and is their choice likely to result in a sense of triumphal challenge or frustration and failure?

It is curious that it may be through the relationships between persons and objects that social anthropologists may most overcome their earlier reluctance to regard emotion as being as important as rights and duties in explaining human behaviour, despite its long understood importance in person–object relations. Work over the last two or so decades has taken two partially overlapping forms. First, there has been research on the relationship between persons and commodities embedded in commercial consumerism, especially in a global context of 'modernity', and summarised by Arce and Fisher (1999: 49) as the idea of commodities being given value through the 'accountability of desires' (see Douglas and Isherwood 1979; Bourdieu 1984; Appadurai 1986; Miller 1987; and Skov and Moeran 1995). Here, economists as well as anthropologists take into account not only global market forces but also people's desire for goods and, say, the honour, shame and envy they might incur in acquiring the objects of desire (Douglas and Isherwood 1979: 3–35). The consumer is attributed with the sentiments which are a condition of consumerism. But, second, some of the titles of studies also indicate a view which not only includes consumer motives but extends to a kind of personalisation of the goods themselves, e.g. *The social life of things* (Appadurai 1986), *Biographical objects* (Hoskins 1998), *Entangled objects* (Thomas 1991), *The world of goods* (Douglas and Isherwood 1979). Not only do these studies show the role of sentiment in people's attitudes to objects, they work to varying extents on the metaphor of life-like objects. This idea of objects becoming in effect an extension of mind is taken from the proposition that persons commonly see themselves emotionally and cognitively through their own and other people's objects. It is most strongly expressed by Gosden in this volume, and is evident in a number of the chapters that wish to move away from the notion of an absolute and intentional human agency operating on a docile environment of objects and to describe instead the way in which people locate their thoughts, intentions and emotions in particular materials and goods around them, which in turn become conceptualised as agents acting on people.

Mind and movement

Gosden recognises that, in saying that we should make mind more material, we may indeed reduce our dependence on purely mentalistic explanations of behaviour but then run the opposite risk of placing too much emphasis on the material. He wants instead to think of things and people as existing within sequences and rates of time: the making of clay pots goes through stages which are as much to do with the changing properties of clay as with the successive skills used by the potter, and his/her changes of feeling and thought. This is not in fact very far from Ingold's idea of the life-course as a world of movement and becoming rather than of a ready-made entity setting out on a journey. Mind for Gosden is then to be understood as social intelligence, not in the sense of a black box existing within a single person's psyche and programmed to undertake tasks, but as solving problems encountered on the way by drawing on an array of skills, values and language such as emerge from interaction with other people and objects. *Social Intelligence and Interaction* is the title of a volume edited by Esther Goody (1995), which relates to the present one and brings together social and biological anthropologists, linguists, primatologists and psychologists and advances the view of human evolution and the development of language as arising from the communicative calculations and transactions characteristic of early social groups which needed to remain coherent in the face of common enemies and needs. Gosden seeks to capture this emergent property of social intelligence by referring to it as a 'between-relation' rather than 'within-relation', as sociability arising from interaction and not a process that simply goes on in the head of an individual. Indeed, Levinson's reference to it as 'interactional intelligence' is perhaps more apt (Levinson 1995: 222).

Developing Gosden's suggestions, we can say that time relates mind, body and historical event, and operates at different speeds. Fastest is synaptic time which is the brain operating throughout our body via the nervous or visceral system and so communicating the unexpected experience of, say, pain or, conversely, the deliberate use of different parts of body skin to touch other skins or objects. Then there is muscular time which operates more slowly and of which we may be aware when we are learning new skills, but of which we are usually unaware, as with different cultural styles of body posture or walking. New or cyclical events, such as rituals or acknowledged crises occurring perhaps every few months or years demand a different engagement of body and mind, as the body–mind prepares, so to speak, for the cold weather or harsh living conditions of the event. Event, viscera and brain together produce our experience of the diversity of duration. It is a diversity which, through individual human cases of experience and somatic change, is the history that includes what we otherwise call evolution.

Dunbar identifies three approaches to the evolutionary study of human behaviour, namely human behavioural ecology (or evolutionary anthropology), Darwinian or evolutionary psychology, and mimetics or gene-culture co-evolution. What is important is his claim that these three should be seen as complementary rather than competing alternatives, or what we might regard as holistically comprehensive. The approach from the assumption of psychological universals is central in bringing together subjective and objective or measurable aspects of cognition, of intentionality and constraint, and in effect asking whether such a distinction is in fact relevant. This is well brought out in his discussion of the emergence of a 'natural' human group size of 150 persons, which is about the limit on the number of interpersonal relationships that can be managed regularly on the basis of trust and reciprocal obligations (with, of course, some more at the core than others). This example brings together the gamut of emotions that are associated with, and sometimes reinforce or stand for, the need for trust (e.g. love, respect, jealousy, betrayal, anger and fear), and a kind of demographic imperative which human sentiment can do little about. It is, moreover, according to Dunbar, the limit on what the neocortex in the human brain can cope with. The possibility nowadays of having hundreds of internet 'friends' seems to reduce the possibilities of such emotional management, since neither time nor the neocortex have expanded correspondingly, leaving the imperative as a kind of universal which is both cognitive and social. Of course, in modern society, institutional means are devised to redeploy the amounts of sentiment, including trust, that go into relationships, as well as the number of such relationships. While there is a limit on the number of people with whom one can regularly experience intense and deeply personal trust, the word 'trust' is used by hugely impersonal organisations such as banks, and insurance and law firms, as well as governments, which attempt to invoke the idiom of reciprocal obligations but which exclude the associated emotions that occur in smaller groups. It is a familiar rhetorical attempt to override the fact that an increase in social scale (i.e. the thousands of clients belonging to a financial trust) lessens interpersonal experience of trust and emotional involvement.

Here, we may point to an area of evolutionary research into social intelligence that provides one of the most fruitful links between anthropology and biology, namely the social brain hypothesis, with which Dunbar is principally associated, having over the years produced a large number of studies (see Dunbar 1998 and 2003 for analyses of his and others' work). This is not the place to try and summarise this corpus of work. But it is relevant to the theme of holism to note how Dunbar draws on the Theory of Mind (ToM as it is known) to propose that the mind evolves through levels of increasing intentional complexity. In doing so he brings together questions concerning the development of the brain and neuronal networks, and of social group size, language and culture, which are otherwise served by other disciplines. Thus, *Homo sapiens* manages through language to operate four levels of intentionality and so provides the basis for religion and culture: 'I *believe* that you *suppose* that there are supernatural beings who can be made to *understand* that you and I *desire* that things should happen in a particular way'(Dunbar 2003: 169–72). Non-religious cognition would involve only three levels: 'I *intend* that you *believe* that you must behave in a way that the rest of us want'. Higher non-human primates would not rise beyond the one or two levels of intentionality (i.e. intending something towards another and assuming that the other will react to that intention).

In his critique of the social brain hypothesis, Mithen wishes to add two other kinds of intelligence to that of social intelligence as accounting for human brain expansion. One is technical intelligence associated with, for example, the manufacture of artefacts. The other is natural history intelligence which he regards as a kind of 'intuitive biology' that became 'embedded within the human genome and did not require learning and/or cultural transmission' to acquire information about the natural world and so in due course resulted in the capacity for sophisticated folk-botanical and folk-zoological knowledge found among latter-day hunter–gatherers (Mithen 2006: S51). Mithen does not reject the claim that replicated social interaction among reasonably dense and stable groups increases intelligence and brain expansion, but wants to see it as only one of the three domains he outlines. What both Dunbar and Mithen do share is a rejection of some kind of general-purpose intelligence, taking instead the view that mental development arises from the kind of specialisation of thought and action that is associated with particular cognitive domains, with perhaps neuro-imaging able to work on such associations.

For social anthropologists, tool-making, botanical and zoological classification, and the complex decision-making that comes from repeated social interaction among the same people, are clearly all aspects of the 'social'. With sociality as their starting-point it is therefore unsurprising that social anthropologists are likely to pay special attention to the social brain hypothesis in human evolution, and to regard artefact manufacture and the classification of nature as no more than complementary, and perhaps lesser, aspects. But this view has been challenged implicitly if not explicitly by a volume which in effect subsumes sociality within the rapidly expanding field of ethnobiology in the evolution and explanation of human behaviour (Ellen 2006). Again, a summary would not do this work justice. Suffice to say that, though the term is not used, it is also an argument for the new anthropological holism as well as one whose starting-point is human understanding of natural history. We are introduced to the view that 'increasingly, the subject matter and methodologies of ethnobiological research address core questions about the character of culture, language, cognition, knowledge, and human subsistence, and how these interact through, for example, long-term processes of co-evolution. ... (and) that ethnobiology stands at an important intellectual junction between biology, culture and sociality' (Ellen 2006: S1). By this view, ethnobiology now seeks to go beyond earlier concerns to elicit local and indigenous conceptualisations and management of animals, plants and their and human environments and to place itself at the centre of anthropology as now concerned with generalisations about humanity at global and not just regional levels, drawing on assumptions of universality in human behaviour. Co-evolution and biocultural syntheses are key methodological concepts. The change from the methodological language of even a generation ago is dramatic and is surely part of the new wave of interest in anthropology as an integration of formerly distinct disciplines for which the designation 'social science' is inadequate or at least obliges us to re-define what we now understand by the term social science. The term life or human science(s) now seems more appropriate for what anthropologists increasingly encompass. It depicts a significant shift from a concern ushered in a generation or so ago. Then, the human body phenomenologically expressed and articulated social relations (as instanced in such expressions as the 'embodiment of power' or 'bodily knowledge'), but this is a view now taken for granted and subsumed within explanations of wider human cognitive–physical capacities.

For instance, the increasing anthropological interest in the senses of smell, touch, taste, hearing and sight (Howse 1996; 2003) and, by extension, the physical dimension of emotions, is being fitted into the new holism. Mention has been made above of the attribution of sentiment to objects in recent studies. But students of human evolution have also become more confident in positing the development and role of emotions, again with interesting cross-over collaboration between anthropologists, archaeologists, psychologists and neuro- and cognitive scientists. Religion is commonly regarded as a sphere of human activity which challenges conventional distinctions between rational and emotional aspects of human action. The presupposition that religion rests on belief in events, entities and objects whose nature cannot be explained rationally is clearly Eurocentric, insofar as what is considered as belief in one cultural context may be regarded as unquestionable proposition and fact in another. The view of religion as resting on belief must then take account of how 'inner states' are at the same time acts of cognition, emotion and aesthetics, insofar as beliefs both strive for and resist congruity.

There is at present a convergence of the popular and the scientific with regard to religion. First, the possibilities for electronic global communication appear to have favoured the popular spread, juxtaposition, self-identification and confrontation of religious ideas, broadly defined. It is perhaps not so much that more people are religious as that they are avowedly so. Second, in partial evocation of classical sociology, some anthropologists have turned again to religion as the domain of humanity which best articulates cognitive, linguistic, aesthetic and socio-cultural developments. As Whitehouse puts it, varieties of religious thinking have for as long as we can discern postulated '*essentialized religious coalitions, supernatural agency* and of life after death, have attributed misfortune and luck to *transcendental causes,* have assumed that certain features of the natural world were *created by intentional design*, have performed *rituals* and endowed them with *symbolic meanings* and have regarded certain kinds of *testimony* or *obligation* as *divinely "given"* and unchallengeable'. These can be the basis of an intuitive ontology of gods, spirits, shamans, divine kings, witches and ghosts. They also allow for the development of counterintuitive concepts which violate the intuitive, such as ghosts or gods passing through solid objects, appearing in different places simultaneously, or divine shrines or statues weeping. These counterintuitive concepts are differentially selected and emphasised to produce the variations of religious expression that we compare across societies. Social anthropologists rightly insist that such features overlap, are found in some but not all religions and so can be compared and classified polythetically rather than in a hierarchical or Linnaean manner (Southwold 1979). Yet, this is in no way incompatible with the claim that they are also an evolutionary play of cognitive, linguistic and emotional hard wiring. Indeed, the play of cultural features that we observe in modern society continues that begun in early religious thinking.

Of course, it might be argued that, while Whitehouse's examples of intuitive ontology are indeed sufficiently widespread over time and place as to be regarded as humanly 'universal' cognitive architecture, they are also too general compared with the much more specific and focused findings of neuroscience, such as are emerging from neuro-imaging testing of emotions, synaethesia, and language competence and learning. The question then is how useful they are in understanding human behaviour, to which the answer is surely that, within an evolutionary context, they may help us understand key stages in cognitive and linguistic development within changing modes of social interaction and density, and that evolutionary feeds into contemporary understanding.

I therefore regard as too simplistic the idea that this is an argument in favour of a so-called universalist approach to the analysis of human behaviour, as in the much cited opposition between universalism and relativism. This latter is in fact a false opposition, since all analysis straddles both. It is true that there are outright claims for one or the other. But methodologically, it is absurd to ask an anthropologist if s/he is a 'relativist' or a 'universalist', since these are of different orders of analysis. In beginning our inductive study, we are relativists to the extent that we assume provisional distinctiveness of the social institutions we observe, for we would not presume to impose on our new data a pattern we know from elsewhere. But we are potential universalists to the extent that we seek generalisations from the plethora of such patterns that we together produce. It is not that we think it likely that we should arrive at universally absolute truths but rather that this remain an objective to which, paradoxically, we wish to draw ever near without expecting to reach it. It is also true that we vary in the extent to which we advocate generalisation or cumulative particular description. The new or (better) re-emergent holistic anthropology starts with problems addressed by many disciplines, fits them to particular socio-cultural circumstances, and returns them to questions of bio-cultural co-evolution and its effect on the present. The danger of biological determinism is averted, Popperian style, by the social anthropological insistence on the one case as testing ethnographically the generalisation or universal claim, rather than the reverse.

Note

1. Such new openness neatly parallels the realisation that the ethnographic human 'other' is not only a fellow voice in an account but also a necessary collaborator increasingly recognised as joint author.

Chapter 1

BIOCULTURALISM

Stanley J. Ulijaszek

Introduction

It is symptomatic of the new anthropological holism that terms, such as bioculturalism, are created to signal the attempt to reconcile divergent sub-disciplines. In biological anthropology, biocultural approaches are those that explicitly recognize the dynamic interactions between humans as biological beings and the social, cultural and physical environments they inhabit. Central to this is the understanding of human variability as a function of responsiveness to social, cultural and physical environments (Dufour in press). Although such concerns were salient at the origins of anthropology as a discipline, they largely fell from consideration when the disciplinary divide took place in the early twentieth century. They re-emerged in the 1950s and 1960s within the adaptability frameworks that placed human evolution and ecology central to the understanding of human biological variation. They became formalized only in the 1990s, when the earlier adaptability framework was shown to need theoretical expansion in explaining how culture and behaviour shape human population biology through economic and political change, modernization and urbanization. Bioculturalism is therefore a return to nineteenth-century concerns by human biologists; however, it does so within frameworks created by important theoretical advances in evolutionary biology, ecology and human genetics in the second half of the twentieth century.

With the adoption of evolutionary and ecological frameworks in biological anthropology from the 1950s onward, some biologists again attempted to make systematic links between biology and culture. A landmark study in this respect was that of Livingstone (1958), who demonstrated links between malaria prevalence in African populations, genetic resistance to this disease in the form of sickle-cell trait, and the adoption of agriculture in prehistory as the environment in which such resistance emerged. Subsequently, the Human Adaptability Section of the International Biological Programme (HAIBP), instigated in the 1960s, aimed to document human biological diversity as fully as possible in many of the world's populations, among them societies seen to be disappearing in the face of global modernization (Baker 1965). Of note is the HAIBP project carried out in Samoa, in which social and cultural environment was considered in relation to human biological variation in more detail than in any other HAIBP project (Hanna and Baker 1979). At a similar time, Katz and Schall (1979) elaborated an alternative version of the Livingstone (1958) model of genetic resistance to malaria, for populations in the Mediterranean region. In this, they proposed a biocultural adaptation involving fava bean consumption, malaria prevalence and resistance to malaria conferred by the Mediterranean variant of the glucose 6 phosphate dehydrogenase (G6PD) deficiency genotype. A number of human adaptability studies of the time attempted to demonstrate the fundamental biological criterion for assessing human adaptation, that of reproductive success. Natural selection was regarded as a much more important determinant of population genetic variation in the 1950s to 1970s than it was by the 1990s (Harrison 1997). Natural selection is difficult to measure and demonstrate in human populations, and investigators increasingly focused on ecological success as a better measure of fitness among humans than that of reproductive success (Ellen 1982). With this came increased emphasis on proximate markers of human biological success, such as nutrition and health, and increased awareness of the importance of social drivers of biological outcomes. Nutrition was clearly as much an outcome of subsistence practice, tradition, food choice and preference as of biological and physiological process. Health and disease could be seen as being socially constructed and/or biomedically defined. The emergent bioculturalism has been viewed in various ways. For example, Wiley (1992) described bioculturalism as biological research with social correlates, while Stinson et al (2000) have stressed the importance of both evolutionary and cultural perspectives in explanations of human biological variation. Furthermore, Goodman and Leatherman (1998a) have pressed for a broadening of biocultural study by integrating political economic approaches.

Current formulations of bioculturalism, as defined by Wiley (1992), Goodman and Leatherman (1998a) and Stinson et al (2000) privilege neither culture nor biology, and unlike sociobiology, do not seek to understand the evolutionary basis of human behaviour and culture. Rather, localized and measurable human biological outcomes are examined in relation to aspects of history, politics and economics, while past evolutionary outcomes are viewed as forming the genetic basis for biological responses to interactive physical, social and biological stresses in the present. The production of health and disease is also central to bioculturalism, and this forms the basis of ecological medical anthropology (McElroy and Townsend 2004). In this article, the emergence of bioculturalism from the adaptationist framework in biological anthropology is examined. It begins with a brief description of adaptationism, and the problems encountered with its use in attempting to understand biological variation in contemporary human populations. It is followed by an examination of bioculturalism as a theoretical framework that has emerged from it. This approach is then applied to the issue of food security among past and present populations of Coastal New Guinea, to illustrate two ways in which this framework can be used.

Human variation and the origins of adaptationism

Biological and cultural variation among human populations was of great interest in the nineteenth century, the Ethnological Society of Great Britain being formed in 1843 with the aim of scientific study of humanity in its broadest sense. Charles Darwin and other biologists such as Alfred Russel Wallace, Thomas Henry Huxley and Francis Galton were members, as was William Pitt-Rivers. Although Darwin (1874) proposed mechanisms of natural selection (Darwin 1859) to have operated to generate human biological variation, ideas of biological difference between human populations had become formalized into notions of race by the nineteenth century. The creation of racial typologies and the use of morphology and classification continued to be the methods of anthropology into the twentieth century, the physical anthropology of the first half of the twentieth century being concerned almost totally with palaeoanthropology, racial origins, typologies, affinities and classifications (Harrison 1997). The ideas of typology and classification were challenged and overturned in the second half of the twentieth century with the empirical testing of evolutionary and ecological mechanisms for human biological variation (Harrison 1997).

From the 1960s, human population biology sought to document and explain processes that contribute to human biological variability. The study of human populations on a comparable scale and intensity to those of plant and animal communities was still poor by the 1960s, and the HAIBP was instigated to extend ecological understanding to human populations. The aims of the HAIBP were defined in 1962 by Lindor Brown and Joseph Weiner as 'a world-wide ecological programme concerned with human physiological, developmental, morphological and genetic adaptability' (Collins and Weiner 1977). The central concept in this field was the idea of human adaptability, the ability of populations to adjust, biologically and behaviourally, to environmental conditions. The HAIBP intigated studies in 93 nations between 1964 and 1974 (ibid).

In the nineteenth and early twentieth centuries there had been many non-medical biologists who sought to engage with broad human themes that considered both social and biological concerns. Similarly, in the 1960s the HAIBP was a point of entry for biological scientists to engage with human themes outside of biomedicine. The majority of work involved attempts to describe and understand human adaptation and adaptability as the ecological processes by which natural selection takes place (Collins and Weiner 1977). Ideas emphasizing plasticity (the ability to alter physiology and morphology within the individual lifetime) as central to adaptation also emerged in various of the HAIBP studies (Lasker 1969).

Adaptationist frameworks and their limitations

The adaptationist perspective is central to evolutionary biology and is one in which genetic, physical, physiological and behavioural characters are seen as being optimized in the adaptation of a species to its environment (Lewontin 1972). When applied to humans, adaptation and adaptability have been defined as processes whereby beneficial relationships between humans and their environments are established and maintained, making an individual better fitted to survive and reproduce in a given environment (Lasker 1969, Frisancho 1993, Harrison 1988, 1993). They have also been viewed as the processes that allow human populations to change in response to changing or changed environments (Baker 1965, Ellen 1982, Little, 1982, 1991, Smith 1993). With the HAIBP, behaviour and culture came to be increasingly incorporated in the adaptationist framework, with genetics and physiology (Ellen 1982, Harrison 1993) (Figure 1.1). In this scheme, genetic adaptation is seen to take place through selection of the genotype, the genetic structure of a population being shaped by migration, and differential fertility and mortality. Physiological adaptation is seen as the shorter-term changes that individuals and populations can make in response to any of a variety of environmental stressors, including heat, cold, low partial pressure

Table 1.1 *The time scale of some human physiological, immunological and developmental adaptive processes (modified from Ulijaszek 1997a)*

Stress	Nature of adaptation	Time needed to observe change
Cold	physiological	immediate – weeks
Heat	physiological	immediate – weeks
Altitude	physiological	weeks – months
Acute nutritional	physiological	months
Infectious disease	immunological	months – years
Chronic nutritional	developmental	years

of oxygen, low food availability, and infection (Table 1.1). Behavioural adaptation includes types of behaviour that can confer some advantage, ultimately reproductive, to a population. Such behaviours may include proximate determinants of reproductive success, for example mating and marriage patterns, types of parental investment (Dunbar 1993b), or patterns of resource acquisition, including food procurement. Cultural adaptation involves the transmission of a body of knowledge and ideas, objects and actions being the products of those ideas (Ulijaszek and Strickland 1993a).

The HAIBP considered the fundamental questions of human ecology to be fitness, selection and population balance, as determined by physiological, developmental, and polymorphic adaptation, while acknowledging the problems associated with accounting for interactions between genetics and environment (Weiner 1966).

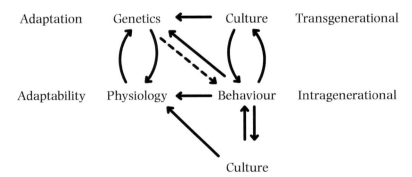

Figure 1.1 *Adaptive relationships (from Ulijaszek 1997a)*

However, operationalizing these questions was difficult. Adaptation can be seen as involving process and change, sometimes but not always in response to stressors, toward reaching accommodation with the environment. If adaptation is a process, then it must be possible to observe the process, or infer it from an observable character or trait. Adaptive processes can only be demonstrated if the duration of research is long enough to observe change; cross-sectional observation will only allow adaptive process to be inferred, not demonstrated. Problems associated with locating possible adaptive solutions of any population become apparent when framed in time and space (Figure 1.2). First, the notion of adaptation as state or trait must be distinguished from adaptation as process and change. The time-scale of human biological adaptation varies from fractions of a second to many generations, while physical states can be observed cross-sectionally at a range of levels, from macro- to micro-level.

Field studies of short duration may be adequate to describe adaptive states, but not adaptive processes, given the long-term nature of many such processes. However, without knowledge of environmental change or stability, it is impossible to say whether the state described is one of adaptedness or not (Dobzhansky 1972). Table 1.1 gives the time scale needed to demonstrate the existence of adaptive processes to a variety of ecological stresses. Research has traditionally been of fairly short duration and rarely beyond a year, and it is of little surprise that adaptive processes have been extensively described in relation to cold, hot and hypoxic stresses (Frisancho 1993). Short-term physiological processes are the most researched and most thoroughly known, not only because they are easier to conduct, but also because they have been useful to the operationalization of military ambitions of various nation states including the United States and the United Kingdom. The understanding of short-term climatic adaptation was accelerated during the Second World War, when military concerns about the efficiency of operation of human military resources placed in extreme environments became important in new global theatres of war (Ulijaszek 1997a). The understanding of variation in human energetics and nutritional adaptation also has its scientific basis during World War Two. For example, the Minnesota starvation experiment was carried out to determine the physiological and psychological effects of human semi-starvation (Keys et al 1950), in an attempt to understand how best to undertake nutrition rehabilitation of starved victims of war. Over a 24 week period, the partial starvation of thirty-two adult male conscientious objectors was observed and physiological and pyschological change extensively documented, prior to nutritional rehabilitation. The value of this study for the understanding of human adaptation was not immediately appreciated by biological

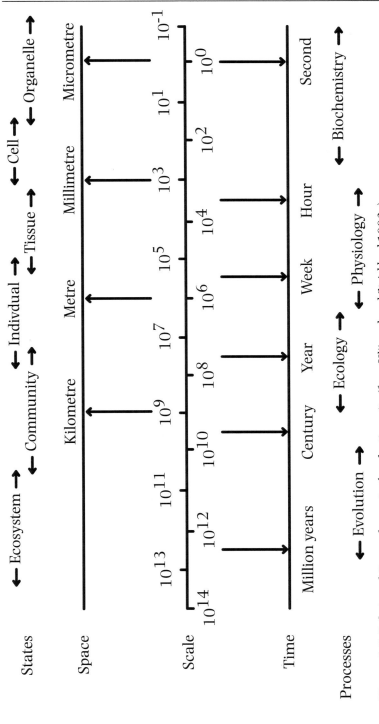

Figure 1.2 *Ordering of time and space in the adaptive suite (from Ulijaszek and Strickland 1993a)*

anthropologists. However, this changed as nutrition and subsistence practices became an increasingly important focus of research with the HAIBP (Ulijaszek 1996).

The question of what constitutes successful human adaptation has remained elusive, however. Since the measure of success is usually taken to be straightforwardly Darwinian (1859), it is necessary to demonstrate that specific alterations favour survival and reproduction. This has proved difficult to demonstrate in human populations (Smith 1993), Darwinian selection being more often inferred in relation to physiological traits which confer advantage. Adaptive processes related to changes in population genetics are cross-generational, and can only be inferred from trait biology or empirical study of distributions of genes or gene products (ibid). The study of trait biology involves examination of morphological and physiological factors that show marked geographical variation in their distributions, the task being to show that variants are each adapted to their own environmental circumstances (ibid). The empirical study of distributions of genes and gene products involves their spatial mapping, and relating these maps to potential selective pressures such as nutrition and infectious disease. An early example of this is Livingstone's (1958) explanation of the linkages among population growth, subsistence strategy, malaria and the distribution of the sickle cell gene in West Africa. Another example is that of populations exhibiting genetic-based lactose tolerance in relation to milk consumption (Flatz 1987).

Another problem is the idea of the population as unit of study, which prior to the HAIBP was seen as synonymous with the idea of a society. Between the 1960s and 1990s, the study of human adaptation and adaptability moved away from essentialized notions of population biology, as such explanations for the existence of species were increasingly replaced by evolutionary ones in biology more generally across the second half of the twentieth century (Sober 1980). Explanations of variation within a species offered by contemporary geneticists involve citations of gene frequencies and the evolutionary forces that affect those frequencies. In the same way that no species-specific essences are required or posited for the current study of biological variation more generally, the understanding of variation in human biology requires no population-specific essence (see chapter by Dunbar, this volume). However, inasmuch as culture is seen as an adaptive force in human adaptability, the population construct has re-emerged in the guise of specific cultures, societies and ethnic groups. These have not undergone similar de-essentialization by biological anthropologists. Definitions of culture might include proximity, history, language and identification (Brumann 1999), as well as shared and socially-tansmitted normative ideas and beliefs

(Alexrod 1997). However, culture as 'norms and rules that maintain heritable variation' (Laland et al 2000, Wilson 2002) as conceived in the adaptability framework has largely excluded the dynamism of social and cultural process. For example, values, beliefs and knowledge might or might not be consensual within a society, and the extent of consensus or lack thereof can have consequences for human population biology. Furthermore, cultures cannot be assumed to be natural, unchanging kinds (Atran et al 2005), leading to questions of how the long-term study of human variation in particular societies might be interpreted and understood.

The idea of environment in the adaptationist framework has also undergone change, increasingly including socially- and culturally-constructed environments. Humans manipulate and change local environments in their use of them and in relation to natural and social stress and social competition. Although some cultural structures may be seen as evolving as adaptive systems in response to environmental factors, culture is not primarily adaptive (Morphy, 1993). Furthermore, while behaviour may buffer against environmental stress effectively, environmental changes induced by behavioural responses often carry with them new stresses. In Wiley's (1992) terms, adaptation in the broadest sense is 'tracking a moving target'.

The reframing of anthropometry

The use of anthropometry in comparative physical anthropology had, in the nineteenth and early twentieth century, been largely to create or reify racial typologies. However, anthropometric descriptions of samples of adults and children have been useful in the determination of health risks of individuals and populations from the early twentieth century onward (Tanner 1981). The new biological anthropology embraced the idea of anthropometry as a measure of plasticity and nutritional health and rejected its use in taxonomy. According to Weiner (1966):

> It is true that anthropologists (of the older schools) have collected data in great abundance but with the avowed aim of making 'racial' and taxonomic comparisons. Consequently (and despite the praiseworthy standardization of technique and the development of statistical method) the data, in their hands, has proved of rather limited biological value. Undue concentration was paid to cranial and facial dimensions; body weight, circumferences, bone, fat, and muscle components were much less often measured. For the assessment of physique, body composition, or growth patterns and their relation to working capacity and to nutritional, climatic, and other

environmental factors – in fact on the general questions of selection and adaptation – the older material is badly deficient.

The reframing of the anthropometric method for adaptability research reflected newer understandings of human physical plasticity and health, as determined by physical human growth patterns, and placing this in evolutionary context (Bogin 1999). Anthropometry is consonant with medical anthropology, in that it is concerned with biological plasticity and its relationship with health.

The HAIBP pulled together a wide range of methods, new and old, by which human biological variation could be measured (Weiner and Lourie 1969). This list grew across the duration of the HAIBP and after (Weiner and Lourie 1981), and with the advent of the new genetics, immunology and immunogenetics, has expanded beyond recognition during the past twenty years or so (Ulijaszek 1997b). Although the emphasis in the second half of the twentieth century shifted from standardized measurements for racial typology to 'designer' tests for each new study according to need (Lasker 1994), anthropometry remained a central measure to the majority of studies of human biological variation (Ulijaszek and Lourie 1994). There are various reasons for this. First, the knowledge that humans can exhibit a high degree of developmental plasticity meant that anthropometric measures could be used to determine responses to environmental stresses. Second, human physiological studies usually needed standardization for body size, and anthropometry remains the simplest and cheapest way to assess body size. Third, a major outcome of nutritional and infectious disease stress was poor child growth, something that could be measured most simply with anthropometry. Thus the new interest in anthropometry among biological anthropologists emerged because the method was cheap, well-understood, and could be applied easily to the new theoretical framework of adaptation and adaptability.

The project to map world-wide variation in physical growth patterns of human populations became one of the most successful of the HAIBP, generating two volumes of growth data (Eveleth and Tanner 1976, 1990). From this, it was possible to identify the key features of between-population variation in child growth in weight, height and skin-fold thicknesses. This component of the HAIBP stimulated a strong interest in studies of growth, body size and proportion in relation to a range of environmental factors. These included: hypoxia and low biological productivity associated with living at high altitude (Frisancho 1993, Demeer et al 1993); chronic nutritional stress across childhood (Torun et al 1996, Golden 1988, Dewey et al 1996), infectious disease experience (Torres et al 2000), environmental exposure to toxins

(Schell 1991a), pregnancy outcome (Kramer 1987) and lactational performance (Prentice et al 1981). Initially, adaptive processes were inferred from cross-sectional data collected on individuals of different ages across childhood, but increasingly longitudinal study designs with repeated measures allowed developmental plasticity to be observed directly. The longitudinal use of anthropometry across one or more annual subsistence cycles within particular communities has also contributed to the understanding of the human ecology of environmental seasonality (Ulijaszek and Strickland 1993b).

Biocultural approaches

The early studies of the HAIBP were largely concerned with the characterisation of populations in terms of genetics, physiology, morphology and development, although the approach varied across study sites. Subsequent to these came the study of processes and complex interactions in human populations, in a search for 'law-like' statements about human adaptation (Thomas 1997), descriptions of interactions between genetics, physiology, behaviour and culture in relation to environment (Figure 1.1) remaining largely ahistorical and relatively undifferentiated in relation to the populations studied. Disappointment in this approach lead to increasing diversity of approaches to the study of human biological variation (Thomas 1998). The study of intra-generational effects and lifespan developmental perspectives became increasingly important (Ulijaszek, 1996), as did the use of biocultural (Katz and Schall 1979, Hanna and Baker 1979, Schell 1991b, Wiley, 1992), political economic (Thomas 1998), political ecologic (Hvalkof and Escobar 1998) and ecological medical anthropological (McElroy and Townsend 2004) approaches. Biocultural approaches came to recognize the pervasiveness and dynamism of interactions between biological and cultural phenomena, and explicitly worked towards integration of biological, sociocultural, environmental, and other kinds of observation. Goodman and Leatherman (1998b) in particular, called for an intensified focus on the social, political and economic forces that affect health.

Current emphasis lies in understanding human physical plastic responses to social structure and process. This includes ways in which political decisions, globalization and poverty are associated with physical growth and development, fertility, morbidity, mortality, and life span. There is also a strong will among human biologists to expand inquiry into problems that remain partially explained independently by study of either human biology or culture. While biocultural approaches generate more holistic explanations than attempted for nearly a century, they remain very difficult to implement. Challenges include the conceptualization of interactions and relationships among the large number of variables potentially involved; the operationalization of both social and biological variables so that they can be measured in ways that are replicable as well as ethnographically valid; and defining clearly what is meant by constructs like poverty, social class and economic inequality (Dufour in press). Further problems lie with the identification of historical events and processes that are important in shaping human biological variation through social and political frameworks, and with developing biologically meaningful ways of incorporating social process in biocultural analyses. The importance placed on such understanding has led to a range of new analyses. These include studies of the human biological responses to uncertainty in Lesotho (Huss-Ashmore and Thomas 1988); health outcomes associated with poverty and pollution (Schell 1991b); secular changes in body size among adults in Papua New Guinea (PNG) (Ulijaszek 1993); health implications of changing agrarian economics in the Andes (Leatherman 1994); the social production of stress and cardiovascular disease (Dressler 1995), relationships between child behaviour and nutritional health in Malagasy (Hardenbergh 1996); the political economy of physical growth status of Guatemala Maya children living in the United States (Bogin and Loucky 1997); socioeconomic status, physical activity and nutritional health among adults in the Cook Islands (Ulijaszek 2001), reproductive ecology and infant health in the Indian Himalayas (Wiley 2004); and impacts of tourism on nutritional health in Mexico (Leatherman and Goodman 2005). In such work, the need for interpretive anthropology remains: for example in understanding uncertainty, poverty and food security in different contexts, and in differentiating the social from the economic in the political economy of health.

In April 2005, the Annual Human Biology Association Symposium in Milwaukee had as its theme 'At the Interface of Biology and Culture: Biocultural Models in Human Biology'. Papers presented there included analyses of reproductive function and health among first and second generation female South Asian migrants to the UK (Pollard et al 2005), the adaptive significance of temper tantrums among teenagers (Flinn 2005), changing secondary sex ratios in India with new reproductive and scanning technologies (Miller 2005), mental health among refugee, street, and non-displaced Afghan youth in the wake of war (Panter-Brick et al 2005), health impacts of environmental pollution among First Nation people in the United States (Schell et al 2005), and food security in historical perspective in PNG (Ulijaszek 2005a). The next section elaborates on this final topic, giving two biocultural analyses of food security in Coastal New Guinea, one in prehistory, the other more recent.

Food security

Food security has been defined as being a human need or right to be understood in biological, social, or cultural terms. Across the past twenty years, food security has moved from being focused on questions of food supply to ones of food distribution and access at individual, household, community, regional and state levels (Murphy 2005). As a population construct, it has been defined by the Food and Agriculture Organization (1998) as 'the physical, social and economic access to sufficient, safe and nutritious food that meets the dietary needs and food preferences of a population, for an active and healthy life'. All definitions of food security are problematic because they rely on physiological, behavioural and cultural criteria for their operationalization. For example, the terms 'sufficient', 'safe', and 'nutritious' are open to interpretation and must reflect changing understandings of nutritional physiology in relation to disease risk and health. Furthermore, the understanding of what an active and healthy life might be, is culturally variant. The understanding of health at population and individual level may be defined biomedically, but this undergoes constant change with new empirical observation, while health is understood differently both among and within different societies. Physiological definitions and understandings of malnutrition and physiological food utilization also continue to change (Jelliffe 1966, Gibson 1990, Waterlow 1992).

Even though difficult to define, food insecurity can undermine human health in a number of ways: by increasing susceptibility to infection (Ulijaszek 1990), impairing reproduction (Ellison 2003), and delaying physical and mental development of children (Grantham McGregor et al 1989). In turn, these problems can reduce the capacity of individuals and groups to secure their livelihoods. For example, persistent uncertainty about food security can push people to adopt short-term economic strategies and to make risk-averse choices that protect a minimum access to food at the expense of riskier investments that would allow much greater possible long-term returns (Murphy 2005). Such social and economic decisions have implications for human biological variation and nutritional health. Food security is an economic concept which lends itself to biocultural analysis because it can be used to examine nutrition, foraging and work as adaptive traits alongside such social and political phenomena as trade, colonialism, social transformation and economic migration. Figure 1.3 gives a framework for the study of biocultural relationships and food security; the linkages examined in this section include food acquisition, work, food consumption, growth and health, and trade in prehistoric, historic and recent Coastal New Guinea.

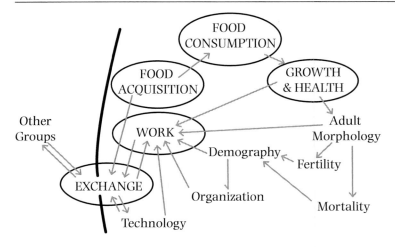

Figure 1.3 *Biocultural relationships and food security (from Ulijaszek and Strickland 1993a)*

While it is difficult to determine whether a population can be considered food secure in the twenty-first century, it remains much more so for past populations. Despite problems of interpretation from scant observation, the understanding of food security is an important one, since much of what can be understood of health and well-being of populations in relation to resources and disease patterns past and recent, rests upon a demonstration of dietary and nutritional well-being, or a lack of it. Biocultural examination of this issue advances knowledge by seeking linkages among historically-based social, economic and biological factors that influence nutritional health (Ulijaszek 2005a). In this section, two aspects of food security are developed and connected in relation to nutritional health of sago-eating populations in Coastal New Guinea: (1) subsistence ecology, cooking, malaria and genetic resistance to it across prehistory; and (2) exchange, trade and urbanism from colonial administration to the twenty-first century. This work follows from that of Townsend (2003), who has pursued a biocultural approach to use of this staple:

> Each of my questions requires help from a different set of specialists – agronomists, botanists, geographers, archaeologists, food chemists, nutritionists, plant physiologists, hydrogeologists, and toxicologists. What can a mere anthropologist bring to such questions? Only, I think, two things: our holism and our persistence. By holism, I mean the willingness to try to bridge these disparate technical specialties in order to gain a broad bio-cultural understanding of a topic like sago. By persistence, I refer to

the fact that our initiation rite of fieldwork, experienced in our youth with a certain amount of pain, engenders a lifetime of commitment to try to understand those things that affect the well-being of the people with whom we did that initial research (and others living in similar situations).

Although the use of sago palm as a means to ensure food security seems unremarkable, the potential toxicity of the staple and the possible implications of poor processing and cooking of sago starch for genetic resistance to malaria bears some scrutiny. The first example concerns prehistoric sago use in Coastal New Guinea in this context. The second example concerns the Purari of South Coast New Guinea, and their changing subsistence ecology in response to colonialism, changing patterns of trade and increasing urban–rural bilocality across the twentieth century. These analyses draw on a range of sources, including: published governmental sources (Annual Reports for British New Guinea between 1891 and 1904; government census reports; village census documentation); published works of anthropologists (e.g. C.G. Seligmann 1910; F.E. Williams 1924, 1940; R.F. Maher 1961, 1984; N. Oram 1982, 1992); archived data, fieldwork notes and diaries of F. Brienl, R.F. Maher, D. Langley and N. Oram; published medical and horticultural data (Hipsley and Clements 1950; Hall 1983); health documentation from Kapuna Hospital, Gulf Province PNG; and published sources, fieldwork notes and unpublished data of the author.

Subsistence ecology, cooking, infectious disease and human genetics

Palm sago (*Metroxylon* species) is a subsistence plant whose centre of diversity was viewed by Rauwerdink (1986) and Flach (1994) to be located in New Guinea, spreading to Malaysia from there. Preliminary genetic studies have confirmed this. Study of genetic variation of eight populations of palm sago in PNG has shown the shortest genetic distances to occur among palms sampled between present-day Lae and Oro Province (Kjaer et al 2002). Furthermore, random amplified polymorphic analysis has shown one population of sago palm growing in the Sepik River region to have the greatest genetic distance from 37 populations of palm sago in the Malay Archipelago (Ehara et al 2002).

Although palm sago may have been used as food in lowlands New Guinea for as long as 20,000 years (Crosby 1976), it is more likely that it may only have become a dominant food source there since the Holocene (Swadling et al 1991). The earliest firm identification of *Metroxylon* species has been at the archaeological site of Dongan, Lower Ramu at between 5,830 and 5,690 years before the present (ibid). Among the staple foods used in New Guinea, palm sago has been particularly important for many populations living on marginal lands, being tolerant of tidal inundation and salinity (Petr and Lucero 1979). Although palm sago is almost totally lacking in nutrients apart from carbohydrate (Ulijaszek 1983), sago palm is an efficient source of dietary energy, sparing time for the acquisition of other food sources that are rich in protein and micronutrients (Ulijaszek 2002). Plentiful stands of sago palm are likely to have provided various past populations of Coastal New Guinea with an abundant staple food whose nutritional short-comings could be supplemented by riverine and foraging resources, including wild pig. Allen (2000) considers it likely that pigs were in New Guinea and parts of the Bismarck Archipelago before the mid-Holocene. However, the earliest directly dated pig remains in New Guinea come from the Kria cave in the Birds Head, Irian Jaya, and date to about 4,000 years before the present (Pasveer 2003).

Present-day New Guinea societies using sago palm as a subsistence plant range from hunter–gatherer bands to more complex systems of subsistence agriculture, as well as societies that are intricately involved in systems of trade. They also differ in the patterns of sago palm management used. Rhoads (1982) has identified three major patterns of sago palm management in New Guinea. The first is the repeated exploitation of palms which helps to maintain the used stands of sago in good condition. The second involves horticulture – the planting of palm seedlings or suckers with limited environmental modification. The third involves palm cultivation with environmental modification such as clearance of rain forest canopy or the creation of artificial swamps.

It is highly unlikely that palm sago could have become a staple food without elaborate processing techniques or cooking. The conversion of sago palm pith into edible starch is an intricate process which has been described for various New Guinea societies (e.g. Townsend 1974, Ulijaszek and Poraituk 1983, Ohtsuka 1983). Comparing the varying technologies of sago extraction throughout PNG, Townsend (2003) concluded that various processing steps have implications for intensity of extraction of sago starch. For example, Dwyer and Minnegal (1994) claim that the beating of the pith is what differentiates the more intensive sago extraction of the Bedamuni from the less thorough extraction of sago practised by the Kubo. Cooking is universal in human society and rich in biological consequences (Wrangham and Conklin-Brittain 2003). The Middle Paleolithic is interpreted as the first time that humans used fire (Wrangham in press). In New Guinea, humans are thought to have used fire for hunting and gathering pursuits from their earliest arrival there, and at least during the past 6,000 years for agriculture (Hope and Golson 1995), and it is possible that some type of cooking of sago starch took place from around this time. Charcoal densities from lowland archaeological sites at which sago palm is likely to have grown in prehistory increase from about 6,000 years ago (Haberle et al 2001), and at the Noreikora Swamp, close to the Lower Ramu, at about 1,580 years before present (Haberle 1996).

The earliest identified use of sago palm, at between 5,830 and 5,690 years ago (Swadling et al 1991) more-or-less coincides with the earliest use of fire in potential sago-using regions (Haberle et al 2001). This may be pure coincidence; alternatively, appropriate processing and cooking procedures are likely to have been needed before palm sago could have become a staple food. Poorly processed, raw, partially cooked, and stale palm sago are variously unpalatable, cause indigestion, and sometimes cause severe disease and death. Universally in my studies among sago-eating peoples of South Coast New Guinea, it was seen as inconceivable that anyone should attempt to cut corners in sago preparation or eat either raw or stale sago. According to the Purari people, the consequences of such acts are likely to inflict on the consumer some combination of nausea, indigestion and illness. Among the Saniyo of the Sepik, Townsend (2003) has written of her long-term observation that many of her informants were unable to eat sago pudding, a commonly used food made from raw processed sago starch in a very quick and simple way. According to Townsend (2003):

> Sago pudding was my translation of the Saniyo word *einei*, sago cooked by pouring boiling water over sago flour and stirring quickly. It could be called sago gel, or, in Tok Pisin, hotwara. About one out of four of the people I asked claimed that they gagged the first time they tried it as a child and thereafter never were able to eat it. This leads to questions about food aversions and about the significance of cooking.

Donovan et al (1977) coined the term 'sago haemolysis' for the severe, acute and sometimes fatal intravascular haemolysis that had occurred on several occasions in the Maprik area and in Western Province, PNG, after the ingestion of apparently 'stale' sago. The relative uncommonness of this condition probably reflects the general aversion of sago-eating communities to eating poorly processed and stored sago starch. If properly processed and dried, sago starch is very stable and can be stored for months with no ill effects to consumers. One example of the aversion that sago-eating communities have to the consumption of poorly processed sago, comes from my fieldwork in the Purari delta in 1997, which coincided with the El Nino of that year. There was virtually no rain in the Purari delta during the months of August to December. Although major rivers remained in flow, smaller streams that provided the clean water usually used for processing sago starch dried up. Major rivers are seen as contaminated, and, if used for sago-making, can lead to food poisoning. Indeed. Petr (1983) carried out various analyses of water quality in the large rivers of the Purari delta, and found them all to carry significant levels of contamination by faecal coliform bacteria. The Purari people ceased to make sago because of a lack of clean water with which to wash sago pith and elute starch, turning instead to a limited range of alternative subsistence options. Despite food shortage, they generally chose to cope with hunger rather than use starch processed with contaminated water from a major river. A number of informants told me that starch resulting from such processing would be unpalatable, have a short storage life, while the few people that attempted it were reported to have experienced digestive and gastro-intestinal disorders.

Palm sago thus emerges as a staple food which must be processed, stored and cooked correctly if it is to be of value as a dominant staple. It contains three polyphenols, DL-epicatechin, D-catechin and procyanidin in high concentration (Okamoto et al 1985, Ozawa et al 1991). All three are strong anti-oxidants, while the former two are cytotoxic at high concentration (Passi et al 1991, Glei et al 2003, Hundhausen et al 2005). All three can be oxidized in the course of successful processing and cooking. The abundance of sago palm in Coastal New Guinea in prehistory could only have been unlocked as a food resource once the techniques appropriate for its safe use had been developed or acquired. The widespread use of sago palm, given its polyphenolic content, has important implications for the emergence of genetic resistance to malaria in Coastal New Guinea. Malaria due to *Plasmodium falciparum* is a major cause of mortality worldwide and is the strongest known force for evolutionary selection in the recent history of the human genome. Genetic analysis of the *P. falciparum* genome sequence and of the speciation of human malaria vectors (Coluzzi 1999; Coluzzi et al 2002) suggests a recent expansion of this *Plasmodium* species within the last 6,000 years from Africa, coinciding with an expansion of both human and mosquito populations brought about by the advent of agriculture (Hume et al 2003). This supports the view of Livingstone (1958) that the practice of agriculture promoted the rise of malaria as an important selective agent for humans. An alternative view, from complete mitochondrial DNA sequence polymorphism data, suggests a date of origin and expansion out of Africa between 100,000 and 10,000 years ago (Conway 2003).

Clark and Kelly (1993) consider malaria to have come to New Guinea with Austronesian speakers and their Gm haplotypes, some 6,000 years ago. Alternatively, Groube (1993) suggested a later presence of malaria in the region, with *P. falciparum* arriving only in the past 1,000 years. Glucose-6 phosphate dehydrogenase (G6PD) deficiency, alpha and beta thalassaemia, and haemoglobins S and C all protect against malaria mortality and malaria-protective genes have been subject to positive selection in recent prehistory (Kwiatkowski 2005). In PNG, genetic resistance to malaria occurs in several forms: alpha and beta thalassaemia, G6PD deficiency, ovalocytosis, and the Gerbich blood group (Serjeantson et al 1992), suggesting that natural selection has been a powerful influence in malarious areas there (Flint et al 1986).

The low antioxidant capacity of red blood cells induced by genetic adaptations such as G6PD deficiency and alpha thalassaemia is protective against malaria (Eaton et al 1976, Cheng et al 2005). Grinberg et al (1997) demonstrated the protective effects of polyphenols against oxidative damage to red blood cells in subjects with beta thalassaemia, reducing red blood cell death rates in those cells most likely to be invaded by malaria parasites. Similarly, Chen et al (2004) showed that supplementation with the polyphenol epicatechin increased intracellular GSH/GSSG ratio and glutathione reductase activity, thus reducing the potential for oxidant stress that red blood cells would be exposed to during invasion by malaria parasites.

In the absence of malaria, limited polyphenol consumption confers no harm, although excessive consumption of epicatechin and catechin in poorly processed sago can damage health. In prehistoric Coastal New Guinea, poorly processed or cooked sago would have increased the antioxidant capacity of the diet. It would have been protective against malaria in individuals with genetic adaptation to it, and would have reduced the intensity of positive selection to malaria in this region.

Sago palm was a plentiful resource in prehistory. However, to ensure food security, populations using it needed processing and cooking technologies to reduce polyphenol and catechins to levels safe for consumption. In so doing, the selective advantage of genetic polymorphisms against malaria, such as alpha and beta thalassaemia and G6PD deficiency, was increased. This example of biocultural adaptation from Coastal New Guinea shows how food security in an area marginal for other forms of subsistence was achieved through the development of processing technologies and cooking, but which is likely to have influenced selection for genetic resistance to malaria by restricting the oral intake of polyphenols associated with the staple food. This has broader implications for the emergence of genetic resistance to malaria among human populations across prehistory.

Genetic resistance to malaria is to be found among all populations exposed to this infection, and the transition to agriculture in Africa has been associated with the emergence of malaria due to *P. falciparum*. These two facts are linked ecologically. Agricultural practice provides both the conditions for transmission of malaria via anopheline mosquitoes, and a resource base adequate for human population expansion. A consequence of *P. falciparum* malaria was high mortality, which would have driven natural selection for genetic resistance to this disease.

It is suggested here that the transition to agriculture is likely to have led to reduced anti-oxidant capacity in most populations undertaking such change. Wherever it took place, the transition to agriculture involved an enormous reduction in plant food diversity (Ulijaszek and Strickland 1993b). Increased dependence on cereal staples especially, and reduced use of flowers, shoots, leaves and fruits would have resulted in reduced intakes of compounds with antioxidant properties, of which polyphenols are a major category. Increased exposure of red blood cells to oxidative stress would have supported positive selection for malaria via the genetic bases for mechanisms that rely on sensitivity to pro-oxidative stress, including the thalassaemias and G6PD deficiency.

Exchange, trade and urbanism

Populations in Coastal New Guinea have managed to adapt the use of sago palm in a way that detoxifies it, but which may have contributed to the selective pressures that drove genetic adaptation to malaria there. In South Coast New Guinea, food security through sago palm use is likely to have allowed significant population growth, but perhaps never to a point that this resource was threatened. In the Purari delta, sago palm is the cornerstone of Purari food security (Maher 1961) and is considered a successful subsistence adaptation in a swampland ecology where other types of subsistence are quantitatively limited (Ulijaszek and Poraituk 1983). Historical records confirm the abundance of this staple there in the late nineteenth and early twentieth centuries. The Annual Report for British New Guinea (1894) describes the first tour to the Purari delta by Administration officers, and notes the presence of much sago in the delta. Patrol officers visited three Purari villages, noting that people lived mostly on palm sago, although in places people grew breadfruit, taro, bananas, and coconuts. In the Annual Report for British New Guinea (1895), W. McGregor stated that 'on the delta and for half a score of miles above the bifurcation (of the delta) there is a greater quantity of sago than I thought at first, in fact, there is much more than even the great population of the delta can ever consume'. In a later year, F.R. Barton (British New Guinea Annual Report 1904) observed that 'the value of the sago to the Gulf native is represented by the amount of work needed to produce it, not by its intrinsic value as a food article, because, of sago, there is an unlimited supply'. During a medical patrol, A. Breinl (1914) found that 'sago making seems to be a flourishing industry in most of the delta villages' and that the 'natives of the sago districts have an easy life when compared with those of the densely populated districts further east, where they are dependent for their daily food on the fruits of their gardens. In the west, nature provides food in abundance'.

Williams (1924) wrote of Purari subsistence in 1913 in the following way:

> It appears that there is enough on the spot to house, clothe, and feed a people of sufficiently primitive tastes – all of it to be had at the cost of little forethought, but none without some toil and trouble. The sago swamp is unsuitable for gardens. The gardens are for the most part situated either on better ground to the north, or else in the nipa areas toward the coast. But, in spite of a somewhat rough-and-ready garden culture, and a desultory planting of coconuts, the native is, as might be expected from his environment, essentially hunter, fisher, and collector.

Accounts of the health of Purari people soon after colonial administration are sparse. The best early observations come from the writings of A. Breinl, a clinician from the Australian Institute of Tropical Medicine, who undertook a journey to the coastal districts west of Port Moresby in 1913 to estimate the distribution of tropical diseases there (Brienl 1914). On this tour, he visited several Purari villages. Speaking of the people in the village of Iari, he observed that 'the natives were, generally speaking, fairly healthy, but numbers of them suffered from various sores on their legs. Yaws was prevalent amongst the children, but malaria fever seemed entirely absent'. In the village of Maipua, he observed that people 'were of very good physique, and apparently free from disease'. In a third village, Kairu, he observed that 'the village is very healthy, although a number of sores were seen', while the village of Kopenairu was 'uninteresting from a medical point of view'. These observations suggest that sago palm use in the Purari was associated with relatively good nutritional health, even if they suffered from a range of infectious ailments.

While food security in the Papuan Gulf was clearly good at that time, there is ample evidence of food shortage elsewhere along the Papuan coast, mostly close to the colonial capital of Port Moresby (Lawes 1876, Chalmers 1895, Pearse 1901, Annual Report on British New Guinea 1891, Oram 1982). The Western Motu people who lived there relied on taro and yams, and often experienced food crop failure, particularly in the late 1800s (Chalmers 1895, Lawes 1876, Annual Report on British New Guinea 1891), sometimes severe enough to cause death by starvation (Annual Report on British New Guinea 1891). The *hiri* trade, in which the Western Motu traded pots and prestige goods for sago, was carried out periodically along the Papuan coast as far as the Purari delta. Although various explanations of this trade are offered, Western Motu food insecurity is the dominant one (Oram 1982, Groves 1972). By the 1950s, the *hiri* trade had been practised for over three hundred years (Oram 1982), reflecting good food security among the Purari for at least this period. Trade in sago starch is well-documented for the Melenau of Sarawak (Morris 1953), which preceded British intervention there. Shortly after the establishment of the Raj in Sarawak, Low (1848) reported the export of village-processed sago from Melenau to Singapore. Unlike the Melenau trade, however, the *hiri* always involved the Western Motu coming to the Purari to trade for sago, never the other way around. The search for food by the Western Motu was the prime mover in the practice of the *hiri* trade (Oram 1982), Barton ((British New Guinea Annual Report 1902–3) noting that:

> In 1870, whatever the situation in more distant times, the Western Motu tapped every available food source. They were restricted to the unfavourable environment in which they lived. There was no adequate alternative to supplementing their food supplies by obtaining sago from the Gulf.

In *hiri* years, traders would leave their villages by canoe (lakatoi) between September and the end of December, to be carried by the southeast trade winds to villages in or bordering the Gulf of Papua. Upon arriving at their destination, pots and armshells were exchanged for palm sago. Quantities of sago traded in any one *hiri* year could be enormous, calculated at between 600 and 680 tonnes (Ulijaszek in press). Purari experience of sago trade was to undergo significant change across the twentieth century, however.

The abundance of palm sago lead Knauft (1993) and Maher (1961) to conclude that lowland Papua has always had the potential to support relatively large population aggregations. However, Purari population decline since colonial rule was severe (Figure 4), largely because of declines in fertility due to male out-migration for labour and increased mortality due to introduced infectious diseases (Ulijaszek 2005b). While the lowered population densities of settlements may have reduced the possibility of transmission of existing density-dependent diseases, new diseases introduced by the European colonizers, as well as by increased internal migration of adult males for work, may well

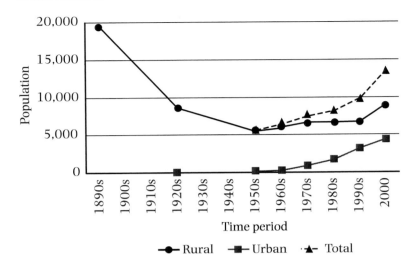

Figure 1.4 *Purari population: decline during colonial times, then demographic recovery and urbanism from the 1950s.*

have more than compensated for this reduction (Denoon 1989). For example, pneumonia was responsible for extremely high mortality rates in early colonial times, especially among indentured labourers (Riley et al 1992). Syphilis became endemic in the Purari delta in the early phases of colonial administration (Hall 1983), while tuberculosis is likely to have been introduced at the time of European contact (Denoon 1989). Associated with these changes came a decline in nutritional health, despite abundant stocks of sago palm. The 1947 Nutrition Survey Expedition attempted to relate nutritional health of New Guinea populations to the subsistence ecologies associated with the use of the dominant staples in different areas (Hipsley and Clements 1950). They chose one village in the Purari delta, Koravake, as representative of New Guinea sago-using ecologies more generally (ibid). They observed that:

> The general appearance of the people at Koravagi (Koravake) was the reverse of well-being. The majority appeared poorly nourished and underweight. Many, including adults, children and infants, had a severe degree of scabies infestation and impetigo, and many of the children had neglected sores.

Empirical evidence for a decline in food security for the Purari between 1910 and 1947 comes from a reanalysis carried out by me of anthropometric data collected by Seligmann (in the Haddon Archive, University of Cambridge), and Hipsley and Clements (Figure 1.5). There was a decline in mean stature of adult males between 1910 and 1947 of just over a centimetre, suggesting some decrease in nutritional status, despite the subsistence diversification that took place across this period. In 1884, Purari subsistence activities were centred around the use of wild sago palm, riverine resources, and some foraging (including pigs, nuts and fruit). By 1913, coconuts and taro had been added to their subsistence options (Williams 1924), the former by the colonial administration. By 1947, banana, sugarcane, cassava, sweet potato, and citrus fruits had been further added (Conrad and Bridgland 1950), under colonial administrative influence. It is likely that out-migration of males for labour to plantations elsewhere in New Guinea placed an excessive work burden on women, such that food supply may have been limited not by resources, but by the work schedules of women. Diversification may also have placed an extra work burden on women, even if the uptake of new crops was made by males, who upon returning from plantation work, wanted to embrace modernization.

Across the same period, the *hiri* trade became less important to the Western Motu and was discontinued by the 1950s (Oram 1982), for two main reasons. The first is that the Western Motu had experienced improved food security with the increased availability of imported food in the Port Moresby region. The second is that the need or desire among the Purari for the pots and prestige goods from the Western Motu declined as they too were increasingly able to buy imported goods (Oram 1982). A third possibility put forward here is that the *hiri* trade represented an increasing and unsustainable work burden on women. I suggest that this is likely to have taken place because of the severe decline in population across the first half of the twentieth century, and the enormous male absenteeism due to plantation labour (Maher 1961). By the Second World War, wage labour had been broadly accepted across the Purari villages, there having been a significant shift from recruitment to voluntary migration for work. In the 1950s, when the Purari population size was at its lowest during the twentieth century, a much greater sago surplus per capita would have been needed to support the volume of *hiri* trade observed in the late nineteenth and early twentieth centuries.

Despite these changes, Purari awareness of the use of sago for trade did not disappear. In 1946, there was a significant indigenous attempt to transform the Purari economy, in the form of the Tom Kabu movement. This attempted, and to some extent succeeded, in stimulating business activities through expansion of existing patterns of sago trade and copra ownership. The charismatic leader, Tom Kabu, intended that the

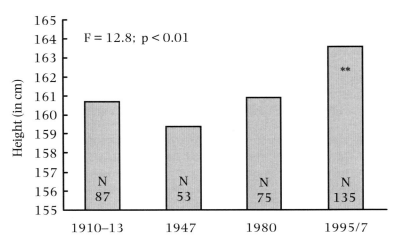

Figure 1.5 *Mean heights of adult Purari males, 1910/13–1995/7; statistical comparison using one way analysis of variance (**p<0.01, post hoc Scheffe test).*

trade with the Western Motu should be commoditized, the Motu and others becoming customers for sago traded into Port Moresby by the Purari (Maher 1984). From his wartime experiences, Kabu saw that the Purari people had been grossly exploited by Europeans. His first step in 1946 was to forbid Purari males to enrol as labourers, and then to set in train his economic programme for the Purari people (Oram 1992). Maher's (1961) assessment of the Purari people immediately prior to the Tom Kabu movement indicated that they were susceptible to such change:

> As their own culture devalued in their estimates of it, things which were European increased in importance, and the Purari's desire for them kept pace. The returns from wage labor were distinctly limited, and although wages were somewhat increased from prewar times, it seems clear that demand for European products had increased considerably more. The ordinary means by which the native earned enough to buy the things he wanted from the white man were more and more falling short of his ambitions. At the same time he had observed the entrepreneurial role of the European and had seen that it offered more rewards. One of these, of course, was greater financial return, but beyond that were independence and prestige. The Purari wanted more of the material goods he had quickly come to value, but the disruptive experience of culture contact had produced other needs which were perhaps stronger. The old sovereignty

and prestige system was no longer in effect, and it was natural for him to turn outward to the European culture as a guide to new things which might be important. Action developed around certain men as leaders, and of these the more important were a few who were among the returnees, particularly a man named Tommy Kabu.

Under Kabu's charismatic influence, traditional longhouses (*ravi*) were destroyed, villages relocated, and houses were built along 'modern' lines for nuclear families. By reducing the crowding in the home, exposure of young children to density-dependent infectious diseases was also reduced, contributing to the reduction in mortality which took place from the 1950s onwards (Ulijaszek 2005b). Sago palm cultivation was initiated in new areas, and village gardens were established, creating a subsistence system of village garden, bush garden, sago and fishing place (Figure 1.6) (Ulijaszek and Poraituk 1983). Bush gardens were areas cleared of nipa, burned over and planted with taro, sugarcane and banana. Village gardens were more productive than bush gardens, and were planted on higher and drier ground. Land was cleared by burning back vegetation during the drier time of year. This was carried out in places where land had been designated for sago palm cultivation, for making small riverside gardens, or for bush gardens. This contrasts with 1947, when Koravake villagers burned off vegetation to make small riverside/bush gardens only (Conrad and Bridgland 1950). In 1980, bush gardens were secondary sites of subsistence, after sago and fishing, and were planted geographically en route to primary subsistence sites. These were harvested on a regular basis on the way to or from sago making, fishing, or crab collecting. After sago-making, the discarded pith, which still has residual amounts of starch, attracts pigs during the night, these being hunted by men. The trunk of the palm, also with considerable starch content, attracts the growth of sago-grubs, which are harvested some two weeks after the sago palm has been felled by either men or women. The only significant change to this system across the second half of the twentieth century was the intensified cultivation of sago palm (Ulijaszek 1991), with retention of cultivars thought to be higher yielding and easier to work (Ulijaszek and Poraituk 1993), and extensive new planting of sago gardens by the late 1990s (Ulijaszek, unpublished observations).

The Tom Kabu movement collapsed in 1955, leaving a small number of smaller cooperative organizations running, with patterns of ownership and inheritance remaining essentially unchanged. It had, however, stimulated an interest among Purari people in enterprises that were connected to European economic structures. Sago cultivation was one response to the call by Tom Kabu for increased palm sago

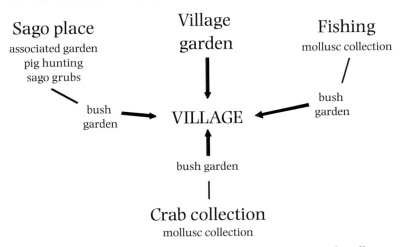

Figure 1.6 *Time–space utilization for subsistence by Koravake villagers, Purari delta, 1980. Adapted from Ulijaszek and Poraituk 1983.*

production for trade to Port Moresby. Others were the establishment of a collecting point for sago in the Purari delta, and of a depot for the collection and storage of sago and other products from the Purari delta in Port Moresby. Rabia Camp arose from the latter need, and was the first systematic entry into urban life for the Purari, and the base for subsequent Purari urbanization. Sago starch was the commodity that allowed Purari urbanism to thrive. The potential market for sago in Port Moresby was enormous at the time of the Tom Kabu movement, competing successfully in price with the imported foods of flour and rice (Hitchcock and Oram 1967). Sago has considerable importance for coastal people living in the Port Moresby area; it is the traditional staple of a significant proportion of the growing urban population, and was used in marriage exchange there into the 1960s (ibid).

Although the Tom Kabu movement had a lifespan of but nine years, it transformed Purari society, opening the door for new forms of trade and of urban–rural bilocality. By the 1960s Rabia Camp was an established settlement for Purari migrants to visit or settle in. Out-migration from the Purari delta during the second half of the twentieth century became extensive and in the year 2000 there were approximately two Purari people in Port Moresby for every five living in the delta (Figure 1.4). The rural Purari population also saw a number of changes, many of them unremarkable in themselves, but which had great impact on their health and human biology. These included the provision of health services, subsistence diversification, cash-cropping and trade of diverse type. Intensification of palm sago cultivation for consumption and trade, the expansion of sago trade to Port Moresby, as well as the initiation of market food trade to urban centres, including Port Moresby, took place at this time, as did the expansion of small-scale quality fish sales for export. Logging of tropical hardwoods was both initiated and extended, while copra production was expanded. Diet also continued to diversify, as imported foods became increasingly available.

Changing food security and bilocality have had major impacts on rural Purari nutritional health. By the 1990s, the vast majority of Purari adults had lived in Port Moresby for at least a year. Between 1947 and 1997, mean stature of rural Purari increased, significantly so between 1980 and 1997 (Figure 1.5). Weight and body mass index (BMI), a measure of nutritional status (Figure 1.7), and the prevalence of obesity among adults (Figure 1.8) also increased greatly between 1980 and 1997 (Ulijaszek 1998). Increased Purari mobility, monetization of the rural economy, and availability and affordability of store foods account for much of this change. While at the national level sago was quantitatively less important than either sweet potato or rice as a staple food in the 1990s, it had became the most important traditional staple used in urban areas (Gibson 2001). In Port Moresby, the urban sago supply has continued to be traded by communities resident along the Papuan coast, including the Purari delta.

I was able to obtain some sense of the nature of sago trade from the Purari delta to Port Moresby in the 1990s by interviewing informants in the Purari village of Ara'ava in 1997. People engaged in trade travelled from Baimuru to Port Moresby by commercial trading vessel, staying with urban relatives usually for month or so before returning to the delta. Each person engaging in trade took between about ten and fifteen bundles of sago, which many would sell whole for twenty kina each. Some traders divided their sago bundles into smaller units which were bagged and sold at markets for larger sums overall, usually between 30 and 40 kina per bundle. People also took other commodities such as bundles of bananas and bags of betel nut for trade, the latter usually weighing around ten kilograms each. The number of banana bundles taken to Port Moresby by traders ranged from zero to six, while the number of betel nut bags taken ranged from zero to about ten. Upon arriving in Port Moresby, these rural traders were usually picked up by relatives in trucks, and they stayed with them until they had sold all their commodities at market. Most rural traders returned to the delta when they had sold everything. The return boat fare from Baimuru to Port Moresby was about 120 kina.

Income from the sale of sago starch, estimated using urban market prices given in Gibson (2001), ranged from 200 to 600 kina.

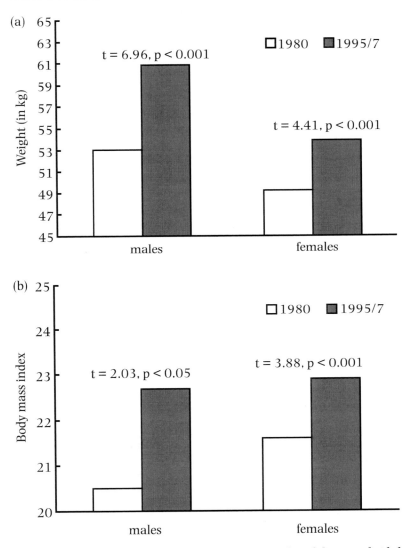

Figure 1.7 (a) Weight and (b) body mass index (weight in kilograms divided by height in metres squared) of Purari adults in 1980 and 1995/7.

The additional sale of bananas and betel nut could triple the overall income. The likely net income gain per trip, after subtracting the sum needed for boat travel from the overall income, is between 80 and 1680 kina. Thus, the financial gain from urban trade could have ranged from virtually nothing, to quite substantial sums, assuming that

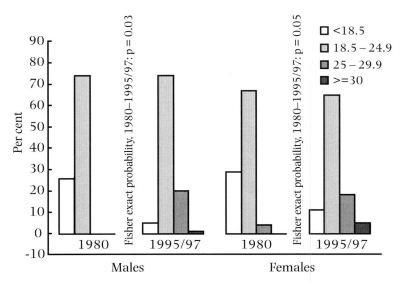

Figure 1.8 *Obesity and overweight among adults in the Purari delta. Percentage of subjects with body mass index below 18.5 (undernourished); between 18.5 and 24.9 (normal); between 25 and 29.9 (overweight); and 30 and over (moderately or severely obese). Chi square, male-female: 1980: 0.5, not significant; 1995/97: 10.6, p<0.05.*

living costs in Port Moresby were totally absorbed by relatives resident there. It was not possible to determine how much of the income from sale returned to the village, either as cash or goods, but it may have been quite substantial in some cases. Such economic transfers are to some extent associated with the accrual of symbols of modernity such as outboard motors and tin roofs. However, they are also associated with greater body size and obesity. Greater income has also increased dietary diversity with increased consumption of imported store foods, and this is associated with greater weight and BMI (Ulijaszek 2003).

The Purari have seen their food security linked with trade for over three hundred years. Since World War Two, these have been reinvented by them, forming both the economic basis of their present-day bilocalism and a driver of change in nutritional health. This analysis goes beyond the urban–rural comparisons that have been more usual in human population biology, focusing on the historical basis for the emergence of bilocality, and giving a longitudinal account of human population biology that is increasingly reported in the fields of economics and human biology (Komlos 2003) and anthropometric history (Floud 1983). Unlike these macro-level approaches, however, the present biocultural analysis is more local, and shows how food security is intimately tied to subsistence practice, colonialism, trade, social transformation and economic migration in the production of nutritional health.

Discussion

The biocultural approach attempts to re-engage with an intellectual stream discarded by anthropology at the turn of the twentieth century, that of understanding human biological diversity in evolutionary, social and cultural contexts. The adaptationist framework from the 1950s acknowledged and sometimes attempted to incorporate cultural factors in its analysis of human variation. This was subsequently extended with the adoption by human biologists of a diversity of approaches in situating human biology and health in its social, economic and cultural contexts. From the 1990s, human biologists have increasingly accepted the importance of understanding social process, often incorporating it into studies of contemporary human variation (Dufour in press). More contextualized study of human biologies provides disciplinary adhesive for medical (Singer 1998) and ecological (DeWalt 1998) anthropology, archaeology (Goodman 1998, Martin 1998), historical demography (Swedlund and Ball 1998) and human ecology (Thomas 1998). This approach has been used to examine how sociocultural and political–economic processes affect human biologies, and how compromised biologies further threaten social structure (Goodman and Leatherman 1998b). While many of the world's populations are undergoing unprecedented social and economic change, bioculturalism offers an approach that can aid understanding of the biological outcomes of such processes. The examination of food security and palm sago in New Guinea prehistory, and across the twentieth century for the Purari of South Coast New Guinea illustrates two possible ways in which a biocultural framework can be used.

Chapter 2

THE BIOLOGICAL IN THE SOCIAL: EVOLUTIONARY APPROACHES TO HUMAN BEHAVIOUR

Robin Dunbar

Introduction

The evolutionary perspective has had, at best, a poor press in the context of social anthropology over the last century. That has, in many ways, been unfortunate, especially given that different disciplines often bring to bear complementary perspectives that can be mutually beneficial. It has been doubly unfortunate, because the distancing of social anthropology from biology occurred at a time (the early part of the twentieth century) when evolutionary ideas within biology were still embroiled in the grand debate between Lamarckian (progressivist) and Darwinian (relativist) ideas about the processes and mechanisms of evolution. For reasons best consigned to a footnote in history, anthropology (both the social kind and what was then known as physical anthropology) took away with it a view of evolution that was firmly rooted in the eighteenth century, and thereby missed out on the radical rethinking of evolution that occurred during the middle decades of the twentieth century when Darwin's theory might be said to have finally reached its maturity after a long (and sometimes troubled) childhood.

As the now standard baseline from which all biologists work, Darwinian[1] evolutionary theory has had two important consequences for biology. First, it has provided a single unifying intellectual framework within which the different disciplines that once made up biology (biochemistry, physiology, botany, zoology, genetics) can interact. One physical manifestation of that has been the gradual amalgamation at many universities around the world of what had once been five or six distinct departments into single schools where disciplinary boundaries have been encouraged to fade away. The old disciplines, while still treading their original distinctive pathways, now see themselves as engaged in a collaborative venture whose success has depended on the coordinated interaction between specialists from different fields. While by no means a seamless garment, the intellectual cloak within which they have become enfolded (Darwinian evolutionary theory) has provided a basis for cross-talk in a way that previously had never been possible. The second advantage of Darwinian theory is its heuristic elegance. Despite the fact that it can be summed up in little more than two dozen words, its theoretical richness has proved to be extraordinary, such that it has become the second most productive theory in the history of science after quantum physics. One reason for this is that it has allowed very precise predictions to be made about how the world might behave. As a result, it has been possible to move very rapidly and confidently through the dialectical processes of conjecture and empirical hypothesis testing that underpin the scientific process (a phenomenon that has come to be referred to by philosophers of science as 'strong inference': Platt 1964).

My aim in this paper is to sketch out the kinds of approaches to the study of human behaviour that have developed out of the evolutionary paradigm within biology, and point to areas in which they may be usefully applied to humans. To avoid misunderstandings, however, it is important that I start by clarifying just what is involved in these biological approaches to behaviour. This is important because many of the discussions that have occurred have been clouded by misunderstandings as to just what an evolutionary approach entails. In the first half, then, I shall sketch out the relevant background to Darwinian evolutionary theory, and then describe the kinds of approaches to the study of human behaviour that have been developed over the past two decades; in so doing, I will try to clarify both how these approaches differ from each other and what it is they are designed to do. In the second half, I shall offer some examples of the kinds of work that has been developed in each of these sub-disciplines.

The philosophical preliminaries[2]

Let me begin on a very general note with the observation that Darwin's theory of evolution by natural selection was intended to explain the diversity of life forms: it was not intended to explain the existence of species *per se*. Species are an outcome of the processes that produce diversity, and biologists commonly use species as a convenient unit of analysis. But if the truth be told, species do not really exist as biological entities. They are abstractions that are convenient in helping us divide the natural world up into manageable chunks and which help us think through the complexities of the real world – a real world that consists only of individuals interacting with each other and with their environments in complex ways. The origin of species happens to be one of the things that can be explained by Darwin's theory, but we need to avoid getting distracted either by the existence of species (as populations of individuals) or by a speciesist view about behaviour and cognition (i.e. one like that current in the ethology of the 1950s in which species are viewed as having distinctively definable species-specific behaviours). Darwinian theory is about variation – variation at the level of the species certainly, but particularly variation at the level of the individual. Without variation between individuals, Darwin's theory simply wouldn't work. So the core of the Darwinian approach lies in individuals and their differences.

However, the biological approach is clearly not just about individuals: biologists obviously talk about genes, and they talk about higher levels of organization (genera in taxonomy, or trophic webs and communities in ecology). The biological world is a multi-layered one in which there is extensive interaction (in reality, as well as in the explanatory world) between the layers. Animals behave in a certain way because their physiology forces them to satisfy certain needs (say, feeding), but they have to do that in a context where they interact (sometimes competitively, sometimes cooperatively) with other members of their own species and with members of other species (including, of course, members of the plant world), and they do so in ways that ultimately affect how many copies of their individual genes get propagated into the next generation. This is a dynamic world of enormous complexity, with webs of interaction that can generate their own dynamics. It is important, therefore, to be clear about the relationship between different levels of explanation within biology. An important starting point here is the theory of evolution itself. Darwin's theory consists, in a nutshell, of just three premises and a conclusion:

> Premise 1: Individuals differ in the extent to which they express a trait.
> Premise 2: Some of that variation between individuals is heritable.
> Premise 3: Variants differ in the success with which they replicate (because of some intrinsic property of the trait in question).
> Conclusion: Because of premises 2 and 3, future populations will come to resemble the more successful individuals.

Notice that this construction of the Darwinian formula, as it is sometimes known, nowhere mentions the word 'gene'. It doesn't do so for the very good reason that Darwin had no knowledge of genes. He knew there must be some kind of mechanism of inheritance that guaranteed some degree of similarity between parents and offspring, but the modern conception of the mechanisms of inheritance in biological evolution (genes, or what later came to be recognized as DNA) only became widely understood half a century after Darwin had worked out his theory of evolution. Nonetheless, the second premise (often known as the 'principle of inheritance') is fundamental to the formulation: without some kind of inheritance, evolution would be impossible because traits can only evolve (that is, change in their relative frequencies over time) providing they are passed on from one generation to the next with some degree of consistency. Inevitably perhaps, biologists have focused heavily on genes in the DNA sense. This is because their interests have focused on mainly anatomical and physiological phenomena, most of which are (relatively speaking) hardwired in the conventional biological sense.

The issue here is that inheritance doesn't have to come about through genes for evolution to be Darwinian. Indeed, it is worth pointing out in this context that when Mendel's theory of inheritance was integrated with Darwin's theory of natural selection during the first decades of the twentieth century (to produce the modern or synthetic theory as we have it now), neither of them knew anything about DNA: Mendel's entire theory of inheritance was based on traits (or phenotypes) and the fidelity of copying that occurred between generations. But fidelity of copying in this context was defined purely in terms of physical similarity, and not in terms of genes. It is important to appreciate that, even though biologists eventually came to identify this with genes in the DNA sense, Mendel never specified the physical nature of the mechanism of inheritance. This was a fortuitously lucky break, because it prevented biologists becoming irrevocably committed to a particular form of inheritance. Learning, as it turns out, is a perfectly good Darwinian process, and acts as a mechanism of inheritance that transmits traits (such as learned rules) reliably from one generation to the next. The rules of propagation are different, of course, and so are the rates of change that this mechanism makes possible. It is purely an empirical question as to which mechanism is in play in any given case. But the process is Darwinian, and Darwinian theory can easily be applied to it.

These points are important, because we need to appreciate that the Darwinian approach is not about genetics: it is about why some traits survive better than others. This has nothing to do with whether or not traits are genetically inherited (which is properly the sphere of Mendel's half of the grand theory). Rather, the question for Darwin is whether successful traits are more likely to be passed on to future generations (premise 2, sometimes known as the *Principle of Adaptation*), and why those traits are successful (premise 3, the *Principle of Inheritance*). We need a mechanism of inheritance, of course, but anything that will do the job will do. Moreover, it doesn't even have to work perfectly – it just has to do better than average. In fact, we can be more prescriptive than that, because if there was perfect fidelity of copying (perfect inheritance), evolution would rapidly grind to a halt. Evolution depends critically on having variation in the population, and variation can only continue to exist if the inheritance mechanism is error prone (a process biologists conventionally refer to as mutation).

This raises an important distinction that biologists draw between the different kinds of questions that arise out of the evolutionary perspective. Conventionally now known as 'Tinbergen's Four Whys', they were in fact first spelled out by Aristotle some two and a half millennia ago. The point can be simply stated: when biologists ask why something is the case, they can in fact be asking any one of four very different kinds of questions. These are questions about mechanisms (what made the dog bark? how does a dog produce a bark?), function[3] (what purpose does the bark serve for the dog? The classic question that addresses the issue of adaptation, as in premise [2] of the Darwinian formula), ontogeny (how does barking come to be in a dog, given that it starts as an embryo?) and phylogeny (by what sequence of changes did barking appear in the dog lineage?). Each of these is logically independent, and the answers we arrive at on one do not in any way influence the answers we give to any other. This last point is important, because it makes it possible to deal with the questions piecemeal without having to worry about the others. If this were not true, it is likely that most biological phenomena are simply too complex to allow us to come to any kind of answer. It should also remind us that we cannot duck the different kinds of explanation, or dismiss them as trivial or irrelevant: we can focus on one for the moment as a matter of convenience, but ultimately, if we are to say we have understood a phenomenon, we must answer all four.

Failure to keep Tinbergen's four whys clearly separated has been the cause of more confusion in discussions between disciplines than anything else. Two in particular may be noted.

Functional and ontogenetic explanations have often been confused, usually because both contain the word 'gene' (respectively, 'barking allows dogs to maximise their genetic fitness' and 'barking is a genetically inherited trait'). However, the word gene does not refer to the same entity in these two kinds of explanation. In ontogenetic statements, it refers to bits of DNA, and contrasts the extent to which a trait is determined by DNA, the environment and learning; in functional statements, it refers to Mendelian genes. To put this another way, the ontogenetic approach explores genes as *causes* of behaviour, while the functional approach explores genes as *consequences* of behaviour. For evolution to occur, the loop must, of course, be closed: but the genes that are selected for in the functional context need not be one and the same entity as the genes that give rise to the trait. This is most obvious in the case of an individual trying to decide how to behave. It makes its choice on the basis of the information available to it, and as a result of its making the right choice, more copies of the genes that allow it to make choices (presumably, those determining its brain) are passed on. The gene that is being selected is the gene for the capacity to make decisions, not the gene for a specific decision. However, what is being selected at the functional level is the correct decision. It is worth pointing out that when biologists use the term gene, they can in fact be referring to any one of four different meanings. They almost never state which definition they are using, because the meaning is obvious from the context. I fear that this has probably helped to sow seeds of confusion among those peering in from outside, but the point perhaps reinforces the anthropologist's dictum that participant observation is essential if one is to avoid unnecessary misunderstandings when visiting new cultures.

The second source of confusion is that between function and mechanism. A common response to evolutionary explanations of behaviour is that humans (in particular) don't decide to behave a certain way in order to maximise their genetic fitness; rather, they behave the way they do because they are motivated by some psychological process (hunger, love, what other people might say, and so on). And the answer is, of course, that's perfectly correct, but an explanation about mechanisms (sometimes known as proximate mechanisms to distinguish them from ultimate functions) is an explanation about mechanisms, and explanations about (genetic) fitness are explanations about function. They are not alternatives, but rather complementary kinds of explanation: selection does not and cannot work directly on genes in that simple sense, because selection acts at the level of the individual (even though it selects *for* a gene); consequently, some mechanism is necessary to produce the appropriate effect. We need motivations to run the system, just as much as we need anatomy. Evolution does not mind too much what kinds of motivations are involved as intervening mechanisms, so long as they produce the desired effect. So the proper question to ask is not 'do I decide to marry in order to maximise my genetic fitness or because I fall in love?', but rather 'how does my falling in love with a particular person affect my genetic fitness?'. The distinction will be familiar as the old one drawn between the -*etic* and the -*emic*. But it plays a particularly important role here because it draws a firm distinction between the processes that cause my behaviour and those consequences that follow from my behaviour. Explanations about evolutionary functions are only and always about the second, but they presuppose the existence of some appropriate mechanism capable of supporting that function.

I mentioned earlier that the inaccuracy of the mechanism of transmission is important to the processes of evolution because it allows for new variants to emerge and be tested. This should remind us that we should not expect all individuals to behave in exactly the same way: some will simply get it wrong. That some individuals get it wrong does not tell us anything about whether or not the evolutionary explanation is true. An evolutionary explanation is necessarily a statistical one: it is about what individuals should do *on average*. By definition, statistical rules cannot be disproved by single cases, so the fact that some individuals get it wrong is evolutionarily interesting (and may have deeply unfortunate consequences for the individuals concerned), but it does not of itself tell us whether the explanation is right. We need to sample several individuals and show that most of them do or do not behave as the hypothesis predicts.

There is one last technical point we need to note about evolutionary explanations. If the evolutionary approach can be summed up in a single word, it is that functional questions are concerned with the strategic approach. The underlying principle is that, if Darwin's theory has any force at all, individuals will tend to behave in ways that maximise the benefits in relation to the costs they necessarily incur. This can best be seen in the now classic formulation known as Hamilton's Rule. Hamilton's Rule was originally produced as part of an attempt to explain the evolution of altruism, but it turns out to have much wider relevance. In fact, it is the evolutionary core to all decisions that an individual ever makes. In its simplest form, Hamilton's Rule states that a gene for altruism will evolve whenever the benefits to the recipient of an altruist's behaviour (when devalued by the probability that they share a specific gene in common, the so-called coefficient of relationship) exceed the cost to the altruist, when both costs and benefits are measured in terms of reproductive opportunities gained or lost.

While this provides an explanation for the evolution of altruism, Hamilton's theory of kin selection highlights four important points. First, when considering how to behave, we always need to consider both the benefits and the costs: as a result, there will be circumstances under which it pays not to behave in the way under consideration. In terms of altruism, for example, Hamilton's theory of kin selection does *not* say that individuals will always be altruistic towards relatives; on the contrary, it states that they will only do so when the benefits of altruism exceed the benefits of behaving more selfishly. Like everything else in biology, Hamilton's Rule is conditional: it is context-dependent, because it is the context that establishes the costs and benefits that drive the balance of the decision. It is important not to confuse this perspective with the methodological individualism of economics: though they share a similar analytical approach (the mathematics of optimisation), economics and evolutionary biology are premised on radically different conceptions of what the criterion by which we cash out these decisions is. Economics, like psychology, focuses explicitly on proximate mechanisms (personal wealth, happiness, capital, and so on).

The second point highlighted by Hamilton's Rule is that an individual is always choosing between at least two alternatives, even if one of those options is simply not doing anything (e.g. simply declining a request for help). Each option has its own set of costs and benefits, and the decision is not just about whether the benefits of doing X exceed the costs, but whether the knock-on effects of doing X are greater than the knock-on effects of doing Y. The net benefit (benefit minus cost) of doing Y is sometimes referred to as the opportunity cost or regret of Y, and forms a crucial part of the decision process.

Third, as a direct consequence of both these two points, we can expect, under the appropriate conditions, to see individuals behaving in diametrically opposite ways despite the fact that they live within the same social group. The contexts in which any two individuals find themselves will differ in any number of different ways (due to their respective ages, their developmental histories, their personal experiences, the chance opportunities that came their way, and so on), and these will all influence either the costs or the benefits or both of the alternative sets of action they have to choose between.

Finally, fourth, this focus on the strategic nature of decisions should remind us that the functional approach that lies at the heart of evolutionary biology is necessarily a multidisciplinary approach. While we might see the individual as choosing what to do, the individual does not do so in some kind of vacuum. The costs and benefits are contingent on the particular circumstances, and a whole suite of influences from both above (society, the wider ecological community, the local climate) and below (one's particular physiology and how it happens to be functioning that day as a result of one's cumulative past history since birth, etc.) play a part. It is important not to confuse the essentially reductionist approach of genetics (ontogenetic explanations, in terms of Tinbergen's Four Whys) with the essentially holistic approach of those who focus on functional (or adaptationist) explanations.

This concludes the essential philosophical issues that we need to consider. What I hope we have been able to do is to dispel a number of misconceptions that have hitherto plagued discussions in the contact area between biological and social anthropological approaches to the study of human behaviour. It is important not to see these two approaches as in conflict, but rather as complementary because they focus on different levels of explanation (or, if you prefer, different senses of Tinbergen's Four Whys). In one important respect, the approaches traditionally adopted by anthropologists can and should play an important role in evolutionary analyses, if only because they provide essential information about the underpinning costs and benefits. However, central to the biological approach is the need to have an extremely detailed understanding of how the system works on the ground. Whether that knowledge comes through ethological observation or participant observation is immaterial: the important issue is that without the detailed knowledge of how the system as a whole works, we cannot construct the web of costs and benefits that are needed to undertake an evolutionary analysis. That much should now be obvious from the fact that evolutionary analyses are always context dependent.

Multilevel selection

Although the focus of the evolutionary approach is firmly on the individual and the effect that behavioural decisions have on his/her fitness, the individual is always embedded within a social matrix. The principal lesson of Hamilton's Rule is to remind us that an individual's decision on how to act has ramifications around his/her entire social network, and beyond. There is no such thing as a decision whose implications are limited to the actor him/herself, although it may be that the way in which fitness consequences of an action ramify through a community attentuate quite quickly as their waves spread outwards from the actor. This is particularly important for humans, because, like all primates, they live in social systems that are based on implicit or explicit social contracts. The social system exists in order to allow its members to solve one or more fitness-relevant problems of life and reproduction more efficiently than the individual can do by living alone.

Species that live in implicit social contracts of this kind essentially trade off short-term losses (giving up their immediate desires and wants) in the interest of a much greater benefit in the long run through group action. Cooperative solutions (mutual defence, cooperative hunting, etc.) all provide benefits that are greater than the sum of the mere parts. By forgoing my immediate selfish interests, I benefit from the trickle-down effects of these group actions. This partitioning of the routes by which fitness accrues can become quite complex, so the practicalities of handling complexity of this kind has often persuaded biologists to reduce the system to the more tractable level of individual returns, plus or minus kin selection (itself an example of multi-level selection at work). Multi-level selection issues are now rearing their heads in a more concerted way, largely thanks to the fact that the individual-level aspects of the system have been explored so successfully over the past three or four decades.

However, to understand intensely social species like primates in general and humans in particular, more intensive attempts are needed to bring the other layers into focus, and this is now beginning to happen. The trade-off between the costs and benefits at different layers seem to be especially important in allowing us to understand some of the emergent properties of social systems, and in particular the reasons why individuals should be willing to accept heavy costs in order to stay in a group. In this context, prosociality (willingness to behave altruistically towards others, over and beyond what one might expect from the more conventional biological explanations for altruism – namely, kin selection, reciprocal altruism, mutualism, pseudoreciprocity and weak altruism) and altruistic punishment (willingness to punish those who infringe social norms, even though at a cost to the punisher) are topics of particular current interest that are generating interaction and collaboration between evolutionary biologists, animal behavioural ecologists, anthropologists and economists.

A unity in diversity

Let me now turn my focus from the general biological approach to the more specific question of how the evolutionary approach has been applied to human behaviour. Once again, more elaborate summaries, together with relevant sources, can be found in Barrett et al (2002) and Dunbar et al (2005).

Given what I have already said about the diversity of levels of explanation within biology, it may be no surprise to learn that there are several different approaches to the evolutionary study of human behaviour. I will highlight three main ones which are now firmly entrenched in the canon: human behavioural ecology (also known as evolutionary anthropology in the narrow sense), Darwinian psychology (also known as evolutionary psychology in the narrow sense) and what for want of a better term I will simply refer to as mimetics (which includes areas more formally known as gene-culture co-evolution, mimetics in the narrow sense, and dual inheritance theory). These differ in a number of important respects, both in terms of theoretical perspective and methodology. However, it is equally important to be aware that they are not entirely separate intellectual streams: many human evolutionarily minded researchers subscribe comfortably to all three.

The first (behavioural ecology) focuses on individual differences in behaviour, its central question being 'Do humans behave in ways that maximise their fitness?' It uses the standard methodology of behavioural ecology (the broad study of animal behaviour) to measure the fitness consequences of behaviour, and commonly searches for correlations (or lack of them) between some trait or behaviour and some appropriate index of fitness (commonly energy intake, matings achieved or offspring successfully reared to adulthood). Typically, human behavioural ecologists are field workers, and often work in traditional societies. Their approach is an observational one, may involve the taking of detailed family histories, and will often involve the same levels of participant observation as one might expect of a conventional social anthropological study. A key assumption is that most species (and humans in particular) exhibit considerable phenotypic plasticity and in some real sense make decisions about how to behave that are contingent on the circumstances in which they find themselves. They focus, in other words, explicitly on functional questions, with some interest in phylogenetic questions (the history by which traits have evolved within – usually cultural – lineages).

Darwinian psychologists, in contrast, focus on the cognitive mechanisms that underpin decision-making. They therefore typically emphasise the universals of behaviour, focus almost exclusively on cognition and tend to use an experimental approach (notably based on pencil-and-paper tests, but sometimes questionnaires of various design) rather than an observational approach. Because Darwinian psychologists are interested in the cognitive universals of how the human mind is structured, they have largely eschewed the fitness-matching methodology of behavioural ecologists in favour of the standard experimental methodology of cognitive psychologists. Perhaps as a result, much of their work has involved the usual workhorses of experimental psychology (i.e. undergraduates), although, increasingly in recent years, these experimental designs have been taken into the field to traditional societies. They have tended to emphasise the modularity of the mind and have tended to defend the view that many aspects of the way the human mind is organised date back to the period of human evolutionary history before the rise of culture (the so-called Environment of Evolutionary Adaptedness, or EEA – a concept that has it origins entirely within psychology of the 1950s, and owes nothing to biology). In short, Darwinian psychologists concern themselves with questions about mechanism.

It is probably important to make it clear that the modularity of the mind is not a necessary prerequisite for this perspective, even though many working in this sub-discipline have tended to make it so. In reality, whether the mind is modular or not is not in itself an evolutionarily relevant question: that is to say, contrary to the claims of some, an evolutionary perspective does not necessarily predispose us to a modular view. So far as evolution is concerned, this is a purely empirical question, and it is one that can only be resolved by developmental psychologists. Whichever way it turns out is equally acceptable from an evolutionary point of view: that is simply the way evolution has chosen to design the system. We can ask questions about the relative efficiency of the two possibilities, and we can ask whether or not phylogenetic constraints have been responsible for evolution having left us with a less than efficient design (and there are many examples of this in biology), but we cannot make any prescriptive judgements from a purely evolutionary perspective.

The third group is that of the broadly defined mimeticists. Their focus is almost entirely on the evolutionary consequences of cultural transmission. In other words, they ask how the existence of two different modes of inheritance (genes and culture) affect the evolution of genetic traits (Mendelian genes) and cultural traits. The perspective is population-based in the sense that it is less interested in individual differences than in the evolutionary dynamics of complex inheritance systems. This is a highly mathematicised discipline, and is not for the numerically nervous. There are a number of distinct strands within this area, which largely reflect the extent to which the two mechanisms of inheritance (genes and culture) are seen as entirely independent of each other or interdependent, and on the role which psychological mechanisms play in the propagation of culture. Infamously or otherwise, this approach is associated with the term 'meme'. However, it is probably important not to read too much into this. We need *some* term to refer to the way culture is inherited in order to differentiate it from the genetic equivalent. Equally, we should not get hung up about the claim that culture is different because it is not inherited piecemeal in the way that biological traits are. In fact, nor are physical traits inherited piecemeal in this way: it does not make sense, for example, to think of a hand in the absence of the arm, or even the body, but this does not mean we cannot focus on the 'gene for the hand' as an appropriate tool for exploring the processes of inheritance and selection. In fact, on more careful analysis, it is clear that this common criticism is based on a fundamental misunderstanding of the processes of genetic inheritance and ontogeny, and is best ignored. Once again, I emphasise that these three approaches should be seen as complementary rather than competing alternatives. They simply focus on different levels of explanation, different senses of Tinbergen's Four Whys.

Some examples

Let me finally turn to some examples of the evolutionary approach to the study of human behaviour. I will limit my examples to the first two approaches, behavioural ecology and Darwinian psychology, and for convenience I will use mainly my own work. I begin with an example of the Darwinian psychology type of approach to cognitive universals. It concerns the way cognition (i.e. our psychological mechanisms) place constraints on our sociality. We have shown that across the primates (including modern humans) social group size is strongly correlated with relative brain size (and in particular neocortex[4] size) (Dunbar 1992, 1993a, 1998). It seems that the computations involved in maintaining social relationships are sufficiently demanding that they are quite costly in terms of neural material. This seems to have something to do with the fact that primate social relationships (in particular) are especially intense (in a person-to-person sense). Humans simply take this primate trend to a higher degree. What this relationship has allowed us to do is to predict what you might think of as 'natural' group sizes for humans, and these turn out to be around 150 in size. This seems to correspond to all the individuals that you know as persons, those with whom you can have some kind of more personal relationship that is based on trust and the expectations of reciprocity and obligation.

These cognitive constraints seem to be mediated by a particularly sophisticated form of cognition, which developmental psychologists refer to as 'theory of mind' (Astington 1993), but which philosophers of mind have described in terms of the hierarchy of intentionality (the mind states associated with beliefs, desires, intentions, etc). This form of 'social' cognition[5] differs from the conventional kinds of cognition discussed by psychologists (memory, inference, etc) because it focusses on an individual's ability to read the minds of those with whom it interacts (hence its alternative names: mindreading or mentalising). It seems that this is a particularly costly form of cognition.

In an extension to this work, we have been able to show that human social networks consist of a set of hierarchically inclusive circles of acquaintanceship. The successive circles seem to have very specific values (5, 15, 50, 150, 500 and 1500 individuals) (Zhou et al 2005).

These circles correlate very closely with both frequency of interaction and the sense of intimacy felt towards the person concerned, and it seems as though we have just so many slots we can fill with persons at a given level of intimacy. The successive circles scale in a surprisingly consistent way, with a scaling ratio of 3. Why they should be so regularly scaled, and why the scaling ratio should be 3, is not at all clear: it could be a time budgeting problem (to maintain a relationship at a given level of intimacy, you need to invest a certain amount of time in interaction with that person, and the time available to invest in social interactions is limited) or it could be some kind of cognitive constraint (e.g. memory capacity[6] or the capacity to manipulate information).

My last two examples both relate to the behavioural ecology approach. One concerns the Hungarian Gypsies or Roma, and I include it because it is the product of a more conventional ethnographic study. The other concerns the Vikings, and I include it here for two reasons. First, it demonstrates that we can approach both ancient, long-extinct cultures in just the same way as we can contemporary ones; second, since it is based on strictly historical (i.e. literary) sources, it also shows that we can apply the evolutionary approach to literature.[7] The summaries given below are based on Bereczkei and Dunbar (1997) for the Gypsies, and Dunbar et al (1995) and Barrett et al (2002) for the Vikings.

Unlike the Gypsy populations elsewhere in Europe, the Hungarian Gypsies were forced by imperial edict to adopt a settled lifestyle during the mid-nineteenth century. To this day, therefore, they live in predominantly Gypsy villages, although over the last century and a half there has been a progressive drift towards urban settlements for the usual economic reasons. Nonetheless, they have been able to retain, in large measure, their traditional way of life, albeit as an economically and politically disadvantaged minority. One of the curious features of their demography is that for the past 150 years they have maintained a consistent female-biased sex ratio, despite the fact that the natural human sex ratio at birth is male-biased (and follows this pattern in the local ethnic Hungarian population). In trying to understand why this might be so, we wondered whether it might be the product of an evolutionary process known as the Trivers–Willard Effect (Trivers and Willard 1973).

The Trivers–Willard Effect offers an explanation for why sex ratios and levels of parental investment should vary within populations, and it is a function of strategic responses to between-subgroup differences in condition (or resources) and the way these influence the ability to produce descendants (i.e. maximise fitness). There are two key components to the Trivers–Willard Effect. One is the assumption that the two sexes differ in their variance in lifetime reproductive output: one sex must show a wider range in completed family size than the other, even though they both have the same average. In polygamously mating mammals,[8] males usually have greater variance than females, because males are more likely than females are not to reproduce at all, and some males will have very large numbers of offspring whereas female reproductive output is limited by their biology. The strength of the Trivers–Willard Effect will be proportional to the magnitude of the ratio of the variances. Given this prior condition, the Trivers–Willard Effect results if parents' investment in their offspring is likely to have different consequences for the number of grand-offspring produced by sons and daughters: parents who can afford to invest a lot should find it advantageous to invest more heavily (or have more of) the more productive sex (i.e. should be prepared to bet on the more risky sex, namely sons), whereas parents who cannot invest so much should be more cautious and prefer the less risky sex (in this case, daughters). To determine whether the Trivers–Willard Effect is the functional explanation for the Gypsies' sex ratios, we need to show that there is a difference in the reproductive rates of the two sexes of offspring, that Gypsy parents do invest more heavily in daughters, and that this genuinely does result in them benefiting by producing more grandchildren via daughters. And we have to do this as a comparison against that part of the population that is economically better off (in this case, the ethnic Hungarians). Notice that we make no claim here that this has anything to do with Gypsy culture, Gypsy biology or anything else to do with ethnic differences between Gypsies and anyone else: rather, the Gypsy and ethnic Hungarian sub-populations are simply being treated as representing two subpopulations within the wider community that are, respectively, economically poorly off and economically well off. So far as this analysis is concerned, Gypsies and ethnic Hungarians are being treated as members of the same community.

The data for this analysis derive from personal histories recorded from 244 women of reproductive age (drawn from four communities of roughly equivalent size and similar economic circumstances: a rural and an urban Gypsy community, and a rural and an urban ethnic Hungarian community), all interviewed individually. These life histories allow us to establish the first premise by showing that Gypsy women who marry into the ethnic Hungarian population produce significantly more children and have higher infant survival rates than those who marry within the Gypsy community. (This is mainly, of course, a function of relative wealth.) Thus hypergamy provides an opportunity for the Trivers–Willard Effect to work because one section of the population can do better reproductively by favouring one sex (in this case, daughters). We can then use the interview data to show that Gypsies disproportionately favour daughters over sons (whereas ethnic Hungarians favour sons over daughters) in three crucial respects: Gypsies have a shorter interbirth interval after sons (an effect that increases the mortality risk for one or both children); they allow girls to breastfeed for about six months longer than boys; and they are willing to pay for secondary education[9] for girls for significantly longer than for boys. Thus, we can confirm the second premise: Gypsies invest more heavily in daughters, whereas ethnic Hungarians invest more heavily in sons.

The critical test is now whether the payoffs for these differences in investment match the investment. For this, we have four communities to consider: urban and rural Gypsy, and urban and rural ethnic Hungarian. When we plot the ratio of payoff (measured as the number of grandchildren produced through sons and the number produced through daughters) against the ratio of investment in the two sexes, we find that the relationship is linear, with a slope close to unity. What this tells us is that the four communities match their investment patterns to roughly what they expect to gain in terms of fitness, and that this decision is fine-tuned with quite extraordinary precision to the circumstances in which each community happens to find itself. This is remarkable for several reasons, not least the fact that it indicates how sensitive humans are to the costs and benefits of their actions and the fact that they can (and are willing) to do something about it if circumstances allow. It is important, however, to bear in mind that our analysis here is strictly limited to the functional level of explanation: we offer no explanation at the proximate level, where the Gypsies' own perceptions, motivations and explanations of what they are doing would be relevant.

My second ethnographic example concerns the Vikings, and is historical in content. We know a great deal about the Vikings because they left us remarkable written accounts in the form of their sagas (or histories). What is particularly useful about these is that they tell us in considerable detail who is descended from whom (partly because rights of land ownership through descent were especially important for them). This allows us to piece together their pedigrees, and thus establish kinship relationships among very large numbers of individuals in the various communities whose histories are detailed in individual sagas. For present purposes, we have focused on paternal pedigrees, since these seem to be more consistently reported. Such pedigrees are, of course, subject to the usual kinds of reporting errors, as well as the vagaries of paternity uncertainty (the fact that, for mammals with internal fertilisation, parental relationships are known with certainty only for maternal lineages). However, we can at least ask whether the

Vikings behaved in accordance with the expectations of evolutionary principles. If they do, we can at least be sure that paternal kinship is (for the Vikings at least) a reliable indicator of biological kinship.

We have looked at three aspects of the Vikings' behaviour, focusing on two historically well supported sagas: the *Orkneyingasaga* (the history of the Viking earls of the Orkneys) and *Njalssaga* (an account of the feuds that took place within one Icelandic community). We extracted from these two sagas all the occasions on which individuals were murdered by members of the community and all the alliances that were formed by members of the community. Our principal concern was to ask whether the Vikings titrated their willingness to murder other members of their community in accordance with Hamilton's Rule. From an analysis of some 48 murders, we were able to show that, when murderer and victim were less closely related to each other than paternal cousins, murder victims were equally likely to be murdered when the benefit that accrued to the murderer was high (e.g. acquiring land rights) as when they were modest (e.g. restitution of minor wrongs) or trivial (the outcome of random brawls). However, close relatives (out to paternal cousins) were likely to be murdered only when the payoff to the murderer was high (presumably high enough to offset the loss of inclusive fitness due to the lost future reproduction of the victim). Similar results came from an analysis of alliances: these were more likely to be granted without preconditions (expected repayment in the future) and to be more stable over time (the grantee did not withdraw his support later) when the parties to the agreement were close relatives (out to paternal cousins) than when they were less closely related.

Those familiar with Viking history will know that some individuals within Viking communities were labelled as *berserkers* (from which we get the work 'berserk'). Such individuals were renowned for their fighting abilities, and invariably welcome on raiding expeditions; but back home, they were the source of considerable problems because of their tendency to strike first and ask questions afterwards, and were much feared. They were responsible for a very high proportion of the murders that took place within a community, and often found themselves banished (usually to England, as in the case of the eponymous hero of *Egilssaga*) or subject to a mass attack by several members of the community. The community that is the focus of *Njalssaga* contained three individuals identified as berserkers. The relatives of murder victims were entitled to demand compensation in one of two forms: by taking revenge on the murderer or a member of his family or by demanding blood money. Since the risks of trying to carry out a revenge murder on a berserker or his family were extremely high (berserkers did not take kindly to the loss of members of their family, and were likely to precipitate vendettas), we can ask whether victim's relatives titrated their choice of compensation in the light of the risks attached to each option. Ecological foraging theory provides a well-grounded basis for predicting that risky options will not be chosen when the costs are high. From an analysis of 38 murders that took place within the community over a 50–year period, we could show that relatives of the victim were more willing to accept blood money than effect a revenge killing (as they were entitled to do) if the murderer was a recognised berseker than if he was not.

The actual existence of berserkers remains something of a puzzle from an evolutionary point of view, since many suffered unfortunate fates prematurely at the hands of exasperated communities. In addition, their disruptive behaviour – often resulting from scant concern for the niceties of social etiquette – placed a great strain on the community, and one might expect there to have been considerable social (and hence evolutionary) selection pressure against them. That they reappear in the historical record with monotonous regularity requires an explanation. One likely explanation is that they and their families benefited through kin selection. In other words, even though beserkers themselves met early and untimely deaths, nonetheless, the family as a whole (and hence the berserker himself) benefited in some way by having increased numbers of offspring. From a comparison of the three berserkers with the rest of the community in *Njalssaga*, we can show that berserker's families suffered about half the number of losses through violence that other families in the community suffered (and this in a context where about half of all the males in the community over a 50 year period came to a sticky end). Moreover, the net fitness gains (indexed as the number of surviving male offspring in the third – or grandchildren – generation when devalued by their coefficient of paternal relatedness to Ego) for the three berserkers was significantly greater than that accruing to individuals who did not have a berserker in their family. In short, for better or worse, under the circumstances prevailing in this particular historical community, there were significant fitness advantages both to being a berserker and to having a berserker in one's immediate family.

Conclusions

I have tried to do two things here. One has been to set the record clear on just what is involved in the evolutionary or Darwinian approach to the study of human behaviour. It is my perception that one of the principal reasons why the evolutionary approach has been resisted so vigorously in social anthropology has been because of misperceptions of what is involved. These have centred on two key misunderstandings. One is that evolutionary explanations are about genetic determinism of behaviour; the other is that evolutionary explanations assume linear or progressivist evolutionary histories. I have tried to show that both of these are wrong, and I have suggested that they arose because the social sciences parted company with the biological sciences before the Darwinian perspective had become widely accepted. The social sciences thus inherited a largely eighteenth century view of evolution based on Darwin's great predecessor Lamarck (mainly thanks, it has to be said, through Herbert Spencer's misreading of Darwin, understandable as this was given the state of understanding at the time). The second thing I have tried to do is to offer just a few examples of the range of approaches to the study of human behaviour that an evolutionary approach offers. In doing so, I have sought to show that the evolutionary approach can involve a number of alternative kinds of explanation which should not be confused with one another. In addition, I hope I have been able to show that an evolutionary approach can provide useful insights into the behaviour of both contemporary and historical peoples. I hope that one important lesson to emerge from this is the fact that the evolutionary approach does not assume that all humans, whether or not they are members of the same community or culture, behave in exactly the same way, even though their different decisions may in fact be based on the same cognitive processes.

Notes

1. I deliberately use the word 'Darwinian' rather than 'Darwin's' here to emphasise the fact that, while firmly founded on the remarkably prescient ideas developed by Darwin (and others!) during the second half of the nineteenth century, modern theory – while still recognisably Darwin's – has developed whole new layers during the 150 years since the publication of his *Origin of Species* in 1859.
2. Most of this section will be given without sources: it is all standard evolutionary theory, and can be found in any evolutionary biology textbook. More readable accounts with specific reference to the study of behaviour can be found in Barrett et al (2002, especially chapter 2), Dunbar (1995, 1996) and Dunbar et al (2005).
3. It is important to appreciate that function in evolutionary biology has only a very tenuous connection with Functionalism in anthropology. Functionalism in the latter sense is a group-level phenomenon, and is based on group selection – one of the core assumptions of eighteenth and early nineteenth century evolutionary thinking (evolution for the benefit of the species or group) that Darwin's theory undermined (though it took just over a century for biologists to fully understand the implications of Darwin's position, which is one reason why the biological sense of functionalism never made the cross-over into anthropology). Functional explanations in evolutionary biology focus on function at the level of the individual, and the correct metric for this is fitness (in the technical genetic sense), hence the

so-called 'selfish gene' perspective (which, for the sake of the record, I emphasise has nothing to do with motives on the parts of genes, since that would be to confuse mechanismic and functional explanations in Tinbergen's Four Whys).

4. The neocortex is the most recently evolved part of the mammalian brain. It constitutes a thin layer on the outer surface of the brain (despite the fact that it accounts for 50–80% of total brain volume in primates). It is broadly associated with what we might think of as the 'smart' mental processes.

5. Again, for a readable summary of the extensive literature in cognitive developmental psychology, see Barrett et al (2002, especially chapter 11).

6. This memory limitation must have something to do with intense personal knowledge of another person, not just memory for faces. Humans are said to be able to put names to around 2000 faces.

7. There have been several recent attempts by literary theorists to use evolutionary theory in this way, including several special journal issues (*Human Nature*, 1998, volume 9, number 3; *Journal of Cultural and Evolutionary Psychology*, 2005, volume 3, number 1), at least one edited volume and a number of individual articles (e.g. Stiller et al 2004).

8. This is purely a consequence of the way mammalian reproductive biology is organised: the Trivers-Willard Effect merely requires that one sex has greater variance than the other. In taxonomic groups whose reproductive biology is organised differently, females may have greater variance than males, and the Trivers-Willard Effect is reversed. The pipefish family (which includes seahorses) is a well-known case in point: in this family, it is males that are pregnant, not females, so males have the more limited reproductive rate.

9. Even under the communist regime, secondary education was not free in Hungary.

Chapter 3

DOMESTICATING THE LANDSCAPE, PRODUCING CROPS AND REPRODUCING SOCIETY IN AMAZONIA

Laura Rival

In an article he wrote at the beginning of his anthropological career, Claude Lévi-Strauss (1950) noted that native Amazonians give preference to semi-wild plant species over fully domesticated ones. Precursory of the later writings where he fully developed the concepts of 'science of the concrete' and 'untamed thinking,' and the theory of the Amerindian mythologising mind, this seminal article inspired many researchers. Philippe Descola (1994, 1996) combined Lévi-Strauss's early insights with the more materialist approaches of André Haudricourt and Maurice Godelier, and proposed a new analysis of the symbolic domestication of nature by Amazonian Indians. In a more post-structuralist stance, Eduardo Viveiros de Castro (1998) argued that Amazonian conceptualisations of humanity are not more monist than modern EuroAmerican ones. Their dualism is as radical as ours, but it sets human culture, not nature, as the prior given; nature is conceptualised as what is made or constructed by cultural subjects. Natural scientists such as the botanist Charles Clement (1999) also rediscovered Lévi-Strauss's seminal hypothesis, which has since been fully supported by the archaeological reconstruction of the origins and subsequent evolution of plant domestication in lowland South America (Piperno and Persall 1998, Bellwood 2005).[1]

The Huaorani share the Amazonian preference for semi-wild forest plants. Subsistence is more than environmental adaptation for them. The economy functions as a moral system and is part of their cosmovision. Until ten years ago, and unlike their indigenous neighbours (all cultivating groups with a strong sense of identity as horticulturalists), the Huaorani chose to cultivate manioc and plantain only sporadically, and mainly for the preparation of ceremonial drinks. Even today, many families prefer to secure their daily subsistence through hunting and gathering. Like most native Amazonians, today's Huaorani cultivate some food crops as part of their subsistence economy. Yet, they continue to define themselves primarily in terms of what they hunt and collect in the forest. Through their cycles of residential mobility, foraging activities, and daily consumption of significant quantities of forest resources, they continue to concentrate useful forest species, and enrich their habitat through marginal modifications, including, for instance, leaving behind hips of fruit seeds upon abandoning a camp or a dwelling site, or weeding around the base of a wild plant whose growth they wish to encourage. The anthropogenic forests they have helped to form through such activities are qualitatively different from those created through shifting cultivation. Experts in reading the signs of past human activity, the Huaorani selectively ascribe transformations in the forest to the deeds of a wide range of agents, be they ancestors, other indigenous groups, or supernatural forces. Whereas the occurrence of ayahuasca vine[2] is systematically attributed to the planting activities of long dead Zaparo enemies, the presence of peach palm[3] groves is invariably considered a legacy from Huaorani ancestors. The forest exists to the extent that humans in the past lived and worked in it, and by so doing produced it as it is today for the benefit and use of the living. In other words, they live their interaction with the forest as a social relation across generations. Trekking is not simply a mundane activity relating to the pragmatics of subsistence and to environmental or historical adaptation, but, rather, a fundamental way of reproducing society through time (Rival 2002).

My aim in this chapter is to show how a more holistic and dynamic perspective on the interactions between Amazonian hunter–gatherers and agriculturalists requires the treatment of ecology and culture as interdependent variables. If the natural environment conditions cultural creativity, it is also true that cultural creativity sets new environmental possibilities. Ecological and biological factors determine what particular plant species are amenable to domestication and the rates at which plants may be selected for favourable traits, as well as the kind of changes in gene frequency occurring in the domesticated plant over time. However, a forest can be transformed through cultural creativity into a manicured manioc plantation, a multi-storey agroforestry system, or any other kind of cultural landscape. Similarly, a cultivator may choose to bring a plant under close control and propagate selected materials until the plant produces the desired characteristics; or she may prefer to manage the plant more indirectly, by encouraging its development through minimal weeding and forest clearance. I review current debates about plant domestication in Amazonia. I start with a section on research guided by the precept that plant domestication is an evolutionary question, before discussing the impact of the Conquest on the evolution of plant domestication in lowland South America. I then show that plant domestication cannot be properly understood without reference to identity politics and to contemporary interactions between foragers and cultivators. I conclude with a few remarks on the kind of holistic approach to human ecology that is needed to further our understanding of plant domestication, and, more generally, interactions between nature and society. A holistic human ecology, which we could as well term an anthropology of life, should integrate, and give equal weight to, the cognitive, historical and political dimensions of human nature.

Plant domestication as an evolutionary question

The fact that Darwin dedicated the opening pages of *On the Origin of Species* to plant and animal domestication is an indication of how important the process of selection for desirable traits by humans has been, and still is, for our overall comprehension of the workings of natural selection (Diamond 1997: 130). Contemporary evolutionary biologists and botanists see plant domestication as a co-evolutionary process resulting from the combined action of natural and human selection (Salick 1995, Elias, Rival and Mc Key 2000). Consciously or inadvertently, people exercise selective pressure on cultivated plants through a number of socio-cultural practices. They select and propagate some plants at the expense of others. Plant selection and propagation by humans are activities that result in genetic modification. Selection and propagation alter the mechanisms for seed dispersal. They also affect seed dormancy, and encourage self-reproduction, either vegetatively or through self-pollination (Diamond 1997: 119–122). There is therefore no doubt that the question 'Why and how did some prehistoric people transform certain wild plants into crops?' is an evolutionary one.

However, scientific accounts of how evolutionary principles caused the transition from hunting-and-gathering to farming differ.[4] Whereas some authors stress the symbiotic mutualism[5] that slowly and progressively developed between humans and the plants that co-evolved with them (Rindos 1984), others prefer to restrict the process of domestication to conscious cultivation, which involves cycles of planting and harvesting in prepared fields clearly set apart from wild, natural habitats (Piperno and Pearsall 1998: 7). Some authors put much emphasis on the fact that people were forced by environmental events or historical circumstances to embark on farming. Hancock (1992), for instance, wonders why the onset of agriculture took so long, given that prehistoric hunter–gatherers had the necessary knowledge and technology to farm long before farming was undertaken. He reasoned that 'hunting and gathering was a very comfortable way of life and humans had to have a very good reason to give it up' (Hancock 1992: 151). For Diamond (1997), that very good reason was the mass extermination of large mammals by early human hunters who migrated out of Africa and colonised Eurasia, Australasia, and the rest of the world. Left with no easily accessible source of wild food, they were forced to innovate (i.e. domesticate plant and animal species), or to conquer those who had invented new food production systems. For Winterhalder (1981, 1993), decisions regarding the use of particular types of natural resources as food, as well as decisions to adopt new or different food sources, are both made on the basis of calculations of relative return rates. Thus for Winterhalder the very good reason that pushed past human ancestors to farm instead of hunting and gathering was either climate change or population growth.[6] Either of these two causes would have demanded a change in subsistence decisions in order to maintain an energetically optimal level of resource use. According to the optimal diet model, resource intensification (i.e. the adoption of agriculture) is driven largely by changes in foraging efficiency and diet breadth. Piperno and Pearsall (1998: 11), who follow Winterhalder's particular brand of evolutionary ecology and flatly deny the importance of socio-cultural factors such as religious ideologies, feasting, or prestige in the birth of agriculture, explain that diet breadth expansion occurs in response to an increasing scarcity of highly ranked resources paralleled by a decrease in the foraging return rate.

In spite of these divergent opinions, there is broad agreement on two major aspects of the overall evolutionary explanation. On the one hand, proto-farming started about 40,000 years ago (that is, during the late Palaeolithic); on the other hand, it did not give way to full-blown agriculture until about 12,000 years ago (that is, during the transition between the end of the Pleistoscene and the start of the Holocene). For Mithen (1996 and 2006) the reason why proto-farming could not develop before the late Palaeolithic is that it involves actions and modes of thought that are exclusively characteristic of

Homo sapiens sapiens. The reason why humans managed and modified the natural environment from at least 35,000 BP but did not start depending on domesticated plants and animals until the last few thousands of years is that this major shift was triggered by climate change. The transition from foraging to farming was thus part and parcel of the profound environmental changes associated with the end of the last Ice Age – between 11,000 and 10,000 years ago. According to Mithen (2006), populations capable of modern human cognition and behaviour, including forms of resource management similar to those found today among modern foragers and incipient farmers, evolved between 35,000 and 10,000 years ago. By accepting Mithen's position, we also accept the fact that previous glacial and interglacial environmental perturbations could not have led to conscious plant propagation by humans. In short, the factors necessary for the emergence of food production probably did not converge until the end of the Pleistocene (Piperno and Pearsall 1998). Piperno and Pearsall, who are the first authors to examine systematically the impact of the last Ice Age on the evolution of food production systems in the Americas, are convinced that agriculture arose in various locations across the world independently, but for the same reason, beginning at about 12,000 years ago.[7] Its sudden, scattered appearance all across the globe was triggered by environmental change, which, in turn, led to an 'important step in the evolving culture of human beings' (Hancock 1992: 151).

In their examination of the impact of the last Ice Age on the Amazon basin, Piperno and Pearsall (1998: 53) note that there have been major natural and human disturbances of the American tropical forest during the late Pleistocene and Holocene periods (*c.* 22,000 years ago to the present). They explain that these natural perturbations drastically changed wild resource density and distribution, and probably called for significant subsistence adjustments by native Americans, particularly during the transition period after the close of the Pleistocene, between 11,000 and 10,000 years ago. During that period, large portions of Amazonia were covered by open, deciduous and dry (seasonal) forest, not with rain and wet forest as it is today. The forest environment was consequently richer in natural resources available to hunters and gatherers, and there were many plant species suitable for domestication. Many important crop plant ancestors were naturally distributed in tropical deciduous and semi-evergreen forests, where the dry season is comparatively long and marked. It is also in these forests that large mammals such as giant capybaras (*Neochoerus*) and giant ground sloths (*Eremotherium* and *Megatherium*) roamed, and where human hunters lived. When the wet tropical forest reoccupied the open terrain that had expanded under the late-glacial climate, the large mammals and open land plants disappeared. Holocene native Amazonians, now faced with expanding rain forests and diminishing foraging options, were forced to develop new food strategies; they started to domesticate available plant species (Piperno and Pearsall 1998: 90–107; see also Keyeux et al 2002).

Piperno's and Pearsall's reconstruction of the Holocene transitional forest and the beginnings of plant domestication in lowland South America is convincing, and certainly more plausible than Diamond's geographical determinism and human over-predation thesis (see in particular Diamond 1997: 96, 103–07).[8] However, they too exhibit the same problematic tendency to reduce human affairs to naturalised ecological economics, presented as the domain of pure efficiency and rationality. Ironically, Diamond is more realistic than Piperno and Pearsall in his assessment of the political tensions caused by emerging inequalities between what he calls 'History's haves and have-nots' (Diamond 1997: 87, 93–113). Although the latter recognise the past and present existence of complex and sophisticated agroforestry systems in Amazonia, they cannot easily reconcile this form of landscape management with their evolutionary continuum of types of food production. They concede that different food production systems may have co-existed after the adoption of agriculture, but envisage this occurrence as a choice forced onto human societies by limiting local ecological conditions (Piperno and Pearsall 1998: 7). The establishment and spread of what they call 'food-producing behaviour' (by which they mean agriculture, as if hunting and gathering were not forms of food-producing behaviour) is envisaged as a purely unilinear progression. The challenge, however, is to differentiate what in human action is conditioned by our common biological make-up, and what is the product of history. This is particularly important in the case of South America, where human migrations are less well understood than they are on other continents (Diamond and Bellwood 2003, Bellwood 2005, Schurr 2004), and where contact with Europeans in the late fifteenth century caused population losses and crop genetic erosion of a magnitude so far unparalleled in human history (Clement 1999, Diamond and Bellwood 2003).

Plant domestication as a historical question

In a recent synthesis of all current information on Amazonian crop genetic biogeography, Charles Clement (1999: 188) notes – conservatively – that at least four to five million people lived in Amazonia at the time of the Conquest, and that 90 to 95 percent died shortly after. He adds that by 1492 native Amazonians already cultivated or managed at least 138 plant species, of which a substantial number were in an advanced state of domestication. He classifies 52 plant species belonging to 27 families as already domesticated, and 41 plant species belonging to 23 families as cultivated and semi-domesticated. More controversially, he inventories 45 species belonging to 17 families as being incipiently domesticated. This survey leads him to conclude that 84 per cent of the 138 crops cultivated or managed in lowland South America at contact most probably originated in the Amazon basin and adjacent lowland regions, representing almost half (45 per cent) of all the plants cultivated in the Americas (Clement 1999). Having classified Amazonian cultivated plants according to their degree of domestication (full domesticates; semi-domesticates; and incipient domesticates) and their particular life history (annuals; semi-annuals; and perennials), Clement distinguishes six plant categories. He then moves on to reconstruct the inter-related historical ecology of anthropogenic forest formations and crop genetic resources, and concludes that if a high percentage (68) per cent of Amazonian domesticates, semi-domesticates and incipiently domesticates are trees and woody perennials, this is not to be attributed to the nature of the forest ecosystem, but, rather, to the high dependence of domesticated annuals on human management. According to Clement, contact triggered two parallel processes: the physical disappearing of human populations and crop genetic erosion. This explains why diversity, especially the infraspecific diversity of cultivars, was reduced shortly after large indigenous Amazonian societies succumbed to world diseases and depopulation. Clement's comprehensive synthesis adds a new dimension to Balée's (1993) estimation that at least 12 per cent of the Amazon rain forest is of anthropogenic origin, in other words, that its present species distribution reflects some sort of human intervention. Recent archaeological studies of anthrosols (dark earth produced through repeated habitation and horticulture) and elaborate earthworks used as habitation mounds and designed to control water for food production (such as raised fields, mounds, and causeways, or tracts of reclaimed wetland savannah) point to the same long-term impact of human intervention on the Amazon's biotic and abiotic landscapes.[9]

Assessment and interpretation of the archaeological data from the Amazon basin is not, however, without difficulties. The literature is full of debates fuelled by disagreements between archaeologists on the existence and the form of pre-Columbian Amazonian chiefdoms, as well as the striking disparity between ethnographic and archaeological accounts. Archaeologists and anthropologists working in the cultural ecology tradition stress the social and cultural discontinuity between pre-Columbian and contemporary Amazonian societies, with their basic social organisation of small, politically independent and egalitarian local groups formed through cognatic ties. They treat high mobility and foraging as indicators of historical change. The nomadic, foraging way of life of interfluvial groups does not reflect, they argue, the pattern that predominated in pre-Columbian Amazonia, where elaborate autochthonous chiefdoms developed and flourished. What is at stake in this debate is the nature of the changes that occurred before, during and after the Conquest, and how we are best to understand the interactions between the natural history of the forest and the eventful, uneven and violent history of human societies in this part of the world.

What kinds of society and what types of cultivation existed in the Amazon prior to 1492? As I have summarised elsewhere the debates on Amazonian chiefdoms (Rival 2002),[10] and as I have already commented on the theory of cultural devolution and agricultural regression, a theory which purports to explain the ecological, cultural, social, and political consequences of post-contact demographic collapse in Amazonia (Rival 2002, 2006a), I simply wish here to point to the problems of analysing the link between large-scale field systems and more complex hierarchical polities or the relationship between domestication, sedentism and social stratification from the premise that Amazonia was first and foremost a land of ancient chiefdoms and intensive agricultural systems.

While I understand the desire of many contemporary archaeologists to acknowledge and assess accurately the level of agrobiodiversity and political complexity created by humans in the Amazon region between the late Pleistocene and European contact, as well as the extent of the erosion that ensued, I lament a tendency found in authors such as Roosevelt (1998) and Heckenberger (2005) to over-generalise the power, stability, and importance of pre-Columbian chiefdoms. Given that the hinterlands were simultaneously used by indigenous populations living in sedentary, densely populated village settlements, and by small, mobile groups dispersed throughout the forest, I prefer to stress, like Denevan (1996: 159–61, 2001), the – almost certainly conflictive – co-existence of various types of society and food production systems in fifteenth-century Amazonia. Renard-Casevitz (2002: 141) uses a similar approach when she cautiously warns that 'there is no necessary connection [in the Bolivian Amazon] between the transformation of the landscape of the savanna and the existence of powerful chieftainships.' She disagrees with the evolutionary reconstruction proposed by archaeologist Clark Erikson (2000), and refuses to interpret the Bolivian earthworks as a proof of the existence of hierarchically centralised polities in this region. In her view, these earthworks were produced by 'sets of farmers settled in dispersed sites varying in size and formed by a reticular system of exchange' (Renard-Casevitz 2002: 141). Finally, we must acknowledge that not all people follow the typically western botanical classification of plants into two distinct categories, wild and domesticated (Rival 2006a and 2006b, Clement 1999: 189).

Errors as unfortunate as those of the 1950s to 1970s[11] will be perpetuated if the assumption is made that, if it had not been for the Conquest, Amazonia's native populations would have continued to develop intensive agriculture and would have increasingly complexified. The consensual view that Europe's invasion of lowland South America caused not only the demographic collapse of native populations but also their massive cultural devolution fails to account fully for the dynamic interaction between history and ecology. Evolutionary/devolutionary processes, which, ultimately, always imply that agricultural intensification is inherently progressive, do not offer the best explanation of the link between the physical world and human societies. If we are to analyse human/environment interactions holistically, we need to take into consideration both the physical environment and the mental world of Amerindians.

Much more promising is an approach that recognises that indigenous peoples actively manipulated the forest ecosystem, enriched the soils, managed and diversified a wide range of plant species, and, in the process, created the material and physical conditions to maintain different social formations. Only some of these were characterised by high population density levels. Moreover, the crucial question of what motivated some groups to gather in large numbers and consume greater quantities of cultivated food crops must be addressed. If we accept Piperno's and Pearsall's thesis that food crops were progressively domesticated between 8,000 and 4,000 BP in Southwest Amazonia by small, fairly mobile family units in house gardens,[12] we must recognise that the relatively sudden intensification of agriculture and the appearance of densely populated and stratified villages occurred only in some very specific areas. Such areas have recently been identified with the Arawak cultural complex (Hill and Santos Granero 2002, Hornborg 2005). I have argued in this section for a dynamic history of plant/human interaction in Amazonia, that is, a history where cultural choices matter. Foraging, incipient horticulture, and intensive, sedentary agriculture were not just alternative modes of subsistence. By choosing one mode of subsistence rather than another, people were also choosing a particular form of life, and a particular identity.

Plant domestication as an identity issue

Native Amazonians, like all peoples, are active shapers of ecological, economic, and historical forces (see Ulijaszek, this volume). Evans-

Pritchard (1940), following in the steps of Beuchat and Mauss (1979[1906]), showed a long time ago that the Nuers' deep sense of identity as pastoralists, although certainly shaped by environmental conditions, could not be reduced to resource economics or energy efficiency calculations. It is only by taking into consideration the autonomous dynamics and rhythms of social life that we are able to offer an explanation of why the Nuer valued cattle herding over all the other subsistence activities they engaged in. A similar argument was put forward by Moore and Vaughan (1994) in their historical reconstruction of Bemba life during the colonial period. Richards (1932) was right to point to the centrality of finger-millet cultivation and food production in Bemba life, but she did not see clearly enough how political the citemene agricultural complex was. A group's adoption of either hunting and gathering or intensive agriculture as the main and valued subsistence strategy represents a collective choice. Integral to the identity formation process, this choice comes to form the basis for the development of historical consciousness. Although Diamond and Bellwood (2003) may disagree, much of the comparative data they present can, in my view, be read in this light. The shortcoming of both the evolutionary and the historical mode of explanation, as argued above, is that they leave no room at all for understanding the subsistence activities of trekkers and foragers in cultural terms, that is to say, for including in the analysis their own conceptualisation of gathering and hunting in cultural landscapes, or their own discourse about their subsistence practices. Archaeologists such as Anna Roosevelt, historical ecologists such as Bill Balée, and evolutionary biologists such as Jared Diamond assume that adaptation is best defined in terms of increasing sociocultural complexity built on increasing population density and sedentariness. These authors tend to think that where the land is arable, horticulture is to be expected. The absence of horticulture, therefore, requires an explanation which automatically locates hunter–gatherers at the lowest stage of cultural evolution and progress. However, we need to ask: What does indirect reliance on past agriculture, rather than on crops cultivated now mean to the non-horticulturalists? What difference does it make, practically and symbolically, to hunt in a pristine, wild forest, or to hunt in forests modified by previous human intervention and management?

Amazonian trekkers and foragers extract semi-domesticates growing in ancient or old agricultural fallows. The issue is not so much whether trekkers and foragers develop their subsistence activities in pristine or culturally transformed forests. We know that humans have lived and survived without domesticates in rain forests (Piperno and Pearsall 1998: 55–61; Bahuchet et al 1991, Hladik and Dounias 1993). What matters, rather, is *how* they cultivate and *why*, that is, for which purposes. What we also need to know is the extent to which the answers to these questions differ for the two groups: those who rely primarily on hunting-and-gathering, and those who produce and trade food crops. Most of the world's contemporary hunters-and-gatherers are directly or indirectly involved in other economic activities such as marginal or sporadic farming activities and wage labour. What characterises them is the way in which they engage in these economic activities, as well as the distinctive social relations they maintain among themselves and with outsiders. Hunting-and-gathering is as much a social and a cultural phenomenon as it is a form of ecological–economic adaptation (Rival 1999). If the regional context in which many Amazonian Indians live is hunter–horticulturalist, some are living according to the hunter–gatherer mode. We need to examine the social and cultural distinctiveness of the latter without starting from the dominant assumption that non-cultivating behaviour is attributable to cultural loss (Rival 2006a).

Hunting-and-gathering is a way of life that human groups may choose to adopt and maintain. Said differently, hunting-and-gathering may be a form of adaptation to the environment, but it is above all a way of life, i.e. a way of organising society and thinking about the world (Rival 2006b). Evolutionary theory and history help us understand how human action has shaped nature, but to understand how nature has shaped human action – that is, how we have domesticated ourselves in the process of domesticating the environment (Dunbar, this volume) – we need to envisage human intelligence as embodied, distributed, and social (Gosden and Ingold, this volume). As mentioned at the beginning of this chapter, palaeo-anthropologists think that the first humans colonised the far north, the Americas, and the islands of the Pacific either in the late Pleistocene or early Holocene, when the last glacial maximum came to an end. It was only in the Holocene, beginning a mere 10,000 years ago, that agricultural economies developed (Diamond 1997, Mithen 1996, 2006), and that the emergence of genetic unity and cultural diversity really started to set in.[13] The early inhabitants of the Amazon basin who first domesticated squash, maize, peach palm and manioc at *c.* 8,000 to 4,000 years ago were fully adapted to, and cognisant of, an extraordinary diversity of environments, which they were able to observe, perceive, classify, understand and discuss with as much sophistication as contemporary native Amazonians do. Moreover, they were as capable of symbolic behaviour and 'cognitive fluidity' (Mithen 1996, Carruthers 2002) as the latter. This is why the apprehension of natural history by either past or contemporary native Amazonians cannot be reduced to mere effective decision making about which resources to exploit in order to gain reproductive advantage. Amazonian environmental knowledge combines in complex ways intuitive biology, anthropomorphic belief and ritual behaviour (Atran et al 2005, Rappaport 1999). The partial autonomy of socio-cultural phenomena is directly related to cognitive fluidity and distributed intelligence. Together, they help us understand why the action of hunters-and-gatherers on the environment is complex, and why hunters-and-gatherers transform nature even if they do not produce in the sense that farmers do, or why human choices and decisions are influenced by social considerations, political orientations and cultural values.

The population bottlenecks that resulted in the twin emergence of genetic unity and cultural diversity cannot be divorced from the ways in which ecology, economy and ethnic identity have become all inter-related to form cultural wholes. Ethnic identity, that is the recognition of a collective difference between 'my group' and 'your group' reflected or not by linguistic difference, is a form of historical self-consciousness, that is, the product between externally attributed and internally experienced qualities, including modes of subsistence, particular landscapes associated with one's mode of life, system of values, and political ethos (Leach 1954, Hornborg 2005). It is by examining the relationship between ecology, economy, and ethnic identity that we will really comprehend the dynamics of landscape and species domestication, as well as the impact of plant and animal domestication on human genetic evolution (Ulijaszek, this volume).

A vast body of ethnographic work suggests that despite clear differences in the intensity with which the Amazon forest is transformed, everywhere we find the cultural centrality of landscape domestication (Wilbert 1961, Denevan 2001). Everywhere, ecological affordances are matched by different subsistence options, and values are attached to economic activities that lead to specific environmental transformations while serving as foundations for ethnic identity construction. The many groups living in the upper Rio Negro left numerous petroglyphs and rock paintings and the Wakuenai continue to create sacred landscapes through ceremonially chanting (Hill 1993). For some groups, such as the Huitoto (Griffiths 2001), the Achuar (Descola 1994), the Curripaco (Journet 1995) or the Makushi (Rival 2001), to name just a few, gardening epitomises human work as a civilising force, which is opposed to wilderness and savagery. While food made out of processed bitter manioc serves as a prime ethnic marker for many groups in northwest Amazonia (Hugh-Jones and Hugh-Jones 1996), the production and consumption of sweet manioc beer is central to the Canelo Quichua's sense of identity (Guzman Gallegos 1997).[14] Alimentary choices (eating forest tubers or garden crops, hunted game or fish, and so forth) are used to draw the boundaries of differentiated moral economies based on, but not reducible to, subsistence activities. In Amazonia, you become what you eat, and the opposition between forest and garden food, or game and fish is used to materialise a wide spectrum of identity positions, or to articulate a range of more or less inclusive or exclusive definitions of humanity.

The association of civilised humanity and gardening commonly found in northwest Amazonia is particularly striking, especially when compared with similar constructions opposing civilised gardeners to wild hunters-and-gatherers found in other regions of the world, particularly in central Africa. The patron–client relationship that unites Tukanoan communities of the Vaupés and the Río Negro with Makú bands is well documented. The Makú, who live deep in the forest, hunt, collect, and garden marginally. They periodically visit the sedentary, fishing, and manioc-cultivating communities of their Tukanoan trading partners, where they receive garden produce, tobacco, and manufactured goods in exchange for their forest produce (especially game), labour, baskets, and blowguns. This relationship, which has economic, political, and symbolic dimensions (Ramos 1980, Jackson 1983), is almost identical to that described by Grinker (1994) for the Efe Pigmies and Lese Bantus. The Tukanoan Indians despise the forest dwelling hunting Makú, whom they see as savages, incestuous and animal-like (Ramos 1980: 166). This moral judgement clearly shows that foraging means more than simple adaptation to the physical environment. In some villages, the Makú are partially incorporated into Tukano society as second-class, marginal citizens, and treated as dependent sons-in-law, even if a Tukano/ Makú marriage alliance would be totally unthinkable. Treated as 'owned' slaves, captives, or co-resident clients, the Makú are seen as sub-human. In fact, their structural position is identical to that of adopted pets (Erikson 1984). For the Tukanos, the Makú do not simply 'make a living;' they live like savage animals. The Makú also perceive their way of life as more than simple adaptation to the forest environment. However, ethnographers tell us much less about Makú understandings of themselves and their relational order than they do about the Tukanos, their values, and their prejudices. Within their communities, the Makú emphasise egalitarianism and the collective appropriation of resources. With the Tukanos, they choose to be elusive. On the surface, they seem to comply with the commands of their non-foraging neighbours. However, as soon as they are back in their forest camps, the Makú make great fun of the Tukanos' airs of superiority. Moreover, no obligation ties them to the latter; they come and go to the gardeners' villages as they please. Only additional research will tell us whether the Makú have yielded control over some aspects of their material and spiritual life to their agricultural neighbours (Grinker 1994). There is nevertheless sufficient ethnographic evidence to support the thesis that subsistence and diet choices play a key role in shaping Makú and Tukano ethnic identities.

In other Amazonian societies we find a positive correlation at the level of discourse between mobility and warfare on the one hand, and peace, gardening, and village life on the other. Journet (1995) notes that the Curripaco, who identify horticulture with peace and the foundation of society, equate the nomadic style of the Makú, seen as antithetical to culture and anterior to civilisation, with warfare, hunting, and autarky. Although the Curripaco were as ready to wage war as the neighbouring groups that they represented as warlike and fierce forest dwellers, they condemned violence morally, and saw themselves as being forced to resort to violence. Fausto's study (2001) of two Parakana groups who chose, after splitting, to live according to two divergent ways of life – nomadism and sedentism – illustrates the same association between pacific village life, horticulture, and sedentism on the one hand, and foraging, warfare, and nomadism on the other. However, the Parakana do not hold the same negative moral judgement on violence. The Tupi–Guarani 'mystical' wars, the more strategic violence practised by Arawakan groups, and the forms of warfare and violence induced by colonial politics are profoundly different. Fighting an enemy recognised as a complete other is not the same as fighting an enemy perceived as a recognisable other (Descola 1993). The volume edited by Hill and Santos Granero (2002) contains numerous references to the moral condemnation of violence as an important Arawakan ethnic marker. The prohibition of endowar, coupled with a strong ethnic prejudice against wild Indians, was central to the development of an Arawakan pan-ethnic ethos. Moral barriers existed not between the lowlands and the highlands of Peru, Ecuador and Bolivia as previously thought, but, rather, between traders and warriors. As Lévi-Strauss (1943) pointed out some time ago, different visions of humanity are implicated in the 'commerce or war' dialectics. What is at stake in the Amazon warfare complex is the definition of humanity. The human condition, as portrayed in Amazonian myths, is essentially a process of humanisation, or, in other words, of domestication. Today, the dual classification nomadic foragers/sedentarised gardeners is no longer closely associated with the opposition between warmongering and peace, but, rather, with the contrast between integrated indigenous communities and communities refusing all contact with outsiders.[15] There are today throughout the Amazon basin individuals and communities who consider themselves 'civilised'. Not unlike their pre-Columbian Tukanoan predecessors, they appropriate the modern discourse of peace and civilisation to force contact with nomadic groups and bring them to their villages to teach them 'how to live as real humans'.

This usually involves educating them in the arts of sedentary village life and horticultural production. The ethnic antagonism between opposing societies that refuse to submit to the authority of chiefdoms and favour autarky over trade and inter-ethnic exchange, and those who accept their incorporation and historical transformation is, as this most recent form of denigration shows, very old indeed.

Amazonian landscapes:
Wild, tamed, and humanised forests

I started this chapter by noting the continuing validity of Lévi-Strauss' perceptive remark on the Amazonian propensity to domesticate forest landscapes, rather than plant species. I then argued that if Clement is right to stress the enormous historical disruptions caused by the Conquest, reliance on semi-domesticates should not be explained away as cultural loss. The intensification of plant domestication, far from being systematic, was highly localised, and conditioned by cultural values. Some authors have attempted to identify historical continuities in the ethos and subsistence practices of socially stratified traders such as those pertaining to the Arawakan diaspora (Honborg 2005). I have similarly argued that some Amazonian trekkers and foragers, far from being devolved agriculturalists, may be characterised by comparable historical continuities expressing values that stand in contrast to those held by their cultivating neighbours. By choosing to contribute to transforming the forest without intensifying the selection and the propagation of fully domesticated plant species, native Amazonians who choose to remain mobile and rely more on hunting and gathering than on cultivation, also choose to transform human society in a way that is not conducive to the reproduction of political hierarchies or economic inequalities.

Ecology cannot be defined with sole reference to the natural environment. A biocultural phenomenon such as plant domestication needs to be placed within its full historical and political context. In Amazonia, the interactions between foragers and cultivators, as well as the dynamics of social change, both historically and in the contemporary context, have involved contrastive and co-existing modes of sociality. As Winthrop (2001) puts it, patterns of economy and belief guide human action with regard to the environment.[16] Politics in Amazonia is characterised by undeveloped hierarchies, weak links between chiefs (hosts) and followers (guests), the importance of ceremonial life and feasting, and the prestige of having large quantities of food to offer. All these aspects have played a significant role in driving food crop domestication. They have also played a part in the use of foods – selected for their nutritional and symbolic importance – as ethnic markers. But it is also true that in many communities, indigenous ideas about space, time, the human condition, and wilderness as the potentially transformable have been used to resist political pressures to develop and increase productivity. Adding to this play of contradictory forces, the needs of long distance trade, and, after the Conquest, European influences, also favoured the evolution of subsistence systems in the direction of agricultural intensification, for instance the extension of manioc or maize monocultures (Steward and Faron 1959: 293). These are precisely the trends that are rejected by those who choose to isolate themselves, and to become 'uncontacted' foragers. In short, there is more to landscape domestication than a linear move towards full agricultural development in a region where dual oppositions of the type fierce/tame abound, and where nature is constructed in terms of its domesticability, that is, its unrealised potential for civilisation.

Plant domestication is an evolutionary, historical and cultural process, which needs to be viewed through the holistic lens of the new ecological anthropology paradigm. Its proper analysis requires the development of a unitary analytical framework that integrates relations between biology, ecology, economy, material culture, language and identity. Whereas ecological studies are concerned with relations between living organisms belonging to different species and their environment, ecological anthropology focuses on the complex relations between ecosystems and social groups. As such, it directs our attention to the ways in which a particular group of people purposely or unintentionally shapes its environment, as well as to the ways in which relations with the environment shape a population's social, economic and political life – in one word, its culture. Put differently, ecological anthropology explores the ways in which the environment is historically and culturally produced through human/nature interactions. Building on Roy Rappaport's (1999) interpretation of culture as a system regulating relations between people and their environments, the new ecological anthropology focuses on the interface between cultural and biophysical factors in terms of integrative, biocultural processes. Given that material factors, tools, technology, knowledge, and productive organisation equally act as powerful mediators between the biophysical environment and human culture, ecological adaptations are never purely 'natural'. Biophysical factors, which are shaped by humans in a material sense, are also culturally perceived. As such, they form part of the ongoing relations of mutual adaptation between culture and material context. Given that the environment is always more than just a set of things to which people adapt, the influences of the biophysical factors on human behaviour are never purely material.

It is now widely accepted that we all share the same biological intuitions (Atran et al 2005, Mithen 2006). Mithen argues that if early humans such as *Homo habilis* already possessed an evolved capacity for ethnobiological knowledge, modern humans alone developed, some 170,000 years ago, a capacity for language and general intelligence. When groups of *Homo sapiens sapiens* started to domesticate plants 15,000 years ago, their minds could process highly metaphoric knowledge, which complemented rather than replaced the previous intuitive physics, psychology and biology that they had inherited from their predecessors. Therefore, the humans who first domesticated plants were capable of cognitive fluidity and creative imagination; they had religious beliefs and expressed their emotions through art forms. Domestication was, and still is, a conscious process. The actions of observing and experimenting, like those of selecting and propagating, are guided by cultural representations. The motivations underlying the actions involved in reproducing plants – or any other form of life, for that matter – are neither purely pragmatic, nor simply aesthetic. Intellectual and scientific curiosity plays a role as well.

Reproductive processes raise a host of questions that directly involve the perception of life. When it comes to plants, where the individual's functional unity is not as straightforward as it is in animals, the observation of morphological differences, the recognition of individual differences, or the capacity to recognise biological variation, whether based on genetic mutation or not, become very complex actions. It is much more difficult[17] to understand the mechanics of heredity in plants than it is in animals. It is perhaps this complexity that led Canguilhem to reflect that:

> [I]t is too easily admitted that there exists a fundamental conflict between knowledge and life, and that their reciprocal aversion can only lead to the destruction of life by knowledge, or to the mocking of knowledge by life. But this fundamental conflict does not lie between thought and life within man; rather, it lies between man and the world within our human awareness of life. Intelligence can be applied to the living only if the originality of life is acknowledged. Thoughts about what lives must be formed from within life itself (Canguilhem 1975: 4).

For Canguilhem, only a holistic approach to the unity of life will restitute the human shared apprehension of life as a biological fact. The anthropologist who wishes to engage with evolutionary thinking accurately and without any reductionist agenda recognises herself in Canguilhem's position. In a similar fashion, Piña-Cabral (2005) recently called for anthropology to re-encounter its universal claims and reaffirm its common ground.[18] As David Parkin (this volume) reminds us, to reclaim anthropology as meta-tradition, we need to start by recognising the openness of social life. In addressing the challenges that face contemporary human societies, we need to acknowledge them as biocultural in part, without loosing sight of the fact that they are moral challenges as well.

Notes

1. See also Lathrap (1970). Both Lathrap and Lévi-Strauss were influenced by the cultural geographer Carl Sauer (1936, 1947).
2. *Banisteriopsis muricata* or *B. caapi, mii* in Huaorani.
3. *Bactris gasipaes, daguenkahue* in Huaorani.
4. For a review of some of the most influential explanations advanced for the transition from foraging to agriculture in the tropics and neotropics, see Piperno and Pearsall (1998: 10–26).
5. For Doyle Mc Key (pers.comm. June 2005), domestication is a co-evolved mutualism, where co-evolution is not purely genetic, but the result of dynamic interactions between genes and culture. Mc Key's model is closely related to Rindos' Darwinian explanation, as summarised by Piperno and Pearsall (1998: 11). Rindos envisages forms of co-evolution which do not involve directed human selection.
6. For Piperno and Pearsall (1998: 12), who note that 'lowland Neotropics may have had the lowest population densities of any region shown to have supported the emergence of food production during the early Holocene,' changes in food production and diet were not responses to population pressure, but, rather, to natural shifts in the abundance and distribution of resources.
7. And perhaps 1,000–2,000 years later in the New World, as humans arrived in North America by around 20,000 BP. By 12,000 BP, they had migrated to the tip of South America. By 9,000 BP, they had domesticated the first American plant in MesoAmerica, the *Cucurbita pepo* squash (Piperno and Pearsall 1998: 168). 'Systematic cultivation of back yard gardens was under way 10,000–9,000 BP in the humid, tropical lowlands of Panama, Peru, Ecuador and Colombia. By at least 9,000–8,000 BP evidence of morphological and other changes (such as larger seed size) associated with systematic cultivation and probably indicating domestication is apparent in some economic plants' (Piperno and Pearsall 1998: 259).
8. Diamond, who does not accept that climate change caused the extinction of large mammals (previous glaciation ages did not bring about the same loss of species), favours the thesis of over-hunting by recently migrated humans. It is only in Africa that large mammals co-evolved with humans, hence evolving defence mechanisms to protect themselves from human predation. Winterhalder, Piperno and Pearsall would not find Diamond's explanation satisfactory, for it assumes human population densities far higher than what they actually were in most parts of the world, that is, except for the Easter Islands on which Diamond bases his generalisation.
9. See in particular Denevan (2001), Petersen et al (2001), Erikson (2000), and all the contributions to Lehman et al (2003).
10. For a contrastive interpretation, see Heckenberger (2005).
11. When the existence of Amazonian chiefdoms was either denied or explained away as failed or short-lived attempts by Highlanders to establish civilisation in

the lowlands. See Rival (2002) for a review of these arguments. See also Wolf (1961).

12. Of proto-Arawak and proto-Tupí stock, according to Clement (person. comm. August 2005). Proto-Arawak groups then moved north and west, and continued to perfect the domestication of sweet manioc and peach palm. Proto-Tupí groups moved east and south, specialising in the domestication and improved diversification of bitter manioc.

13. Mithen (2006: S48) usefully reminds us that '[H]uman genetic diversity is highly constrained, with significantly greater differences between chimpanzees separated by a few kilometres in Africa than between humans living at the opposite ends of the earth and engaged in quite different lifestyles.'

14. Similarly, changing alimentary markers are used to signify the choice of new political and economic alliances, particularly inter-ethnic trade. For the Matsigenga who have controlled an important long distance trade route for several centuries, to consume salt is to be human. Salt has also become an important ethnic marker among Ecuador's lowland Quichua and Shuar speakers. And when the missionarised Huaorani speak of 'civilising' uncontacted Huaorani groups such as the Tagaeri, they always mention that these wild Indians must now eat proper food like sugar and rice. Traditionally, the Huaorani identified as eaters of boiled monkey meat. Old Huaorani still refuse to eat salt, or meat other than monkey and forest bird.

15. See *The Belem Declaration on Isolated Indigenous Peoples* signed on 11 November 2005, and the creation of the International Alliance for the Protection of Isolated Indigenous Peoples.

16. '[T]he economy of any society always defines an important aspect of human relationships with the environment. Beliefs and values regarding the natural world and humanity's place within it provide powerful motivations both with regard to economic practices and other types of human actions' (Winthrop 2001: 205).

17. Or, rather, it was, at least until the advent of Mendelian science.

18. 'All human "others" can only be "others" to the extent that they are the same in a very important way. But the search for that sameness involves us in a whole range of theoretical wrangles that most of us prefer to avoid. The result has been a single-minded emphasis on "difference" as the factor defining our field' (Piña-Cabral 2005: 126).

Chapter 4

THE BIOLOGICAL IN THE CULTURAL: THE FIVE AGENTS AND THE BODY ECOLOGIC IN CHINESE MEDICINE

Elisabeth Hsu

The three bodies and the body ecologic

The first article in the first issue of *Medical Anthropology Quarterly* by Nancy Scheper-Hughes and Margaret Lock (1987) outlines theoretical angles whence medical anthropologists are exhorted to approach the anthropology of the body. The authors explicitly say that they wish to prevent researchers from taking the common approach to the body that is grounded in Cartesian mind–body dualism. The 'three bodies' they outline are not topical bodies (as conceptualised by other authors who spoke of five, six or seven bodies). Rather, the understanding of each of the 'three bodies' arises from a different theoretical approach towards the study of the body. Thus, an investigation informed by phenomenology explores the 'individual body', a study informed by structuralist analysis of symbolic representations describes the 'social body', and a post-structuralist / postmodern Foucaultian approach assesses the 'body politic'. To be sure, the boundaries between the three bodies are fluid, and the social body and body politic, in particular, show overlappings. The triad is, then, to be understood as a holistically integrated fan of perspectives.[1]

This article presents a fourth theoretical approach towards the body, the 'genealogical approach', which further extends the holistic image. This genealogical approach consists of uncovering layers of past meanings contained in currently used body concepts which allude to ecological experiences. A study informed by the genealogical approach describes what I propose to call the 'body ecologic'.[2] In many medicines, humans are considered co-substantial with the natural environment, and accordingly, as is argued here, many key terms, such as hot and cold or wind and fire, convey culture-specific knowledge about experiences of ecological processes. How exactly such knowledge about ecological realities is contained in contemporary medical terminology is not a straightforward matter, however. It certainly would be futile to assess it by means of ethno-scientific tables only. Nor would a cognitive scientific approach that seeks for intrinsic qualities in the superiority of, for instance, dry over wet prove fertile to explain the esteem that the quality *jangala* (dry) enjoys over *anupa* (wet) in Ayurveda. Rather, inspired by Zimmermann's (1987) historical approach to cultural geographies, I advocate a genealogical method for investigating contemporary body concepts that ultimately are derived from ecological experiences. I argue that 'ecological realities' contained within contemporary medical terminology have become worked into elaborate learned languages (so-called 'symbolic systems') in the course of complex historical processes. It is the task of anthropologists and historians alike to unravel these complex histories.[3]

In recent years, several thinkers (three of whom are mentioned below) have emphasized that the past is contained in the present, that history is made into nature, and that accordingly, anthropology is a form of engaging in historical research. Rather than essentialising culture and culturalising contemporary social practices, anthropologists have increasingly become interested in the contiguous social and political histories of the localities that have produced these cultural practices.

How exactly an anthropologist accounts for the diachronic dimension contained in contemporary practice and usage of current indigenous terminologies depends on the particular problems investigated. This study, which concerns medical reasoning in terms of the five agents (*wuxing*) – wood, fire, earth, metal and water – in contemporary Chinese medicine (for details, see Table 4.1, p. 101), is inspired by Brian Morris's (1990) idea of engaging in a 'historical sociology', Michel Foucault's (e.g. [1971] 1991) 'archaeologies' and 'genealogies' of knowledge and Reinhart Koselleck's (e.g. 2002) 'conceptual history' (*Begriffsgeschichte*). Morris, Foucault, and Koselleck all emphasize that people's usage of concepts has distinctive histories, and that certain aspects of the history of how a concept was used is important for understanding its current meanings. Although people may use the same linguistic term in different time periods, nuances and shadings of meanings of any such term are bound to change over time. Both Foucault and Koselleck are interested in explaining the present by unearthing meanings of previous time periods that currently tend to be overlooked. It is not only situational circumstance that imbues these terms with meaning but importantly also the (unknown) histories of how people used them in the past.

Regardless of whether or not a human propensity for creating systems of correlative thinking can be demonstrated by neuro-biology (Farmer et al 2000), this body-ecological account aims to find answers in the history of the culture-specific ways in which common ecological, climatic and seasonal realities were initially understood and later systematised. In other words, it attempts to account for the biological in the cultural through a historically sensitive study.

A note on methodology

Brian Morris (1990) would not regard himself as a specialist in Chinese medicine, but when confronted with its contemporary technical terminology, he advocated that anthropologists engage in 'historical sociology' to elucidate the meanings of currently used Chinese medical terms. 'Historical sociology' is a project that explains the meaning of currently used terminology in the light of its sociology in a previous historical time period. For instance, it has variously been pointed out that in the Han dynasty (206 BC to AD 220) the concepts of the Han administration like sovereign, minister, general and the like described the functions of the heart, lungs, liver and other viscera (*Suwen* 8). Of anthropological concern here is that medical contents of this kind continue to be taught in the People's Republic of China (PRC) as basic knowledge of Traditional Chinese Medicine (TCM). It would be futile to explain the contemporary usage of these terms in a structuralist manner by alluding to the administrative institutions of the PRC. Contemporary physicians invoke Han times, the period of the formation of what Porkert (1974) called the 'medicine of systematic correspondences'.

The leap back to the Han has produced many master narratives, and in his article on the 'historical sociology' of Chinese medical terms, Morris replicated some. The historical sociological approach has to be valued for making the anthropologist aware of diachronic dimensions in contemporary terminology. However, the historical sociological approach insufficiently accounts for the fact that meanings have been modified continuously for two thousand years, and that they have a history that predates the period of the master narratives. These histories, with their many complications, interest the anthropologist who investigates the 'body ecologic' because they are relevant for current understandings of the terminology in question.

In this context, Foucault's idea of 'genealogy' becomes important. In contra-distinction to 'master narratives' that often assume a linear progression and a continuous development from a point of 'origin' to contemporary practice, Foucault emphasized that genealogies uncover unknown histories of how people use concepts. Foucault saw sharp discontinuities in the history of knowledge, (a stance he apparently had adopted from Gaston Bachelard, Georges Canguilhem and Louis Althusser), and he did so in contrast to the *Annales* school that postulated slow transitions and long-term continuities (Hacking 1986: 29–30). His concept of history, in accordance with Nietzsche's, was not one of a linear trajectory controlled by 'destiny' or 'regulative mechanisms'. Rather, it resulted from responses to 'haphazard conflicts' (Foucault 1991: 88). The histories that emerge from the genealogical approach are opposed to the history that sets out to discover the 'origin' of a tradition and 'roots' of current identity. Accordingly, a genealogy of contemporary Chinese medical terminology does not jump back into the Han dynasty for elucidating contemporary meanings. Rather, it sifts through 'a vast accumulation of source material' (ibid: 77) to uncover unknown events relevant to its current understanding.[4]

In addition to the Foucaultian inspiration, the body ecological exploration presented here will build on methodological considerations that allow for a distinction between linguistic and non-linguistic events. Foucault's 'discursive practices' do not differentiate between non-linguistic and linguistic events, for 'discourse' comprises both. Moreover, Foucault does not give much methodological guidance on how to engage in genealogies of linguistic terms. However, if one considers the 'five agents' a linguistic term, one can differentiate between linguistic and non-linguistic events, and make use of the methodological considerations Reinhart Koselleck outlines in his 'conceptual history'.

In his work on the conceptual history of mainly political terms ('crisis', 'democracy', but also 'marriage', 'emancipation', etc.), Koselleck (e.g. 2002) thought extensively about the interrelation between language and non-linguistic events in history. His conceptual history is not a history just of ideas, precisely because it takes seriously social institutions and social practices, i.e. non-linguistic events in their relation to the spoken/written word. His understanding of history contrasts two 'temporal structures', namely the 'repeatability of linguistic phenomena' versus the 'uniqueness of the sequence of events' (1989: 656). He posits that semantic structures change at a slower rate than historical events and that, due to their greater durability, linguistic terms can re-appear in different time periods, seemingly static, when people then invest them with new meanings (ibid: 657). He emphasizes that concepts have a 'diachronic thrust' that cannot be fully controlled by the speakers, and that they therefore have an 'internal temporal structure' distinct from that of events, 'events that they [the concepts] help bring about and that they are supposed to comprehend' (ibid: 659). A conceptual historical account of the term 'five agents' would thus uncover implicit meanings of the currently used term's internal temporal structure.[5]

In summary, I have sketched out three very different possibilities of how to account for the 'diachronic thrust' in contemporary medical terminology, namely Brian Morris's 'historical sociology', Michel Foucault's 'genealogical approach' and Reinhart Koselleck's 'conceptual history'. The following account, partly inspired by conceptual historical considerations, outlines a genealogy, in Foucault's sense, of one aspect of the body ecologic in Chinese medicine, namely reasoning in terms of the five agents.

The five agents in Chinese medicine

Reasoning in terms of the 'five agents' (*wuxing*) is generally considered an aspect of a natural philosophical system of 'correlative thinking'.[6] It puts different domains of experience more or less systematically in correlation with each other. It divides the universe into five great rubrics – of wood, fire, earth, metal, water – which each are co-substantive with many different aspects/entities of the universe that stand in correlation with each other. It is a cosmological scheme that has attracted the interest of many Western scholars.[7] In Chinese medicine, reasoning in terms of the five agents often explains change, for instance, devices of treatment are formulated in terms of specific interrelations between the five agents.[8] One may therefore wonder why yet another article should be devoted to this theme. The argument put forth here is that reasoning in terms of the five agents, with several layers of historically grown meaning aspects, ultimately represents a culture-specific variation on a common ecological theme, namely the seasonality of illness.[9]

The genealogical study in what follows begins with an exploration of contemporary medical practice and corroborates the well-known viewpoint that medical reasoning in terms of the five agents has been accorded the status of a *scientific theory* only as recently as in the communist–socialist interpretation of Chinese medicine, i.e. in TCM, since the late 1950s. As one sifts through textual material of the medical archive, it becomes obvious that reasoning in terms of the five agents had already an important *epistemological* significance in the Ming dynasty (1368–1644), namely as a 'heuristic device' for enhancing one's knowledge by correlating hidden processes with externally observed ones. However, if one goes back a millennium, from the Ming dynasty to the Tang dynasty (618–907), it appears that reasoning in terms of the five agents in the Tang dynasty was not primarily valued as a heuristic device or a scientific principle, but rather as an idiom that expressed a *moral concern* of a status-conscious elite aiming to live a 'life style' endowed with prestige. Working backwards from there five hundred years to the Eastern Han dynasty (AD 25–220), one finds that reasoning in terms of the 'five agents' satisfied the Han preoccupation in governmental regulation through the *politics of prognostication*. This genealogical study will show that it was by means of collapsing temporal and spatial concerns that Han physicians were able to refashion already given ecological and medical knowledge in the language of prognostication. By doing so, these Han physicians for the first time in medical history reasoned in terms of the five agents. However, contrary to the widespread assumption that it was reasoning in terms of the five agents that had them see a correlation between seasons and illnesses, this genealogical study will show that they elaborated, in fact, on an ecological theme that pre-Han physicians (before 206 BC) had already attended to, namely the seasonality of illness. To be sure, the seasonality of illness is a phenomenon cross-culturally known to many peoples, not only the ancient Chinese. Accordingly, correlative thinking in terms of the five agents in Chinese medicine is best viewed as a historically grown, culture-specific elaboration of a cross-cultural common ecological experience.

By providing evidence that in medicine ancient elite physicians' interests were ecological, this study provides an alternative to Joseph Needham's (1956: 243) master narrative that locates the first mentioning of the five agents in so-called 'proto-chemistry', in the chapter called 'Great Plan' (Hongfan) of the *Book of Documents* (*Shangshu*).[10] The 'Great Plan' passage has been extremely influential throughout Chinese history, and continues to be widely cited in Western scholarship (e.g. Unschuld 2003: 102, Lloyd 2004: 78), although it is now generally considered a late addition to the *Book of Documents* (Sivin 1987: 71) that has little to do with the concept of the five agents discussed here (Sivin 1995a: 16, n20).

It is likely that the pattern of reasoning in terms of the five agents arose in other contexts than medicine, probably that of the prognosticatory arts as practised at court during the Warring States (475–221 BC),[11] where 'ecology' may or may not have played as important a role as it did in medicine.[12] It is noteworthy that once reasoning in terms of the five agents was imported into medicine, by Han physicians, it took on a prominent role, particularly in the *Basic Questions* (*Suwen*), the first book of the *Yellow Emperor's Inner Canon* (*Huangdi neijing*), which to the present day has remained the most revered scripture in Chinese medicine.[13] It is conceivable that due to the (potentially empirical) validity of prognostications of seasonal illness occurrence, medical reasoning in terms of the five agents was very successful, and that therefore it was much elaborated in medicine. It is not inconceivable that, at a later stage, it may have been exported in its elaborate form from medicine into other fields of learned knowledge and practice.

The genealogical approach

Contemporary TCM education is the starting point for the genealogical exploration that follows, which, as one traces a genealogy, works from contemporary to ancient times. If TCM is innovative in that it considers correlative thinking in terms of the five agents a 'scientific theory', wherein lay the significance and purpose of reasoning in terms of the five agents in earlier time periods of Chinese medical history? The study investigates book structures, chapter structures, sentence structures and word structures in the Ming, Tang, Han and Warring States periods in order to uncover the layers of meaning of the texts that outline the core contents of 'The Theory of the Five Agents' in TCM. Each layer of meaning will be shown to reflect time-period-specific attitudes of physicians towards reasoning in terms of the five agents.

The five agents (*wuxing*) are presented as universal principles of 'The Theory of the Five Agents' in the opening chapters of the two main introductory TCM textbooks called *Interpretation of the Inner Canon* (*Neijing jiangyi*; Cheng 1984) and *Fundamentals of TCM Theory* (*Zhongyi jichu lilun*; Yin 1984). The introductory textbook *Interpretation* reproduces the entire classical Chinese text of, first, *Suwen* chapter 5 and then, *Suwen* chapter 4 (in this sequence), under the heading 'The Theory of Yin Yang and the Five Agents' (*yinyang wuxing xueshuo*).[14] The text of *Suwen* 5 and 4, found on pages 21 through to 42, forms the core of this genealogical study (that focuses on this one single text of TCM education). At the core of this text, on pages 26 through to 30, there are two sections, namely chapter sections *Suwen* 5.3 and 4.3, which present 'The Theory of the Five Agents' in a very systematic way.[15] They constitute the core of the theory which students have to memorise.

Strangely, 'The Theory of Yin Yang and the Five Agents' is not discussed in combination with the contents presented in the following chapters of the introductory TCM textbooks, entitled either 'Organ Clusters' (*zangxiang*) or 'Five Organs' (*wuzang*). Although everyone would agree that the 'organ clusters' and 'five organs' are an aspect of the 'five agents'. However, the introductory TCM textbooks discuss them in separate chapters. The 'five agents' are presented as universal principles of a theory on the workings of the universe, and the 'organ clusters'/'five organs' as comparatively materialist entities within a body-enveloped-by-skin.

In my previous research I found that the structure of knowledge presentation, i.e. the sequencing of chapter headings, in the introductory TCM textbooks is much the same as that given in the *Canon of Categories (Leijing)* of 1624 (Hsu 1999: chapter 6). There was continuity for three hundred years between the *Canon of Categories* and the TCM textbooks, but the *Canon of Categories* consisted of a radical re-ordering of all text passages in the *Yellow Emperor's Inner Canon (Huangdi neijing)*. The *Canon of Categories* discussed the text passages that form the core of 'The Theory of the Five Agents' in TCM, namely *Suwen* 5.3 and 4.3, under the heading of *zangxiang* (*Leijing* III and IV). In contrast to introductory TCM textbooks, which discuss *Suwen* 5.3 and 4.3 in separate chapters, correlative thinking in terms of the five agents constituted an integral part of the discussion of *zangxiang* in the *Canon of Categories*. The notion *zangxiang* in the *Canon of Categories* thus must have had slightly different meanings from *zangxiang* meaning 'organ clusters' and, for reasons given in more detail below, has been translated as referring to 'the hidden and apparent'. Correlative thinking in terms of the five agents, I argue, was useful to physicians who were interested in recognising how apparent phenomena in the universe resonated with hidden ones inside the body-enveloped-by-skin; the use of reasoning in terms of the five agents was that it was a 'heuristic device' for the enhancement of the scholar-physician's knowledge of the body ecologic.

As already stated, the *Canon of Categories* of 1624 consisted of a complete re-organisation of the contents of the *Yellow Emperor's Inner Canon* and did away with the latter's subdivision into the two books *Suwen* and *Lingshu*. The *Suwen* had been edited by Wang Bing in 762 (and re-edited in 1067 under Li Lin), the *Lingshu* is of no further concern to us here. In Wang Bing's *Suwen* edition, the text passages in question, *Suwen* 5.3 and 4.3, appear among the five opening chapters *Suwen* 1–5, which are mainly concerned with principles of self-cultivation. In *Suwen* 1–5, as will be shown below, reasoning in terms of the five agents appears to have had the main purpose of providing a proscriptive exhortation to a moderate life style.

The sentences in the *Suwen*, as some have argued (e.g. Keegan 1988), are composed according to Han dynastic grammar. By investigating the structure of all the sentences mentioned in *Suwen* 5 and 4, yet another layer of meaning contained in contemporary 'Theory of the Five Agents' is uncovered: a careful analysis of the patterning of those sentences shows that Han dynasty physicians used it particularly in those contexts of medical practice that concerned the seasonality of illness, i.e. in the contexts where they put seasons into correlation with the occurrence of specific illnesses. The numerology of five predominates in those sentences because the primarily spatial notion of the five 'directions' (north, south, east, west, and centre) represented the temporal notion of the 'seasons'. This was possible in Han dynastic medical cosmology because time and space were not conceived as different dimensions but as an intrinsically co-substantive continuum.

The genealogical method uncovers that the core of 'The Theory of the Five Agents', as given in *Suwen* 5.3 and 4.3, interrelates the five directions (implicitly meant to refer to the five seasons) with ecological and pathological changes within the 'body ecologic', but not with nosological entities such as 'cough' or 'intermittent fevers'. The correlation between seasons and specific illnesses is given in other sentences of *Suwen* 5 and 4, but not in the core theoretical texts *Suwen* 5.3 and 4.3. The genealogical method thereby demonstrates that physicians' observations that specific illnesses occur during certain seasons is fundamental for the emergence and historical development of 'The Theory of the Five Agents', but, paradoxically, no longer explicitly contained in its core texts.

An analysis of the structure of the words occurring within *Suwen* 5 and 4 highlights that reasoning concerned with the seasonality of illness pre-dated correlative thinking in terms of the five agents in medicine: sayings relating to the seasonality of illness alluded to a numerology of four rather than five. This suggests that the seasonality of illness was recognised by physicians before correlative reasoning in terms of the five agents became prominent in medicine.

Inspiration from the conceptual historical method can lead the genealogist only so far. The genealogy highlights many layers of meaning contained in 'The Theory of the Five Agents' today, but it cannot explain why correlative thinking in terms of the five agents became prominent within medical language during the Eastern Han dynasty. Based on social historical considerations, the article then postulates that reasoning in terms of the five agents was initially integrated into medicine in those contexts where physicians had already recognised regularities that could be used for formulating prognostications. It suggests that medical reasoning that adopted the language of the arts of divination and prognostication, which was cultivated among retainers at the courts of kings and nobles (Sivin 1995b), enhanced the prestige of physicians. Medical practice, which always tends to be relegated to a manual skill and denied scholarly status, thus may have gained the recognition of a courtly art among the elite of Han China by excelling in the application of the terminology of the prognosticatory arts. The medical insights that lent themselves to the formulation of prognostications in terms of the five agents built on a pre-Han recognition of the seasonality of illness.

The genealogist furthermore observes that in this process of elaborating reasoning in terms of the five agents, medical practitioners became more sensitive to the subtleties of visceral changes. Accordingly, the importance of concepts that account for such subtle changes, like *qi* and *zang* (viscera/organs), which are central to the 'five agents theory' in TCM but not in sayings dating to the Han, must have been enhanced in those contexts of medical reasoning that were framed in terms of the five agents. Ironically, this happened at the expense of neglecting the concepts that initially had made possible the adoption of this pattern of reasoning into medicine, namely the seasons and the seasonally specific illness entities, and their correlations.

The genealogical exploration of the five agents as an aspect of the body ecologic in Chinese medicine that has been sketched out above will now be discussed in more detail, thereby uncovering layers of meaning inherent to 'The Theory of the Five Agents' in contemporary TCM.

A genealogy, inspired by conceptual history, of layers of meaning contained in the contemporary concept of the 'five agents' (*wuxing*)

TCM textbooks of 1984: the five agents as universal principles of 'The Theory of the Five Agents', a highly elaborate and culture-specific learned language

The so-called 'Theory of the Five Agents' (*wuxing lun or wuxing xueshuo*) figures prominently in TCM education, and also in clinical practice; it is considered scientific (*kexuehua*).[16] The first year students learn from the *TCM Fundamentals* cycles of change and these scripts of how changes occur in cycles are indispensable for formulating complex considerations of treatment (Hsu 1999: 210). First year students furthermore learn the correlates of each of the five agents (*xing*), ranging from tones (*yin*), flavours (*wei*), colours (*se*), types of transformation (*hua*), kinds of *qi*, directions (*fang*), and seasons (*ji*) to inner organs (*zang*), bowels (*fu*), orifices/offices (*guan*), kinds of tissue (*xingti*), feelings (*qingzhi*), [human] sounds (*sheng*), and [pathological] movements (*biandong*) (*TCM Fundamentals* 1984: 20, reprinted in Hsu 1999: 203). The second year students read the *Interpretation of the Inner Canon*, which quotes and annotates *Suwen* 5 and 4.

The contents of the 'The Theory of the Five Agents' that TCM students learn are given in Table 4.1. *Suwen* 5.3 and 4.3 are remarkable for the systematic way in which they postulate correspondences between the five directions and their correlates. In Table 4.1, only the correlations of one direction, the east, are given, but *Suwen* 5.3 and 4.3 also spell out the interrelations for the other four directions. They provide most of the information contained in the tables of the five agents and their correlates in modern TCM textbooks.[17] No doubt, these correlations represent a highly sophisticated culture-specific understanding of the natural world, but it is difficult to see how exactly they relate to an immediate ecological experience. Hence the genealogist attempts to uncover the relevance of these correlations

Table 4.1 *The contents of the 'The Theory of the Five Agents' that students of Traditional Medicine learn*

Suwen 5.3 begins with a direction (e.g. the east), which is said to give rise to a climatic illness factor (e.g. wind), which gives rise to an agent (e.g. wood), that in turn gives rise to a flavour (e.g. sourness), that gives rise to a viscus (e.g. the liver), that gives rise to a tissue (e.g. the sinews), that in turn gives rise to another viscus (e.g. the heart). The text then mentions the aperture (e.g. the eyes) that is governed by the viscus. This is followed by an enumeration of the corresponding climatic illness factor in heaven (e.g. wind), the corresponding agent on earth (e.g. wood), and the corresponding tissue (e.g. the sinews), viscus (e.g. the liver), colour (e.g. blue), tone (e.g. *jue*), [human] sound (e.g. to shout out), movement (e.g. to shake), aperture (e.g. the eyes), flavour (e.g. sourness), and intent (e.g. anger). Thereupon follow the interrelations between the intent (e.g. anger) harming the viscus (e.g. the liver) and the intent (e.g. grief) that can overcome this intent (e.g. anger); the climatic illness factor (e.g. wind) harming the tissue (e.g. the sinews) and the climatic illness factor (e.g. dryness) that can overcome this factor (e.g. wind); the flavour (e.g. sourness) harming tissue (e.g. the sinews) and the flavour (e.g. acidity) that can overcome this flavour (e.g. sourness). These correspondences are systematically given for wood, fire, earth, metal, and water. The text in *Suwen* 4.3 provides extensive information on the interrelations of direction (e.g. the east), colour (e.g. blue-green), viscus (e.g. the liver), aperture (e.g. the eyes), illness (e.g. convulsions), flavour (e.g. sourness), agent (here referred to as *lei* rather than *xing*; e.g. herbs and wood), animal (e.g. the rooster), grain (e.g. wheat), star (e.g. Jupiter), seasonal *qi* (e.g. spring *qi*) in tissue (e.g. the head), tone (e.g. *jue*), number (e.g. eight), tissue (e.g. the sinews), and smell (e.g. foul smell, as that of urine), with slight variations for each of the five entries.

by viewing them as a historically grown system of knowledge. The following comparison of the contents of *Suwen* 5.3 and 4.3 suggests that the five agents have been interpreted in increasingly internalising ways (Young 1976).

Suwen 5.3 contains more extensive correlations than *Suwen* 4.3, and includes also information on the interrelations between each of the five agents, namely giving birth (*sheng*) and overcoming (*ke*). Moreover, *Suwen* 5.3 refers to aspects inside the body-enveloped-by-skin not mentioned in *Suwen* 4.3, namely the apertures (*qiao*), the different kinds of intent (*zhi*), and [pathological] movements (*bian dong*). However, *Suwen* 4.3 mentions correlates in the outside world, not mentioned in *Suwen* 5.3: the animals, grains, stars, numbers, smells as well as a seasonal *qi*.

It is difficult to know the exact date of the composition of each of the text passages recorded in the *Suwen*. Parts of *Suwen* 5 are sometimes said to belong to the *Suwen* chapters of uncertain origin.[18] Therefore, *Suwen* 4.3 may represent an earlier stage of reasoning in terms of the five agents in medicine than *Suwen* 5.3. If this were the case, one could point to a tendency to emphasize aspects of the five agents' correspondences that refer to processes inside the 'body-enveloped-by-skin', at the cost of neglecting aspects of the outside world; one could speak of an historical development away from an externalising medicine towards an internalising one (Young 1976).

The tendency to provide an internalising interpretation of the five agents is particularly blatant in the contemporary textbook *TCM Fundamentals*. Introductory lectures for TCM students before mid-term examinations in the first year centre on so-called physiological–functional (*shengli zuoyong*) processes inside the body-enveloped-by-skin (Hsu 1999: table 6.8), most importantly, those of the five organs (*wuzang*): the liver (*gan*), heart (*xin*), spleen (*pi*), lungs (*fei*) and kidneys (*shen*).[19]

On a village health station, by contrast, I overheard people talking of fire, wood and water when they were speaking about their bodily states (Anning, September 1989). On another serendipitous occasion, I met with acupuncturists from rural Henan, who presented me with a picture of the human body with acupuncture points that referred to the five agents. This representation of the body showed no channels, but instead depicted five central acupuncture points in the centre of the abdomen: the earth in the middle (at the position of *guanyuan* or *zhongji*) and the fire, metal, water and wood around it. It also showed various other spots of the body onto which acupuncture points were projected in a similar concentric way. These acupuncturists thought of bodily processes in terms of earth, wood, fire, metal and water, which they knew were co-substantive with the five organs, but they did not explicitly name the latter (Kunming, December 1989).

In summary, while most people compare and contrast TCM primarily with Western medicine, and therefore consider correlative thinking in terms of the five agents typical of a comparatively 'holistic medicine', the above suggests that if one compares TCM to some contemporary rural practices of medicine, it displays tendencies of an internalising medicine. It would seem likely that the emphasis in TCM on internal bodily concepts, like the five organs, results from biomedicine being the dominant medicine practised in contemporary China. However, a close analysis of introductory TCM textbooks reveals that the foundations for such an internalising interpretation of the body were laid already three to four hundred years ago, before Chinese medical doctors had come into close contact with Western medicine. By paying attention to the footnotes and sources of the citations given in the textbooks on the *Interpretation of the Inner Canon* (*Neijing jiangyi*) and the *TCM Fundamentals* (*Zhongyi jichu lilun*), in the fashion of Foucault's meticulous genealogist, I found that TCM textbook compilers frequently referred to the *Canon of Categories* (*Leijing*).

Zhang Jiebin's Leijing *of 1624: the five agents as an epistemological heuristic device for the enhancement of the scholar-physician's knowledge*

In the *Canon of [ordering knowledge according to] Categories* (*Leijing*) of 1624, Zhang Jiebin (1562–1640) completely re-organised the knowledge presented in the *Yellow Emperor's Inner Canon*. He said it was necessary to re-order it in a thematic way (*Lei jing* ([1624] 1985: 1–8). Interestingly, the thematic chapters or, in his words, the 'categories' (*lei*) he created, continue to structure the overall presentation of medical knowledge in the introductory textbooks *TCM Fundamentals* and *Interpretation of the Inner Canon* (Hsu 1999: table 6.4). There are variations, no doubt, but nevertheless it is noteworthy that introductory Chinese medical books have maintained the same overall structure of knowledge presentation, despite the enormous political upheavals that China has seen in the last three to four hundred years.[20]

The notion of *zangxiang* figures prominently in the *Canon of Categories* of 1624 and also in the TCM textbooks of 1984. The conceptual historian expects that the same linguistic term has been reapplied within a different programme of action. This is indeed so. Rather different text extracts from the *Yellow Emperor's Inner Canon* are assembled under the respective chapter headings *zangxiang* (see Hsu 1999: tables 6.6 and 6.9). Accordingly, the contents differ: the text passages assembled under *zangxiang* in the *Canon of Categories* concern a 'body ecologic', while the *zangxiang* chapter in the *Interpretation* contains text passages that allude mostly to a 'body-enveloped-by-skin'. To be sure, in TCM *zangxiang* also relate to variables outside the 'body-enveloped-by-skin', but, as demonstrated above, there is an undeniable tendency to interpret the five agents in an internalising way.

Zangxiang in TCM has been approximated as 'orbs', 'visceral systems' or 'organ clusters', but what meaning did Zhang Jiebin himself invest into the notion of *zangxiang*? In his comments on *Suwen* 8, which he cites in the first section of the *zangxiang* category, he says that he uses the notion *zang* in the sense of *kucang*, which means 'to store' (*Leijing* [1624] 1985: 30). In the context of commenting in the second section of the *zangxiang* category, when commenting on *Suwen* 9, he asks: 'What are *zangxiang* like? [*zangxiang he ru?*]' '*Xiang*', he answers, 'is the appearance/ image/ configuration of a form' [*xiang xing xiang ye*]. 'The *zang* are located on the inside [of the body], [their] forms appear on the outside, hence one speaks of *zang xiang* [*zang ju yu nei, xing jian yu wai, gu yue zang xiang*] (ibid: 33). These comments suggest that Zhang Jiebin assembled textual extracts from the *Yellow Emperor's Inner Canon* under the heading *zangxiang*, which accounted for the resonance of external and internal bodily dynamics, hidden and apparent ones.[21] His preoccupation with the inner and outer, the hidden and the apparent, is obvious also in his choice of the textual extract from *Lingshu* 3 for the third section in *zangxiang* category. It concerns the inner and outer (*biaoli*) aspects of the *zangxiang* (ibid: 34–35). *Zangxiang* in Zhang Jiebin's sense seems to allude to apparent and hidden aspects of the body ecologic (for more detail, see Hsu 2000a: 175 and 178–183).

In summary, Zhang Jiebin discussed the textual extracts of *Suwen* 5 and 4 in two different categories, *yinyang* and *zangxiang*, depending on whether they were framed in a numerology of two or five. He had the body ecologic in mind, and used reasoning in terms of the five agents as a heuristic device for correlating the apparent to the hidden. Despite the striking continuity in the overall structure of knowledge presentation, which arises from comparing the chapter headings in the *Canon of Categories* of 1624 and the introductory TCM textbooks of 1984, subtle variations in the regrouping of the textual extracts discussed under the chapter headings in question reveal important differences in the interpretation of the five agents. Continuities are found in the attitude of the doctors and in the significance they attributed to reasoning in terms of the five agents that was valued then, as it is now, as knowledge enhancing.

Wang Bing's Suwen of 762: the five agents as a proscriptive device outlining an honour-seeking status group's life style

Whereas the footnotes and citations in introductory TCM textbooks led the genealogist from TCM textbooks to Zhang Jiebin's *Canon of*

Categories, Zhang Jiebin himself explicitly refers to the *Yellow Emperor's Inner Canon*, which consisted of two books, Wang Bing's *Suwen* edition of 762 and a *Lingshu* edition of no further concern to this study. Strictly speaking, a genealogy would focus merely on the analysis of *Suwen* 5.3. and 4.3, because they form the core texts of 'The Theory of the Five Agents' in TCM. However, the significance of *Suwen* 5.3 and 4.3 becomes evident only if one widens the focus and examines the context in which they are mentioned. How far should one widen the scope of context? Should one discuss merely *Suwen* 5 and 4, or examine these two chapters together with the preceding three? I eventually found that *Suwen* 5.3 and 4.3 contained textual contents that thematically formed a continuum with others discussed in the five opening chapters in Wang Bing's *Suwen* edition.[22]

Table 4.2 compares the positions in which *Su wen* 5.3 and 4.3 are mentioned in the *Su wen* of 762, the *Canon of Categories* of 1624 and the TCM *Interpretation* of 1984. It shows that *Suwen* chapters 1 and 2 are discussed in the first category of the *Canon of Categories* but at the very end of the TCM *Interpretation*, in its chapter 9. *Suwen* 3 is neither in the *Canon of Categories* nor in the *Interpretation* discussed in the opening chapters. *Suwen* 5, by contrast, is in the TCM textbook *Interpretation* discussed first, followed by *Suwen* 4. This would suggest that in TCM the contents of *Suwen* 5, which concern the 'The Theory of Yin Yang and the Five Agents', are valued highly; they are 'scientific'. By contrast, Wang Bing esteemed particularly the contents of *Suwen* 1. So, what were the contents of *Suwen* 1 that mattered so much to Wang Bing?

The contents of *Suwen* 1 and 2 emphasize, in the words of contemporary TCM doctors, 'preventive health principles' (*fangzhi yuanze*). Considering that in the *Suwen* these contents are mentioned in the first chapter, rather than a later one, 'preventive health' appears to have been a preoccupation of the editor Wang Bing in the Tang dynasty. The fact that 'preventive health' is discussed in the very last chapter of the introductory TCM textbooks would suggest that TCM textbook compilers put more emphasis on therapy. It is well known that internalising medicines tend to be therapy-oriented. This again may come as a surprise to those who generally compare TCM with Western biomedicine and hail it as a medicine that endorses preventive health. But if TCM is compared to the medicine advocated in Wang Bing's *Suwen* and Zhang Jiebin's *Canon of Categories*, it is therapy-oriented.

The contents of the following *Suwen* 3 emphasize the importance of *yangqi*, but these contents are not mentioned among the opening 'categories' (*lei*) of the *Canon of Categories* (but as late as in category 13). One wonders why. It is likely that Zhang Jiebin's understanding of *yinyang*, and particularly that of *yangqi*, differed from Wang Bing's. It is possible that in Late Imperial China the gender-specific aspects of

Table 4.2 *Chapter sections of the first five chapters in the* Suwen *edition of 762 as cited in the* Categories *(1624) and the* Interpretation *(1984)*

Suwen (Han/Tang/Song) (*Basic Questions*) Chapter sections 1.1– 5.4.4 according to Ren (1986)	Leijing (Ming) (*Canon of Categories*) Roman no. for categories Arabic no. for sections	Neijing jiangyi (PRC) (*Interpretation of the Inner Canon*) Chapters 2.1–9.2
Suwen 1.1 *shanggutian zhenlun*	*Leijing* I.1 (*sheshenglei*)	*Neijing jiangyi* 9.1 (entire *Suwen* 1)
Suwen 1.2	*Leijing* I.2 (*sheshenglei*)	
Suwen 1.3	*Leijing* III.13 (*zangxianglei*)	
Suwen 1.4	*Leijing* I.3 (*sheshenglei*)	
Suwen 2.1 *siqi tiaoshen dalun*	*Leijing* I.4 (*sheshenglei*)	*Neijing jiangyi* 9.2 (entire *Suwen* 2)
Suwen 2.2	*Leijing* I.5 (*sheshenglei*)	
Suwen 2.2 (end)	*Leijing* I.6 (*sheshenglei*)	
Suwen 2.3	*Leijing* I.6 (*sheshenglei*)	
Suwen 2.3 (end)	*Leijing* I.7 (*sheshenglei*)	
Suwen 3 *shengqi tongtian lun*	*Leijing* XIII.5 (*jibinglei*)	—
Suwen 4.1 *jingui zhenyan lun*	*Leijing* XV.27 (*jibinglei*)	**Neijing jiangyi 2.2** (entire *Suwen* 4)
Suwen 4.2	*Leijing* II.5 (*yinyanglei*)	
Suwen 4.3	**Leijing III.4 (zangxianglei)**	
Suwen 5.1 *yinyangyingxiangdalun*	*Leijing* II.1 (*yinyanglei*)	**Neijing jiangyi 2.1** (entire *Suwen* 5)
Suwen 5.2	*Leijing* II.1 (*yinyanglei*)	
Suwen 5.3	**Leijing III.5 (zangxianglei)**	
Suwen 5.4.1	*Leijing* II.2 (*yinyanglei*)	
Suwen 5.4.2	*Leijing* II.2 (*yinyanglei*)	
Suwen 5.4.3 (1st part)	*Leijing* II.3 (*yinyanglei*)	
Suwen 5.4.3 (2nd part)	*Leijing* II.4 (*yinyanglei*)	
Suwen 5.4.4	*Leijing* XII.8 (*lunzhilei*)	

yinyang had become more pronounced, and that therefore *yin* and *yang*, more emphatically than before, were seen as a pair. In medicine, the women's department *(fuke)* gained importance after the Song dynasty (Furth 1999), in addition to the canonical medical view of taking men's bodies as the model for the ungendered body (e.g. Despeux 1996: 107); likewise, in the context of self-cultivation practices, manuals specifically for women's meditative practices started to be published in the Qing dynasty (Valussi 2003); and in pulse diagnostics differences between women's and men's pulses were emphasized not so much in the Han as in Late Imperial China (Hsu 2000b). No doubt, *yin* and *yang* formed a pair already in Han and Tang China, but in Late Imperial China the *yinyang* dualism was perhaps more stressed than before. In *Suwen* 3, *yang* is clearly imbued with positive qualities; by contrast, *yin* often alludes to the shady, dark and hidden, and sometimes even the pathological. The understanding of *yangqi* that seemed directly relevant to well-being for Wang Bing in the Tang dynasty does not seem to have been shared by the physician Zhang Jiebin in the Ming dynasty nor by contemporary TCM textbook compilers.

Suwen 5 and 4, and *Suwen* 5.3 and 4.3, in particular, have already been discussed in detail since they constitute the core of 'The Theory of the Five Agents' in TCM. What, however, was Wang Bing's aim in mentioning reasoning in terms of the five agents among the opening chapters of the *Suwen* notably, not in the first chapter but the fourth and fifth? Catherine Despeux (2001) and Paul Unschuld (2003) provide an answer. Despeux (2001: 129) cites Wang Bing as declaring in the preface to his *Suwen* commentary: 'In my youth, I liked Daoism and the techniques for tending the vital principle.' Unschuld (2003: 41) corroborates this: Wang Bing's commentary on the *Suwen* emphasizes self-cultivation. Unschuld furthermore remarks that in the process of his restructuring and amendment of the *Suwen*, Wang Bing apparently moved the first chapter sections there from a later chapter (ibid: 48), and downplayed sections on prognostics by moving them into less a prominent position and by renaming them (ibid: 45).

Notably, the opening chapters of the *Suwen* are concerned with 'techniques for tending the vital principle' and 'self-cultivation'. Likewise, Zhang Jiebin's *Canon of Categories* also discusses the contents of *Suwen* 1 and 2 as aspects of the first category called *shesheng*, 'self-cultivation',[23] and the *Interpretation*, chapter 9, as *yangsheng xueshuo*, which means 'theory of nurturing life'. Only the *TCM Fundamentals*, chapter 8, discusses the same contents under the heading 'preventive health principles'.

It is not irrelevant that the same textual contents were once conceived as self-cultivation, and now as preventive health care. While self-cultivation and preventive health can both be framed as medical practices, they importantly also have moral and political implications. Preventive health care is a public health practice; self-cultivation practices, by contrast, evolved in a different moral and political order. Preventive health ideally should apply equally to every citizen in a nation-state, but self-cultivation, for reasons given below, was probably an aspect of a 'life style' fostered among a group of people who sought 'distinction' from others.

I use the word 'distinction' in the sense of Pierre Bourdieu (1984), who showed how taste and aesthetics rather than wages and salaries segregate people into different groups, and I refer to the notion of 'life style' in the sense of Max Weber, whose definition differs sharply from the current common sense notion of 'life style' and its definition by the World Health Organization in that it alludes to a notion of 'honour' (*Ehre*).[24] 'Distinction' and 'life style', in the sense used here, both allude to aesthetics and the judgement of taste, which according to Bourdieu shaped 'social capital' and according to Weber expressed 'social power'. Since Bourdieu's ethnography concerns late twentieth century Europe, while Weber had also premodern societies in mind, I will use the latter's notion of 'life style' in what follows. If reasoning in terms of the five agents can be shown to have been relevant for carving out a particular 'life style' within the moral order that prevailed in the feudal bureaucracy of Imperial China, rather than being used as a 'heuristic device' for enhancing knowledge, yet another layer of meaning inherent to the contemporary 'Theory of the Five Agents' becomes apparent.

Strictly speaking, Max Weber used the idioms of 'life conduct' (*Lebensführung*) and the 'stylisation of life' ('*Stilisierung' des Lebens*), words that have been rendered in translation as 'life style' and have, more recently, been re-translated into German as '*Lebensstil*'. Weber ([1921]1980: 535, 537) mentions these notions only briefly in his essay on 'Political communities', in the context where he features three distinct groups of people – classes, status groups, and political parties – identified as such by the power distributions within a community. Weber points out that there are qualitatively different forms of authority and power in society: classes are identified in respect of economic power, parties in the realm of political power, and status groups in respect of power in the social domain. Within the social domain, Weber declares, power takes the form of prestige, and the notion of 'honour' (*Ehre*) is crucial. Status groups, he says, express 'honour' usually in the form of a certain 'life style', which is concerned with social interaction that is not primarily economically oriented.

Weber's allusion to 'honour' and 'status groups' in his discussion of 'life style' lends itself very well to the analysis of the social order of much of the Tang. If one accepts that the members of the various elite groups in the Tang formed a status group and not a class, 'honour' and prestige may well explain adherence to peculiar elite medical practices.[25] One can then read the opening chapters of the *Suwen*, and their insistence on self cultivation, as indicative of an elite status group's preoccupation with endorsing and expressing its power/honour through a certain life style. Self-cultivation, as presented in the opening chapters of the *Suwen*, is then understood to emphasize a certain life style. Perhaps, for Wang Bing, the significance of the *Suwen*, in addition to being a medical treatise, was also as a manual for etiquette, advising elite status group members on how to endorse/express their power/honour?

It has variously been noted that the *Suwen* contains ample information on life style, appropriate conduct in respect of age and season, proper diet and physical exertion (sexual conduct), together with information on principles of treatment, medical ethics, and the workings of the universe. Western researchers generally stress life style as an aspect of preventive health and emphasize self cultivation for the sake of longevity. Without denying the longevity enhancing aspects, it needs to be kept in mind that self cultivation has a social and moral significance that goes beyond their medical purpose. The Tang edition of the *Suwen* may well have provided prescriptive guidance for persons seeking to behave in accordance with a certain status. The emphasis on life style in a book otherwise known as a medical treatise may have appealed to an honour-seeking status group.

In other words, the opening chapters of the *Suwen* were perhaps not so much preoccupied with the modern idea of 'preventive health', as many modern doctors and researchers stress, but with prestige, etiquette and life style of an honour-seeking status group. The genealogist notes that 'The Theory of the Five Agents' as outlined in chapters 4.3 and 5.3 is mentioned in the context of self cultivation in Wang Bing's *Suwen*. The systematic correspondences that *Suwen* 4.3 and 5.3 outline prescribe regularity and moderation, i.e. a distinctive life style. Rather than being valued as a heuristic device for epistemological purposes, as in the Ming and as a science in TCM, correlative thinking in terms of the five agents may have been esteemed for its prescriptions of a certain life style in the Tang. To be sure, in TCM, 'The Theory of the Five Agents' is also understood to proscribe a regular and moderate life style, although in the PRC its medical rather than its status-enhancing aspect is stressed.

Sayings in the Suwen *from the Han dynasty (206* BC *to* AD *220):*
the five agents as an ecological prognostic device for the regulation of
government

Keegan (1988) found that the sentences of the *Suwen* are written in Han dynasty grammar. Thus, while the overall organisation of the chapters of the *Suwen* may date to the Tang, the sentence structures may well date to the Han. The genealogist interested in uncovering the layers of meaning contained in the contemporary 'Theory of the Five Agents' as given in *Suwen* 5.3 and 4.3, may now set out to examine specific sentences. Again, a focus on the chapter sections *Suwen* 5.3 and 4.3 proves too narrow, while interesting findings result from keeping the scope of analysis wide enough to include the entire chapters of *Suwen* 4 and 5 (or of *Suwen* 1–5 as done in Hsu 2001a: chapter 3, which yields basically the same results).

The main problem that now arises is how one recognises that a specific sentence concerns reasoning in terms of the five agents. There are sentences, that explicitly mention one of the five agents – wood, fire, earth, metal, and water -, but they are too few to make the analysis interesting. This in itself is a worthwhile finding; it suggests that although everyone speaks of 'The Theory of the Five Agents', the 'agents' (*xing*) themselves were not a central concept within this pattern of reasoning in its early stages.

Rather than focusing on a particular linguistic term, the examination of Han dynastic sentences was undertaken by investigating their patterning: if sentences succeeded each other with the same syntactic structure more than twice,[26] and if they mentioned one of the correlates/terms known from the core texts *Suwen* 4.3 and 5.3, I considered them to relate to reasoning in terms of the five agents. This has led to the finding presented in Table 4.3.

Table 4.3 lists paragraphs with phrases of grammatically identical structure that are sometimes four, sometimes five, and sometimes six lines long. With one exception (namely *Suwen* 4.1.a), they mention a term relating to the outside world in the beginning of each sentence, such as the 'eastern wind' (*Suwen* 4.1.b), 'spring *qi*'(*Suwen* 4.1.c), 'spring time' (*Suwen* 4.1.d), and the like, and they refer to aspects of or processes arising inside the body-enveloped-by-skin at the end of each sentence, such as the 'neck and head' (*Suwen* 4.1.b), the 'head' (*Suwen* 4.1.c), 'nose bleeding' (*Suwen* 4.1.d), and the like. These phrases thus establish a correlation between aspects of the external and internal world (with the skin as dividing line between the two). In a first approximation, the phrases in table 4.3 appear to be epistemologically relevant and do much the same as 'The Theory of the Five Agents' in TCM and the text passages assembled in the *zangxiang* category of the *Canon of Categories*.

There is a notable difference, however. In most cases, the sentences in table 4.3 establish an interrelation between an ecological variable and a specific illness. *Suwen* 5.3 and 4.3, which enumerate many correspondences between macrocosmic and microcosmic aspects of the universe, do so as well, but not as evidently (see table 4.1). A close analysis of the text passages in table 4.3 suggests that these sentences set up correlations between seasons and illness entities (see *Suwen* 4.1.b, 4.1.c, 4.1.d, and 5.2.6). They mention seasons at the beginning of a sentence and specific illness entities at the end. *Su wen* 5.2.6, for instance, reads in translation:

> If in winter you get harmed by the cold, in spring there must be a warmth disorder (*wenbing*),
> if in spring you get harmed by the wind, in summer there will be diarrhoea (*canxie*),
> if in summer you get harmed by the heat, in autumn there must be an intermittent fever (*kenüe*),
> if in autumn you get harmed by the damp, in winter there will be coughing (*kesou*).

This is an interesting finding that does not directly emerge from reading *Suwen* 5.3 and 4.3. Neither *Suwen* 5.3 nor *Suwen* 4.3 mention illness entities like warmth disorders, diarrhoea, intermittent fevers, or coughing. *Suwen* 5.3, in particular, which is hailed as the most representative text of 'The Theory of the Five Agents' in TCM, does not even mention the seasons or seasonal *qi*!

The sentences recorded in Table 4.3 clearly suggest that reasoning in terms of the five agents was grounded in ecological experiences. Han elite physicians were aware of the seasonality of certain illnesses, and they used reasoning in terms of the five agents to account for such seasonality.

Seasonality of illness is a subject that human ecologists have extensively studied and documented. Malaria (which, *inter alia*, may have been meant by the term 'intermittent fever' in the above quote of *Suwen* 5.2.6) is a prime example of such seasonal illness occurrence; it typically arises in the rainy season. According to Ulijaszek and Strickland (1993b), diarrhoea is another seasonal illness which has its peak in the wet season, while coughing and other diseases of the respiratory tract occur in particular during the dry season, when ritual events are numerous and crowding is frequent. According to Harrison (2004), not only infectious diseases, but also affective disorders, like depression, can occur in seasonal cycles.

The seasonality of illness is a phenomenon known not only to modern scientists. Chinese physicians formulated the sentences in

Table 4.3 *The repetitive phrases alluding to one aspect of five-phase theory in chapters 4 and 5 of the Basic Questions*

4.1(a)   The sequence of seasons overcoming each other

春勝長夏   spring overcomes the long summer
長夏勝冬   the long summer overcomes winter
冬勝夏   winter overcomes the summer
夏勝秋   summer overcomes autumn
秋勝春   autumn overcomes spring

(b)   The interrelations between wind, season, organ-*shu*, complaints

東風生於春 病在肝俞 在頸頭	if the Eastern wind arises in spring, the illness resides in the liver *shu*, in the neck and head
南風生於夏 病在心俞 在胸脅	if the Southern wind arises in summer, the illness resides in the heart *shu*, in the chest and flanks
西風生於秋 病在肺俞 在肩背	if the Western wind arises in autumn, the illness resides in the lung *shu*, in the shoulders and back
北風生於冬 病在腎俞 在腰股	if the Northern wind arises in winter, the illness resides in the kidney *shu*, in the waist and thigh
中央為土 病在脾俞 在脊	the centre is earth, the illness resides in the spleen *shu*, in the spine.

(c)   The interrelation between the *qi* of a season and a symptom

春氣者 病在頭	if there is spring *qi*, the illness is in the head
夏氣者 病在藏	if there is summer *qi*, the illness is in the viscera
秋氣者 病在肩背	if there is autumn *qi*, the illness is in the shoulders and back
冬氣者 病在四支	if there is winter *qi*, the illness is in the four limbs

(d)   The seasonal propensity of illnesses

春善病鼽	in summer one has a propensity to ail from nose bleeding
仲夏善病胸脅	in mid-summer one has a propensity to ail in the chest and flanks
長夏善病洞泄寒	in the long summer one has a propensity to ail from diarrhoea and internal coldness
秋善病風虐	in autumn one has a propensity to ail from wind-induced intermittent fevers
冬善病庳厥	in winter one has a propensity to ail from obstructions and numbness

Table 4.3 *continued*

3.3	Introductory remark: 五藏應四時

extensive interrelations of directions with ... see Table 4.1

4.4.4	Interrelation between climatic factor and pathological condition in the body

風勝則動	if wind predominates, then there is agitation
熱勝則腫	if heat predominates, then there is a swelling
燥勝則乾	if the arid predominates, then there is dryness
寒勝則浮	if coldness predominates, then there is oedema
溼勝則濡寫	if dampness predominates, then there is a moist discharge

5.2.6	Interrelation between season, climatic factor, illness

冬傷於寒 春必溫病	if in winter you get harmed by the cold, in spring there must be a warmth disorder
春傷於風 夏生餐泄	if in spring you get harmed by the wind, in summer there will be diarrhoea
夏傷於暑 秋必痎瘧	if in summer you get harmed by the heat, in autumn there must be an intermittent fever
秋傷於濕 冬生欬嗽	if in autumn you get harmed by the damp, in winter there will be coughing

5.3	Extensive interrelations between direction and ... See Table 4.1

End remarks on *yin* and *yang* (notably, the seasons are not mentioned)

3.3.3	Interrelation of various kinds of *qi* with six viscera

天氣通於肺	heavenly *qi* connects with the lungs
地氣通於嗌	earthly *qi* connects with the throat
風氣通於肝	wind *qi* connects with the liver
雷氣通於心	thunder *qi* connects with the heart
谷氣通於脾	grain *qi* connects with the spleen
雨氣通於腎	rain *qi* connects with the kidneys

Table 4.3. Likewise, the ancient Greeks were well aware of the seasonal occurrence of certain illnesses. The *Epidemics* in the Hippocratic corpus record 'constitutions' in which reference is made to seasonal and climatic factors, followed by an enumeration of various fevers and other illnesses (Lloyd [1950]1983). Not only the ancient Chinese and Greeks, but also pre-modern African peoples were aware of the seasonality of illness. Eva Gillies (1976: 384) writes in a footnote to a footnote: 'The Somali of Zaila seem to have attributed malarial fever to mosquito bites in 1853, well in advance of Ross and Manson. Burton comments wisely in a footnote that 'the superstition probably arises from the fact that mosquitoes and fevers became formidable at the same time'.' (Ironically, the 'superstitious' Africans knew better than their later conquerors.)

The sentences in Table 4.3 may refer to details about the seasonal occurrence of illness that are inaccurate according to biomedicine. This should not deter the genealogist from the important issue, which is that these sentences concern a cross-culturally acknowledged ecological reality, namely the seasonality of illness. This finding gives reasoning in terms of the five agents an ecological dimension and grounds it in the daily life experience of people who live in geographical areas where there are seasons.[27] It shows that Chinese physicians were interested in regularities (contrary to Don Bates's impression, forthcoming), namely patterns of seasonal regularity. It suggests that reasoning in terms of the five agents may well have been integrated into medicine primarily within the context of ecologically motivated reasoning, namely the seasonality of certain illnesses.

Suwen 4.3 and 5.3, which are considered by TCM textbook compilers as presenting the most systematic account of reasoning in terms of the five agents, do not begin their sentences by referring to the seasons. The first term they both mention in a paragraph on one of the five agents (e.g. wood) is a direction (e.g. the east, *dongfang*). Both chapters sequence the five directions in the same order – east, south, centre, west, north – and from this sequencing it is easy to see that the directions represent the seasons – spring, summer, long summer, autumn and winter.[28] However, why should the directions rather than the seasons be mentioned in *Suwen* 4.3 and 5.3? The answer is probably best found in numerological considerations: the seasons were originally – and still are – conceived to be patterned within a numerology of four, while by Han times the notion of there being five directions was well accepted.

John Major (1993) and Wang Aihe (2000: 23–74) have made a strong case that reasoning in terms of the five agents built on an understanding of space derived from Shang (sixteenth to eleventh century BC) conceptions of the four directions (*sifang*) and the centre.

It is this spatial division of the universe that laid the foundations for the late Zhou and Han cosmologists, who adopted the numerology of five in Chinese cosmology. By Han times, this cosmology collapsed spatial and temporal dimensions into one.[29] It cannot be overemphasized how intertwined the temporal and spatial order are in Han cosmologies, and already some pre-Han ones (e.g. Granet 1934: 113). Processes taking place in time are intricately linked to their movement through space. This applies also to Han Chinese medicine (e.g. Hsu 1994). An illness, for instance, as it becomes protracted in time, moves from spatial locations on the body surface, such as the skin, flesh and channels, to internal ones, such as the viscera and bones. Likewise, seasons (*shi*) were intrinsically related to directions (*fang*) (e.g. Hsu 1999: 81–82 and 110–11).

The ecological variable that relates directions to seasons is wind. Wind provides the key to understanding why directions and seasons should be aspects of one and the same rubric: winds can effect weather changes, and they are often closely linked to seasonal changes. They are often conceived as predominately coming from a certain direction during a certain season, as described by Pandya (1993) for the Ongee on the Andaman islands. In Chinese medical writings it is implicitly given, as for instance in *Suwen* 5.3 and 4.3, where the winds of the five directions are mentioned in place of the seasons.

In summary, sayings from the Han dynasty (listed in Table 4.3) pertaining to correlative thinking in terms of the five agents reflect an ecological concern and account mostly for the seasonality of illness. Since seasons were originally and still are generally framed within a numerology of four, it became common practice in medicine to refer to the five directions instead of the four seasons in the context of reasoning in terms of the five agents, as a careful reading of *Suwen* 5.3 and 4.3 would suggest. The collapse of the spatial and temporal dimensions into one made this possible in Han cosmology. Seasonal regularity is yet another diachronic thrust contained in the 'Theory of the Five Agents' of TCM. However, today it is generally not known that the predominant pair of correspondences that Han physicians emphasized linked a specific season to a specific nosological entity like diarrhoea and intermittent fevers. The genealogical method uncovered this.

Pre-Han idioms and words in the Suwen (c. third century BC): the seasonality of illness, a cross-cultural 'ecological reality'

From investigating the structure of the sentences in *Suwen* 4 and 5, it became apparent that reasoning in terms of five agents was primarily used for accounting for the seasonality of illness. However, if physicians used reasoning in terms of the five agents in order to account for the seasonal regularity of certain illnesses, why did they allude to five agents when they explicitly referred to the 'four seasons' (*sishi*), an idiom that pre-dates Han medical writings (e.g. *Lüshi chunqiu*)? As the above cross-cultural examples suggest, peoples all over the world developed an awareness of the seasonal occurrence of certain illnesses, and this also seems to have been the case in ancient China, long before reasoning in terms of the five agents became predominant in medical language.

Interestingly, the idiom 'four seasons' (*sishi*), and not 'five seasons', is invariably used to refer to the seasons, even if five seasons are then enumerated. The 'four seasons' are often associated with *yin* and *yang*, whereby spring and summer are classified as *yang* and autumn and winter as *yin*, or, in terms of directions, the east and south are associated with *yang* and the north and west with *yin*. The idiom 'the four seasons, *yin* and *yang*' (*sishi yinyang*) suggests that the four seasons were framed in *yinyang* cosmology, before reasoning in terms of the five agents became predominant in medical language. Furthermore, the four seasons are delimited by mono-syllabic terms, spring (*chun*) and autumn (*qiu*), winter (*dong*) and summer (*xia*), while the fifth one is a compound word, the 'long summer' (*changxia*), which suggests more recent coinage. Thus, by focusing on particular words and idioms, the genealogist uncovers yet a further layer of meaning contained in the texts currently presented to TCM students as fundamental to 'The theory of the Five Agents'.

The fifth viscus, the 'spleen' (*pi*), which correlates with the 'long summer', was probably added to an already existent four at a later stage. This is generally accepted wisdom among historians of Chinese medicine. There are text passages (e.g. in *Suwen* 2.1 and 2.2, see Hsu 2001a: table 3.2) where the four viscera are put in correlation with the four seasons, and where neither a fifth season nor a fifth viscus is mentioned. *Suwen* 4.1.b also shows such an intermediary stage (see Table 4.3). It systematically correlates the winds from the four directions with the *shu*-areas of the viscus in which the illness resides,[30] and with the corresponding body parts affected, and in the fifth line correlates the 'centre' with the spleen, but the rhythm of this line is irregular in comparison to the previous four. There is little doubt that this fifth line represents a later amendment to a well-established earlier saying.

There are also various other text passages in the *Yellow Emperor's Inner Canon*, that hint at the possibility that the spleen became established as one of the five viscera only at a fairly late stage. Thus, in *Suwen* 9.5 the spleen does not figure as one of the five viscera. Rather, the heart, the lungs, the kidneys and liver are grouped together, followed by a comment on *piwei* (the spleen and stomach), the large and small intestine (*dachang xiaochang*), the triple burner and the bladder (*sanjiao pangguang*). This text passage refers to four viscera, and the spleen and stomach do not belong among them.

It may well be that the stomach rather than the spleen was originally the fifth viscus. Thus, *Suwen* 17.7 lists as five viscera kidneys, liver, stomach, lungs and heart and mentions them as opposites to the centre of the abdomen (*fu zhong*), the diaphragm (*ge*), the spleen (*pi*), the chest (*xiong zhong*), and the centre of the chest (*dan zhong*). This suggests that the stomach rather than the spleen was considered on a par with the other four viscera. Notably, the stomach is also considered more important than the spleen in the Mawangdui vessel texts. Thus, there is a vessel (*mai*) called the 'vessel of the stomach' (*wei mai*); it is the 'foot's great *yin* vessel' and its course begins in the stomach (Mawangdui medical manuscripts 1985: 11).[31]

The above suggests that the fifth season was the long summer, and the fifth viscus the spleen or stomach, and that physicians already had an arsenal of sayings that pertained to the seasonality of illness before reasoning in terms of the five agents became predominant in medicine. This is a finding that only the genealogist is able to make with respect to 'The Theory of the Five Agents'. It is a meaning aspect not much emphasized in TCM. The question that then arises is: why were Han elite physicians prepared to adopt reasoning in terms of the five agents, with the numerology of five, into their medical reasoning that was sensitive to the seasonality of illness in respect of four seasons? The conceptual history approach cannot answer the above question with the textual material at hand.

Summary

So far, we have seen how the five agents have been singled out as rather disembodied universal principles of 'The Theory of the Five Agents' in TCM. This 'theory', which builds on *Suwen* 5.3 and 4.3, is paradoxically presented in a different chapter than that called *zangxiang*, which discusses the five organs (an intrinsic aspect of the five agents) in comparatively materialist ways and with a focus on the body-enveloped-by-skin.

In a genealogical manner, we then traced reasoning in terms of the five agents back to the *Canon of Categories* of 1624, and found that the text passages which formed the core of 'The Theory of the Five Agents' in TCM, *Suwen* 5.3 and 4.3, were mentioned within the *zangxiang* category in the *Canon of Categories*. Already in the Ming, correlative thinking in terms of the five agents was valued in particular for its epistemological purposes and use as a 'heuristic device' for enhancing knowledge: it put the apparent in correlation with the hidden. By contrast, the editor of the *Suwen* of 762 discussed *Suwen* 4.3 and

5.3 in the context of self-cultivation practices that we interpreted as prescribing a moderate 'life style' for an honour-seeking status group.

As the genealogist dug deeper, and analysed the sentence structure of the texts assembled in *Suwen* 5 and 4, which reflected Han dynasty grammar, it became apparent that reasoning in terms of the five agents was primarily used in the context of prognosticating the seasonal occurrence of certain illnesses. Yet, as, in conceptual historical manner, we analysed the idioms and words in those sentences, it became apparent that Chinese physicians had already formulated sayings that accounted for the seasonality of illness before reasoning in terms of the five agents became integrated into this domain of medicine. This happened presumably in pre-Han times, i.e. the Warring States. The question that then arises is: why did Han physicians adopt correlative thinking in terms of the five agents theory into medicine at all, why did they not just reason in terms of the four seasons? To answer this question, we cannot scrutinise the text passages in question any further in a conceptual historical fashion, but must turn to social history.

A social historical consideration

In the medical context, five agents correlations are already recorded in the so-called iatromantic manuscripts of Shuihudi (iatromancy concerns the art of predicting medical events), which date to the third century BC (Harper 2001). According to these manuscripts, diviners made use of reasoning in terms of the five agents in combination with the system of the ten 'stems' and twelve 'branches'. The latter was well-established within divinatory practices by the fourth century BC (as testified through manuscripts unearthed from Baoshan). They combined the two for making medical prognostications about a given morbid condition of 'slight curing', 'great curing' or 'life and death'.[32] This would suggest that reasoning in terms of the five agents was primarily adopted in the context of medical prognostication in the Shuihudi manuscripts. Those prognostications concerned the course of a given illness, and in particular whether its outcome was lethal or not.

It has variously been noted that not only a diviner's but also a physician's ability to prognosticate death provided legitimation for medical practice. The physician Chunyu Yi of the second century BC, for instance, refused to treat any patients whom he prognosticated to have a lethal illness, and infallibly cured all the patients he decided to treat (Hsu 2001b). Prognostication was not an exclusively medical practice. Much as statistics is held in high esteem among government planners today, reasoning in terms of the five agents was often used in the context of prognostications that regulated government in Han and pre-Han times. Astronomers and other diviners who were kept as retainers at the court of a king, or other nobility, made use of highly sophisticated schemas of prognostication, often within the framework of the five agents (Sivin 1995b). The numerology of five alluded to the five rubrics of space and the five directions. It is to be expected that medical doctors who were able to make medical prognostications within the framework of the five agents were aspiring to a similarly prestigious social standing.[33]

Reasoning in terms of the five agents may have been adopted in medicine primarily in the context of predicting the seasonal occurrence of certain illnesses. The mentioning of either the five directions or the winds coming from the five directions when commenting on the seasonality of illness helps explain how it was feasible to adopt the pentic pattern of correlative thinking from the prognosticatory arts into medical reasoning. Prognostications for the seasonal occurrence of certain illnesses, for which there might have been an empirical basis, may well have become one of the most successful and most respected, and therefore most elaborate, aspects of elite medical practice.

Five agents prognostication
and the visceral language of *qi*

In *Suwen* 4.1.b the seasons are correlated with illnesses through the intermediary of the viscera (or, more precisely, the *shu*-areas of the viscera), i.e. each of the five sentences begins with mentioning a seasonal aspect of the illness (e.g. the east wind arises in spring) and ends with naming a certain kind of illness (e.g. an illness residing in the neck and head); in the middle it mentions an intermediary (e.g. the liver-*shu* area). One could say that in these sentences the viscera represent what Unschuld (1988) has called 'mediating links'. Reasoning in terms of 'mediating links' allows one to get away from the directly observable, and speak in more general or abstract ways about the topic in question. It is noteworthy that most sentences concerned with the seasonality of illness in *Suwen* 5 and 4, do not accord the viscera a prominent role (see Table 4.3), while the viscera and their correlates inside the body-enveloped-by-skin figure prominently in *Suwen* 5.3.

In other words, it is conceivable that doctors initially recognised seasonal patterns of certain illnesses, like diarrhoea and intermittent fevers, and that initially the viscera were not important for recognising those seasonal patterns. Considering how prominent the viscera are in *Suwen* 5.3 and 4.3, where five agents theory is very elaborate, it is likely that the viscera gradually gained in importance within the framework of medical reasoning in terms of the five agents. This is a generally accepted view among historians of Chinese medicine, and the genealogical method reconfirms this with new evidence.

One could furthermore point out that ecological correlations, which emphasized the prevalence of certain illnesses during certain seasons, gradually fell into oblivion. *Suwen* 5.3 and 4.3 are explicit about various aspects of the viscera and their correlates, but mention neither seasonal illness entities nor the seasons (seasonal *qi* is mentioned in chapter 4.3 but not in 5.3). In other words, correlative thinking in terms of the five agents enhanced reasoning relating to visceral states at the expense of reasoning that concerned easily observable seasonal patterns of illness occurrence.

Why should reasoning in terms of the invisible 'mediating links' have become more interesting to medical doctors than reasoning that built on the observation of season-specific illness patterns, which, as cross-cultural examples have shown, are often known to lay persons and experts alike? I suggest that precisely their invisibility and subtlety made them useful entities for correlative speculation in terms of the five agents. Since visceral changes and *qi* are not easily perceived, but require specialists adept in the diagnosis of pulse (*mai*) or complexion (*se*), prognosticated changes are not easy to falsify. By working with entities like *qi* and *zang* (viscera), whose subtle changes are difficult to discern, the regularities imputed to them predominate over any blatantly obvious irregularity. Precisely the subtlety of the recognition of visceral changes allowed doctors to systematise and present them in an internally consistent manner.

Contrary to Don Bates's impression that the Chinese were not interested in regularities, Chinese physicians' preoccupation with prognostications shows that they were. However, they accounted for them, not in terms of purposeful organic mechanism, but in terms of subtle potentialities that were captured by the language of *qi* (Hsu 2001b). Unlike the Greek philosophers Plato and Aristotle, who distrusted the tangible material world and spoke of 'purposeful instruments' (i.e they imputed mindful purpose to the instruments they described), Chinese physicians seem to have had an unbroken relationship to matter. *Qi* and *zang* (viscera) were matter, and simultaneously exerted agency; they were subtle 'matter-agencies'. The Chinese physicians who reasoned in terms of the five agents were interested in the regularities imputed to these subtle matter-agencies.

In this context, it is interesting to note that the notion of *qi* and reasoning in terms of the visceral states (*zang*) became prominent within the same medical lineages. This close interrelation between the language of the atmospheric (*qi*) and the visceral (*zang*) goes against the intuition of the modern practitioner who stresses that *qi* flows within the vessels (*mai*). However, the Mawangdui vessel texts of the early second century BC do not report on *qi* circulating within the *mai*.[34] It needs to be borne in mind that the language of *qi* became important to Han physicians only as they became interested in the dynamics of the visceral states, *zang*.[35] *Qi* starts to be perceived to be in the vessels, *mai*, only after the viscera, *zang*, are connected to *mai*. The earliest evidence for this can be dated with fair certainty into the mid-second century BC and is recorded in Chunyu Yi's (*215 BC) medical case histories (Hsu 2001a, 2001b and 2005).[36]

In summary, medical reasoning which postulated the seasonality of certain illnesses provided a suitable framework for promoting correlative thinking in terms of the five agents within medical language. As it became more elaborate, the terms for the four seasons were replaced with terms that implied the seasons but explicitly referred to the five directions (as in *Suwen* 5.3 and 4.3). Moreover, nosological terminology referring to 'warmth disorders', 'diarrhoea', 'intermittent fevers', and 'limpness and numbness', which testified to pre-Han medical doctors' interest in seasonal illness occurrences, was eventually no longer mentioned in the context of 'The Theory of the Five Agents' (nor does it occur in *Suwen* 5.3 nor 4.3). In the course of elaborating reasoning in terms of the five agents, medical specialists focused on the invisible and subtle, namely subtle atmospheric and visceral changes. This made them sensitive to potentialities and allowed them to make prognostications of regularities that are not easily falsified.

Discussion

The above genealogical approach to 'The Theory of the Five Agents' in TCM uncovered, step by step, layers of meaning contained in the contemporary notion of the 'five agents' and resulted in the description of one aspect of the body ecologic in Chinese medicine. To be sure, correlative thinking in terms of the five agents represents but one facet of the Chinese medical body ecologic. It is to be expected that in Chinese and other medicines further experiences of ecological realities, encoded in highly learned language, can be elicited through a genealogical study.

The genealogical approach that results in an assessment of the body ecologic is meant to represent an addition to Scheper-Hughes and Lock's 'three bodies' in that it provides a non-Cartesian approach to engaging in an anthropology of the body. While the 'three bodies' outlined by Scheper-Hughes and Lock (1987) can be assessed through the study of synchronous dynamics in society, the genealogical approach uncovers meaning aspects of earlier time periods in currently used medical terminology and focuses on their diachronic thrust. As scholarship in the social sciences has emphasized in recent years, there is an increasing awareness that contemporary social practice is history turned into nature, that the past is contained in the present, and that contemporary usages of current terminology have a diachronic dimension. This applies also to the anthropology of the body.

The Foucauldian genealogical approach aims to uncover unknown events relevant to its current understanding, and thereby has the potential to unmask master narratives of a historical sociological kind. The unknown event found in this study is that physicians in pre-Han times were already aware of the seasonality of illness before correlative thinking in terms of the five agents became predominant and that, as correlations between the five agents were elaborated, the initial correlation between a certain season and the occurrence of a certain illness, which is a cross-cultural ecological experience, was no longer mentioned.

This study dealt with a highly complex learned language that has a long history, and the analysis has therefore been protracted. The concept of time was defined through the events that had occurred in time (e.g. the time of the compilation of the *Canon of Categories*, the time of the edition of the *Suwen* chapters, the time of composition of the sentences contained in those chapters, etc.), and not by clock time, and it importantly did not assume linear trajectory. 'The Theory of the Five Agents' is one of the most elaborate aspects of Chinese medical reasoning and it is likely that a genealogical approach to other body concepts may result in a body ecological description that is not as technical.

The method for making possible the genealogical approach in this study was inspired by conceptual history and Koselleck's observation that there exist two separate temporal structures between linguistic phenomena and non-linguistic events. Thus, Koselleck (1989: 660) maintains: 'Concepts' [or rather: 'linguistic terms' (EH)] ... 'are of extraordinary constancy and are capable of repeated application, even in cases where, in practice, they help ground completely different programs of action.' Accordingly, people may imbue the same term with different meanings, depending on the text and the authors', compilers' and readers' attitudes towards the text in which it is mentioned, which often are characteristic of specific historical time periods.

The article furthermore insists that those interested in how biology is contained in culture have to turn to history. It is through complex historical processes that ecological experiences become integrated into highly elaborate systems of cultural signification. The genealogy given here started with TCM, which comprehends the 'five agents' as universal principles of a 'theory' that should explain the workings of the universe, and discusses them separately from the 'five organs' that are understood in more materialist terms. While this understanding of the five agents differs from that of the Ming due to its undeniable tendencies towards an internalising and therapy-oriented medicine, it nevertheless resembles it in that it attributes the five agents epistemological significance. In the Tang, Han and pre-Han periods, by contrast, reasoning in terms of the five agents was shown to have primarily a ritually prestigious, government regulatory and medical ecological significance. Reasoning in terms of the five agents as an aspect of a body ecologic was used for prognosticatory purposes and for regulating human conduct, as is characteristic of externalising and preventive medicines.

Notes

1. This article synthesizes ideas developed over the last decade that were presented in London 1997, Cambridge 1998, Singapore 1999, Taipei 1999, Paris 2000 and Montreal 2003, and in parts published in Hsu (1999: 78–83 and 2001a: chapter 3). The discussion of Traditional Chinese Medicine (TCM) recapitulates Hsu (1999: chapter 6 and 2000a), but the framing of the project as a 'genealogical approach' is new, thanks to a perceptive remark by Stefan Ecks and help from Lewis Mayo. I am indebted to Erling Høg for unrelenting encouragement as well as Barbara Gerke, Ann Lever, Geoffrey Lloyd, David Parkin, and Katherine Swancutt for valuable comments on an earlier draft.

2. Although researchers of the Chinese medical body have not specifically referred to the article by Scheper-Hughes & Lock, one can retrospectively discern their theoretical approaches to the three bodies as follows: Ots' (1990) discussion of the vocabulary of patients' complaints, often identical to expert terminology, throws light on the individual body in Chinese medicine; Unschuld (1980: 62; 2003: 133), who compares the functions of the viscera to offices of the Imperial administration, highlights aspects of the social body in Chinese medicine; and Farquhar's (1999) discussion of the recent sub-discipline 'men's medicine' (*nanke*) alludes to the body politic in post-Maoist China (see Hsu 2001c and 2003 in German).

3. The study of the 'body ecologic' undeniably also has a thematic aspect in that it accounts for ecological knowledge and its culture-specific perception. Its defining aspect, however, is the theoretical approach that consists of exploring in a genealogical fashion the diachronic thrust in contemporary social practice.

4. The above summary of some points Foucault ([1971]1991) raised in Nietzsche, Genealogy, History barely touches on power relations. However, a genealogy not only rearranges evidence into new configurations that provide new insights (Flynn 1994: 33), but is also interested in power relations (ibid: 36). Foucault's works that contain genealogies, such as *Discipline and Punish* ([1975] 1979) and *The History of Sexuality*, vol. 1 ([1976] 1990), become fully intelligible only when one considers how they deal with issues of power and knowledge, regardless of whether they take the form of an 'archaeology', a 'genealogy' or a 'problematisation' (e.g. Rabinow [1984] 1991, Hacking 1986, Flynn 1994).

5. Gry Sagli (2003) and her supervisor, Christoph Harbsmeier, drew my attention to Reinhart Koselleck.

6. *Wuxing* was in translation first rendered as 'five elements', in analogy to the four Greek elements (Matteo Ricci cited in Sivin 1987: 73). Richard Wilhelm spoke of '*Wandlungsphasen*' in German and in medicine, Manfred Porkert (1974) coined the phrase 'five evolutive phases' or 'five phases'. More recently, Kalinowski (1991: 111), Harper (1998) and Unschuld (2003) have started to use the term 'five agents' to refer to *wuxing*.

7. E.g. Granet (1934), Needham (1956), Henderson (1984), Graham (1986), Kalinowski (1991, 2003), Major (1993), Queen (1996), Wang (2000), and many others.

8. E.g. Porkert (1974), Unschuld (1980, 2003), Sivin (1987), Farquhar (1994), Hsu (1999), Despeux (2001), and many others.

9. It takes issue, for instance, with Unschuld (2003: 99), who postulates an ecological reality for the numerology of two of *yin-yang* reasoning (shady and sunny side of a mountain), but none for that of the five agents: 'In contrast to the dualism underlying the *yin-yang* doctrine, the pentic numerology of the five agents [*wuxing*] doctrine lacks an obvious antecedent in man's natural environment.'

10. Graham (1989: 326) suggests that 'The *xing* [the five agents] would seem to be the processes specific to each material', but Sivin (1987: 71) claims that 'the word refers not to aspects of the physical world but to five moral qualities'.

11. Correlative thinking was mentioned in the context of government at least as early as in the third century BC (e.g. Queen 1996: 3), and is, for instance, recorded in the *Lüshi chunqiu* (Mr Lü's Spring and Autumn) of the third century BC. It is often assumed that it was elevated to a politically relevant notion of world order during the Western Han (e.g. Wang 2000: 129–172). However, Queen (1996: 100–104) makes a convincing argument that the texts attributed to one of its main architects, Dong Zhongshu (*c.* 179–*c.* 104 BC), probably date to a later time period. They are continuously documented only from as late as from the sixth century AD onwards.

12. Manuscripts from the third century BC (Harper 2001, see below), which testify to the use of the five agents for making medical predictions, show no explicit ecological awareness; they are medical from a modern viewpoint in that they concern illness (in particular the prediction of its course and outcome), but they may have been conducted by another group of retainers rather than the physicians who actually treated illness.

13. According to Unschuld (2003: 106), twenty-six of the seventy-two pre-Wang Bing chapters in the *Suwen* allude to reasoning in terms of the five agents. There are seven chapters, namely *Suwen* 66–71 and 74, which are considered later additions by the editor Wang Bing of the eighth century (Unschuld 2003: 393, though consider also p. 100). They constitute one third of the *Suwen* and concern reasoning in terms of the *wuyun liuqi* (five circulatory phases and six seasonal *qi*), discussed as 'phase energetics' by Porkert (1974). See also Despeux (2001), Zheng and Tessenow in Unschuld (2003: 395–488) and Feng (2003).

14. The *Suwen* (Basic Questions) and *Lingshu* (Divine Pivot) each comprise 81 treatises/ chapters, and form together the scripture called the *Huangdi neijing* (Yellow Emperor's Inner Canon). The standard references on its complicated history are Ma (1990) and Sivin (1993). Probably, it was first compiled in the Western Han (206 BC to AD 9) with some text passages that date to the Warring States (475–221 BC), yet in its rendition relevant for its extant version in all likelihood dates to the Eastern Han (AD 25 to 220; Unschuld 2003: 5).

15. The concordance to the *Huangdi neijing* of 1986, edited by Ren Yingqiu, divided all *Suwen* chapters into thematic sections. This numbering is adopted here.

16. This point has been made univocally by Unschuld (1980), Sivin (1987), Ots (1987), Farquhar (1994), Hsu (1999), Scheid (2002), Taylor (2005). Strictly speaking, the

common word for 'theory' is *lilun* in modern standard Chinese; the term *xueshuo* can mean 'learning', 'doctrine', as well as 'theory'.

17. Tables are ubiquitous in the secondary literature on Chinese medicine. Rather than drawing up yet another one, I have translated verbatim what the canonical texts actually say, which form the core of 'The Theory of the Five Agents' in TCM education.

18. See notes 13 and 14.

19. Evidence for this internalising interpretation of the five agents comes from the recording of the themes of the introductory lectures (Hsu 1999); the analysis of diagrams of textbook representations of the correlates of the five agents, which showed in the 1984 edition the five agents at the centre of the diagram, but in the 1988 edition the five organs at its centre (figure 6.3); and from conversations with and observation of TCM practitioners during the clinical encounter (fieldwork 1988–89).

20. What motivated Zhang Jiebin to re-order the *Inner Canon*? Had printing produced such a wealth of knowledge that it had to be newly ordered? And why was the notion of category (*lei*) considered useful for ordering knowledge? Li Shizhen reorganised *materia medica* knowledge in terms of categories (*lei*) (Métailié 2001). Finally, why did Zhang Jiebin's reorganisation of medical knowledge, despite enormous socio-political changes, remain in place? We observe a tension between non-linguistic events of drastic change and a basically unchanged linguistic event.

21. My translation of *zangxiang* as 'hidden and apparent' stresses the meaning aspect of the concept as one concerned with external as well as internal processes of the body ecologic. No doubt, *zangxiang* also had the meaning aspects of 'viscera' and 'organs'.

22. The contents of *Suwen* 1–5 are listed in detail in Hsu (2001a: chapter 3, table 3.1).

23. The exception is *Suwen* 1.3, which Zhang Jiebin moved into the *zangxianglei*.

24. The WHO Health Education Unit (1986: 118) defined life style as: 'A general way of living based on the interplay between living conditions in the wide sense and individual patterns of behaviour as determined by socio-cultural factors and personal characteristics.' This definition does away with Weber's notion of 'honour'. Yet precisely this notion of 'honour' is relevant for understanding self-cultivation practices as a form of 'life style' in Chinese feudal bureaucracy.

25. McMullen (1988), without explicitly opposing these terms to each other, provides information on the sociology of Tang scholarship that would characterise it as a status-conscious social group rather than a class.

26. Incidentally, *Suwen* 4 and 5 contain many sentences on *yinyang* interrelations. Some scholars consider '*yinyang* theory' an aspect of 'five agents theory', but historically viewed, *yinyang* and *wuxing* (five agents) were two distinctive doctrines (e.g. Queen 1996: 3). Therefore sentences framed in *yinyang* complementarities will be left aside in this analysis.

27. This finding in itself is not new (e.g. Kuriyama 1993), but the genealogical method has produced detailed textual evidence.

28. Notably, seasons are mentioned neither in *Suwen* 4.3 nor in 5.3, which form the core of 'The Theory of the Five Agents' in TCM. Seasonal *qi* is mentioned in *Suwen* 4.3, but not in *Suwen* 5.3. Instead, *Suwen* 5.3 and 4.3 speak of directions. Ironically, Sivin (1987: 209, table 1.2) does not mention the five directions, despite their indisputable importance in contemporary TCM.

29. See, for instance, the *Zuozhuan*, as cited in *Shiji* 60 ([1959]1975: 2115): 'The land of the son of heaven has an ancestral altar. In the east, it is bluegreen, in the south, it is red, in the west, it is white, in the north, it is black, on the top, it is yellow.'

30. The *shu*-areas are mentioned in *Shi ji* 105 (1975: 2811), discussed in *Huangdi neijing lingshu* 1 (1986: 265 and 267–8), today known as 'alarm points'.
31. Unschuld (2003: 109) maintains that in *Shiji* 105.2 [case 15] the stomach was treated as though it was a viscus, associated with the colour red. The case in question concerns a damaged spleen and mentions *qi* coming from the stomach that is yellow (not red!) (Hsu forthcoming). The evidence is insufficient to make the former statement, and the latter statement is incorrect.
32. The interrelations of directions and colours in those manuscripts are with few exceptions (Harper 2001: 111, fn 42) identical to the ones in the *Suwen* 5.3 and 4.3 and *Shiji* 60, see note 29 above.
33. This would refute Don Bates' impression (forthcoming 77) that the credibility of Chinese doctors did not depend on them being natural philosophers.
34. Harper (1998) and many others state that it does without, however, providing any textual evidence from a primary source that explicitly mentions the circulation of *qi*.
35. This happened as emotions became medicalised or medicine became psychologised (Hsu 2001a).
36. The resonance of *qi* resonating with the viscera (*zang*), rather than the *mai*, is also variously given in phrases of the *Suwen* 3.3.3: 'The *qi* of the four seasons, when they *gengxxx*, they injure the five viscera' or *Suwen* 5.4.4: 'The noxious influences from heaven, when they resonate, then they harm the five viscera of the person.'

ON THE SOCIAL, THE BIOLOGICAL AND THE POLITICAL: REVISITING BEATRICE BLACKWOOD'S RESEARCH AND TEACHING

Laura Peers

Over the past decade in Britain, human remains have emerged as a sensitive category of objects whose value and meanings to science and to families and communities of origin have been widely contested.[1] At one level the nature of this sensitivity has been played out as a power struggle over who should have control of such material, although such control would seem to rest on the ability to define and categorize human remains in one way or another. Increasingly, it would seem, human remains in scientific collections cannot be defined solely as biological, nor can they be defined solely as social in meaning. They are both, and very political as well.[2]

If one of the fundamental problems surrounding human remains today is their multiple sets of meanings, and the tensions between these, then they seem a useful focus for thinking about a new holism in anthropology. The idea of holism is not new in anthropology, of course, but has been integral to the discipline since E.B. Tylor's 1871 definition of culture as 'that complex whole which includes knowledge, belief, art, morals, law, custom, and any other capabilities and habits acquired by man as a member of society.' Anthropology as a discipline was similarly comprehensive from the start, embracing biological, linguistic, material, social and cultural aspects of human life and the inter-relations between them. A holistic perspective acknowledges that however one might analyse the elements of human society, they are always bound up together, often mutually constitutive, and virtually impossible to disentangle from one another. Anthropology has since developed in specialized directions, making it difficult to maintain this all-encompassing approach to human life, but those of us who teach on related degrees in these different fields in the School of Anthropology at Oxford find ourselves sharply aware of the links – and tensions – between biological, social, cultural, and material elements of the discipline and of these perspectives on human societies.

My central thesis is that it is not just human societies which require a holistic perspective, and in which social, biological, political, and material elements are inter-related. The information collected by anthropologists (in whatever form), and the work done by anthropologists with their subjects of study, also requires a holistic perspective. While anthropological research has been intended as a focus of scientific study and a means of understanding humankind, anthropologists have been sharply reminded in recent decades that such study has never been apolitical and that scientific research, analyses, and conclusions have always been embedded in and constructed by social and political factors – just as mutually constitutive, just as entangled, as elements of society in Tylor's definition. This new anthropological holism has been highlighted in regards to the material products of anthropological research, possession and interpretation of which have been and continue to be contested by the communities from which they were generated. As Curator for the Americas collections at the Pitt Rivers Museum, as well as a lecturer focusing on material culture and museum anthropology, and specializing in relations between indigenous peoples and museums, my work requires, on a daily basis, shifting between cultural, theoretical, pragmatic, and political meanings and interpretations of the material products of anthropological research. In thinking about the tensions between meanings that have been given to things by anthropologists and meanings given by source communities, and in negotiating the politics arising from these tensions, it seems to me that both the strength and the great difficulty of anthropology is its holism, and specifically the problem that meanings cannot be entirely isolated and privileged, one from another.

The boundaries between all of us, in various sub-fields and across cultural borders, are very porous. Meanings leak from one compartment to another. Indeed, they are apt to shift suddenly from one register to another, to be contested between conceptual compartments. Partly this is a problem of post-modern authority, or the lack thereof, but partly also it is a situation in which we have learned to value the co-presence of multiple meanings and the tensions between them. As I discuss in this paper, what were thought in the nineteenth and early twentieth centuries to be biological data and measurements turn out to have been equally indices of social identity, historical experience, and cross-cultural politics all along.

I focus here on work by Beatrice Blackwood, a former Pitt Rivers Museum staff member and lecturer in anthropology at Oxford, and specifically on materials collected by her during a field trip across North America between 1924 and 1927. Much of the data she acquired on this trip, in the form of photographs, drawings, hair samples, and genealogical information connected to these, are held in the Manuscripts and Photographs department of the Pitt Rivers Museum. Over the past several years, I have been exploring the legacy of her work on this trip for First Nations and Native American groups today. Blackwood's collections provide a useful lens through which to understand the multiple meanings, past and present, of such information and objects to anthropologists and to source communities, and prove that such collections cannot be seen as just biological, just social, or just political. They are all three, and more. If we acknowledge holism as a valid perspective on human societies we study, we need also to acknowledge it within our profession.

Beatrice Blackwood, anthropology, and Oxford

Born in London in 1889, Beatrice Blackwood rejected the usual pattern of marriage for women of her family's status and studied at Oxford instead, graduating with an undergraduate degree in English Language from Somerville College in 1912. She returned to Oxford in 1916 to begin studying for the Diploma in Anthropology, which she completed in 1918.[3] She then began an academic career, first as a research assistant for Professor Arthur Thomson in the Department of Human Anatomy, which was located in the University Museum of Natural History. In 1920 she was promoted to Departmental Demonstrator there. In 1924, she began a three-year research trip in North America to explore the relationship between intelligence and 'race'. When she returned to Oxford in 1927, Blackwood became a University Demonstrator in Ethnology and in 1935 her post was transferred to the Pitt Rivers Museum, where she worked until her death in 1975. She did a great deal of teaching from 1930 onward and was promoted to Lecturer in 1946.

Blackwood is best known in anthropological circles for her 1929 Melanesian fieldwork and collecting, for which she was awarded the Rivers Memorial Medal by the Royal Anthropological Institute in

1943. However, she has remained a minor figure within the history of anthropology. She never became interested in the theoretical developments occurring within anthropology after she graduated from the Diploma, preferring to focus on material culture. In the 1920s and after, and even after her promotion to Lecturer in 1946, she preferred to teach on this and on 'ethnology' (defined then as the comparative study of the different groups of mankind, and seen as somewhat old-fashioned) rather than on the new social anthropology taught by others in the department.

Blackwood's North American fieldwork

Funded by a Laura Spelman Rockefeller Memorial Fellowship in the social sciences, Blackwood's 1924–27 North American trip involved physical measurements and mental tests of different cultural groups across North America, focusing particularly on women.[4] Over three years, Blackwood travelled from New York to Alert Bay and from northern Manitoba to the American Southwest by train, canoe, mule, car and truck. Her research subjects included African-Americans, poor and middle-class whites, members of over a dozen American Indian and First Nations groups, and residents of a home for disabled and mentally ill people.

At most of her stops, Blackwood recorded physical measurements from subjects on detailed forms (see for example Figure 5.1). She sometimes also obtained samples of hair from people whom she measured. She carefully noted basic information about these people on the forms and the envelopes in which the hair samples were placed; this usually consisted of the names and racial identities of the person's parents: for example 'mother is half-breed'. She also took referentially anthropometric photographs – paired frontal and side views – of many people, and images showing the communities she worked in.

Blackwood and 'race': the biological *as* the social and political

Blackwood's research focus on this trip arose from her interest in physical anthropology, developed on the Diploma in Anthropology course which, as her student notebooks reveal, included a great deal of work on physical anthropology, human evolution, and measurement. Her perceptions of Native American peoples were very much those of her time and of the earlier salvage paradigm in which she had been trained, focusing on methods of classifying and comparing different

177

No..................................

Race ....

| Full Name | Sex |

| Age: yrs.   mos. | Date of birth: day   month   yr. |

Birthplace   Occupation

Father's birthplace   Mother's

Father's race or nationality   Mother's

Father's ancestors came from

Mother's ancestors came from

Other data on ancestry

Span	1	Skin Colour.				1-2 Rel. Span
Stature	2	N	R	W	Y	3-2 Rel. Shld. Ht.
Shoulder height	3					4-2 Rel. Arm L.
Mid. Finger	4a					5-2 Rel. Leg L.
Arm length	4	Hair Colour.				7-2 Rel. Sit. Ht.
Ht. to ant. sup. il. sp.	5	black dk. brn. med. brn. lt. brn. fair v. fair gray lt. red bright red dk. red				8-2 Rel. Shld. W.
Ht. to iliac crest	6	Hair Form.				9-8 Rel. Hip. W.
Sit. ht.	7	straight low waves dp. waves curly frizzly woolly				11-10 Ceph. I.
Shoulder width	8	Hair Texture.				23-10 Vert. I. L.
Width bet. iliac crests	9	coarse med. fine				23-11 Vert. I. B.
Head length	10	Eye Colour.				12-11 Fr. Pa. I.
Head width	11	dk. brn. lt. brn. neutral hazel green blue gray				13-11 Ceph. Fa. I.
Min. frontal	12					12-13 Zyg. Fr. I.
Bizygomatic	13	Eye fold.				14-13 Zyp. Con. I.
Bigonial	14	abs. trace med. mkd.				17-13 Up. Fac. I.
Nasal width	15	Intercanthus width.				18-13 Tot. Fac. I.
Nasal height	16	narrow med. wide				15-16 Nasal I.
Upper facial ht.	17	Nose.				22-21 Hand I.
Total facial ht.	18	Bridge: low med. high Profile: convex str. concave Nostril axis: ant-post. obl. transverse				
Lip thickness	19	Prognathism.				
Mouth width	20	None slight med. mkd.				Pathological conditions.
Hand length	21	Bite.				
Hand width	22	overhung edge-to-edge underhung				
Head height	23	General Condition.				
		Good med. bad v. bad				

Notes

Where measured   Date

Figure 5.1 *Blackwood's form for recording physical measurements.*
(PRM Blackwood Papers box 21, folder 2.)

human populations and on assumed divisions between 'traditional' and 'modern' culture. Intriguingly, like many of her colleagues, Blackwood tended to blur the categories of social and biological analysis in her work. This blurring equated human physical characteristics with cultural ones, and the 'purity' of physical traits with cultural 'purity' or authenticity (a quality usually expressed in the term 'traditional'). These ideas have become entangled with the anthropological salvage paradigm, in which authentic was seen to equal pre-contact, undiluted, as it were, by European influence in thought or material culture – or by admixture of European blood. Blackwood's photographs and notes illustrate this very well. What Blackwood looked for and recorded in her notes and photographs was, within this system of thought, a set of indices, both physical and social, which revealed either purity and traditionalism, or hybridity and change. Thus, in her notes on the children's drawings that she obtained at Nett Lake Reservation in Minnesota state, she writes: 'This reservation is one of the most isolated in Minnesota. There was no road into it till about 10 years ago. There is some white blood but much less than in any other village and the people are more primitive in their habits than elsewhere in Minnesota'. Similarly, a diary entry during her visit to the Blood Reserve in southern Alberta links physical traits with cultural ones around the key term 'traditional': 'They are far more like the traditional Indian than the Crees are – tall, big-boned, large faces with very high cheekbones – and big hooked noses, the men wear their hair in two long plaits tied together in front on their chests. The women all wear shawls except some who had European dress' (Pitt Rivers Museum Blackwood Diary 1924–27, 3 August 1925).

Blackwood's referentially anthropometric portraits of First Nations people, which used frontal and side views but without measuring sticks and retained details of the environment in which she photographed rather than isolating the subject, are especially indicative of this blurring of physical and cultural indices. Thus, a pair of photographs of shaman Billy Williams at Kispiox in British Columbia, in his regalia and with his small daughter by his side (Figure 5.2), became, in the caption for her lecture slide, 'Man wearing Chilkat blanket. Side' (PRM Blackwood Papers, Box 13).

Such blurring and conflation serve as a strong reminder of the need for holistic perspectives when trying to understand our forebears' work. While anthropology developed as a science, neither its categories nor its tools of classification were ever neutral and objective; nor was the analysis of biological data unrelated to social and political dynamics. Both racial classification and cultural description functioned to quantify difference between peoples, and were always linked in the broader public mind to intellectual and moral qualities and to assumptions about hierarchical relationships between peoples. As Annie Coombes, Faye

Harrison, and others have shown, the analysis and display of human remains, body casts, anthropometric photographs and other data within nineteenth century scientific and museum contexts functioned to authenticate narratives of race and legitimated the popular belief in the superiority of certain class elements of the 'English race' (as it was called), over others (Coombes 1994; Harrison 1995: 52).

If Blackwood's blurring of physical and cultural categories of analysis was typical of anthropology, it was especially interesting given the extremely political context in which her particular research was located. From the very beginning of her work in North America, Blackwood was forced to face the interrelationships between the biological and the political. Much of her first winter of 1924–25 was spent at African-American colleges in the American South, where she was disturbed to discover the discrimination faced by blacks and began to grapple with the political implications of standard measures of intelligence and racial difference. While based in Nashville during spring 1925, Blackwood recorded in her diary episodes of racism she encountered, such as the refusal of white colleagues to receive her in their homes because she was working with and living near blacks (PRM Blackwood Diary 1924–27, 16 April 1925). She also recorded racial conflict and activism, including riots between the Ku Klux Klan and blacks.

This was not a neutral environment for Blackwood's particular work, and at several points during this period she had to explain her research to the black leaders of these colleges, who were 'very suspicious of mental tests' (PRM Blackwood Diary 1924–27, 7 March 1925, see also entry for 29 April 1925) because they feared she was trying to equate race with intelligence, a potential link which might be used against them in the racist context of American society. Blackwood was, of course, exploring the links between race and intelligence, although she quickly became aware of the problematic dynamic of racism in such studies, and of the potential for findings to be misused. She was also forced to think about the connotations of terminology for physical characteristics, choosing the term 'mixed' (as in 'mixed-race') instead of 'mulatto' or 'octaroon' (PRM Blackwood Diary 1924–27, 29 April 1925), terms which had been used in the slave trade. At one point, Blackwood found herself lunching with members of the local 'Interracial Commission' at the Tuskegee Institute in Alabama (a college for African-Americans), discussing 'tests & their legitimate uses' (PRM Blackwood Diary 1924–27, 7 June 1925).

It was after these months that she began working with Native American people, and she quickly discovered that they faced many of the same problems as African-Americans. By the time she began working in Native communities, she was alert to some of the social, economic, and political realities Native people faced, and became aware

Figure 5.2 *Frontal and side portraits of Billy Williams with his daughter, Kispiox Village, 1 September 1925. Photographs by Beatrice Blackwood. (Pitt Rivers Museum, University of Oxford, PRM BB.A4.32, 33).*

that such factors and prejudice counted for far more in determining what people's lives and abilities were like than inherited factors did.

Despite this, she maintained her research framework for the duration of the trip. As she moved across the continent taking physical measurements, recording genealogies, measuring skin colour, and cutting and labelling hair samples, she worked with the scholarly concept of race every day. She did so within a broader context in which she discussed, almost daily, applied theories of race with the missionaries, Indian agents, school principals, and other colonial officials who made her work possible by giving her accommodation, driving her around, and sharing genealogical information for her to cross-check her interview data. These individuals had firm views about how to deal with the 'problem' (as it was then referred to) of Native peoples – in other words, how to manage what were assumed to be inferior races during the period of their decline. Thus, when she 'talked shop with Dr Ralph Linton' at the Field Museum in Chicago on 24 June 1925, Linton – who later went on to publish a major monograph on acculturation – stated strongly that, regarding African-Americans, 'the solution of the future lay in complete absorption of the negro into the white stock' (PRM Blackwood Diary 1924–27, 24 June 1925). Similarly, Blackwood paraphrased the attitudes of Reverend Atkinson, the missionary at Oxford House in northern Manitoba, as: 'The only possible future for the Indian in Canada is complete assimilation with the whites – in blood as in culture – this is going on pretty rapidly' (PRM Blackwood Diary 1924–27, 29 June 1925). Whatever biological data she got was sticky with political context and meaning.

Hair samples, science, and cross-cultural politics

This frustrating entanglement of meanings and categories of meaning is demonstrated most clearly by one particular collection made by Blackwood in one particular community: the hair samples she obtained in the Ojibwe community of Red Lake in northern Minnesota.[5]

In the late nineteenth and early twentieth centuries, some scientists used hair colour and texture as one indicator of racial identity. While such meanings were intended to be biological and scientific, they complemented other meanings and uses of hair within broader Victorian and Edwardian society: as standing for the person (e.g., mourning jewellery made of hair), and thus as a powerful form of control and punishment (as in the shaving of prostitutes' and prisoners' heads). Hair as a symbol of cultural identity was manipulated cross-culturally in colonial encounters: thus, the deliberate cutting of traditional braids into 'ladylike' bobs and 'hygienic' buzzcuts, was used in schools for Native American children as part of a process designed to separate them from what was seen as their contaminating culture. For Ojibwe people today in communities where Blackwood worked, such uses of hair to assault traditional identity and tribal sovereignty are recognized, along with older cultural meanings that hair can be used magically to harm the person from whom it comes (see, for instance, Densmore 1979 (1929): 107; Hilger 1992 (1951): 160).

Blackwood arrived in Red Lake in early November 1925, after her stint in the American South. She was lured by the idea that the communities in this area were culturally traditional. Her work at Red Lake was supported by government officials, school staff, and missionaries. Miss Deedie, the Matron of the school, assisted her in making physical measurements of people there (14 November 1925), and when it turned out that she would be in the community during the annual payment of treaty annuities on 16 November, she took full advantage of the situation: as she noted in her diary, 'Set up my instruments in a room in the office & caught a number of the women as they came for their payment.' She may have been doing careful biological research, but she did so within a coercive political system in which it was possible for her to 'catch' research subjects, children as well as adults. With the cooperation of teaching staff, Blackwood obtained 29 hair samples from schoolgirls at Cross Lake Indian Boarding School in Ponemah and 11 samples at the Red Lake Indian Day School. [6] She sealed them in small envelopes, and wrote the name of the child each was from and their parents' racial identification on the outside. The samples reside today in the collections of the Pitt Rivers Museum.

Since most of my previous research has been on historic Ojibwe culture (e.g. Peers 1994), I was aware that people in Red Lake might be concerned about the potential of the hair to do magical harm. This posed a curatorial dilemma, for the Museum frequently receives requests for permission to conduct various scientific tests on hair samples in its collection, for things ranging from mercury levels to nutritional analysis and DNA studies. I therefore thought it necessary to consult with community members before I allowed this collection to be tested.[7]

The consultation was a powerful and difficult experience, precisely because it involved bringing together all the different meanings of the hair samples – biological, racial, cultural, political, and cross-cultural. In the process, the samples became highly charged, and their meanings shifted rapidly and often abruptly from one to another: from the very personal to externally controlled, from person to object, from biological data to the product of systems of political control. In one particular case, hair sample PRM 1994.15.1073 'became' the Ojibwe elder Mrs Goldie Johnson, who was, in the autumn of 1925, a six-year old girl named Julia Sigana who started school just two months before Beatrice Blackwood arrived at Red Lake.

Cross Lake Indian Boarding School, where Blackwood encountered Julia Sigana, was, like many other residential schools, intended to assimilate tribal children and to strip their culture from them, and one standard element in that process was forbidding children to speak their tribal languages in school. Like many Ojibwe children, Julia Sigana spoke no English when she arrived at school, and her older sister attempted to prepare her for this by teaching her to recognize the English phrase, 'What is your name?' and to respond, in English, 'My name is Julia.' When the school principal asked her this and she proudly told him, however, he replied, 'I think we have too many Julias in school this year. I think we'll call you Goldie.' Her hair sample is labelled, 'Goldie Sigana, age 6, Primer Class, Female.'

The traumatic and multi-generational effects of such schools for Native American children have been well documented.[8] Mrs Johnson's experience of having even her name taken from her is part of the Ojibwe histories of Blackwood's collection, a completely different set of meanings than Blackwood intended for them. That Blackwood had obtained the Red Lake hair samples in the coercive environment of the school gave them, from the perspective of Ojibwe people today, a powerful set of negative connotations. While these are scientific samples intended by Blackwood to provide data about 'race,' they are also documents which tell us much about cross-cultural relations and about the powerlessness and disenfranchisement of early twentieth-century Ojibwe life. Indeed, they evoke Lindman and Tarter's powerful statement (2001: 2), written about bodies in colonial America, that

> Bodies are not only physical phenomena but surfaces of inscription, loci of control, and transmitters of culture. They are never unmediated; they are related but not reducible to cultural concepts of differentiation, identity, status, and power ... Encompassing both the physical and the symbolic, [the body] is ... enmeshed in the social relations of power.

In this especially holistic view, Lindman and Tarter acknowledge that the biological can never be separated from its social and political contexts. The schools in which Blackwood obtained the hair samples can be seen as colonial contexts in which the dynamics identified by Lindman and Tarter were fully in play. The deliberate separation of name from person and body is directly related to colonial relations of power, not only in Mrs Johnson's experience but more broadly in issues regarding human remains and their contested fates today. Blackwood's carefully labelled envelopes of hair are an exception; very few biological specimens, whether skeletal, of tissue, or of hair, arrived in museums with the names of the persons to which they had belonged. In part, this was a reflection of poor relations between source communities and collectors, so that the collectors were unable to establish the names or other affiliations of the collected; partly also it reflected European collectors' beliefs about human physical 'types', so that names of individuals were deemed less important than the identification of the type ('Tasmanian skull'); also, scientific practice has tended to separate the physical phenomenon, which has been given a whole new set of names (e.g., 'crania') from the named person, so that again the name is less important than the idea or condition which the remains are being used to represent. Once in the museum, human remains were given new identities signalled by their classification, and were further distanced from the persons they had once been. Like mourning rituals, which separate the living and the dead, museum procedures and scientific analysis intervened between remains and persons.

So too did the use of fieldwork data for teaching. While she almost always recorded the English names of individuals she photographed, measured, or took samples from, Blackwood tended to drop these in her use of images and data for teaching to emphasize anthropological categories of meaning and thus translate portraits of individuals into scientific data. One image of Kainai men harvesting, from shortly after Blackwood's time in Ojibwe communities, became translated, for a lecture on 'Physical types of Plains Indians', from a list of English names in her field notes to a list of traits in her lecture notes: 'They are among the tallest of the Indians. ... The Plains type I took on the Blood Reserve in 1925 is, on the whole, more homogenous than are the Indians in other parts of the country' (PRM Blackwood Papers Box 23 'Lands and Peoples' lecture series, 'Plains Indian' lecture, p.10). My recent fieldwork revisiting Blackwood's work amongst Ojibwe and Kainai people suggests that the very ability to drop names in such contexts is an index of colonial power in which the production of scholarly theory was embedded. Ojibwe and Kainai people today dispute the validity of knowledge produced through traditional scholarly means within such political contexts.

Much of the tension within the UK scientific community over the past few years regarding the fate of indigenous human remains has focused on the potential definition of those remains as ancestral persons rather than as biological specimens. Names have been important in the debate, although this has seldom been articulated. Even institutions which have taken a very hard line on these issues have indicated that if names were attached to human remains in their collections – as, in fact, they are inked on some crania in major British museums – then those remains would be available for repatriation.[9] Names shift human remains from one category – biological data – to another – that of persons, with kin who can legitimately and often legally repatriate. Along with this shift in categorization comes a shift in control and authority, from the scientific community to the source community.

The ability to remove names from persons, as in Julia Sigana's case, or from human remains, as in many other cases, reflects not only an intellectual stance but very real dynamics of power and control. If mapping, or place-naming, is one of the mechanisms of nationalism, according to Benedict Anderson's theory, then so is un-naming the indigenous inhabitants of colonized areas, not just their place names but their personal names. We have all seen historic photos of a named white colonial official or military officer with a large group of anonymous natives; such systematic un-naming was part of, a marker of, a broader process. Un-naming facilitates scientific analysis, transforming human remains from person to data. It was a rather powerful bit of colonial magic which took human populations, enmeshed in social and political relations with European powers, and made those social and political contexts apparently disappear to produce biological specimens. Presumably this is what has fuelled certain scientists' objections recently to proposals made by the Working Group on Human Remains, which suggested that descendant populations have rights in indigenous human remains, and that remains will therefore need to be provenanced as well as possible to facilitate negotiations with legitimate claimants. Responding to this, Professor Robert Foley of the Leverhulme (Duckworth) Centre for Human Evolutionary Studies at Cambridge objected to 'the sheer amount of time dedicated to researching the provenance of material and contacting possible descendants – time and money that could be spent on productive research' (Jenkins 2003). Chris Stringer of the Natural History Museum similarly tried to maintain human remains within scientific categories of control, stating that the report of the Working Group did not place sufficient emphasis 'on the scientific importance of these collections and their potential benefits' (Stringer 2003), and Tiffany Jenkins (2003), writing for a civil liberties watchdog, claimed that the import of the Working Group's recommendations was that 'rather than researching remains and improving understanding for the future, it will mean dredging up the past provenance of remains.' From a curatorial point of view, in which museums and scientific institutions have a professional obligation to research the provenance of their collections, these perspectives seem very odd; and one might have thought that scientific research on topics such as population movements and diet might find provenance information rather useful. The real meaning of such statements, of course, is the desire to prevent the movement of human remains from the category of scientific data – the biological – to that of persons, and the social, where repatriation to documented kin groups might be a possibility. Research to provenance remains even with the name of the social or ethnic group from which they came, undoes the un-naming procedures of colonial collection which so handily produced those specimens in the first place, and begins to shift the nature of the relationships between scientific institutions and indigenous communities to one of slightly greater equality.

The wilful refusal by some scientists to acknowledge the social and political constitution of some remains defined as biological specimens, and the struggle by this group to maintain the boundaries of biological categories of analysis, has had one further dimension in recent UK debates. This is that scientists have managed to define so-called 'replaceable' body parts, such as nail clippings and hair samples, as not in the same category of human remains as skeletal material or tissue. The Human Tissue Act (2004), for instance, excludes hair and nails, and despite earlier inclusion of such materials in a definition of human remains for museum collections, the Department of Culture, Media and Sport (DCMS) are now leaning toward using the Human Tissue Act definition (see DCMS 2005). Perhaps unsurprisingly, historic hair samples are an emerging pot of gold for geneticists who now have techniques to extract and amplify DNA from hair. By this trick of defining 'replaceable' remains as different, Blackwood's hair samples thus fall outside recent attempts to provide guidance on the care of indigenous human remains, and are legitimate objects of scientific analysis: they remain biological rather than social. Goldie Sigana Johnson's experience, and those of her female classmates, don't matter in this definition; and their hair, under these guidelines, is not subject to their or their children's or their community's control. Blackwood's collections of hair samples have been defined as being under the control of British scientists, no matter what the individuals from whom the hair was taken might say. Thinking quite holistically now, such attitudes suggest the legitimacy of Ojibwe beliefs that hair can be used magically to harm or control the person from whom it comes. 'Magical harm' may occur in more than one form, and the cultural and scientific arrogance involved in the continuation, for research purposes, of white scholars taking and controlling Ojibwe body parts without the permission or involvement of Ojibwe people, is not at all different from traditional Ojibwe concepts of the damage one can do to another using hair and nail clippings. As tribal groups in North America have expressed very forcefully, disempowerment – including being written out of the research process – has contributed much to the overall ill-health faced by tribal communities today: little wonder that people in these communities complain of being, quite literally, 'studied to death' (on which see Warry 1998: 245–46).

Hair and identity politics in Minnesota

The hair samples, and Blackwood's research project, were linked to tribal disempowerment around Red Lake in the 1920s in another way, for hair and genealogical information were used in Minnesota to classify Ojibwe individuals as full or mixed-blood, and this classification determined whether tribal members could sell tribal lands. Based on assumptions about the relative intelligence and 'civilization' of lighter- and darker-skinned peoples, US federal policy in the early twentieth century deemed Native peoples less intelligent and less competent than whites (and see Beaulieu 1984: 289). On this basis, a Minnesota State Act of 1906[10] permitted mixed-blood people to lease or sell their reservation lands or timber, but made it illegal for full-bloods to do so. The act resulted in an enormous amount of fraud, with full-bloods being encouraged by white entrepreneurs to pass as mixed-blood and sell lands. Just three years later, 90 per cent of the land at one reservation in Minnesota had been sold (Meyer 1994: 160).

To end the fraud, in 1914 state officials hired Aleš Hrdlička, curator of physical anthropology at the Smithsonian Institute, to create a scientific definition and test for 'full blood' and 'mixed blood' people (Beaulieu 1984: 293; Meyer 1994: 168), and in 1915, Albert E. Jenks, professor of anthropology at the University of Minnesota, was also hired to work on such a definition. Facial shape, cranial measurements, and skin colour, but especially hair colour and texture (lighter and curlier, it was believed, for mixed-blood, and darker and straighter for full-blood), were used as markers of racial identity in these enquiries.

Jenks's involvement in these cases links them to Blackwood's work, for it was Jenks who suggested which Ojibwe communities Blackwood should visit in Minnesota. Jenks mentions the Act, the subsequent land sale fraud, and his involvement in the ensuing court cases in Jenks 1916, and presumably, when she talked with him on two occasions in October 1925, Jenks spoke to Blackwood about his attempts to determine 'race' through physical measurement, but she does not mention anything about the controversy in her notes.[11] She was only in Minnesota for 20 days, but the controversy was ongoing at the time in the communities she visited; it seems unlikely that she knew nothing about it. That she said nothing about it suggests her determination that her hair samples be seen and used solely as biological samples. Of course, they were not. In their original context, the samples meant politics as much as anything else. They represented the weakening of tribal sovereignty, the alienation of tribal lands, the desperation caused by unemployment and racism, and the imposition of dominant-society power to define and control Ojibwe people.

Things do, of course, hold different meanings simultaneously and, as I said at the beginning of this paper, this is especially true of human remains. Core theory on material culture has explored the multiple, shifting meanings of artefacts across their biographies although this theory has focused less on the dynamics of power involved in such shifts. Nor have we gone much beyond noting the transitions of meaning across the life of an artefact, or of human remains. We might modify this recent body of theory by proposing that for ethnographic artefacts it constitutes a new form of cross-cultural historiography, for while artefacts continue to acquire layers of meaning along with each stage in their histories, what those layers consist of are the parallel, and very different, histories and experiences of indigenous and settler societies. As Chris Gosden has noted, these material things embody (sometimes literally) the relationships between peoples, the productive and stimulating elements of these relationships as well as the controlling and damaging ones.[12]

Blackwood, categories, uncertainty

Intriguingly, despite her insistence in getting it, Blackwood's use of her biological data gathered on the 1924–27 fieldwork suggests that she was well aware of its social and political entanglements. Her disenchantment with terms such as 'race' and 'intelligence' is made clear in the monograph which was the primary product of this research trip (Blackwood 1927). Blackwood began this report by acknowledging that scores on mental tests 'vary in direct ratio with the social status of the subject' (1927: 8), and she concluded by stating that 'intelligence … can be defined only as what is measured by the tests' and that '"race" should carry a biological definition only' (Blackwood 1927: 111).

Nor, other than this monograph, did she really draw on her measurements and other data during her later career and teaching. She did publish some of her findings on skin colour and methodology for recording it (Blackwood 1930). Her photographs were printed as pairs of frontal and side portraits, and became part of a reference collection for the Pitt Rivers Museum, but she never published on them. The hair samples are still in the little envelopes she placed them in, and have never been opened. The children's drawings did not come to the Museum until after her death, and she never published on them. The slips of paper on which she recorded physical measurements were never deposited in the Museum's collection.

Blackwood did draw fairly extensively on the material she collected on this trip in her later teaching. She taught on physical anthropology and issues of race as well as on cultures and on what were seen then as determinative links between race, environment, and culture. However, she avoided shallow generalisations about race in her teaching, and updated her lectures with new findings on blood groups, archaeology, and other research which helped to refine theories about human

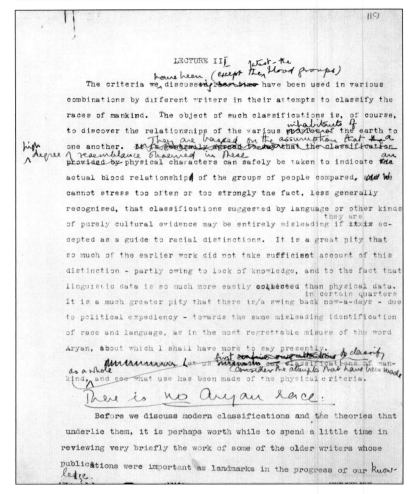

Figure 5.3 *Blackwood lecture notes, 'THERE IS NO ARYAN RACE.'*
Blackwood Papers, lecture III, box 21.

populations and their relationships. Even here, where she might have focused on her biological data, the legacy of her disquiet with ready associations between 'race' and intelligence and other factors, which she expressed in her diary for the 1924–27 field trip, may be seen in a poignant pencilled insertion, in large letters, in a lecture on ethnology which she gave during the war years of 1942 and 1944 (Figure 5.3): 'THERE IS NO ARYAN RACE.'

Conclusion

Holistic perspectives illuminate the often unexpected connections between entities that we might prefer to think of in simpler terms as discrete units. Within museums, the increasing expectation that curators will consult with source communities has brought to the fore not only the existence and nature of very different meanings of anthropological collections, but the impossibility of categorizing them as only one thing or another. Not only are conceptual boundaries permeable, but it turns out that different meanings have constituted one another. The tensions arising from acknowledging the co-presence and relations between anthropological and Native, social and biological and political meanings of these collections, affect relations not just between museums and indigenous peoples but between cultural and biological areas of anthropology.

A holistic perspective on the products of anthropological research, whether these be notes, measurements, human remains, or museum collections, requires that we see them in the broadest possible way, and that we acknowledge the co-presence of and interconnections between their various sets of meaning. Human remains do not cease to be socially constituted even when they are in the laboratory. Indeed, biological specimens such as the hair samples collected by Blackwood are defined as being of interest to science and are retained in museums and laboratories for study by the accumulation of social and political relations over time; their existence and use documents cross-cultural and racial politics across time as much as they document biological phenomena. In the face of this complex reality, the insistence by some segments of the British scholarly community on defining human remains solely as biological data seems not only simplistic, but quite obviously intended to retain a certain social and political control over them which carries over from colonial relationships. Holistically, of course, neither we nor the people we work with ever stop being persons, and the products of our research – whether in our offices, in archives, in museums, or in laboratories – reflect this.

Notes

1. Several groups have been appointed by government in recent years to consider human remains, including the Retained Organs Commission, which examined issues connected with the retention of post-1948 medical specimens in England; the Church Archaeology Human Remains Working Group, which focused on burials from Christian contexts in England dating from the seventh–nineteenth century AD; and the Working Group on Human Remains, of which I was a member, which focused on overseas indigenous remains from 1500 to 1948 AD. The Retained Organs Commission report is at: www.nhs.uk/retainedorgans/. The Church Archaeology Human Remains Working Group report is at: www.english-heritage.org.uk/default. asp?wci=Node&wce=8246. The report of the Working Group on Human Remains is at: www.culture.gov.uk/global/publications/archive_2003

2. Several ideas developed in this paper have been worked out in other publications for quite different purposes and contexts: see Peers 2004, 2003, and Brown, Peers et al. 2006. I have recombined and further extended my thinking for the purpose of the present paper and would like to thank David Parkin and Stanley Ulijaszek for giving me the opportunity to do so.

3. On details of Blackwood's life and career, see: Knowles 2000; Knowles 2004; Penniman 1976.

4. Little documentation has survived which describes Blackwood's own understanding of its goals, or which sheds light on the mental testing elements. Following the trip, she published the results of mental tests she conducted on different groups as *A Study of Mental Testing in Relation to Anthropology* (Blackwood 1930).

5. The Ojibwe, an Algonquian-speaking people, still inhabit their historic territories around the Great Lakes and west onto the prairies, in Canada and the US. They call themselves in their own language *Anishinaabeg*, and have also been called Chippewa and Saulteaux.

6. I am grateful to PRM volunteer Ina van der Veen, whose careful archival research and correlation of documents proved the sources of the hair samples, which are not mentioned in Blackwood's field notes or diary.

7. Consultation began in 1999 and involved a member of Red Lake Nation (Nokomis Paiz) travelling to Oxford to work with PRM collections, followed by a visit by myself to Red Lake in 2000. These visits were made possible with funding by the AHRB, University of Oxford Astor Fund, and the Minnesota Historical Society, and by the efforts of Marcia Anderson, Head of Collections at MHS, to all of whom I am profoundly grateful.

8. See, for instance, Child 1998, Miller 1996.

9. On the issue of names and human remains, see also Hubert and Fforde 2002: 12. While otherwise strongly retentionist, the Duckworth Laboratory in Cambridge has made it policy 'to return any individual skeletons or skulls of named individuals' (cited in WGHR Report 2003: 60).

10. This was the Clapp Act, amended in 1907. See also Meyer 1994, Beaulieu 1984.

11. The two field diary entries relating to her conversations with Jenks say simply, '(13 October 1925, Minneapolis, University of Minnesota) Talked to Dr Jenks, Professor of Anthropology, who schemed out a trip for me to Indian Reservations. The one where there is most mixture is at White Earth ... Another, the Turtle Mountain Reserve ... a good place to study the amalgamation process' and '(20 October 1925) Saw Dr Jenks and got my marching orders for the Indian trip.' In her teaching papers (BB B12.12 Physical Anthropology notes), which date from after the 1924–27 trip, Blackwood had notes from her readings and fieldwork comparing blood quantum with physical measurements and with eye and skin colour. One of these

notes compares her findings with those of Professor Jenks from his work with a number of Minnesota Ojibwe communities, but again does not mention legal or political contexts for Jenks' research.

12. And see Gosden and Knowles 2001: 4 on the position of artefacts in the centre of relationships. These ideas are explored in greater depth in Brown, Peers et al 2006.

Chapter 6

ANTHROPOLOGICAL THEORY AND THE MULTIPLE DETERMINACY OF THE PRESENT

Howard Morphy

Introduction

Zygmunt Bauman, justifying a second edition of his book *Culture as Praxis*, twenty-five years after the publication of the original, reflects on the tendency in contemporary social theory for ideas to be buried before their time or to be remembered in a way that distorts the senses they had in their own time. The ideas become simplified, removed from the complexities of the discourse of which they were a part, encapsulated in an ordering process which often masks continuities with the present.[1] 'We proceed nowadays not so much by continuous and cumulative learning as through a mixture of forgetting and recalling' (Bauman 1999: viii). There is a tendency for theories and concepts in anthropology to be presented as if they develop sequentially rather than cumulatively – rather than being modified and added to, they tend to replace one another holus bolus. Recent developments in anthropological theory have problematised the boundaries around things; people are not acting in the environment but are integral parts of the environment; knowledge is embodied and so on. Relationships that were once thought of as mediated are now conceived of as direct. The language that was associated with mediation – structure, symbolic or semiotic system, system of knowledge, culture – has been replaced by a language of interconnectedness. People have become partible;

agency has become distributed, material objects relational. Associated with this development has been a move away from differentiating between levels of reality and levels of structure, from the separating of the physical from the mental, and of persons from things. The individual has either disappeared or become everywhere. The reaction against structure and culture, as mediating processes, occurred in part because the boundaries between phenomena had been too firmly drawn – had been reified – rather than being understood as emergent, complex, multiply determined, transforming, produced and reproduced by relationships. While at a very general level a relational perspective ought not to be deterministic – nothing exists except in relationship to something else – in much recent anthropological theory it has become determining. Sometimes this has been in a weak sense – the determining level of reality as opposed for example to concepts of structure – sometimes in a stronger, narrower sense – the determining nature of the social and hence of social relationships.[2] Many of the relational concepts that have been developed are useful, but in the move away from levels of analysis, levels of reality, there is a danger that they can obscure rather than illuminate the complexity of human motivation and action.

Towards a concept of relative autonomy

Almost any meaningful human activity or artefact can take an anthropologist on an interpretative journey that connects it to most other aspects of its society and indeed to aspects of human societies in general. These 'thick descriptions' are not so much part of the method of anthropology but rather a descriptive outcome that is made possible by anthropological analysis.[3]

If after a long and bumpy journey along a dirt road someone says to a Yolngu woman within the hearing of her brother that they hope she does not feel sore, considerable offence will be caused. In order to understand why requires an analysis of brother–sister relations in the context of the overall set of kinship behaviour in Yolngu society. A full explanation will have to account for the emotional and psychological impact of the question in sociological terms. It will require an understanding of Yolngu religious beliefs and the nature of clan organisation. It will lead into an analysis of gender relations and the division of labour and the place of violence in Yolngu society.[4] It will also require a subtle understanding of the relationship between context and consequence, for although such a question is always likely to cause offence, in different circumstances and with different people it can have either severe or moderate consequences.

Likewise, if when watching a Yolngu painting being completed with fine cross-hatched lines the anthropologist focuses his or her attention on the *marwat*, the brush of human hair that is used to perform the task, a similar journey of explanation occurs. It will touch on the division of labour, on the technology of painting, on the sensuality and aesthetics of paintings, and more abstractly on Yolngu conceptions of self. Hair establishes a connection to the head and in turn the fontanelle, which to Yolngu is the fountainhead of wisdom, a bodily manifestation of the clan well from which knowledge and understanding are derived. What we might provisionally refer to as the deep semantics of the *marwat* also touches on brother–sister avoidance, since the hair on the brush should, though it does not always, come from women of the clan to which the painting belongs. There is no necessary connection between these different dimensions of the significance of the *marwat*. Its functional suitability to producing sequences of even parallel lines is not influenced by the gender of the hair-provider. The symbolic significance and functionality of the brush are *relatively autonomous*. This does not mean, however, that they are neatly separated out in Yolngu conceptions of the *marwat*. The symbolic load of the brush is as important as the pigment that it carries in expressing the essence of paintings: on the one hand, that Yolngu paintings are a product of the mind and, at the same time, that they are manifestations of the clan's spiritual identity (see e.g. Morphy 2005).

I find the concept of *relative autonomy* a useful one. The term has a considerable history in Marxist theory and my use of the term overlaps to an extent with its use in Althusserian structural Marxism. However, I use the term in a much less deterministic sense, and I do not intend to imply a systems model of society. I use the term as a way of simultaneously avoiding dualisms and acknowledging the difference between different domains of existence, different frames of action, different orders of reality – mind and body, the symbolic and the material, technique and form, and even the biological and the cultural. The implication is that that which is relatively autonomous is of epistemological significance and reflects something that from a particular perspective can be considered to have properties of its own. The relative signifies that one domain is influenced by others – the what of symbolism by the how, the methods of production by the technology available, the materials used in manufacture by their symbolic value and by their physical properties. The relationships are multiple; determinacy is not excluded but involves multiple factors, which echo in complex ways across different domains. Theories of coadaptation and coevolution both fit well with the concept as I am using it since ultimately no domain of existence is isolated from all others. The domains can never be treated as if they are autonomous

– as if they are outside the context of action, uninfluenced by other domains or conceived of as entirely divorced from the events which provide the context for their continued existence.

In this paper I do not intend to fully explicate the examples I introduced above, though I will return briefly to them. My analysis presupposes that there are structures, patterns of behaviour, bodies of ideas, that make the observations meaningful. An understanding of avoidance relationships requires an understanding of Yolngu kinship, marriage arrangements and clan organisation. An understanding of the hair brush requires both knowledge of the techniques of painting and of the symbolic ideas connected to hair. Clearly explanation is not limited to how those events and objects are experienced by Yolngu; however, the explanations and structures must be consistent with the ethnography. A Yolngu explanation of brother–sister avoidance is likely to be phrased in terms of feelings of anger and shame. People are socialised from birth into particular kinds of relationships with kin that foreshadow aspects of those relationships later in life. For example, children in a potential spouse relationship know from early on that it is safe to play 'mother and father' games together, whereas from an early age brothers and sisters will be very reserved in each other's company.[5] Such relationships are learned through experience and observation but also through verbal instruction. Avoidance relationships are terminologically marked and can be formulated by Yolngu as a set of rules that can be communicated to outsiders. While the verbal, the psychological and the behavioural are relatively autonomous there is no reason to give one logical priority over the other in the reproduction of the patterns of behaviour observed. Embodied behaviour, while resistant to change, can clearly be modified as the ideas associated with it change. People can reach a point where they no longer think it appropriate or necessary to avoid their sisters.

Similarly, in the case of technical tasks, very different skills and bodies of knowledge can be brought to the task of producing a particular object. There is no question that people develop certain skills through a process of embodiment, by learning to handle clay, by learning dance movements, how to handle the bow or cradle the cello, but it is equally the case that this is not all there is to it. The process may also include reflective moments or reference to external information, plans, designs, templates and so on.[6] Moreover, individual performance is usually part of a larger event in which other people play a part in different ways. In Yolngu society, the capacity to appreciate music or the principles of painting can be acquired by those who have never developed the ability to perform at a high level. And indeed these may be precisely the people who determine the sequence of songs to be performed or the correct form of the design in painting. The initial form of a design may be set by people who are acknowledged not to have the skill to produce the finished form of the object. What they do possess is the knowledge and authority to determine the correct pattern.

Holism and agency

The very breadth of the journey that an anthropologist undertakes to explain a particular event, his or her holistic approach, is both the discipline's greatest strength and the origin of many of the conceptual difficulties that anthropologists have faced. One response has been to narrow down the domain of the subject. Radcliffe-Brown, for example, notoriously achieved this by severing off certain dimensions of human existence as the province of other disciplines, making social structure and social relations the core of anthropology. The problem with such an approach is that in studying humans it is difficult to separate the social from the historical, from the psychological and from the biological. Much of the critique of anthropology in recent years has involved the inclusion of what was once excluded: history, colonialism, psychology in as much as it includes emotion, affect and bodily experience, and so on. What is included or excluded has an impact on the theoretical frameworks of the discipline. Over-rigid determining models of structure were problematised and replaced by ones more sensitive to process, transformation and change.

Complementing, and to an extent contradicting, the broadening critique has been an increasing tendency to shift the focus of anthropological theory to action in context, not through the micro-method of ethnomethodology but, ironically, through a more interpretative and assertive anthropology in which the anthropologist's personal experience of being in the world turns out to be synergistic with those he or she is studying. The relational framework has in some cases become all-encompassing – assuming the status of a theory in which the human beings and the objects of their social environment can be seen as being equivalent, agentive subjects (see for example Gell 1998).

Certainly from a Yolngu perspective there is no absolute boundary between the human and the non-human world. Material objects are an integral part of people's worlds and can be thought of in some cases as extensions of the person, extensions of a person's agency or the agency of spiritual powers incarnate in the landscape. However, to treat the relationships between persons and things as if they are relationships between people is insufficient. Relationships between people involve mutual intentional agency between thinking beings with different degrees of shared knowledge about each other. While in some contexts Yolngu may behave towards animals, rocks or trees as if they have agency, that does not mean that they conceive of them in the same way that they do human beings, nor does it mean that they relate to trees or rocks in general as if they had agency. A particular tree can be incorporated into a nexus of causation that impacts on the human world – by causing a death, or manifesting ancestral properties – but most are not. Yolngu distinguish between animals in their ordinary or mundane sense (*wakinngu*) and animals in a sacred aspect (*maḏayinpuy*). It is with the latter that Yolngu have quasi-social relationships, as opposed to incorporating them within social relationships as food items or objects of exchange. The emu that runs away will be shot, killed and eaten. One that walks fearlessly into a camp will be treated with respect and have kinship terms applied to it: 'Welcome brother, feel at home'.[7]

How is the emu in this case thought to have agency? To what extent is the relationship with it the equivalent to the relationships between people? Such questions have been part of anthropology since its inception and I would argue that the complex answers that they require are a prerequisite to understanding why people relate to emu in different ways in different contexts. The explanation requires precisely that same journey of exploration we have undertaken in the case of brother–sister avoidance and the *marwat*: an analysis of Yolngu concepts of the nature of the world and its ancestral determination, the moiety system, Yolngu kinship terminology and so on.

Parallel to the renewed relational focus in anthropological theory has been a continuing critique of the concept of culture, a concept that has never been central to British social anthropology.[8] This is not the place to engage in detail with the extensive debates over the concept. My position is that a concept that covers the terrain occupied by the various uses of the term culture is necessary to understanding human societies, and that many of the problems with the term are caused by trying to make it do too much, by opposing it to concepts such as society and habitus, rather than seeing it as an idea that can readily complement other concepts. I also see anthropology's difficulty with the concept of culture arising out of a failure to deal with complexity and the multi-determined nature of events. In essence, culture as I use it is the ideational dimension of meaningful behaviour. In this sense culture includes information, knowledge, ideas and concepts that are shared, communicated, experienced and learnt. However, it is acknowledged that each of these terms is used in a qualified and relative manner; the boundaries around many concepts are fuzzy and overlapping just as are the boundaries around groups. While some ideas and concepts are widely shared and easily communicated, others are not, and knowledge and experience itself are variables across time and space and vary from individual to individual. As ideas, 'a̲ culture' and 'a̲ discrete body of cultural knowledge' are misleading parodies or a consequence of inadequate theorisations of the concept. Part of the objective of anthropology is to discover the parameters of variation and to develop models that are able to account for that variability. Culture, in the sense I am using it, is a flag for those ideational components that enable action in context, which, together with local and global social and political structures and relationships, in part create the context in which action occurs.

Thus a central part of my argument is that in order to understand behaviour or material artefacts in context it is necessary and useful to include in one's analysis both structural and cultural components. However that does not mean that in themselves they are determining. Ideas, institutions, and relations are reproduced by action in context, even if they are not derivable solely from action in context. To assert that would be to fall into a synchronicity that is recognised, correctly, to be a major problem with over-rigid models of structure. We have brought into our 'thick descriptions' different and relatively autonomous orders of existence that cannot be wholly explained in the relational matrix of a particular context but that depend on pre-existing structures, bodies of knowledge, semantic categories, and local and regional histories. We need to be able to place the events that we observe in a multi-dimensional space where they exist simultaneously in the context of very different domains and histories. The relationships that are needed to fully understand agency in context largely exist outside any particular context but are implicated in the very possibility of the action itself.

The structures and bodies of knowledge we are concerned with are part of events as they unfold but they are simultaneously complex abstractions. A holistic anthropology cannot be reductionist but must recognise the multi-determined nature of reality and the relative autonomy of different domains or components of reality. It is the *relative autonomy* of these different domains that requires analysts both to step away from the context of action and simultaneously to be present where the action happens. It is only by engaging in this double movement that we gain the perspective that allows us to understand behaviour in context, and appreciate the role of agency in influencing the trajectories of dynamic but structured processes – be they cultural, social or biological – that precede any particular presence in the world.

Method and abstraction

The very methods of anthropological practice that yield the data from which models of social structure are produced have a dimension of abstraction to them that has to be explicitly acknowledged or their status will be fundamentally misunderstood. For example, the genealogical method is a tool which can be used, among other things, to explore kinship terminologies and behaviour. Its use is not motivated by the implication that the persons most closely connected by descent are of equivalent relationship to each other or more significant than more distantly related individuals. The compilation of a genealogy may reveal distinctions which place people in different categories – in different spiritual universes (as in the Yolngu moiety system), or as marriageable and unmarriageable – even though they are equally closely related to ego from a genetic viewpoint. A genealogy creates a framework for posing questions, for determining whether or not there is a systematic relationship between genealogical relatedness and the relationship terminologies that people apply to each other. The recording of a genealogy is the beginning of the exploration of kinship terminology; it is not necessarily the case that genealogical connection is fundamental to understanding kinship terminology, though usually it is a significant component of the analysis. There are clearly many other ways in which one can approach kinship terminologies. It may even be that there are societies in which genealogical connections are unrecognised and hence irrelevant to the analysis of relationship terminologies (as Storrie 2003 suggests for the Hoti). But it would be counter-intuitive to ignore the fact that Yolngu women call their children *waku* and their brother's children *gäthu* and that their brothers use the same terms for the same children.

Action, agency and context

The key area for social theory in recent years has been set at the locus of action – appropriately focusing on human agency in context. Action is seen as the fulcrum that connects the past with the future. Yet the context of action is an arbitrary moment in a socio-cultural process taking place over time. It is no more or less *real* than the structures, concepts, bodies of ideas and knowledge, and sets of dispositions that precede it. Individual action flows through contexts. While at the moment of action the individual may seem to act immediately and unreflexively, following embodied movements, time for reflection soon enters the process. The throwing of the clay to produce the body of a pot is, in the hands of the accomplished potter, an almost automatic process. However, the potter still requires those moments of reflection during which he or she might contemplate and accept or reject the form of the pot. Over the long term, reflection and recursion are integral to social and cultural processes. To a considerable extent these are the prerequisites for action – action that often appears to the observer to flow through context. Modelling these processes in the context of action is vital to the anthropological enterprise. But understanding them also requires the analyst to step outside the immediate context.

For the remainder of this paper I will centre my analysis on a particular object, a *yingapungapu* sand sculpture used in Yolngu mortuary rituals. I will explicate the form and significance of the sand sculpture by engaging in the two-way process I have outlined above. I will initially provide a broad, ethnographically-based summary of its significance to Yolngu. I will argue that the *yingapungapu* sand sculpture, as a significant object in its social and cultural context, is subject to multiple processes of determination. I will analyse the way in which it is used in Yolngu rituals from a performative perspective, and then place it in the context of Yolngu social organisation and social structure. Finally I will consider the semantics of the *yingapungapu* by considering how it is represented in paintings by the Yolngu artist Narritjin Maymuru. I will argue that his paintings demonstrate the ways in which reflective and recursive action and thought are integral to the dialogical processes that determine the trajectory of human societies. Individuals weave pathways through the complexity of a multi-determined present. However, at any given point in time those pathways are, relatively speaking, structured by the requirements of collective action, of intersubjective communication, by shared conceptions of the nature of the world. I would go further than that and say that these structures, the patterned associations that underlie the trajectory, are in many cases located in explicit metamodels of society – root metaphors – that are integral to the recursive process.[9]

For anthropologists models exist in the space between abstraction and the 'real world'. In many cases indigenous metamodels occupy an analogous space. Different societies are likely to have different metamodels; clearly they are as variable as the anthropologist's own models – more than one is likely to exist at any time and there will be relative degrees of fuzziness around their edges. The language of durability, of template, of replication, reflects a fundamental meta-model in Yolngu society and at this moment in history provides a model by which people continually reconstruct their society. However, Yolngu also have metamodels for networks of connection, pathways and amalgams. Anthropologists must look for areas where models *of* and models *for* coincide.[10]

Yingapungapu: narratives of origin

A *yingapungapu* sand sculpture is used by clans of the Yirritja moiety centred on the region to the north of Blue Mud Bay. The sand sculpture is *garma*, that is, part of the public ceremonial law of the region. A *yingapungapu* can be made to enclose the shade where a body lies prior to burial, or it can be constructed as part of the purificatory rituals that follow the burial ceremony (see Figure 6.1). The word *yingapungapu* can be applied to the state of pollution of participants in the ritual and to objects closely associated with the dead person. Clans of the Dhuwa moiety in the same region have a different sculpture, *wukidi*, which is used in ceremonies of that moiety. Sand sculptures are central components of Yolngu ritual and help to define the stage around which events take place. The *yingapungapu* sculpture may be in place for the duration of the ceremony or it may be in existence for only part of a day, depending on the phase of the ceremony in which it is employed. At the conclusion of the ceremony what remains of the sand sculpture is danced out of existence.[11]

The *yingapungapu* sand sculpture, like all Yolngu ritual forms, has its origins in the ancestral dimension or *wangarr*. A group of *mokuy* ancestral women, the Wuradilagu, travelled from Groote Eylandt to the

Figure 6.1 *A* Yingapungapu *ground sculpture at Yilpara, Blue Mud Bay, 2000. The sand sculpture was made for the purification ceremony of a senior member of the Madarrpa clan. It is positioned in front of the hut or shade where the body had previously lain before burial. In the evening following the purificatory rituals the hut was set alight in a final ceremony. (Photograph Howard Morphy.)*

mainland in Blue Mud Bay (Figure 6.2). They were shy and hid from
men. They caught fish and feasted off wild plums that they knocked
from the trees with their digging sticks. They journeyed north and
established camps on three of the main peninsulas that extend into
the northern waters of the Bay – Garrapara, Yilpara and Djarrakpi. A
fourth *yingapungapu* place is some distance away to the north, on the
island of Lunggurrtja on Buckingham Bay. When they finished eating
their meals of fish they buried the remains in an elliptical hollow
scooped out in the soft sand of the beach. The shape was that of the
yingapungapu. At each of the places where the Wuradilagu settled
they established relationships with male *mokuy* who lived in the area,
whom they referred to as their brothers. At each place they have a
separate identity and their own sets of names.

   The men went out to sea fishing and hunting for turtle and dugong.
When they returned the fish were cooked on the open fire and shared
with the women and the remains buried in the sand. The fishing
trips were sometimes hazardous: storms developed and the might of
the open sea, Mungurru, threatened to overturn the boat. On most

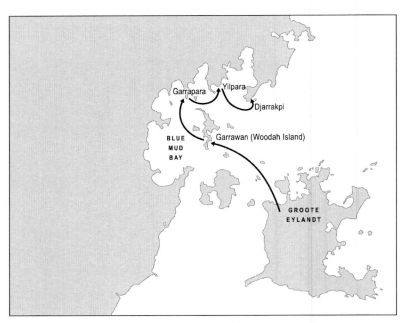

Figure 6.2 *Map of the journey of the Wuradilagu. The map shows the journey
of the Wuradilagu ancestral women as they travelled from Groote Eylandt to
the mainland and then journeyed to each of the peninsulas: Garrapara, which is
associated with the Dhalwangu clan, Yilpara which is associated with the Madarrpa,
and Djarrakpi which is associated with the Manggalili. (Map by Katie Hayne.)*

occasions the hunters returned drenched by the sea and rain but rejoicing in the calm that followed and ready to share their catch with the Wuradilagu women. However, in one episode of the myth the boat failed to return. The ancestral women stood on the top of the dunes looking out to sea. They saw great cumulus clouds rising above the horizon and feared the worst. The empty canoe was washed up on the shore and later the dead body of one of the ancestral men was found stranded on the beach. The women made a large sculpture in the sand in the form of the *yingapungapu* and laid the body of their dead brother in it. They were beside themselves with grief and, deep in mourning, cut their heads with their digging sticks and the blood flowed into the *yingapungapu*.

The three *yingapungapu* places on Blue Mud Bay are each associated with a different clan of the Yirritja moiety – Garrapara with the Dhalwangu, Yilpara with the Madarrpa and Djarrakpi with the Manggalili. The fourth place, Lunggurrtja, which is outside the regional community and will not be considered any further here, also belongs to a Yirritja clan, the Birrkili. The landscape in each place is redolent with memories of the Wuradilagu women. The high sand dunes are transformations of the mountains of possum fur string that they spun to make bags and sacred objects, patches of jungle are places where they hunted and gathered, the thin delicate forms of the whistling trees represent their bodies along the shoreline looking out to sea. At Yilpara and Garrapara the shape of their *yingapungapu* is still visible, and at Djarrakpi the brackish waters of the lagoon behind the dunes hints at their mourning blood. Each place also became the site for burials of people from the Yirritja moiety.

Yingapungapu: the ritual performance

The myths of the Wuradilagu and their brothers form the basis of the purificatory phase of contemporary mortuary rituals associated with the *yingapungapu* sculpture. Yolngu mortuary rituals are complex events lasting for several days or even weeks. The ceremony has a number of complementary themes (see Morphy 1984). The central structuring theme is the return of the deceased person's spirit to the ancestral dimension, to the clan's sacred well. The spirit is encouraged on this journey by ancestral beings connected to the dead person. Songs, dances, paintings and sacred objects are combined in performative sequences that map out the journey of the soul. The grave itself represents the clan's sacred well, its *djalkirri* (foundational) place. A *yingapungapu* sand sculpture may be made at the beginning of the entire ceremony to mark off the area where the body is held, almost literally as a container of pollution. However, the main ritual action centred on the *yingapungapu* takes place towards the end of the ceremony after the body has been buried. I can only provide a brief summary here.[12]

The *yingapungapu* ceremony is designed to purify people and objects that have been contaminated by close association with the dead person and to return them to a state of normality. Closeness includes both physical closeness – preparing the body for burial, placing it in the coffin and so on – and genealogical closeness – in particular mothers, wives and sisters. The performance is explicitly cathartic, designed to lift people out of their feeling of loss and to make them part of the community again. The performance will continue until the ceremonial leader has sensed maximum participation, until the closest relatives, those most overwhelmed with grief, join in with the performance. Quite literally, life returns to normal at the conclusion of the ceremony. The community shop, if there is one, will be opened again, and prohibitions are lifted so that people can go hunting.

The narrative of the *yingapungapu* ceremony follows that of the successful hunt. It begins with songs about the journey of the fishermen out to sea and the spearing of fish, in particular *yambirrku* (parrot fish). Clouds rise up on the horizon and a storm breaks out. The participants are gathered together in the centre of the sand sculpture and purification by water (*liyalupthun*) begins. Men and women are initially washed separately. The singing describes the course of the storm and the state of Mungurru, the great body of Yirritja moiety water that moves from the deep sea to the shore. The storm abates and the hunters paddle their canoe towards the land. They hear the sounds of life on the shore and glimpse the distant flight of parrots.

The hunters return to the shore and begin to cook the fish in the fire. The group of singers sits beside the sculpture and a fire is built in the centre of the sculpture where the washing has taken place. The men who are in a state of pollution (also *yingapungapu*) sit in a circle around the fire. They perform a series of dances on their haunches enacting the cooking, eating and sharing of fish. The fire is lit and blazes up, branches of ironwood leaves are thrust on the fire by men and women. The younger men bravely thrust their chests into the flames. Men and women seize the branches and hit themselves and their neighbours with them, showering sparks everywhere. Some women will dance around the assembled company with smouldering branches waving smoke in their direction. Pots and pans, eating utensils – anything that has been used to feed people during the burial ceremony – will be brought into the *yingapungapu* and smoked. This may be the occasion when the vehicle that was used to carry the dead body to the grave is driven up to the *yingapungapu*, washed, smoked and smeared with red ochre.

The time has arrived for the final phase of the ritual. A series of themes are interwoven: death, decay, regeneration, remembrance and forgetting. The re-enacted myth centres on the burial of fish remains in the sand after a meal. Maggots come and consume the flesh leaving the bones clean, sand crabs scavenge the remains and bury them in holes in the sand, and birds scour the intertidal zone spearing the scavengers with their beaks. Finally the tide moves up the beach, sweeping it clean. Like all Yolngu myths it is difficult to separate the ancestral dimension from an almost romantic reflective poesis of landscape, linking it to the emotions and experience of human life.[13]

The final sequence of dances places a strong emphasis on joy and forgetting, though the underlying struggle with the negative emotions of death is still present and can potentially emerge more strongly expressed. Continuity is provided by the transformational dances of the maggots. The sequence begins with a group of dancers, with men at the front followed by the women, dancing as maggots consuming the rotting remains. They dance on their knees crawling forward, wiping out the contour of the *yingapungapu* sand sculpture, leaving behind a patterned trail in the sand (Figure 6.3). They stop at the entrance to the shade where the corpse has lain. There then follow dances with spears as men oppose one another, thrusting the spears towards one another and flicking them into the ground – they hint at the scavenging *guluwitjpitj* birds, and the *mokuy* spearing *yambirrku*, but never far behind is the idea of vengeance and the anger felt at the death. In the final dances the maggots have become flies and take to the wing. The dance is performed competitively by young men and women who dance around the shade and in the final sequences move ever closer to its entrance. As they dance they sing out the names of the places where the maggots have flown, the three *yingapungapu* sites of Garrapara, Yilpara and Djarrakpi and the island of Woodah jointly owned by the three clans, the Dhalwangu, Madarrpa and Manggalili. When the dancing has concluded, usually after a suitable interval, the men enter the shade and remove any items left behind. In the evening a final ceremony is performed which ends with the shade being set ablaze. It burns with an intensity that lights up the whole area surrounding it.

The description of a typical *yingapungapu* ceremony clearly shows how the ritual achieves certain objectives and acts as a vehicle for the expression of the emotions, and how it connects different domains of experience. The ceremony allows for the coordination of different domains of reality in the same expressive moment. There is a relative autonomy between the content of the ritual, the mythic reference of

Figure 6.3 *The maggot dancers, Yilpara, August 2001. On this occasion the* yingapungapu *sand sculpture was built at the start of the burial ceremony and contained within its shape the shade where the body lay. Following the burial a* yingapungapu *cleansing ceremony was performed. The performance shown here represents the penultimate phase of the ceremony as men and women dancers, as maggots, move forward on their knees towards the shade. In front of them two men dance with spears, thrusting them into the ground in front of the shade. The marks impressed into the ground by the dancers represent the tracks of the maggots as they approach the shade. In paintings the maggot's tracks are represented by dashed infill. (Still from film by Howard Morphy.)*

the songs and dances, the ritual event being performed – purification or the movement of the body – the primary theme of the particular phase of the ceremony – the spirit's journey, the expression of vengeance – and the sociological dimension of the ritual and psychological states of the performers. The core structure of the ceremony – based on the movement of the body from place of death to place of burial followed by the purificatory rituals – provides a basic script for a coordinated performance that enables these other components of the event to be expressed, produced or manifested.

The movement of a dead person may in general have psychological effects on the bereaved. In the Yolngu case such moments provide the context for an apparently 'uncontrolled' outbreak of grieving from female relatives. It is the time when they will throw themselves on the ground, attempt to cut their heads, and keen songs of lament. The movement of the body provides a cue to switching from one *madayin* or body of ancestral law, or a particular episode, to another. Sociologically it may provide a moment when relationships to the dead person are revealed, when a group of *waku* (sisters' children) step forward to lift the coffin or sisters throw themselves on the ground. It is a moment of apparently coordinated action, when people know that certain things are going to happen, when certain emotions will be expressed. However, that moment is never exactly the same and each time the particular episode is performed it may be performed in a different way, involving different ancestral beings and different myths.

Yingapungapu: positioned in Yolngu social relations

The *yingapungapu* is one way that one set of clans perform the purificatory stages of mortuary rituals, but it is only one of many possible ways of doing it. The variety is required in part by the nature of Yolngu social organisation and its ancestral determination. The *yingapungapu* ceremony can only be performed by clans which have inherited rights to it, but other clans have equivalent rituals that structure the emotions in analogous ways. If we simply focus on the purifying action of fire, the variety of ways in which it can be introduced is considerable. In the *yingapungapu* ceremony fire is introduced through the mythic narrative of cooking fish. However, in other purificatory rituals fire can be the fire used by 'Macassans' to forge metal, or the bush fire that burnt the ancestral crocodile's nest, or the fire carried by *djirrikitj* the quail and so on.[14]

Every sand sculpture and painting produced, every song sung or dance performed, provides a context for demonstrating the rights that people have, and these in turn reflect the structured pattern of relationships between people. Yolngu ritual law is a resource capable of making fine discriminations at almost any level of social organisation. Using connection to the *wangarr* it is possible to place people in encompassing crosscutting sets or to isolate them as individuals. However, underlying this flexibility is a structured process that operates to create and reimpose categorical distinctions and ordered sets of relationships. The moiety division is an absolute one. Myths, lands, names, places, people, animal species, afterworlds and so on are divided on a moiety basis into Dhuwa or Yirritja. The *yingapungapu* sand sculpture is one of the sculptures of the Yirritja moiety. The moiety itself, however, comprises sets of clans that are interrelated on a range of different bases. The substance of ceremonies is not shared at the level of moiety but at that of clans within the moiety and it forms an overlapping pattern of connection. Rights in the *yingapungapu* are not vested in the moiety as a whole but in the clans who can claim rights to it through ancestral connections – in Blue Mud Bay the Dhalwangu, Maḏarrpa and Manggalili. The performance of a *yingapungapu* ceremony and the making of the sand sculpture are an exercise of clan-based rights. There is considerable overlap in the details of the *yingapungapu* but in each case there are also many differences. The locational references of the myths differ, the names of the ancestral beings differ, there are minor variations in the form of the sand sculpture – in the number of small circles that can be represented at each end of the ellipse – and the power names associated with the big sea Mungurru differ in one case.

Clans of the same moiety can be connected on a number of different bases, through geographical contiguity or proximity, relationships of descent, position in the regional marriage system, mythological connection and so on. The *yingapungapu* sand sculpture is seen as evidence of the strong connection between the Dhalwangu, Maḏarrpa and Manggalili clans. It marks them as a set of closely related clans who cooperate together. Their estates are geographically contiguous and the sand sculpture and ceremony can be used to express this relationship. However, although the clans are close geographically and share much sacred law in common, they are separated from one another in the regional system of marriage alliances. Manggalili are a *märi* group to Dhalwangu and Maḏarrpa, who in turn are *gutharra* clans to Manggalili. The *märi–gutharra* relationship between clans is referred to as the 'backbone'. *Märi* is a kinship term that refers to mother's mother and mother's mother's brother. Men marry their mother's mother's brother's daughter's daughters. The *märi* clan is seen as a provider of mothers-in-law to men of their *gutharra* clans. A series of things flow from this relationship. People receive names from their mother's mother's clan, generally have permission to use the resources of that clan's country and are in a strong position to succeed to their *märi*'s country should that clan become extinct. In mortuary rituals and circumcision ceremonies the *märi* clan plays an organising role in their *gutharra's* ceremony.

The marriage relations between Yolngu clans are clearly socially produced and reproduced, and must change over time. However, Yolngu ideology holds that the relationships are fixed and are derived from or follow relationships between the lands themselves, and the ancestral beings incarnate in those lands. An analysis of genealogies does indeed suggest great stability in the pattern of marriage relationships over time and Yolngu act to ensure that any changes that do occur are reframed to accord with ancestral relationships between lands.

The *yingapungapu* sand sculptures provide a focus for the relationship between these sets of clans. They will perform the ceremony jointly, the sand sculpture will be oriented to reflect the geographical relationships between the clans, with the two ends and the middle being identified with each of the places concerned. In the concluding maggot dance each place is danced in turn. When the groups come together to perform a *yingapungapu* ceremony they are referred to collectively as Yithuwa (maggot people). Yet the *yingapungapu* can also provide a basis for differentiating the clans from one another within a closely related set. Manggalili, the *māri* clan, possesses a unique set of names for Mungurru while Madarrpa and Dhalwangu share the same set. In discussing the relationship between the *yingapungapu* places, people can order them in different sequences according to context. The Wuradilagu women travelled from west to east, from Garrapara to Yilpara and Djarrakpi; mothers-in-law and names move from east to west – Djarrakpi, Yilpara and Garrapara. When ceremonies are held at Yilpara then that location is central and the other places peripheral, and the flies spread to Garrapara and Djarrakpi.

The fact that each clan owns a *yingapungapu* sand sculpture is seen by Yolngu as a reflection of a long and durable regional relationship between a set of clans of the same moiety. People make sense of it in terms of the regional system of social organisation. It accords with the fundamental division of the world into two spiritually segregated moieties, it can be thought to represent the connubium of marriage relations between the clans in the north of Blue Mud Bay (including the Dhuwa moiety clans that have roles in the ceremony determined by relationship traced through their mother's clan). However, it can also be used to express the difference of the clans from one another and the separate nature of their rights.

Yingapungapu: one artist's response

In the final section of this paper I will look at the ways in which Narritjin Maymuru represented the *yingapungapu* sand sculpture in his paintings produced over a period of 35 years.[15] I will show how his paintings amplify and elaborate on the mythology of the Wuradilagu and the form and content of Yolngu mortuary practices. More generally they reflect the ways in which the ancestral world is included within the imagination of a Yolngu elder. An analysis of the paintings shows how the *yingapungapu* becomes a symbol, conveyed to others through his paintings, in the context of discourse, experience and reflection over a lifetime. Narritjin played an important role as a ritual leader in passing the ceremony on in a particular form – he was one of those who would organise the sequence of songs in ceremonies, who was actively concerned to direct the emotions of the participants and to influence the ways in which participants experienced the performance. 'Passing it on' involves instructing people about the correct form of sand sculpture and the set of rights vested in it, but it also involves influencing attitudes towards death. In producing these paintings Narritjin reveals psychologically deep aspects of the emotional structure of Yolngu society that are both painful and in a sense liberating; he stretches towards the edge of a universe of meaning that connects deep structures of Yolngu society with deep structures of human emotional thought and expression.

The pattern of production, the authorship of *yingapungapu* paintings, is similar to other Yolngu works. Generally they are produced by members of the clan owning the particular manifestation of ancestral law concerned – the *yingapungapu* in its location. Occasionally a senior artist will paint their mother's clan design – indeed in a ritual context a *waku* (woman's child) will set the form of the sand sculpture. More rarely a person may paint a design belonging to his or her mother's mother's clan. The artists of the Dhalwangu, Madarrpa and Manggalili clans paint their own versions of the *yingapungapu* but they will occasionally include references to those of the other clans.

The earliest surviving example of Narritjin's *yingapungapu* sand sculpture paintings was made in 1946 for Ronald Berndt. The painting represents the sculpture made by the ancestral women at Djarrakpi. The women are shown with their digging sticks and carrying baskets, and the structure of the painting marks out features of the landscape at Djarrakpi. The hatched and dashed design which covers the surface of the painting is used to represent the process of decay (Figure 6.4). In subsequent paintings Narritjin explored most aspects of the symbolism of the *yingapungapu* and its connection to ritual.

The paintings can all be read at different levels or according to different narratives. Some paintings represent the ancestral women as they hunt and gather on the beach using their digging sticks to climb up and down the dunes, their heads covered out of modesty by an inverted carrying basket. Some represent the hollow scooped out in the sand where the remains of fish were buried. Others show the fishermen out at sea. The great storm that rose up was caused by the ancestral turtle coming in with the monsoon winds. The boat can be seen floating upturned in the water, the drowning men are shown being tossed around by the waves, their paddles scattered. Yet others show the body on the shore laid out in a *yingapungapu* sand sculpture. We can see the ceremony in progress, with groups of singers beside the sculpture. The ancestral women sit beside the sculpture,

Figure 6.4 'Yingapungapu' *by Narritjin Maymuru. This painting was made in 1946 for the anthropologist Ronald Berndt. It represents the land associated with the ancestral* yingapungapu *at Djarrakpi. The ancestral woman Nyapililngu is represented in the bottom left of the painting with her carrying basket on her head. Above her can be seen a representation of a* yingapungapu. *A representation of Nyapililngu's digging stick runs up the centre of the painting. The digging stick also symbolises the journey that ancestral beings took in travelling to Djarrakpi and a sacred tree associated with the ancestral Guwak, the brothers of Nyapililngu who 'drowned' at sea. The two figures to the top right represent the women in mourning. The background dashed pattern has a multiplicity of connotations including the maggots that consumed the remains of rotting fish left over from Nyapililngu's meal (for a detailed analysis of the iconography of these paintings see relevant chapters in Morphy 1991). (Berndt Museum of Anthropology, University of Western Australia, Reproduced with the permission of Buku-Larrnggay Mulka, Yirrkala.)*

distraught in mourning, cutting their heads with their digging sticks so that their blood flows into the hollow. The paintings often locate the *yingapungapu* in relation to other features of the landscape, in particular to the head of the Djarrakpi peninsula where the ancestral *yingapungapu* is sited. In one painting we can see the beach where turtles move up to lay their eggs in the sand, and Gungunbuy, the beach named after the sand crab (*gungun*), and the place where the empty boat was washed ashore after the drowning.

So far I have been drawing attention to descriptive elements in the paintings, many of which will be readily identified in figurative representations in Figures 6.5 and 6.6. In Yolngu epistemology these are the most 'outside' level of interpretation. They are reflected in the order of the ritual performance, and in the names of places and people – the places can be visited, the evidence seen. However, Narritjin's paintings also elaborate on some of the symbolic themes that carry the intellectual content of the ritual performance. The paintings show fish remains being eaten by maggots, with the fish sometimes shown white or in skeletal form and the maggots represented by the dashed infill of the clan design. Sand crabs are shown gathering together little balls of sand and flesh and rolling them into the holes in the sand into which they retreat. Sometimes we can see *guluwitjpitj* birds on the beach pecking at the crabs. Through the activity on the beach the paintings show images of decay, cleansing, growth and regeneration, a chaos of activity inscribed in the sand, washed away each day by the incoming tide. The images are the ones danced out with great emotion in the final stage of the *yingapungapu* ceremony and while the emphasis in the paintings is different – more on acceptance than joy – the message is complementary. [16]

The themes of death and regeneration are echoed elsewhere in Narritjin's *yingapungapu* paintings. The ancestral turtle is associated both with the death of the *mokuy* at sea and with birth and fertility. The turtle lays its eggs by burying them in the sand. The eggs themselves are both a source of food for Yolngu hunter–gatherers and a source of new life. As we shall see, for Narritjin the fertility of the turtle had a particular resonance.

However, the most powerful symbol of death and regeneration, even rebirth, is the *yingapungapu* itself. The *yingapungapu* carries obvious connotations of female sexuality and birth. The sand sculptures that are used in Yolngu mortuary rituals can all be seen to have this dimension. They represent such things as a crocodile's nest, the body of a female shark, a fish trap – to Yolngu all these are images or containers of fertility. The possible connections between the *yingapungapu* and the female body are densely portrayed in Narritjin's paintings, in particular through the image of Nyapililngu,

Figure 6.5 *'Yingapungapu' by Narritjin Maymuru, 1974. The central figure is a* yingapungapu *sand sculpture. The imagery within the* yingapungapu *centres on the chain of connection that links the remains of fish with the maggots that feed off them, and the sand crabs which in turn eat the maggots and other left overs, before they in turn become the prey of sea birds scavenging along the beach. The pattern on either side of the* yingapungapu *represents the marks made by turtles as they move up the beach to lay their eggs. A smaller representation of the sand sculpture is contained within each corner of the painting. In the lower section the* yingapungapu *represent the shallow hollow scooped out in the sand by the Wuradilagu women to bury the fish remains. In the upper sections there is a switch of scale and people can be seen gathered around the sand sculpture at a mortuary ritual, dancing and singing. The women in the top left are beside themselves, hitting their heads in grief. The image at the top of the* yingapungapu *represents the sacred tree under which the ancestral Guwak would sit. (National Museum of Australia, Canberra. Reproduced with the permission of Buku-Larrnggay Mulka, Yirrkala.)*

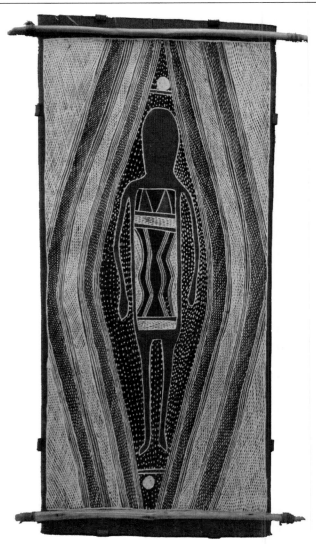

Figure 6.6 *'The Spirit Returns' by Narritjin Maymuru, 1981. This poignant image is one of the last paintings that Narritjin produced before his death. The painting shows a body lying within a* yingapuŋapu *awaiting burial. The person's chest has been painted with a Manggalili ancestral design associated with the Milky Way, the Yirritja moiety land of the dead. The body is contained within the 'womblike'* yingapuŋapu. *The dashed background design represents the processes of bodily decay and the crawling maggots. But in this case the pattern also represents the multitude of stars in the Milky Way and the painting evokes the process of transubstantiation that is believed to occur after death. (Buku Larrngay Mulka, Yirrkala. Reproduced with the permission of Buku-Larrnggay Mulka, Yirrkala.)*

the Wuradilagu woman who made the first *yingapungapu* at Djarrakpi and whose blood flows into it. I will simply illustrate a number of these patterns of association that he develops.

The imagery of Nyapililngu strongly connects her to the themes of the *yingapungapu* ritual and to the overall mythic narrative (Figure 6.7). At either end of his paintings of the *yingapungapu* Narritjin often painted anvil-shaped cloud symbols. The clouds connect Nyapililngu with the storm at sea. An analogy is made in Yolngu song between the clouds and the billowing breasts of the ancestral women. The anvil-shaped cloud design frequently has a cross incorporated within the motif. The cross represents the possum fur string breast girdles that women wear in addition to being a symbol of the cloud. The digging stick with which the women collected wild plums and dug the ellipse in the sand to bury fish can also be combined with the carrying basket to represent the women themselves.

The connection between the carrying basket and a womb is a general feature of Yolngu symbolism. The phallic connotations of the digging stick are fairly clear and explicitly alluded to in many of Narritjin's paintings (Figure 6.8). The carrying basket can be represented by an elliptical sign, as can the gash in Nyapililngu's head where she cut herself in mourning. The lagoon at Djarrakpi, into which her blood flowed when she mourned her dead brothers, is a source of conception spirits for the Manggalili clan. The paintings abound with imagery that connects the blood that Nyapililngu shed in mourning with the continuity of the Manggalili clan. Manggalili people are cradled in a *yingapungapu* sand sculpture as they return to the spiritual dimension to become a source of future souls.

However, rather than always opposing the digging stick to the ellipse in a simple male-female opposition, Narritjin's iconology quite often merges the boundaries between them. The digging stick itself can be seen as an elongated form of a *yingapungapu* sand sculpture and in his paintings Narritjin often plays on the relationship between the two. The *yingapungapu* can represent the ancestral women and so can the elliptical design.

A painting which initially appears to be an abstract geometric composition can be seen to refer in multiple ways to the ancestral woman (Figure 6.9). The central figure has the shape of the *yingapungapu*. On either side two anvil shapes are represented, the clouds from the storm that overwhelmed the boat, that became a sign to the women of the events that took place out at sea. However they can equally be seen to be representations of the women themselves standing on the dunes looking out to sea for the men to return. The anvil shapes represent the women's bodies. In another painting Narritjin represents the womens' bodies in the form of an ellipse

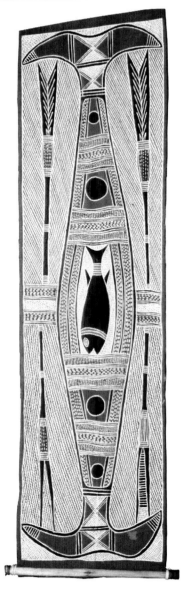

Figure 6.7 'Yingapungapu *and clouds' by Narritjin Maymuru, 1978. A simple painting of a* yingapungapu *with fish remains. However the anvil-shaped symbols at either end represent the clouds that arose with the storm at sea and caused the boat to overturn, drowning the Guwak. The clouds also represent the ancestral women, Nyapililngu, standing beside the* yingapungapu *mourning their dead brother. (Private collection. Reproduced with the permission of Buku-Larrnggay Mulka, Yirrkala.)*

Figure 6.8 *'Nyapililngu's carrying basket' by Narritjin Maymuru, 1966. This deceptively simple painting contains multiple references to Nyapililngu. The central figure represents a digging stick of the kind Nyapililngu used to scoop out the shape of a* yingapungapu, *and with which she cut her head in mourning. It also represents a ceremonial object with feather string arms that stands for Nyapililngu herself. The two figures on either are representations of Nyapililngu (who is both singular and plural). Their heads are covered with the inverted bent stringy bark-carrying basket, though we are able to see through the ends of the baskets to her face beyond. The structure of the painting also alludes to the shape of the basket. The semi circles top and bottom are the sand dunes at Djarrakpi, but they also refer to the ends of the basket produced by the inward folding of the bent bark. (National Museum of Australia. Reproduced with the permission of Buku-Larrnggay Mulka, Yirrkala.)*

containing a digging stick. In this case the Nyapililngu are said to be pregnant (Figure 6.10).

The blurring of distinction between male and female in the case of the *yingapungapu* paintings and the emphasis on female creativity reflects the deep structures of Yolngu symbolic thought. Nyapililngu is a female being of the Yirritja moiety. The fact that the sand sculpture represents an ancestral womb of the person's own moiety is entirely consistent with Yolngu religious beliefs. A person is conceived from conception spirits belonging to his or her own clan, that spiritual identity is reinforced throughout their lives by the separateness of the moieties and on their death their spirit is reincorporated within the ancestral world of their own moiety – Yirritja moiety souls can be seen in the stars of the Milky Way. Yet in the actual world people are born of women of the opposite moiety and sexual relations within the moiety are prohibited. The ambiguities in Narritjin's paintings and in the performance of the *yingapungapu* ceremony hint at deeper levels of metaphysical speculation – reflections on the limits of the autonomy of the clan, the lack of control over its reproduction, the tensions of sexual relations in a society with a moiety-wide incest taboo. It is not inconceivable that in the context of death and the fears, intense emotions and concerns that it raises, a field of speculation is opened up that creates the possibility of other worlds – worlds that can never be real but are part of the underlying logic of the ancestral or spiritual dimension.

These speculations are not going to be central to most people's engagement with a *yingapungapu* ceremony and are never made explicit. The sexual connotations of aspects of the ritual, while acknowledged, are implicit; the eroticism of the dances is normally constrained and controlled. However, as the dances progress towards the conclusion of the burial ceremony, young men and women dance almost in competition with one another, often in an atmosphere of laughter and barely contained ribaldry. The idea of continuity, of regeneration, of the joys of life for the living are clearly themes that operate in dialogue with the sense of loss, sadness and decay. The paintings work through these relationships, as does the ritual performance.

While the forms of, and inspiration for, paintings are spoken of by Yolngu artists as if they are set forms passed on from one generation to the next, following an ancestral design, they allow for considerable individual variation. There are set patterns, design elements and contents that belong to individual clans. However, I have argued elsewhere that the Yolngu conception of transmitted knowledge is not routine replication but more the emergence of ancestral design. Yolngu art provides considerable space for an individual's life experiences to

Figure 6.9 'Yingapungapu, *digging sticks and clouds' by Narritjin Maymuru, c. 1976. A geometric version of the previous painting. The central figure is again the digging stick, but in this case broadened to form the shape of the* yingapungapu. *On either side are two figures representing the Nyapililngu standing beside the* yingapungapu, *with their arms and legs outstretched. The elliptical signs to either side of their bodies represent their digging sticks. The background pattern of wavy lines in the top and bottom segments represents the pattern of the sea and the marks made by the tide in the sand. (Museum and Art Galleries of the Northern Territory, Reproduced with the permission of Buku-Larrnggay Mulka, Yirrkala.)*

Figure 6.10 *'Nyapililngu and Digging Sticks.' by Narritjin Maymuru, 1976. The central figure represents both the digging stick sacred object and a* yingapungapu *sand sculpture. The figures on either side represent the two Nyapililngu. The inverted carrying basket can be seen on their heads. Their body appears to comprise a digging stick nested within a* yingapungapu *shape and was interpreted as such by Narritjin. However he also explained to me that the design represented the pregnant Nyapililngu. The ancestral* yingapungapu *that Nyapililngu made is today a lake and a source of Manggalili conception spirits. (Private Collection. Reproduced with the permission of Buku-Larrnggay Mulka, Yirrkala.)*

be reflected in the details of their art. Narritjin spent much of his early life travelling by canoe along the eastern Arnhem Land coast; he was a renowned turtle hunter and had survived many storms at sea. Narritjin had himself come close to drowning on a number of occasions. During World War II he hitched a ride on a naval patrol boat that was sunk by the Japanese. He went down with the boat, his leg entangled in a rope, before breaking free and rising to the surface, where he played a major role in rescuing the other survivors. Narritjin's conception totem was that same turtle who created the storm at sea that overturned the *mokuy's* boat. His conception followed a hunting trip by his three fathers out into the deep sea. They came back with a boat loaded with turtle and parrotfish, chased by storm clouds that followed them to the shore. Narritjin was born of turtle and parrotfish, the very quarry that overturned the boat of the ancestral hunters and resulted in their deaths. In a very literal sense in everyday life, turtles, as large marine animals, are a major source of sustenance for the community but can also endanger the lives of the hunters. Yolngu symbolism builds on experience and moves thought in particular directions. Thus Narritjin's personal experiences reinforced for him the significance of the *yingapungapu*, perhaps structuring his interpretations of myth, instilling a fatalistic attitude to danger, encouraging him to look death in the face. Yet this facing of death is characteristic of Yolngu society in general. It takes the form equally of preparing, almost nurturing the dying, so that they will be prepared for their spiritual journey, yet encouraging the living to re-engage with life.

Conclusion

In his paintings of the *yingapungapu*, Narritjin takes us through precisely the form of thick description that an anthropological analysis requires, by elaborating on the symbolic and sociological dimensions of the *yingapungapu* sand sculpture. In producing the paintings he is enacting the relationships between the *yingapungapu* clans; in representing the *yingapungapu* in different contexts he presents it as an emergent but abstract idea, a template connected to all aspects of the mythology of the Nyapililngu, to the symbolic connotations of its different elements. In a sense, none of Narritjin's paintings are complete. They are all part of a work in progress, representing an individual's dialogue with his own past, bringing forward knowledge and experience and conveying it to others whose lives overlap with his own.

My intuition is that the social theory of the future will emphasise concepts that transcend the divisions between present, past and future, and between the individual and the social: concepts that occupy a 'space in between', that refer to states of the relationship, that contain the idea of a trajectory, that capture the idea of a multi-dimensional and multiply determined ongoing process, which combines in the same sequence of action relatively autonomous components.

One way of modelling the relationship between an event or object and its multiple determinants may be to imagine them simultaneously existing in different dimensions or systemic locations. The *yingapungapu* sand sculpture, as a design, is the product of a design differentiation system, a system of encoding meaning, that enables it to be recognised, known and used. However, the design generation system is relatively autonomous from the particular form of the *yingapungapu* (it would exist without it). Each production of the design is an instantiation of an object that exists in the variety of different contexts in which it is produced. The sand sculpture is a design that is always produced in a context, although it can be separated from any particular context. In the ritual context of the *yingapungapu* ceremony, it is an integral part of the performance connected directly to the purposes and organisational structure of the ceremony. Yet the ceremony itself (that is, a purificatory ceremony) can be performed without a *yingapungapu* and it can incorporate a quite different mythological complex. And the *yingapungapu* exists in the context of myths that are relatively independent of the particular ritual context (purification following burial). The *yingapungapu* in context is an instantiation of elements of Yolngu social organization: the moiety system, the kin-based rules for the performance of roles in the ritual, and so on. Again, that domain of kinship behaviour, extremely complex and interconnected though it is, is relatively autonomous from many other aspects of the *yingapungapu*, the mythology and design generation system. Clearly there are enormous crossovers. Over time the design generation system has developed very precise and subtle ways of articulating with the structure and process of group formation and differentiation. They are relatively autonomous but implicated in the same trajectory.

Just as an anthropologist is able to abstract different instantiations or attributes from an object or even place them in systemic contexts, so too, clearly, can Yolngu. These multiple determinations are part of the reality, the multidimensional nature of social process. Clearly, all these dimensions come together in the context of action and the context of action is a moment in the reproduction of society over time. At the moment of action most of the determinants are in sync with each other; action flows almost unconsciously. The moiety association of the *yingapungapu* is not going to be thought of unless it is used in a way that fundamentally contradicts its past – for example being used as a Dhuwa moiety object. At that moment the unthinkable becomes instantly thinkable. Such world changing moments do occur. In 1974 when Frances Morphy and I were recording a Yolngu circumcision ceremony (in our case for the first time), it was the first occasion on which a woman took over the painting of one of the boys who was to be circumcised. The action was so unprecedented that people who were not present denied that it could possibly have happened. Women generally sit separate from the men and the painting of clan designs in ritual contexts had been until then an exclusively male preserve. While on most occasions Yolngu still follow past practice, with women sitting separately and taking no part in the painting, the event has changed the acknowledged possibilities for action. The unthinkable has become thinkable and, on two other occasions that we know of, women have painted young men. Such events however can be seen to be foregrounded long before they occur, in changes that are occurring elsewhere in the society. The diagnosis of that process of change is a fundamental part of the job of anthropology – to show how, and in what contexts, the unthinkable becomes thinkable.

The perspective that I have adopted on the relative autonomy of different determinants of social action clearly has implications for the disciplinary boundaries of anthropology. The *yingapungapu* ceremony cannot be understood separately from psychological aspects of human behaviour, the response to death, the emotions death generates, and ways of dealing with those emotions. In the ritual, Yolngu have developed ways of dealing with these emotions that are part of their way of life, an integral part of their cultural trajectory. Anthropology must take into account these psychological factors by entering into discourse with psychology over them. But anthropology will in turn provide the essential background for a cross-cultural psychology. The relative autonomy of the different determinants of human action and behaviour means that they can only be understood through an analysis that is sensitive to context, since it is in the context of ongoing social process that the particular form of the determinants is set.

Notes

1. Bauman's most extended example is that of Lévi-Straussian structuralism: 'The ordering passion of social sciences extends to their own playground, and so Lévi-Strauss was promptly dubbed a structuralist (just like the revolutionary edge of George Simmel's sociology was blunted, tamed and effused for years by classifying him as a 'formalist'); but this strange structuralist did more than any other thinker to explode the orthodox idea of structure as a vehicle of monotonous reproduction, repetitiveness and sameness. In Lévi- Strauss's vision structure has turned from a cage into a catapult ... Lévi-Strauss hotly denied the existence of anything like *the* structure of a 'society' or 'culture': while it is true that all human activities

    – from myth-telling through the selection of marriage partners to pet-naming and cooking – are *structured*, the idea of '*structure* as such' is but an abstraction from this non-randomness of the infinitely varied kinds of human interactions' (Bauman 1999: xxvii).

2. A perspective reflected in the introduction to Alfred Gell's *Art and Agency*: '[the subject matter of anthropology is] 'social relationships' – relationships between participants in social systems of various kinds' (Gell 1998: 4).

3. Clifford Geertz 'Thick description: towards an interpretative theory of culture', in his *The Interpretation of Cultures* (1975).

4. For a relevant analysis see Victoria Burbank (1985).

5. Yolngu men marry women they refer to by the kin term *galay*. While preference is for marriage with an actual mother's mother's brother's daughter's daughter any female *galay* is a potential marriage partner. The kinship reciprocal for *galay* is *dhuway*, the term by which women refer to their husbands.

6. My position thus differs from Ingold's in that I see no reason to give embodied action priority over ideas in the production of artefacts. Ingold (2002: 59) writes: 'The form of the pot emerges from the movements of the potter's hands, which respond at every moment to the feel of the clay ... This is not to deny that when people set out to make things, they may lay plans and formulate intentions; and may even construct models and blueprints. But it is not from such plans and blue prints that the forms of artefacts arise, but from the skilled sensuous activity of those who make them.' In my view Ingold artificially separates out components of complex processes, by the qualifying buts.

7. Relevant examples are discussed in more detail in Morphy (1995).

8. for example Kuper (1999) and Kahn (1995)

9. In anthropology Mary Douglas in particular has used the concept of root metaphors productively (e.g. Douglas 1973).

10. Compare for example Keen (2000) and Morphy (1999).

11. Morphy (nd.) analyses a *yingapungapu* sand sculpture being used in the contemporary context of an exhibition at the National Museum of Australia. Ian Dunlop's 1986 film, *One Man's Response*, includes the performance of a *yingapungapu* ceremony. Berndt (1966) provides a transcription of the Wuradilagu song cycle.

12. The account here is the summary of a number of ceremonies recorded between 2000 and 2003. The *yingapungapu* sculpture was the subject of an exhibition that I curated with Pip Deveson for the opening of the new National Museum of Australia (Morphy in press).

13. Fiona Magowan provides a rich analysis of some Yolngu song texts that in effect create a dialogue with the landscape: 'it is the potential for these forms to be recreated through their patterning in performance that affords it potency through the fluid movements of the landscape and seascape which are imaged in song, animated by dance' (2001: 25).

14. Praus from Macassar in South Sulawesi used to visit the Arnhem Land coast each year during the wet season to collect trepang to trade with people to the north (see Macknight, 1978). They established close relationships with Aboriginal groups who worked for them and traded with them. The trade was stopped by the Australian Government in 1907. However the Macassans remain an important component of Yolngu historical memory and there are significant Macassan references in Yolngu ritual.

15. Limitations of space mean that I can only exemplify my argument here in relation to a very few of his paintings. Narritjin Maymuru was born around 1916 some 20 years before the establishment of the first mission station in the region (Yirrkala in 1935). His earliest known paintings were collected by the anthropologist R.M. Berndt in 1946. He continued painting until his death in 1981. A documented

database of Narritjin's art is published in Morphy, Deveson and Hayne (2005). A detailed analysis of Yolngu art, which includes an anlysis of the iconography of Manggalili paintings is presented in Morphy (1991).

16. Narritjin tended to emphasise acceptance of the inevitability of death and the process of coming to terms with it through a process of forgetting that removed the more immediate memories of the dead.

Chapter 7

HOLISM, INTELLIGENCE AND TIME

Chris Gosden

This chapter represents an exercise in speculation, not just concerning the notions of mind and intelligence, but also concepts such as material, materialism and materiality, which might have seemed to complement or oppose insubstantial mental operations. In considering the issue of human intelligence I am inclined to do away with the concept of mind, but also to rethink notions of the material which are well entrenched within attempts to rethink mind. I shall explore how anthropology and archaeology might be able to help in such a radical form of rethinking.

Is intelligence a mental phenomenon? This would once have seemed an obviously counter-intuitive question. Even more surprising is the fact that many now would answer in the negative. Critique is turning to the central locus of thought, objectivity and meaning: the mind itself. But also and importantly the body is seen in a much more positive light than previously. An emphasis on the skills of the body and the power of material culture to shape our lives has led to key new concepts, especially on the part of philosophers working with notions of externalism or extended mind. Andy Clark (1997), Mark Rowlands (2003) and Mike Wheeler (2005) have built on longer philosophical traditions going back to Heidegger and Marx to develop concepts of extended mind or externalism. These ideas see mind not as located in our heads, but as something which comes about through the interactions of the whole human organism with its world, so that intelligence resides in action as much as thought and in the social use people make of the object world. Neuroscientists are also exploring the body, pointing out that the mind has an ambiguous relationship with the brain, so that the mind somehow derives from the workings of the brain, but forms an immaterial abstract space impossible to map onto the physical workings of neurons directly. The brain is obviously an organ of the body and thus linked to its broader workings, mapping the body's physical and emotional states. If the operation of the brain cannot be understood apart from the working of the body, but the brain is linked to the mind, then this must mean that the overall operations of the body are relevant to the workings of the mind. As scholars have long agreed, Descartes' disembodied notion of mind becomes very hard to sustain at this point. Philosophers, neuroscientists and a host of others such as roboticists all attempt to bring the mind out of the head and into the body; the workings of the body in turn cannot be understood in an abstract manner but only in relation to other people and material things. It is in studying material and social relations that archaeology and anthropology can make a contribution to the complex project of redefining intelligence and what it means to be human. These disciplines are less inclined to use the vocabulary of thought and cognition.

Making mind more material is an obvious swing of the intellectual pendulum away from mentalism, but we need to worry about the concept of the material too, as this was created initially as the opposite or counterpoint to the mental. One possible strategy is to concentrate on time and temporality as a key aspect of the relationship between people and things.

Important though these ideas focusing on distributed or extended cognition are, I feel that they are still reacting to older thoughts about mind, saying that the mind exists not in the head but in the interaction between people and the world. They are also too rooted in a problem-solving individual, albeit one more richly embedded in an environment than previously. Notions of externalism, extended or distributed intelligence all play with spatial metaphors, taking the inner space of the mind and following it out into the world, in the process allowing the world to have a determinant influence on thought. But another set of metaphors are open to us which are perhaps more disruptive of older views of mental operations – and these derive from an emphasis on time, rather than space.

I shall try to make two key points in this chapter. First, that intelligence exists as a between-relation, not a within-relation. That is to say, intelligent action and thought derives from a complex network of relations between people and people, and people and things. Individual problem solving, where it occurs, draws on a broader set of cultural resources, such as language, but also learned physical skills of making, using and giving value to things. The emphasis on intelligence as a between-relation might seem to take us back to a spatial view of human action, such as those which I have just criticised. However, relations between people and things never happen simultaneously, but unfold in particular sequences and rhythms. An important part of the temporality of action derives not just from people, but from things. Using a particular material, such as wood, stone or clay, necessitates a sequence of actions deriving from the materials, some of which impose stricter conditions than others. The plasticity of unfired clay allows a potter to start again in making their pot if things go wrong. No such luxury is allowed by stone, where an ill-judged blow may represent a point of no return, necessitating starting again. In what follows I want to explore time as it derives from both people and materials. The influence of objects on people in the longer term should not be underestimated and this is because some materials last longer than people, so that we are all born into material settings that pre-exist us. People are socialised by objects to a considerable degree, so that we become the people we are through early and sustained interaction with a material world of a particular cultural shape. The qualities of things are internalised within us as a sense of the possibilities that the world holds for us.

An important part of this argument equates intelligence and sociability, which we need to briefly explore before returning to the main issues to be raised. The most challenging element to being human is that we are sociable beings. Many animals are social, but humans are social in a peculiar manner in that we create and build our social relations through shaping the material world. Without food, clothing, housing or ritual paraphernalia we would have no social life. Conversely, although all the materials I have mentioned fulfil functional purposes, none are purely functional. Food is imbued with many cultural values and forms of aesthetic as well as nutritional properties. Eating roast pig in Papua New Guinea, as I have been lucky enough to do, one is aware of the whole weight of social relations and cultural values condensed into such an act. Pigs are killed and eaten in large numbers in exchange ceremonies of various types throughout New Guinea and are an indispensable element of such ceremonies. Such ceremonies take place in a cyclical manner in which the group hosting this pig feast may become the guests at the next and will judge that feast against their own performance. Companionship between those gathered and the sensory enjoyment of the food are given an edge by questions of protocol, hierarchy and reciprocity – what is the appropriate response to those putting on the feast and should it take the form of words, actions or gifts? Human action unfolds within two dimensions at once (which are ultimately less separable than time and space): the material and the social. The New Guinea pig needs a series of physical skills to bring it to readiness. It needs to be bred, nurtured, grown, killed, butchered, cooked and divided up appropriately. All these moments of the process involve skills that I do not possess, nor (I would guess) do most readers of this chapter. For events to be socially effective they need to work in their physical dimension – a half-cooked pig, or one too small for the assembled company would have the opposite social effect to that intended.

At the heart of being human is a basic transubstantiation: the changing of objects into social relations. To effect this transubstantiation we need a grasp of the physics, chemistry and biology of the world together with the social impact of the material. The truly effective social actor in New Guinea can organise the labour of others and themselves to create the root crops needed to sustain a pig herd, bring the herd to maturity at the right social moment, but then organise the theatre of ceremony in such a way that the dress of the participants, their songs and dances together with the rhetoric of the organiser are used to work the crowd and send them away impressed by the overall novelty, lavishness and spiritual depth of the event. For the analyst, a roast pig is a total social and material fact, so that one can start here and work out towards the organisation of the landscape and of labour, or to the history of speech and rhetoric within a given group or to the metaphorical connections made between the body of the pig and the spirit world of the human ancestors. For such an analysis to do justice to a pig feast the material and the social should blend together, be given equal weight and disappear as separate categories. It is hard for the analyst, especially if they are an outsider, to grasp and render the overall feel and style of the event if they lack the embodied knowledge of which it is composed. A feel of rightness or lack of style is hard to grasp or to convey, but is one which blends the material and the social.

It is a testimony to the complexity of all our lives that the social and material lives of others look impossibly difficult and this is because for the outsider the skilled actions requisite to any occasion have to be listed and anatomised, whereas to the actor so much is internalised, habitual and unthought. After a large ceremonial event in New Guinea, people will sit down and endlessly talk through what worked and what didn't; but these discussions take for granted a series of embodied logics unavailable to an outsider.

There is a lot of intelligence at work in a New Guinea feast, which, as elsewhere, draws on a long history of action and socialization. Crucially, this intelligence operates as a between-relation rather than primarily within people's heads. Intelligent action occurs between people and things or people and people, or, invariably between things and people (both of these terms being in the plural). The Cartesian dictum 'I think, therefore I am', which makes sense to Westerners who have a heightened sense of individuality compared to many in the world, can be replaced with 'You are, therefore I am', where many of the significant others in this statement are things as well as people.

Intelligence and time

Time is a dimension of human intelligence that has not been explored as productively as might be possible. My key argument in this chapter is that human consciousness and intelligence come about through our continuing attempts to bring together times operating at different speeds. The fastest human times are the synaptic responses in our brains making connections in fractions of a second. Synaptic times are counterposed at the other end of the temporal scale by slowly evolving traditions of creating and using material things unfolding over centuries and millennia. Furthermore, time is a quality rather than a quantity, so that it is not just a question of actions, reactions and processes operating at different speeds, but rather how these speeds are used by the society in question. These rather mysterious statements need exploring and explicating.

Bodily times

The body can be seen as having a variety of speeds of time operating through it. The fastest of these we might call synaptic time. As is well known, the human brain is made up of nerve cells known as neurons, separated by gaps called synapses. An electrical impulse passing down a neuron causes the release of a chemical neurotransmitter which crosses and closes the gap with a neighbouring cell. Synaptic transmission is at the basis of all brain function and some have consequently seen the synapses as the foundation of the self (Ledoux 2003). Pairs of neurons are not connected in isolation. Rather neuroscientists are increasingly aware that circulation systems exist in the brain. The speed at which such patterns of connection occur within the brain makes it technically difficult with present scanning technology to understand the full scope and nature of the connections.

Synaptic connections are made at a speed greater than consciousness can grasp, so that we are never aware of all the things happening to our organism, presumably because too detailed knowledge would impede rather than aid our ability to exist in the everyday world.

The brain is distributed through our body in the form of our nervous system, with impulses again moving through the system in fractions of a second. The brain helps map the ever-changing states of the body, ranging from its position in space, as judged from the states of tension within the muscles, to its chemical constitution so vital to mood and emotion. A series of complex interacting systems exist to monitor and map the changing states of the body. Damasio (2000: 149–153), for instance, identifies three interacting systems: the internal milieu and visceral division; the vestibular and musculoskeletal division; and the fine touch division. The first of these senses changes in the chemical environment of the cells throughout the body, which takes place partly through the brain monitoring the chemical composition of the blood directly and partly through impulses travelling along nerve pathways 'to carry signals that we eventually perceive as pain' (ibid: 151). Impulses are also sent from smooth muscles in blood vessels and the main viscera to the brain via the spinal cord. The musculoskeletal division conveys information about muscles and the position of the bones they are connected to, which are muscles under our conscious control, contributing to a kinaesthetic or prioproceptive sense of the body. Fine touch represents a third division of the somatosensory system , describing alterations in the specialized receptors in the skin due to contacts with objects (ibid: 153).

Operating rapidly, but still at a much slower rate than synaptic time, is muscular time. In carrying even simple operations our muscles need to be activated in the right sequence and often at high speed. Even a two-fingered typist such as myself engages a very complex range and sequence of muscular activity in the arms, hands and fingers, so that I can type competently enough to concentrate on the words I write rather than the muscles I use to produce them. We are most aware of muscular activity in the process of learning to work with the world. Once sequences have been learned they reside in muscular memory, rather than being mainly or purely directed by conscious thought. It is only through the retention of memories in the muscles that we can walk, whistle and (sometimes) think simultaneously. Famously, Marcel Mauss pointed out that bodies are taught unconsciously to carry out basic operations in ways that vary due to unthought cultural conceptions – Americans walk differently to French people, styles of swimming vary nationally even when using the same stroke, and tools which work for one set of muscles are confronting for others, so that French and British soldiers could not use each others' shovels and spades when digging trenches in the First World War (Mauss 1979). Our bodies are educated when young in ways that become deeply internalized, to become part of what we are rather than part of what we know. Much of this education takes place through objects such as shovels and spades, which provide a powerful set of silent lessons.

One could follow through slower bodily times to the whole biography of the human being, but also looking at the periodicities of group life on an annual or longer cycle, which activate different sets of bodily intelligences. Really big exchange events in places like the Highlands of New Guinea may only take place every five years or so, but necessitate continual work with pigs and to obtain exchange valuables. The relatively brief period of the feast brings out forms of dancing, speech and consumption which mark the event as special because they are used rarely. Big events entail an infinitely complex combination of on-going, low-level muscular skills and those learnt and used at very special times. Groups of bodies regularly act together in ways that are carried beyond biographical times, but here the binding qualities of things are vital.

Times of things

A key point made above is that human temporality derives not just from our actions, but from the forms of time deriving from objects. Like the times of the body, these can be seen as unfolding from the very fast to the terribly slow. Imagine a person sitting down to knap a set of flint tools. Knapping often involves taking a core and preparing it in various ways through the removal of prior flakes. Such a process of flake removal takes place through a rhythmical series of blows and turning the core. Working a core in order to produce flakes of particular types involves a series of steps and stages, which has a temporal sequence and periodicity. There are nanotimes wherein the molecules of the stone part one from another as a flake is removed. These are equivalent to the synaptic times of the human body in their speed, being way beyond the speeds of human consciousness. But there are also product times which in flint knapping are due to the interaction of human muscles and the nature of the material. Flint knapping has a variety of different rhythms depending on the skill of the knapper, the nature of the material and the form of the desired end result. It is a reductive process, systematically preparing a core and then removing flakes from it, so that each future step is influenced by the previous ones. Options narrow as the core reduces and with good core preparation techniques, for instance when making Levallois flakes, the sequence is designed towards a desired shape of flake. A mistake at one step of the process may be hard or impossible to redeem.

But think now of someone making a pot. There is a series of steps to be followed from digging out the clay and preparing it, to finding and adding temper. The pot is then formed either by hand or on a wheel and mistakes in forming can be remedied up to the point when the pot is fired. After this point the plasticity of clay gives way to the hardness and fragility of a pot, which can then be used or broken (see the generalized sequence below, taken from Hodges 1964: 19):

CLAY DEPOSIT   digging   UNPREPARED CLAY   preparation   CLAY BODY

TEMPER

Forming   CLAY SHAPE   drying   HARD SHAPE   firing   FIRED SHAPE

Metallurgy has a different set of times, from digging the ore to cleaning and roasting it through to smelting and casting. The series of steps involved in metalworking is long and invariable and many other sets of materials are needed (see generalized sequence for copper working taken from Hodges 1964: 64):

Mining   ORE STONE   Preparing   ORE   Smelting   INGOT   Refining/casting

GANGUE   SLAG

THE CASTING   Hot and Cold working   FINISHED OBJECT

The series of steps have to be followed in the right order (with constant minor improvisations). The big difference when compared with pottery is that the application of heat to the metal does not change its state for ever, but rather the finished object can later be melted down and formed anew, with this process continuing infinitely, so that it might well be that jewellery from today contains metal from the Bronze Age.

One could carry on looking at wood, textiles, bone, antler, glass, leather, dyes, pigments and so on, each of which have their own series of steps and stages in making, which include varying points of no return. Neither the human actor nor the materials are totally dominant, with a process of negotiation being set up between people and things where the material nature and skills of both parties interact to create an end result. Such negotiations are carried out within cultural contexts in which various forms of ends and effects are aimed at and desired. Activities need to be carried out in the right order, for sufficient lengths of time and in a proper rhythm for them to be efficacious. Practices of everyday life involve sequences deriving from the capacities and skills of the body through infinite numbers of muscle activations, the deployment of sight, touch, taste and the kinaesthetic sense. But temporality of action also derives from the nature of the material being worked. A swift blow will detach a flake of a particular size and shape depending on the granularity of the stone, flaws in the rock or the shape of the core. A series of material factors meet, with the mechanics and biochemistry of the body encountering the shape and structure of the rest of the world. One of the key elements of human action is that it can be effective, producing a desired and predictable result despite the variability of materials and of human skills. There exist long-term traditions of making which have some stability to them over long periods, helping to create predictable transformations of materials. As a number of authors have pointed out, forms of temper used for pottery may be very resistant to change, with types of paste (a particular combination of clay and temper) which may have a very long history. More recently, it has been realized that temper might be added to pots because of the associations it has to particular places, so that objects contain within them complex references to other places. The use of the same materials over long periods does not require, but does encourage, continuity of action in making and perhaps in use, so that generations of potters may learn how to pot from their materials. The material helps provide a constant thread linking human generations.

Production techniques form long-term histories, but these will primarily affect the people making objects. Stable finished products, on the other hand, will influence all those who use these objects. Finished forms have conventionally been understood through typology. Adams and Adams Typology has been basic to archaeological approaches to material culture since the early nineteenth century, when it became the foundation for chronological understanding of Europe's prehistory in the shift from stone to bronze to iron, providing the basis for the so-called Three Age system. Typology and the Three Age system have both been roundly criticised for reifying basic types which then create an overly rigid distinction between one period and another when much continuity as well as change can be seen between the Neolithic and the Bronze Age or the Bronze and Iron Ages. The Three Age system undoubtedly produces a prehistory which is too compartmentalised, but this is not my concern here and I would rather celebrate the typological urge for a moment, due to what it can tell us about things individually and as a mass.

To get some sense of how typology works, let us take one of the most famous recent explorations of types and their changes: that of Deetz and Dethlefsen (1966, Deetz 1977) looking at gravestones on the eastern seaboard of the United States. They and others created a series of tombstone typologies for New England and the eastern seaboard more generally, which defined types of tombstones in terms of their decorations and epitaphs, together with their changes through time. The great advantage of tombstones for creating a time series is that they have on them the date of the person buried. Many can also be attributed to individual carvers, as some are signed and other producers provide indications of their activities through diaries, accounts books and other forms of archival record. Nor did tombstones move far from their point of manufacture, with a 30 mile radius encompassing most movement of tombstones, which were usually made in a town and then exported out to the countryside. Between 1680, when the first stone tombstones were carved (before then memorials in wood were common), and 1820 three basic forms of design are found, each of which derives from a different form of religious sensibility: death's heads, urn and cherubs, and willow trees. Tombstones help make links between people's feelings for the world and material forms.

These overall trends can be described by so-called battleship curves which chart the coming into being of a new style, its rise in popularity and decline when succeeded by a further style. Such curves have been used to describe the history of styles in a whole range of artefacts, prehistoric as well as historic, seeming to capture general tendencies in the history of types. Styles often go through processes of initiation, florescence and decline and analogies have been made with biological organisms (Clarke 1978). We can see in general that people were born into worlds of material culture which lasted longer than it took to replace human generations. In the case of the gravestones, each form lasted for at least 40 years and often a lot longer, considerably more than the conventional time period given for a human generation of 25 years, although not quite as long as a human lifetime (although life expectancy might not have far exceeded the lifetime of the style). We are able to see constant change, looking back in time, but for those contemporary with the things made and used, things would have represented a series of stable or slowly changing entities through which to build social relations, or, as in this case, relationships with the divine. The nature of intelligent action was refracted and made effective through material forms of some stability and durability.

Many forms last for much longer than the gravestones. Styles of pottery, such as Beakers, carried on for hundreds of years with subtle changes of form. As some have pointed out, objects can be seen to use human muscles to reproduce themselves, so that human generations come and go, but help perpetuate objects in recognisable forms.

Human life is a between-relation, played out between groups of people and groups of things, all of which have their own temporal properties. Creating and coping with time is a matter of attempting to bring together and harmonise disparate temporal relations deriving from the characteristics of things and of people. The in-betweenness of human life is key to its effectiveness, allotting values to all parties, some of which outlast human time-spans. Intelligence is not primarily about an individual confronting a puzzling world, but groups of actions, which may at once be problems and solutions, unfolding in time.

Discussion

The old mind–body distinction was primarily a spatial one. Ideas originating in the interior space of the mind are enacted by the body on the external world. In such a scenario the mind proposes and the body disposes. One problem with such inside: outside metaphors is that there is a discontinuity but it is not clear where this occurs. Does the inside space exist within the head, is the skin the boundary between the self and the rest of the world or does the intelligent self project itself outside into the world in some way? Externalism retains the notion of mind and retains a spatial metaphor, but without positing any boundary between self and the rest. A key example here is the blind person and their cane, where the person walks along, possibly talking or otherwise engaged, but is also continuously sensing obstacles and changes of level with the cane. Is it possible to disaggregate the assemblage of person and cane and, if so, what are the points of disaggregation? Do these lie at the point where the hand holds the cane, between the cane and the pavement or at some other point? The lesson of the story as it is generally told is that there is a continuity of person and instrument, which is inseparable from them in the act of sensing. This is a very fair point, but it doesn't get away from the feeling that human intelligence and representation starts in an interior space and ends up out in the world without encountering a barrier or point of transition.

If we replace an emphasis on space with a consideration of time, then both the human organism and the world generally are made up of a mass of times in complex relationship with each other. The tiny times of synaptic connections are paralleled by the molecules parting in a knapped flake, both occurring in a fraction of a second. Such instants mix with longer-term histories contained in the muscular memory of the body, many of which are laid down in childhood. The body, in turn, is educated through the long-term histories of material forms which might last decades or centuries. Often we cannot know synaptic times in the present, much less in the prehistoric past, but we can see how the hyper-malleable work of synaptic circulations is rendered solid by objects.

The idea of extended mind takes an individual and places her or him in a world which poses problems to be solved. For instance, advocates of extended mind see that such an individual is able to get from the train station to a meeting not because they keep a full and accurate map of the route in their head, but because when they turn a corner a new scene provides memory prompts which guide their feet. The world is a vital part of human intelligence and it is the interaction between people and things which provides the possibility of intelligent action. Mind is enacted rather than being the locus of inner representation and thought. This is an inspiring vision in many ways. However, the world of the extended mind is a lonely one in which individuals navigate competently or make up memory deficits through physical prompts. But such individuals rarely play with their children, fight or have any fun. It is a world created in reaction to an older notion that cognition only happens in the head and is to be applauded for its subversive intent. But an emphasis on spatial extension or distribution can only take us so far in breaking up models of mind.

In this chapter I stress two key points: intelligence emerges in group interaction where the group is always made up of people and things; interaction is most provocatively explored in terms of time, which brings out the unfolding and contradictory nature of these interactions. The durable nature of things themselves and the potentially long-term patterns of practice needed to make and use them provide a trans-generational element which gives rise to continuity.

My initial target was the concept of mind, which despite attempts to give it more extended and material form still carries a set of associations of a disembodied mental space, which we find hard to discard. Having become sceptical about mind, it was hard not to harbour doubts about what is often seen to be its opposite – the material world. The mental vs. the material has been a very productive dichotomy in western thought and we must remember that one term helped give birth to the other. We are comfortable currently with the idea of the material, but it is hard to sustain this concept without some counterbalance in the form of the immaterial world of mind, meaning and spirit. Discarding mind could well mean a deeper questioning of the concept of the material. Given the deep-rootedness of these concepts in Western thought, rethinking both the mental and the material will not be easy. One route is to stress the complex temporal set of interactions that unfold between people and things, as well as the values that attach to each in this process. As in evolution and ecology (Ulijaszek, this volume), interactions range between the nanosecond and millennia. In the considerable effort needed to shift our ontological views of mind and materials, both anthropology and archaeology have a serious role to play.

Chapter 8

MOVEMENT, KNOWLEDGE AND DESCRIPTION

Tim Ingold

> As individuals and groups we are made of lines,
> lines that are very diverse in nature.
> (Deleuze and Guattari 1983: 69)

What do walking, weaving, observing, storytelling, drawing and writing have in common? The answer is that they all proceed along lines of one kind and another. In what follows I would like to share some ideas for a programme of work that I have still to carry out, and that will be occupying my attention over the next three years.[1] My overall aim is to undertake a comparative and historical anthropology of the line, and through this to forge a new approach to understanding the relation, in human social life and experience, between movement, knowledge and description. So far as I know, nothing quite like this has been attempted before. We have anthropological studies of space and place, of perception and cognition, and of orality and literacy, but not of the production and significance of lines. Yet it takes only a moment's reflection to recognise that lines are everywhere.[2] As walking, talking and gesticulating creatures, human beings generate lines wherever they go. It is not just that line-making is as ubiquitous as the use of the voice, hands and feet – respectively in speaking, gesturing and moving around – but rather that it subsumes all these aspects of everyday human activity and, in so doing, brings them together into a single field of inquiry. This is the field I seek to delineate.

The project has its intellectual roots in my earlier work on livelihood, dwelling and skill (Ingold 2000a). Here I sought to establish an alternative to the view that the human being can be understood, *in toto*, as a compound of three complementary parts, respectively of body, mind and culture.[3] Drawing on a combination of 'relational' thinking in anthropology, 'developmental systems' thinking in biology and 'ecological' thinking in psychology, I put forward a conception of the human being as a singular nexus of creative growth within a continually unfolding field of relationships. This process of growth, I suggested, is tantamount to a *movement along a way of life*. By 'way of life', however, I did not mean a corpus of rules and principles (or a 'culture') transmitted from ancestors but rather a path to be followed, along which one can keep on going instead of coming to a dead end or being caught in a loop of ever-repeating cycles. It is along such paths, I argued, and not from within the confines of bounded places, that lives are lived, skills developed and understandings grown. These paths are the lines of my inquiry. In the pursuit of this inquiry I have been led to explore three further areas that, although foreshadowed in my earlier work, were not fully elaborated there. These concern: (i) the dynamics of pedestrian movement; (ii) the linearity of writing, and (iii) the creativity of practice. I begin by reviewing each of these areas in turn; the connections between them will become apparent later on.

The dynamics of pedestrian movement

Studies of human cognition tend to assume that thinking and knowing are the achievements of a stationary mind, encased within a body in motion.[4] This assumption, I suggest, has its foundation in three related areas of technological development that, in the history of western societies, accompanied the onset of the modern era. The first was in footwear, particularly in the constriction of movement and sensation imposed by the stiff leather boot. The second was in paving and road-building, leading to the creation of hard thoroughfares that remain unmarked by the passage of human life. The third was in transport, by which travellers could be 'carried across' from a point of departure to a destination, rather than making their own way as they go along (Ingold 2004b). Although these might not be the only reasons why we have come to 'think about thinking' in the way we do, they have undoubtedly exerted a powerful influence. Together, they contribute to our ideas that movement is a mechanical displacement of the human body across the surface of the earth, from one point to another, and that knowledge is assembled from observations taken from these points. Of course there are forms of pedestrian movement, most notoriously the so-called striding gait, that approximate to the ideal of pure transport. However, the stride, a rigidly mechanical, straight-legged oscillation from the hips, with eyes gazing steadfastly

ahead rather than downcast, really only works with booted feet on a
paved, levelled surface. It enacts a bodily image of colonial occupation,
straddling the distance between points of departure and arrival as
though one could have a foot in each simultaneously, encompassing
both – and all points in between – in a single, appropriative movement.
But the striding gait, once thought to be the quintessential human
locomotor achievement (Napier 1967), is not typical of ordinary
movement on foot. Far from marching out in heavy boots across
the paved surfaces of the world, its human inhabitants have made
their way for the most part lightly, dextrously and usually barefoot.
Nor were the feet used exclusively for walking. They could be used,
in conjunction with the hands, for creeping, crawling, climbing and
a host of other purposes (Watanabe 1971). It is in these dextrous
movements along paths of life and travel, I contend, and not in the
processing of data collected from multiple sites of observation, that
inhabitants' knowledge is forged. Thus locomotion and cognition are
inseparable, and an account of the mind must be as much concerned
with the work of the feet as with that of the head and hands.

The linearity of writing

My interest in this area has arisen particularly through a critical
engagement with the extraordinary work of the French archaeologist
and anthropologist André Leroi-Gourhan (Ingold 1999, 2004c).
In a brilliantly original yet tantalisingly inconsistent chapter in his
monumental treatise *Gesture and Speech* (1993: 187–216), Leroi-
Gourhan argues that for as long as human beings have been talking
and telling stories, they have also been drawing lines. These lines are
traces left by the manual gestures that routinely accompany the flow
of spoken narrative. Leroi-Gourhan calls this kind of line-making
'graphism'. The organisation of early graphism, he claims, was radial
rather than linear, spiralling out from a focus. Only with the advent
of alphabetic writing was graphism 'linearised' to conform with the
linear organisation of the speech sounds it purported to represent. This
argument, however, flies in the face of Leroi-Gourhan's own contention
that in their original contexts of oral narrative, the rhythms of speech
were so intimately coupled with those of gesture that the former can
have been no more linear in their organisation than the latter. Indeed
he goes so far as to suggest that our assumptions about the linearity
of speech may be a *product* of our familiarity with alphabetic writing.
Only because we are so accustomed to the sight of letters do we come
to think that the sounds of speech succeed one another like beads on
a string. Thus, to recover the original unity of speech, gesture and

inscription we have first to remove the straitjacket that literacy has imposed upon our perception of speech. As Jacques Derrida has put it, with acknowledgement to Leroi-Gourhan, we have to 'de-sediment' from our minds the deposit of four millennia of linear thinking (Derrida 1976: 86). This argument, however, begs the question of what we mean by linearity. How can the continuous lines traced by early graphism have been 'non-linear'? And how, conversely, can the discrete letter-forms of the printed page be regarded as the epitome of the 'linear'? In short, how can the line be non-linear and the non-line linear? The answer, I suggest, lies in a critical distinction between two kinds of line: the *gestural trace* and the *point-to-point connector*. The first is exemplified by graphism, the second by the line of print. The linearisation of thought and expression that many scholars attribute to modern forms of literacy is actually a transformation from one kind of line to the other.

The creativity of practice

In his *Creative Evolution* of 1911 Henri Bergson declared that 'the living being is, above all, a thoroughfare'. Though presenting the appearance of a self-contained entity, in reality 'the very permanence of [its] form is only the outline of a movement' (1911: 135). Like a growing root, the organism creates itself endlessly, trailing its history behind it as the past presses against the present. By the middle of the twentieth century, Bergson's vision of evolution, as a mesh of intertwined thoroughfares along which organisms follow their respective ways of life, had been comprehensively discredited. A resurgent Darwinism had dismissed the key idea of the vital force, *élan vital*, as a metaphysical delusion that could in no way account, as Bergson had claimed, for the creation of novel forms. In its place it substituted an equally metaphysical concept of the gene, as a particle of information that could somehow be inserted into the organism-to-be before its life in the world had even begun (Ingold 1986: 173–221). The creativity of evolution was thus ascribed to the potential for mutation and recombination of these elementary particles in the formation of a *design* for the organism, the genotype, in advance of its subsequent phenotypic 'expression', in one form or another, through growth in a particular environment. The latter was understood as a mechanical process of transcription that did not, in itself, generate anything new.[5] This same logic is as prevalent in the fields of art and architecture as it is in that of biology: thus the creative essence of the work of art is said to lie in an original conception in the mind of the artist, and that of the building in the architect's design. In every case, the effect is to deny the creativity of the processes of environmentally situated and perceptually engaged activity through which real forms – whether of living beings, buildings or works of art – are generated and held in place. To recover this creativity we have to show, as Bergson tried to do, how the movements of everyday life give rise to the forms we see around us: how walking, for example, can be a practice of architecture, or manual gesture a practice of art. It is, in short, to explore the generative potentials of the line. Such exploration suggests a reconfiguration of the relations between anthropology, art and architecture. In place of the conventional anthropologies *of* art and architecture in which the latter are reduced, as for example in the writings of Alfred Gell (1998), to assemblages of 'works' conceived as *objects* of analysis, we need to recognise that art and architecture are, like anthropology, modes of investigative practice whose synergy lies less in their products than in their respective ways of working.[6]

Lines from the past

In May 2003 I presented a series of six public lectures, in Edinburgh, under the title *Lines from the past: towards an anthropological archaeology of inscriptive practices*.[7] The series was my first attempt to set out an agenda for the comparative study of the line, and it took me into a number of fields with which I was quite unacquainted, including classical archaeology and medieval history, and the histories and philosophies of art, music and literature. I began from a nagging problem that, on the face of it, had nothing to do with lines at all. It was the problem of how we have come to distinguish between speech and song. The fact is that this distinction, in the form in which we recognise it today, is relatively recent in the history of the western world. So long as speech had not finally been distinguished from song, or language from music, the written word must also have been a form of written music. Hence, I reasoned, the difference between writing and musical notation, which seems so obvious to us today, was not given from the outset but has rather emerged in the course of the history of writing itself. There can therefore be no history of writing that is not also a history of musical notation. In thinking about what form a comprehensive history of notation might take, I realised that – since any notation consists of lines – a history of notation would have to be part of a general history of the line. It soon became clear, however, that what was at stake was not merely the lines themselves, and their production, but the nature of the relation between lines and the surfaces on which they are drawn. Distinguishing between threads and traces, and drawing on a wide range of ethnographic material dealing with weaving and embroidery as well as calligraphy,

I showed how traces are transformed into threads in the dissolution of surfaces, and how threads are transformed into traces in their constitution. Whether as a thread or a trace, however, the line is perceived as something that moves and grows. I went on to show how, in the course of its history, the moving, growing line, inscribed as the trace of a gesture, was gradually displaced by a line of a quite different kind, namely the point-to-point connector. Such lines are not trails that can be followed but components that can be joined up, into network-like assemblies. The kind of linearisation that made a break with the consciousness of the past, I argued, was one of point-to-point connections.

With this, writing ceased to be a practice of line-making and was finally dissociated from the craft of the calligrapher or scribe. It was not, then, the advent of alphabetic lettering that fragmented and 'linearised' the non-linear trails of gestural inscription, as Leroi-Gourhan thought, but rather the technology of print by which letters and words, through the work of the compositor, came to be assembled on the page. At the same time, writing came to be clearly differentiated from drawing on the grounds of an emergent distinction between technology and art.

Life on the line

In preparing my Rhind Lectures on *Lines from the past* for publication (Ingold 2007), I realised that I had only scratched the surface of a vast intellectual terrain. In particular, I find that the contrast between the gestural trace and the point-to-point connector, already introduced in regard to the linearity of writing, holds the key to the relation between movement, knowledge and description, and its historical transformations. The inspiration for this contrast comes from the notebooks of the painter Paul Klee, where he distinguishes between two kinds of line. The first arises from a point that sets itself in motion and is free to go where it will. Such a line, as Klee famously remarked, 'goes out for a walk'. Another kind of line, however, takes the shortest and quickest route from one predetermined point to another. Its appearance, says Klee, is 'more like a series of appointments than a walk' (Klee 1961: 105–9). Now whereas the first line is the trace of a gesture, the second is a chain of point-to-point connections. The former, like a *walk*, always overshoots its destinations. Wherever it has reached, and for as long as life goes on, there is somewhere further it can go. The latter, by contrast, does not grow or develop but joins things up, linking the points it connects into as *assembly*. Once the

Figure 8.1 *Two kinds of line, after Klee. One (above) goes out for a walk; the other (below) keeps a series of appointments.*

assembly is complete there is nowhere further for the line to go (Figure 8.1).

I propose that it is fundamentally along lines of the first kind that human beings inhabit the world around them. These are the 'wandering lines' or 'efficacious meanderings' by which Michel de Certeau (1984: xviii) distinguishes the tactics of everyday practice from the strategies of society's master-builders, which are planned and implemented as assemblies of connected elements. The strategists' architectonic world is built to be occupied, and its lines are of occupation, not habitation. Yet as inhabitant tacticians continue to thread their ways through the cracks and crevices of the built environment, they both contribute to its erosion and reincorporate its crumbling fragments into their own ways of life. Precisely how they do so will be the subject of my inquiry, and I cannot of course anticipate its conclusions. I can, however, spell out its premises. These lie in the reversal of a certain logic, deeply sedimented in the canons of modern thought, which seems bent on converting the paths along which life is lived into boundaries within which it is contained. I call this the logic of inversion (Ingold 1993: 218–19). Through inversion, beings originally open to the world are closed in upon themselves, sealed by an outer boundary or shell that protects their inner constitution from the traffic of interaction with their surroundings. My aim is to reverse this logic. Life having been, as it were, turned 'outside in', I now want to turn it inside out again in order to recover that original openness to the world in which inhabitants find the meaning of existence.

To explain what I have in mind, let me present you with a simple illustration. Imagine an organism or a person. We might depict it like this:

But in this apparently innocent depiction I have already effected an inversion. I have folded the being in on itself such that it is delineated and contained within a perimeter boundary, set off against a surrounding world – an environment – with which it is destined to interact according to its nature. The organism is 'in here', the

environment 'out there'.[8] But instead of drawing a circle, I might just as well have drawn a line. So let us start again. Here is an organism-person:

In this depiction there is no inside or outside, and no boundary separating the two domains. Rather, there is a trail of movement or growth. Every such trail traces a relation. But the relation is not *between* one thing and another – between the organism-person 'here' and the environment 'there'. It is rather a trail *along* which life is lived: one strand in a tissue of interlaced trails that together make up the texture of the lifeworld. That texture is what I mean when I speak of organisms being constituted within a relational field. It is a field not of interconnected points but of interwoven lines; not a network but a *meshwork* (Figure 8.2).

Of course the depiction of the single line is an oversimplification. For lives generally extend along not one but multiple trails, branching out from a source. We should imagine the organism-person, then, not as a self-contained object like a ball that can propel itself from place to place, but as an ever ramifying web of lines of growth. The philosophers Gilles Deleuze and Félix Guattari (1983) famously likened this web to a rhizome, though I prefer the image of the fungal mycelium. A

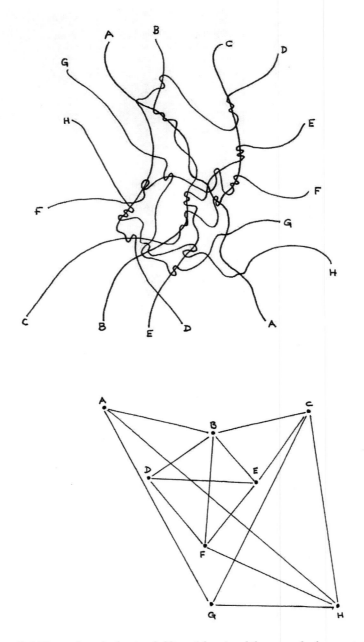

Figure 8.2 *The meshwork of entangled lines (above) and the network of connected points (below).*

mycologist friend once remarked to me that the whole of biology would be different, had it taken the mycelium as the prototypical exemplar of a living organism (Rayner 1997, Ingold 2000a: 426, fn. 7). By starting with a model of the mycelial person as a bundle of lines, I believe our understanding of social life can be similarly transformed (Ingold 2003b). I shall now offer a brief sketch of how this transformation may be effected in five topical areas. These concern: the dynamics of movement, the integration of knowledge, modes of description, place and environment, and history and genealogy. In each case, as I shall show, the transformation hinges on the difference between our two kinds of line: the trace and the connector.

Movement

In my earlier discussion of pedestrian movement I introduced the distinction between transport, as a mechanical displacement of the body from one site to another *across* the surface of the earth, and the dextrous footwork by which the ordinary pedestrian finds his or her way *along* the myriad trails of everyday life and experience. I refer to this quotidian trail-following as *wayfaring*. Perhaps an analogy might be drawn in the plant world, with the growth of roots and runners that trail behind their ever-advancing tips as the latter grope for a path through the tangle of vegetation above or below the soil. Like growing roots, wayfarers are instantiated in the world as their paths of movement: they and their lines are one and the same. This movement is moreover a process of self-renewal, and in that sense organic rather than mechanical. Wayfarers work out their paths as they go along, continually adjusting their pace, posture and orientation in response to an ongoing perceptual monitoring of their surroundings. In transport, by contrast, the route is predetermined, laid out even before embarkation as a connection between points of departure and arrival. Thus whereas the wayfarer quite literally takes his line for a walk, the lines of transport are point-to-point connectors. Pure transport, if it were practically possible, would have no duration, as though the traveller could take successive points in his stride and, straddling them all, contrive to be – and to see – everywhere at once. But precisely because it is *not* possible, in practice, to be everywhere at once, pure transport is an illusion.[9] Getting from one place to another always takes time, and life continues to unfold *en route*. Inhabitants are wayfarers, however much their physical movements are bound and regulated by the mechanisms and infrastructure of transport. The question, then, is: how are the lines of wayfaring and transport, or trails and routes, interpolated? How are ways of life enmeshed in a networked world of lines and connectors?

Knowledge

Now, to the contrast between wayfaring and transport, I argue, there correspond different models of knowing. Transport, as I have already shown, implies a distinction between locomotion and cognition, the one mechanical the other intellectual, achievements of body and mind respectively. As the body moves *across*, from site to site, so the mind builds *up*, assembling the observations or materials collected from each site into overarching structures of ever-increasing scope and generality. Thus locomotion and cognition are separated on orthogonal axes running, in turn, laterally and vertically. Knowledge, in this model, is constructed in the same way that the surveyor makes a map, by joining up into a complete picture observations taken from multiple sites while discarding, or 'pushing into the wings' (de Certeau 1984: 121), the experience of getting from site to site. One should not allow such experience to intrude upon site-specific observations, as cartographers and scientists are routinely warned, for fear of compromising their objectivity. But pure objectivity is as illusory as pure transport, and for much the same reasons. Just as there can be no knowledge without observation, so there can be no observation without movement, entailing a coupling, in perception and action, of the observer with the things or persons that occupy his or her attention. Following James Gibson's (1989 [1976]: 195–7) insight that environments are perceived not at successive points but rather along *paths* of observation, I suggest that the knowledge of inhabitants is not so much built up as forged *along* lines of movement, in the passage from place to place and the changing horizons along the way (Ingold 2000a: 227). For them, moving is knowing. It is through the practices of wayfaring, then, that knowledge is integrated. Inhabitants do not so much construct or assemble their knowledge as grow into it, in their movements along ways of life. One way of putting it would be to say that inhabitant knowledge is not vertically but *alongly* integrated.

Description

Now, in the vertical integration of knowledge, it is supposed that data extracted from each successive locus of observation are inputted into higher processing centres in the mind, where they are sorted and assembled in terms of attributes that are given independently of the particular contexts in which they are encountered. In short, such integration presupposes a project of *classification*. Yet this project severs the very relations that bring people and things to where they are, at any place or moment, such that their paths converge and observation can proceed. These relations, as we have seen, go along and not up, and are characteristically described in the form not of a classification but of a story. Thus alongly integrated knowledge is *storied* knowledge. In a story, things do not exist but occur – they are not objects but topics. As the wayfarer goes from place to place, the storyteller goes from topic to topic. Each topic is identified by the things that paved the way for it, that are concurrent with it, and that follow on, along the line of the story. Or in short, stories always, and inevitably, relate what classifications divide. For in the storied world every being, far from serving as a vector for attributes received in advance, enfolds in its own constitution the relational trails along which its life is lived. Yet, as Leroi-Gourhan showed, storytelling always involves gesture, and gesture may leave a trace or graph. In what sense, then, might such graphism be regarded as writing, and how does the line-making of the storyteller resemble, or differ from, that of the writer? The calligrapher may tell a story in the movements of the pen or brush, just as the dancer does in the movements of the feet. Indeed so long as it is regarded as a practice of inscription, writing is very similar to storytelling. But the writer of today is not a calligrapher or scribe but a wordsmith. His script is not woven from flowing lines, as the original metaphor of the text implies, but assembled from discrete elements: letters into words, words into sentences, sentences into the complete composition. Thus, rather than focusing exclusively on the contrast between orality and literacy, as has been the convention in the past, the more important question is to discover how and why the flowing line of the storyteller or scribe came to be replaced by the connecting, point-to-point lines of the pre-composed plot

Environment

Let me return for a moment to the logic of inversion. This logic, as we have seen, converts the lines *along* which life is lived into enclosures *within* which it is contained. The fate of the concept of place offers a good example of inversion at work. Inhabitants, it is supposed, live *in* places, each a bounded hub from which radiate the spokes of a network of connections to places elsewhere. As wayfarers, however, inhabitants do not live in places but around them, and along the ways to and from other places. Thus places are not containers for life and knowledge, nor – for that reason – can inhabitants properly be

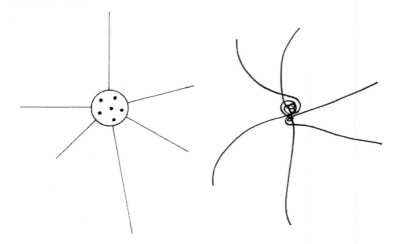

Figure 8.3 *The hub-and-spokes model of place (left) compared with the place as a knot of entangled life-lines (right).*

described as 'locals'. Every place is like a knot tied from the multiple and interlaced strands of growth and movement of its inhabitants, rather than a hub in a static network of connectors (Figure 8.3). But if life is not enclosed within a boundary, neither can it be surrounded. What, then, becomes of our concept of environment? Literally, the environment is what surrounds an organism, person or place. You cannot, however, surround a knot without drawing a line around it, and that would immediately be to effect an inversion, turning the bindings that comprise the knot into boundaries that contain it. We can imagine, however, that lines of growth issuing from multiple sources become comprehensively entangled with one another, rather like the vines and creepers of a dense patch of tropical forest, or the tangled root systems that you cut through with your spade every time you dig your garden. What we have been accustomed to calling 'the environment' might, then, be better envisaged as a domain of entanglement. It is within such a tangle of interlaced trails, continually ravelling here and unravelling there, that beings grow or 'issue forth' along the lines of their relationships. This tangle is the texture of the world. It has no insides or outsides, only openings and 'ways through'. Thus an ecology of life must be of threads and traces, not of nodes and connectors.

History

I have argued that the knowledge of inhabitants, far from being assembled into the received categories of a system of classification, is continually forged in the process of moving around. This, in turn, gives us an open-ended way of thinking about history as a flow in which people and their knowledge undergo perpetual formation and re-formation. It is a way of thinking that contrasts radically with the genealogical conception of history built into conventional models of biological and cultural evolution. According to this conception, every individual is endowed with the essential specifications for carrying on a particular form (or, more strictly, a certain range of forms) of life, independently and in advance of its growth and development in an environment. It follows that while the individual may be depicted geographically as making a sequence of strategic moves across a plane surface, rather like a piece on a gaming board, from a genealogical perspective its entire life may be condensed into a single point. It is no wonder that Charles Darwin, in the only illustration in *The Origin of Species*, chose to depict the phyletic line as a series of dots (Darwin 1950 [1859]: 90–91). In the very similar diagrams constructed by anthropologists to depict human genealogies, the dots are replaced by equally punctual symbols (triangles for men and circles for women) that are connected by lines. These lines, instantly recognisable as point-to-point connectors, are not, however, indices of growth or movement. They are rather lines of genetic or cultural transmission, down which is supposed to pass not the impulse of life but information for living it. In connecting points, they resemble the lines of a transport network. But whereas transport lines mark out an individual's moves on the plane of the present, lines of transmission connect the sources and recipients of information in diachronic sequence. Transport and transmission are arrayed upon the separate axes of synchrony and diachrony (Figure 8.4). However, just as pure transport is an impossibility, so too is pure transmission. It is no more possible to be everywhere at once than it is to receive the specifications for life in advance of living it.[10]

Following the imagery of Bergson rather than Darwin, I suggest that every being is instantiated in the world not as a bounded entity but as a thoroughfare, along the path of its own movement and activity. The passage of generations would then be depicted not as a succession of points connected by lines, but as a plait of lines, alternately convergent and divergent (Figure 8.5). Of course, the depiction is highly schematic, but it does serve to illustrate the possibility of thinking of history as a trans-generational flow rather than a succession of discrete generational states. It also gives us a way

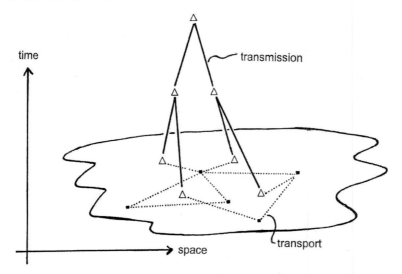

Figure 8.4 *Lines of transmission and transport. Lines of transport connect locations arrayed synchronically in space. Lines of transmission connect individuals in a diachronic, ancestor-descendant sequence, irrespective of spatial location.*

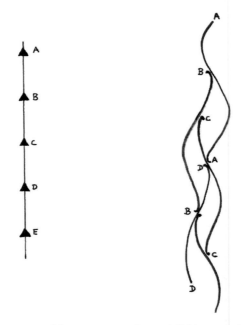

Figure 8.5 *A sequence of five generations depicted (left) as a series of point-to-to point connections and (right) as a series of interlaced and overlapping life-lines.*

of describing ancestry and descent which, I believe, better accords with the way people generally talk about such matters – in terms of the narrative interweaving of present and past lives rather than the application of classificatory schemata.

A holistic anthropology?

I would like to conclude with a few words about holism in anthropology, since my argument runs directly counter to some of the senses in which the concept of holism has been promulgated as a desideratum of anthropological scholarship, both within this volume and elsewhere. Specifically, I believe it is crucial to dissociate holism from a concern with wholes. Holism is one thing, totalisation quite another, and my argument *for* holism is, quite directly, an argument *against* totalisation. Or more precisely, it is against the particular conception of part-whole relations that totalisation implies. It is so in three ways. First, in thinking of the relations between movement, knowledge and description in terms of organically growing lines, I have stressed the open-endedness – rather than closure – both of the world we inhabit and of our own attempts, as inhabitants, to know and understand that world. We are not and never will be, as so many grand theorists have claimed, on the point of opening the last envelope, when the world and our knowledge of it will be complete. Secondly, I imagine the world, in the terms of the physicist David Bohm (1980: 149), as an *implicate* rather than *explicate* order: that is, as a world of movement and becoming, in which any thing, caught at a particular moment, enfolds within its own constitution the history of relations that brought it there. In such a world we can understand the nature of things only by attending to their relations, or, in other words, by telling their stories. Thirdly, and following from this, I have stressed the primacy of process over structure or form. In this view, knowing does not lie in the establishment of a correspondence between the world and its representation, but is rather immanent in the life and consciousness of the knower as it unfolds within the field of practice set up through his or her presence as a being-in-the-world (Ingold 2001b: 143). In short, we must recognise our own immersion in the world we seek to know, and that our own processes of knowing are woven into its ever-weaving texture. Thus the aim of a holistic anthropology, in my view, should not be to bolt together components of being – such as mind, body and culture – into which it should never have been carved in the first place. In a world of ever-growing lines loose ends proliferate. Our job is not to join them up into an integrated and complete totality but to make the most of the possibilities they afford, both scholarly and political, for *keeping life going.*

Notes

1. I gratefully acknowledge the support of the Economic and Social Research Council, which has awarded me a Professorial Fellowship for the period 2005–2008 to undertake this work.
2. Lines turn up in all sorts of forms: a rough taxonomy could include traces, threads, rods, cuts, cracks and creases. One of my tasks will be to explore this diversity, and to consider how different kinds of line relate to, or transform into, one another. In this I shall be able to draw on the pioneering studies already undertaken by artists such as Wassily Kandinsky (1982: 617–36), Paul Klee (1961: 103–20), and Richard Long (2002). Such exploration, however, lies beyond the scope of the present chapter.
3. Many anthropological advocates of holism, including several represented in this volume, appeal to some notion of what I call the 'complementarity thesis', under the rubric of 'bioculturalism' (Ulijaszek) or similar hybrid terms. I disagree with them. In a number of recent publications (Ingold 2000b, 2001a, 2002, 2003a, 2004a) I have sought to show why this thesis is ill-founded, and have argued instead for an 'obviation' approach that does away with the conventional distinctions between body, mind and culture.
4. This assumption is not stated explicitly. It is rather implicit in a language of cognitive science that draws on the metaphors of information processing, computation, mapping and mental representation, all of which entail that the mind gets to work on data already extracted *from* the world in order to form ideas that do not themselves change as one moves from place to place (Ingold 2000a: 18). Thus the body's movement through the world, though necessary for gathering the 'raw material' of perception, has no bearing on how the mind works in the formation of representations.
5. The neo-Darwinian agenda is elegantly summarised in this volume by Robin Dunbar. As he makes clear, the 'genes' it adduces, and that together make up the genotype, are not to be confused with bits of DNA in the genome. They are rather so-called Mendelian genes, each of which specifies a *trait* regardless of how it comes to be expressed, or of whether it is expressed at all, in the life-history of the organism. In reality, as components of a virtual, context-independent specification, these genes can exist nowhere save in the imagination of the biologist. The logic by which neo-Darwinism reads 'into' the organism a set of specifications abstracted from the range of observed developmental outcomes, such that development itself can be understood as the reading 'off' of these specifications under particular environmental conditions, is of course entirely circular. The circularity is carefully hidden, however, by an insistence on the logical independence of questions of ontogeny and phylogeny that can only be sustained on the assumption that in the life history of the organism, design precedes the processes that are otherwise supposed to give rise to it. As Dunbar's exposition of 'Tinbergen's Four Whys' shows, confusion in biological thought does not present itself openly but rather hides behind the back of neat and tidy distinctions in terms on which everything seems to be already sorted out (Ingold 1996). Any criticism from interlopers such as myself, 'peering in' on biology from the outside, is interpreted as lamentable misunderstanding. Denouncing critics for the error of their ways is, of course,

no more than a crude defensive reaction that absolves zealots of any obligation to respond.

6. For this reason I would take issue with anthropologists of art and material culture, including both Howard Morphy and Chris Gosden (this volume), who seem to believe that persons and things, and their mutually constitutive interactions, together comprise *all there is*. We live in a world not just of objects, whether made or found, but of generative processes, of which these objects are but the more or less ephemeral precipitates.

7. These were the Rhind Lectures, sponsored by the Society of Antiquaries of Scotland. I am most grateful to the Society for offering me the opportunity to develop, and to 'try out' on an audience, ideas that at the time were still in a very embryonic state of development.

8. For simplicity, and for purposes of illustration, I have focused on the 'level' of the individual organism. I could have focused 'down', say, on the cell and its intra-organismic environment, or 'up' to a community of organisms and their shared environment. Combining these foci into a single, multi-levelled projection would yield something like a series of concentric circles. This does not affect the logic of the argument. It does, however, raise an issue about levels. For the idea that life is lived on different levels of inclusiveness rests on the very same logic of inversion that converts lifeways into boundaries of inclusion in the first place.

9. It might be argued that modern communications technologies (mobile phones, email, the worldwide web) have turned what was once an illusory dream into a practical reality. Perhaps, in cyberspace, we *can* be everywhere at once. I would argue, however, that the world of cyberspace is not one that we can inhabit as the living, breathing and sensing creatures that we are.

10. This is the root of my objection to the notions of genetic and cultural 'inheritance' continually and casually invoked by neo-Darwinian theorists, including Dunbar (this volume). It is their insistence that individuals inherit 'traits' prior to their possible 'expression' in an environment that leads them to suppose that each individual is pre-endowed with a design, and to speak of evolution as a design agent. Indeed it is ironic that in the current controversy surrounding the doctrine of 'intelligent design', the existence of such design is the one thing that both sides are agreed upon. The dispute is over whose intelligence is to be granted the higher authority: that of Science reflected in the mirror of Nature, or that of Christian Theodicy reflected in the mirror of God. In this clash of fundamentalisms, there is little to choose between them.

Chapter 9

THE EVOLUTION AND
HISTORY OF RELIGION[1]

Harvey Whitehouse

In his 1917 Presidential Address to the Folk Lore Society, Marett eloquently distinguished two major approaches to the study of culture, both of which could be substantially traced to pioneering figures in Oxford. One he labelled the 'historical method', exemplified by Sir Laurence Gomme. Gomme wanted to show that culture is transmitted, among people and across generations, through processes of imitation and learning – and thus through the cumulative storage of information and habits. His method involved painstaking description and collation of historiographical evidence over vast expanses of time and space. The other main approach Marett described as 'anthropological'. This approach, he believed, was exemplified by the work of Sir Edward Tylor (among others). The emphasis of Tylor's anthropology, Marett observed, was not on the local and transient *particularities* of human behaviour but rather on patterns of cross-cultural and historical *recurrence*. Like Tylor, Marett believed in the psychic unity of humankind – and in that unity he saw a key to what he called the 'uniformities' of human culture. Universal features of human psychology were to be explained with reference to processes of biological evolution. But this did not mean that cultural *variables* were to be explained solely with reference to historical accidents or prior patterns of learning and transmission. Marett argued for a synthesis of historiographical and anthropological methods, based on sound psychological assumptions. After all, he pointed out, Laurence Gomme couldn't possibly account for patterns of cultural transmission without recourse to more or less explicit assumptions about the psychic unity of our species. Nor indeed could Tylor explain a given custom without recourse to prior histories of cultural transmission. The two projects, Marett argued, were mutually implicated.

If Marett could somehow be raised from the dead, I suspect he would be astonished at the progress that has been made in the scientific study of culture. Far from having overturned all the central ideas of Victorian scholarship, modern scientific methods have garnered overwhelming support for at least some of the central insights of Marett's generation, as we shall see. But Marett would also have been disappointed, I think, to discover that certain branches of the study of human nature, including much of social and cultural anthropology, had become progressively detached from the natural sciences, and most crucially from the *biological* and *psychological* sciences in the course of the twentieth century.

In Marett's day, major theoretical advances in our understanding of social and cultural phenomena seemed to be inextricably wedded to the future of scientific enquiry. But this optimism gradually evaporated as the consensus of opinion in the social sciences and humanities favoured the partitioning of all things cultural from the rest of the world (so that culture now seemed to be explainable only with reference to phenomena of the same order). We might classify this doctrine as a form of 'idealism' (though of course it took on many different guises and did not consist of a single coherent ideology). The obvious next step, for many students of society and culture, was to relinquish their scientific aspirations altogether. There are various ways in which this intellectual shift could be narrated and illustrated, and it would be easy to conjure up a rich variety of shifting intellectual coalitions, even-handedly populated with villains and heroes. But let us put all of that to one side, and consider where it has left us at the beginning of the twenty-first century.

Towards a new holistic Anthropology

Many contributors to this volume, myself included, are seeking a new kind of anthropology, one that looks outwards to surrounding disciplines with at least as much excitement as it countenances internally driven debates and disputes. For some of us (though not necessarily all) this search beyond our disciplinary boundaries is driven by a growing awareness that a revolution is taking place around us in the human sciences, and especially in various fields of biology and scientific psychology. The last few decades have seen a veritable explosion of powerful new theories and methods in such fields as neuroscience, genetics, cognitive, developmental, and evolutionary psychology, and linguistics. Disciplines responsible for tracking and evaluating such developments from the sidelines, such as the history and philosophy of science (and especially the philosophy of mind) have been racing to keep up, while many others have simply been left behind. It seems to me that the discipline of sociocultural anthropology has tended to straggle. Many of its practitioners are wary of biological and psychological reductionism and there are probably a number of reasons for this.

Some of the difficulties may arise from misunderstandings. In this volume, Robin Dunbar answers the kinds of misplaced objections that are commonly raised by sociocultural anthropologists in response to theories of human behaviour and culture in the contemporary biological sciences. Many such misunderstandings (if that is what they are) stem from the fact that anthropology and evolutionary theory parted company before Darwinian approaches had fully matured and, consequently, the criticisms of anthropologists may be pointlessly targeted at outmoded (e.g. Lamarckian) models of evolutionary theory. The points that Dunbar makes in his 'philosophical preliminaries' are surely correct and there is little I would wish to add. But it may be worth tackling head on a couple of issues that Dunbar sets aside, but which probably also contribute to the unease with which contemporary anthropologists countenance the biological and cognitive sciences. The first has to do with the stereotyping of scientific research on human nature and the second is mainly about protectionist urges within the professional guild.

Science suffers from an image problem, at least among many anthropologists. For instance, science is often seen as the servant of imperialistic ambitions or related forms of political domination and economic exploitation. There is (unfortunately) considerable evidence to support these stereotypes, although it is equally easy to find examples of more positive contributions of science to humane, liberal and even politically radical projects. Much more dubiously, however, some may assume that if science can serve the wicked then it must itself be a wicked ideology.

An example of how science has got itself a bad name is provided in this volume by Laura Peers' thought-provoking biography of Beatrice Blackwood. Peers shows that Blackwood's extensive investigation of the relationship between 'race' and intelligence in the 1920s has left a legacy of moral and political dilemmas. Quite apart from the threat Blackwood's research once posed to black activists struggling against notoriously extreme forms of racism in the American South, the fate of the hair samples she gathered from Ojibwe children in northern Minnesota continues to raise concerns among those now elderly persons from whom the samples were taken.

It is tempting to argue that Blackwood's work was an example of 'bad science', driven as it was by a scientific agenda on the decline and subsequently overturned by new discoveries in the biological sciences. The very idea of searching for a connection between race and intelligence is, from a twenty-first-century vantage point, somewhat absurd since culturally prevalent racial categories simply are not founded in biologically significant clusters of differences.[2] But thanks in large part to Blackwood's scientific training, she gathered her data in a highly systematic fashion and therefore her work continues to be of potential value for modern research. For example, in this volume Stanley Ulijaszek explains that anthropometric data, of the sort collected by Blackwood in North America, provides an effective means of assessing environmental stresses, with potentially significant implications for public health policy in a range of areas. Even though the hair samples Blackwood gathered are still stored in unopened envelopes in the Pitt Rivers Museum, it is conceivable that they too may have some genuine scientific value in the future.[3]

Thus, the moral and political implications of biological (or more generally scientific) approaches to the study of culture are much less straightforward than it may first appear. Scientific theories, and particularly the rigorous methodologies upon which they rely, give rise to knowledge that can be used for good or ill. Good science, in and of itself, is neither good nor bad in moral terms, and neither reactionary nor radical in its political orientation. It is only a means to knowledge which, though provisional, is (by virtue of its rigour, precision, and testability) more *reliable* than other kinds of knowledge. What we do with that knowledge is another matter.

Another cluster of concerns among anthropologists, however, relates to the position of their professional guild among surrounding sciences. Some may fear that scientific reductionism is rapaciously imperialistic, seeking to overtake and swallow up any friendly disciplines that are foolish enough to let it in. The cognitive sciences are currently in the throes of a revolution, embracing a broad coalition of subject areas that take the evolution of specialized psychological capacities in our species as axiomatic and assume that the systematic testing of precisely formulated hypotheses must provide the bedrock of further theory building. Researchers in such fields as experimental psychology, neo-Darwinian evolutionary biology, and the neurosciences are increasingly working with a broad range of social scientists, philosophers, archaeologists and others to develop a robust and testable body of knowledge about human nature, and in particular to explain our uniquely human capacities for cultural innovation and cumulative transmission. In doing so, these researchers trespass ever more deeply into topics that lie historically in the heartland of social and cultural anthropology.

What should we, as anthropologists, do about these developments? One option would be to ignore them. But such a strategy could carry heavy costs. As our relevance to surrounding sciences diminishes we may find our own abandoned agendas being taken up successfully by our competitors. And if we do allow our intellectual and institutional heritage as a discipline to be plundered by others, then what would remain for us? Having abandoned our most valuable explanatory tools we may be condemned to endless *descriptions and re-descriptions* of cultural phenomena, enlivened only by speculative interpretations and reinterpretations.[4] If, as anthropologists, we side exclusively with interpretive and hermeneutic traditions, we run the risk of becoming merely an irrelevance to potentially powerful allies, and a feeble adversary to our real rivals.

Alternatively, we may elect to join the revolution. The reason many of the cognitive sciences are growing so fast is because their theoretical frameworks are increasingly integrated, sophisticated and empirically productive. We can both gain from and contribute to this process. We can gain by rebuilding confidence in the questions we once asked, refining them, and seeking more convincing answers (with the help of others). What are the causal dynamics that govern kinship relations, exchange, communication, technology, art, gender relations, religion, and so on? What are the limits of institutional and behavioural variation in these and other domains? To what extent do differing contexts of development and learning impact on the way we think? Anthropologists were among the first to pose such questions and we can still help to answer them.

We (anthropologists) arguably know more than anybody else about continuities and differences in human culture, at least in the modern world. Taking that body of knowledge together with the findings of historians and archaeologist this constitutes quite a lot of information. We also have our own distinctive methodologies for gathering data. Long-term, intensive fieldwork in a single location allows in-depth observation and empathetic learning which provides a *necessary* backdrop and corrective to many other types of investigation (e.g. quantitative or experimental). There is also great scope for refinement of our ethnographic techniques. Generalizations about what people do and say are no substitute for systematic study of how declarative knowledge differs by age and gender, for instance, or how it may be primed by subtle differences of context or developmental history. The usefulness of ethnography for other disciplines will always depend on our capacity to be precise about such matters.[5]

Aside from the data it commands, anthropology has another valuable gift to contribute – and that is its intellectual breadth. Others specialize in particular aspects of human nature: our minds, our societies, our economic behaviour, or the way we exercise power, for instance. Anthropologists study all those things and more. As such, we have a potentially major role in the new integrative movement. Indeed, we should be at the very centre of it.

Re-framing Marett's problem

Approximately 50,000 years ago, humanity underwent what archaeologists commonly refer to as the 'Upper Palaeolithic Revolution'. Up to that point, evolved changes in behaviour (as is typical of evolutionary processes in general) tended to correspond closely to changes in *anatomy*. From about 50,000 years ago, however, behaviour began to show unprecedented plasticity against a background of *minimal anatomical change*. This behavioural plasticity heralded both cultural diversification and the transmission across generations of potentially *cumulative* bodies of cultural knowledge. Another way of putting this is to say that whereas behavioural variation in our archaic human ancestors is most effectively tracked in evolutionary time, behavioural variation in modern humans is to be explained in terms of both evolution *and* history. On this fundamental point Marett was surely correct. My aim in what follows is to identify some of the general contributions of evolution and history to the development of culture, and to illustrate this argument with reference to the domain of *religion*. I choose religion mostly because it is my own area of specialism but it is doubly apposite since religion was a principal interest of Marett's as well.[6]

Much recent research in experimental psychology and the neurosciences suggests that the human mind incorporates a complex repertoire of specialized mechanisms. These mechanisms are the outcome of a common evolutionary history in our species and they are fundamentally the same regardless of differences of culture and ecology. There is, as Marett and Tylor imagined, a bedrock of psychological commonalities among members of our species. The challenge confronting us now (as in the past) is to show that significant features of the content, organization, and spread of religious phenomena can be explained in terms of the ways in which these evolved psychological mechanisms are activated. Part of the challenge is clearly to explain religious *universals*: much of what we have learned from modern ethnography, historiography, and archaeology (for instance) points to a massive amount of cross-cultural recurrence not only in human behaviour but in the form and content of religious phenomena. Our first task is therefore to consider how universal features of human psychology serve to shape and constrain the repertoire of religious thought and behaviour in our species. But we must also rise to the challenge of explaining religious *differences*: why do religious ideas and practices vary from one tradition to the next? This question holds particular importance for anthropologists like myself who have devoted extended periods of their lives to understanding particular local traditions and wondering why they have the distinctive features they do. Let us approach these two questions in turn.

Evolved cognition and religious Universals

I would venture that certain features of religious thinking and behaviour are universal and ancient. Humans everywhere (and throughout the opaquely visible past) have entertained notions of *essentialized religious coalitions, supernatural agency* and of *life after death*; have attributed misfortune and luck to *transcendental causes*; have assumed that certain features of the natural world were *created by intentional design*; have performed *rituals* and endowed them with *symbolic meanings* and have regarded certain kinds of *testimony or obligation as divinely 'given'* and unchallengeable.

If we concede that there is indeed an invariable core of all religious thinking and behaviour – a universal religious repertoire, if you will – then it seems to me that this is potentially explainable as an outcome of biases in our species' evolved cognitive architecture. A useful starting point is provided by the psychological finding that people acquire certain basic assumptions about the nature of the world around them according to a linked series of universal stages, or 'developmental schedules'. This kind of knowledge emerges in a series of distinct domains. For instance, in the domain of knowledge concerned with the behaviour of *physical* entities, people everywhere expect unsupported objects to fall earthwards (a principle known as intuitive gravity). We also expect objects to move in continuous paths, to displace each other in space, etc.[7] In the domain of knowledge concerned with *biological* phenomena, we assume that organisms have essential properties that assign them immutably to particular classes of natural kinds. From an early age, children reason that although an artifact can be altered so drastically that it becomes a legitimate member of an entirely different class of artifacts (e.g. a kettle can be converted into a bird feeder, thereby ceasing to be a kettle), natural species cannot be transformed in this way.[8] Thus, no matter how convincingly a cat may be transformed (e.g. by means of radical surgery) to appear exactly like a dog, subjects assume that it still possesses some hidden essence of feline qualities that prevent it from joining the dog category. The origins of these domain-specific systems are ancient and we have increasingly detailed accounts of their specialization in the course of hominid evolution.[9] Research in developmental psychology on the emergence of these systems in childhood[10] has recently been augmented by evidence of how these systems operate at the neurological level and also how they malfunction in cases of brain damage and disease, based on both clinical observations and experimental research.[11]

Closely related to intuitive thinking about natural kinds is the way we reason about social categories. Although there has been some debate about whether our folk notions of the social domain rest on intuitive biological reasoning or constitute a distinct type of intuitive ontological knowledge in their own right, what is not in doubt is that people everywhere treat the differences between classes of fellow humans as *similar* to the differences between natural species, at least insofar as they are endowed with heritable essences.[12] Such reasoning appears to lie at the core of racial thinking – in particular the idea that there are invisible essentialized components to the differences between races that are somehow passed on from parent to child. But such reasoning also figures prominently in the way religious specialists and coalitions are cognized. Religious thinking typically postulates distinct classes of persons defined by heritable essences in virtue of which they are entitled to assume sacred office (e.g. in the case of shamans, divine kings, emperors, etc.) or by means of which their persecution may be justified (e.g. in the case of witches, heathens, untouchables etc.).[13] The same intuitive reasoning commonly underpins our representations of religious coalitions, for instance the way Catholics and Protestants in Northern Ireland or Muslims and Jews in the Middle East construe the differences that divide them.[14]

Intuitive ontology becomes important in religious thinking in other ways as well. For instance, cognitive processes that *violate* intuitive ontological expectations may be referred to as *counterintuitive* ways of thinking.[15] Counterintuitive concepts figure prominently in the domain of religion, and they come in two main varieties. First, there are concepts that entail *breaches* of our intuitive expectations. For example, many supernatural agents (ghosts and gods) are assumed to think and feel in much the same way as ordinary human beings but are accorded special physical properties, such as the ability to pass through solid obstacles or to appear in more than one place at a time. Second, there are violations that entail the *transfer* of properties from one intuitive domain to another. For instance, inanimate objects (statues of gods or paintings of saints) might be accorded properties normally restricted to the domain of biological organisms (the ability to weep or bleed). Recent experimental evidence suggests that simple counterintuitive concepts are easier for people to recall than simple intuitive concepts, regardless of cultural differences.[16] This would help to explain the ethnographic finding that simple counterintuitive concepts are globally recurrent and historically ancient features of religious thinking.[17]

Another feature of human cognition that impacts substantially on the universal religious repertoire is our unique capacity (indeed nagging obligation) to reflect on what others may be thinking. This capacity involves a number of complex psychological mechanisms that have come to be known as 'Theory of Mind'[18] (or ToM), which leads us to make continual inferences about the mental states of other people, to adjust our behaviour in light of those inferences, and to plot and scheme on the basis of what we think others may or may not know (including what we think they know or don't know about our own intentions).

Some recent *evolutionary* accounts of the emergence of ToM have emphasized the reproductive advantage conferred on individuals capable of tracking the strategic interests of allies and enemies and to manipulate social relations accordingly.[19] These evolutionary models are complemented by evidence of ToM operations at the level of brain function.[20] Some of the neuroscience literature is directed to the study of pathological conditions.[21] Serious deficits in ToM capabilities are associated with the condition diagnosed as autism.[22] We have some evidence from ethnography that ToM mechanisms develop and operate similarly in different cultural environments though much more research in this area is needed.[23]

ToM capacities appear to play a crucial role in the production of 'afterlife' concepts. Recent experimental research suggests that people are strongly biased to attribute mental states (desires, sensory responses, intentions, etc.) to dead persons, based on basic ToM operations, even though they are readily able to represent biological and physical functions as having terminated.[24] Part of the reason for this bias may be the impossibility of representing one's own consciousness as 'no longer existing' even though one can readily imagine (or directly experience) the loss of particular biological and physical capacities. Our bias to represent dead persons as having mental/emotional capacities that outlive their physical bodies provides a compelling foundation for notions of free-floating agency, separable from any corporeal anchorage. Such a notion in turn affords the possibility of other kinds of bodiless agents, such as deities and primordial ancestors.

Much recent research has focused on the role of ToM operations in the construction of concepts of extranatural agency. Counterintuitive constructs (based on violations and transfers of intuitive ontological knowledge) enjoy a mnemonic advantage over intuitive concepts in laboratory conditions but that may not be sufficient to explain why simple counterintuitive concepts become culturally widespread. What we find in the global ethnographic record is not simply a host of counterintuitive concepts (e.g. artifacts that resemble organisms) but, much more strikingly, a plethora of *agents* that have special (counterintuitive) powers. A counterintuitive agent is far more salient than a counterintuitive artifact or plant. This appears to be because an agent has a *mind* that can process information of strategic importance.[25] More importantly, a counterintuitive agent can access and utilize information in ways that ordinary mortals cannot. For instance, a spirit capable of overcoming the physical constraints of gravity and solidity will be able to move around with superhuman speed and stealth – flying through walls or appearing invisibly in more than one place at a single moment. Such counterintuitive abilities allow spirits to listen in on conversations or to observe misdemeanours in a way that human surveillance normally cannot. Consequently, spirits tend to know very much more about what is going on than the rest of us could possibly hope to do. Such a conception of supernatural agency clearly requires ToM operations. We have to be able to represent the spirit as taking an interest in what we are up to – and paying attention in particular to those behaviours that have consequences for others. Typically, we imagine that spirits use this kind of information to mete out punishments and rewards. In order produce such concepts, we must attribute a mind (i.e. intentions, beliefs, and desires) to our supernatural construct. Often, extranatural agents are construed as having special kinds of minds – capable of reading our thoughts (rather than having to infer them from our behaviour) or being able to see into the future (and thus to provide warnings or to lay traps).

ToM capacities are also clearly essential for representations of spirit possession and mediumship. Here, the idea is not merely that a person's mental/emotional capacities can live on after the body has expired but that, in virtue of being separable in this way, minds and bodies can be temporarily dislocated and recombined. Minds can leave bodies and be replaced by other minds (for instance the minds of dead persons or deities), before being restored to their original location. For such a process to make any sense, those who experience or observe possession episodes must be able to represent their own and other people's minds as discrete entities whose identities can be revealed on the basis of complex signals.[26]

In the construction of religious concepts a crucial role is also played by psychological mechanisms dedicated to the detection of agency. The Agency-Detection System develops at a strikingly early age in humans.[27] Even newborn infants have rudimentary biases to distinguish animate agents from inanimate objects and this early predisposition rapidly develops into a system that treats a wide range of inputs as possible signs of agency.[28] Children and adults alike are highly susceptible to the overdetection of agents in their environments. It is all too easy to see the outlines of faces in the striated patterns of a rockface or the changing configurations of clouds in the sky. And we rapidly attribute agency to unexpected or ambiguous noises or movements. It has long been appreciated that such a system would have been highly adaptive in an environment replete with dangerous predators.[29] This would help to account for the hyperactivity of the system in question: the costs of raising the alarm when detecting harmless agents (or sounds and movements not caused by agents at all) would, one might surmise, have been a small price to pay for the successful avoidance of genuinely dangerous creatures.

Although the Agency-Detection System is not capable in itself of creating a full-blown concept of extranatural agency, it appears to play a supporting role in persuading people (who have already acquired such concepts) that spirits and deities really are around, lurking in the environment. Of course, many instances of agent overdetection are readily dismissed: it turns out to be a rustling of leaves or the whistling of the wind. But not all unexpected sounds and movements are traceable to obvious causes and if somebody were to claim that even one such occurrence had been caused by ghosts, it would be well nigh impossible to disprove such a claim. Thus, the Agency-Detection System is capable of supporting concepts of supernatural agency generated by the ToM system.

Supernatural agents, however, are also quintessentially *moral* agents. They do not simply supervise or monitor our behaviour, by means of their special powers; they punish us when we transgress and reward us when we behave well. Whereas rules of convention are highly variable cross-culturally, moral rules exhibit a number of universal features.[30] For instance, moral thinking everywhere delivers the intuition that *harming others* is wrong.[31] Moral infractions are universally treated more seriously than violations of convention. Of special significance is the intuition that moral rules are not contingent on authority in the same way as rules of convention. Regardless of whether figures of authority forbid or condone harming behaviours, those behaviours are still intuitively judged to be immoral. This applies equally to supernatural and worldly authorities alike. For instance, an early study of moral reasoning among Armish youths revealed that the conventional rule forbidding labour on the Sabbath was contingent on God's authority whereas harming behaviours (use of violence to achieve one's goals) were perceived to be wrong whether or not they were subject to divine sanction.[32]

Moral thinking, together with the operation of ToM mechanisms, plays an especially prominent role in the way people manage their *reputations* in the eyes of others. The maintenance of alliances and support networks of all kinds, and perhaps most crucially (in terms of gene transmission) the task of attracting a mate, depend upon the successful management of one's reputation (through the suppression of harmful information about one's behaviour and the promulgation, where possible, of a virtuous self-image). [33] A person of dubious moral integrity (with a history of harming others whether through physical abuse, treachery, stealing, or character assassination) runs the risk of exposure and thus of becoming saddled with a poor reputation in the community. Religious thinking provides unique opportunities for this kind of management. First, it may serve to inhibit antisocial behaviour (by postulating extranatural agents with special capacities to observe and punish wrongdoing). Second, those who can convince others of their moral fibre through costly displays of religious devotion may derive the benefits of a high reputation (whether or not their concealed thoughts and behaviours are congruent with a laudable public image). Third, religious thinking can provide a means of restoring damaged reputations (or forestalling and thereby limiting potential damage) through mechanisms of confession, absolution, reconciliation, expiation and so on. All these processes depend, of course, on the presence of a moral thinking system as well as an awareness (based on ToM capacities) that others are capable of monitoring one's intentions and making judgements of character on that basis.

These are just a few examples of the ways in which our species-specific cognitive systems may give rise to universal features of religious thinking. Much more could be said on this subject and of course there are other features of the universal repertoire that I have not even touched upon. But this should suffice to give a flavour of the ways in which the cognitive science of religion is beginning to provide precise and testable explanations for cross-culturally recurrent religious concepts, commensurate with the findings of surrounding sciences.

Let us move swiftly on to another, equally daunting but potentially soluble problem: the causes of religious *variation*. To put it concretely, how might our knowledge of the kinds of minds we have help us to explain what makes the richly textured and distinctive features of Yolngu religion and cosmology, as described by Howard Morphy in this volume, *different* from those that might prevail among parishioners of an Oxford church?

Historicized cognition and religious variation

Some species-specific behaviour is highly stereotyped and *fixed* by biological design features. Other behaviours are more malleable and diverse within the species. One way of grasping this point is to distinguish between 'open' and 'closed' behaviour programmes.[34] 'Closed' behaviour programmes are ones that churn out much the same outputs in all known environments. Obvious examples in humans would include the programmes responsible for such universal behavioural displays as sneezing, flinching, laughing, crying, and so on. We might reasonably compare such responses to the behavioural repertoires of other species. Some behaviour programmes are more 'open' than others in that they can undergo significant modification through processes of learning. We know from studies of bird behaviour, for instance, that despite the presence of species-typical vocal repertoires there may also be subtle *regional* differences in birdsong that are the outcome of local innovation and the transmission of distinctive vocal patterns among individual birds.[35] Such patterns of innovation and transmission are even more striking among our closer primate relatives, like chimpanzees – who are now known to invent and pass on a variety of skills, for instance involving simple tools.[36] But in modern humans, these same types of processes operate on an altogether different scale. Not only are humans highly inventive creatures (just like some of our primate cousins) but crucially we also have highly developed methods of *storing*, both by means of cognitive memory and through the use of various kinds of external repositories, the innovations and discoveries of our forebears. And for this reason many features of human culture are capable of developing *cumulatively* over time. Instead of having to rely more or less *exclusively* on behavioural repertoires that are characteristic of the species as a whole, and thus forged in *evolutionary* time, humans are able to master massive bodies of skills and information gradually assembled by their ancestors in the course of *locally distinctive histories* of transmission.

The accumulation of cultural knowledge over time constitutes a source of quite dramatic ecological change. It is not simply that, in building on the shoulders of our ancestors, we have transformed the landscape or built skyscrapers and jumbo jets. Of course we have certainly done this, with increasingly grave consequences, as cultivable land diminishes, as non-renewable resources become scarcer, as levels of pollution rise, as climate change accelerates, and so on. But in addition to this, humans have created significant changes in the way social relations are conceptualized and reproduced. Consider, for instance, David Parkin's discussion in this volume of the implications of changing levels of density of interaction and effervescence for patterns of conflict, alliance, co-operation, and competition in human populations. And there are other examples in the present collection of essays. Consider Tim Ingold's reflections on the possible impact of literacy on conceptual development and embodied skills or Chris

Gosden's observations on the way our uses of artifacts can shape and channel social relations.

Environments (including patterns of social interaction and culturally distributed knowledge and tools) may well be capable of influencing some features of the development of our cognitive architecture.[37] But it also seems likely that varying ecological contexts serve to *prime* and *constrain* the way our universal cognitive capacities are activated. This latter hypothesis has proved to be an especially fertile area of research in recent years and holds great promise for further investigation.

While there is currently a range of candidate hypotheses with regard to the cognitive causes of religious diversity, much of my own work has focused on domain-general features of the human mind and, in particular, our capacity for conscious remembering. By 'domain-general' I mean that any kind of information we consciously recall can (at least in principle) become the trigger for any other, regardless of the domain to which that particular knowledge relates. For instance, your telling me that this chapter needs cutting could in principle remind me that my lawn needs mowing, even though texts and gardens belong to different ontological domains subject to different types of intuitive expectations and inferences. Being able to create novel *connections* of this kind is part of the key to understanding religious innovation. And being able to *store* those connections and *pass them on* is the foundation for cumulative religious transmission, and thus of the history of religion. The challenge, as I see it, is to isolate the principal causes of creative innovation in religious traditions and to identify the core mechanisms by which those innovations are preserved in memory and transmitted to others (both horizontally, across populations, and vertically, across generations).

It is probably useful to distinguish a number of different kinds of religious innovation but let us consider two. First, there is a kind that we might describe as 'revelatory' or 'epiphanic', whereby in a flash of insight (often attributed to some kind of divine or miraculous intervention) the religious innovator comes to see things in a radically new and persuasive light. Second, there is a kind of innovation that is more incremental, involving stepwise advancement from one idea to the next until a new network of connections is completed.[38] These two types of innovation are often intimately entangled – epiphanic revelations can give rise to gradual reworking of complex doctrinal problems and, conversely, more incremental changes in a doctrinal framework can trigger sudden and consequential moments of insight. But it also seems to be the case that these two types of innovative responses can be primed and suppressed in ways that are socially regulated.

Consider, for instance, the area of ritual performance. One of the defining features of ritual actions is their irreducibility to technical and intentional motivations.[39] Whereas all the constituent procedures of technically motivated actions contribute in some intuitively graspable way to a given outcome, many of the procedures entailed in ritual performances do not. The relation of such procedures to the outcome is opaque. Why do the ritual participants have to dress up in peculiar clothes (not just any clothes, but these particular clothes)? Why do they have to repeat this phrase or that action three times rather than just once? Why perform the procedures in this sequence rather than that? The question of how ritual actions contribute to particular outcomes (assuming those outcomes are specified, which is not always the case), is somewhat mysterious. Given that humans are inveterate 'mindreaders' (forever wondering what intentions lie behind the behaviour of others), rituals present another distinctive kind of problem: *who* told us to carry out the rituals a certain way, and *why*? It is clearly insufficient to say that the priest or the shaman told us to do it because we assume that any religious authorities in the present acquired these rules from their predecessors, going back into ancestral time, thus inviting an infinite regress in search of the answer. The riddle of intentionality posed by ritual behaviour[40] can invite four types of response. First, one might initiate a search for intentional meaning but more or less immediately give up and simply say that this is 'the tradition' or 'the will of the ancestors or gods'. Second, one might accept at face value whatever the religious authorities declare to be the meaning of the ritual procedures (or indeed of the ritual as a whole). Official exegesis of this sort may well provide a substitute for independent exegetical rumination and thus be combined with the 'giving up' response. Third, one may generate some kind of off-the-cuff speculation as to the meaning behind the ritual procedures (for instance in response to the badgering of anthropologists who want to fill their notebooks!). Fourth, one might engage in prolonged spontaneous exegetical reflection resulting in a rich and complex body of interpretations of a personal and idiosyncratic kind.

These types of responses to the puzzle of what rituals might mean are not randomly generated. It is quite possible that, due to personality differences, for instance, some people may be more inclined to accept official exegesis whereas others might be more ruminative and creative.[41] But there are also features of the way ritual performances are organized and carried out that affect how we respond to problems of exegesis at a population level. Rituals that are very frequently performed eventually come to be encoded in procedural memory and are thus capable of being carried out as entrenched embodied habits without any need for deliberate thought or concentration.[42] Once there is no longer any need for conscious thought about *how* to conduct the ritual, we are considerably less likely to wonder *why* we have to do it in a particular way.[43] Consequently, routinization of ritual procedures tends to be associated with the suppression of exegetical rumination (the 'giving up' response). At the same time, frequently-performed rituals provide opportunities for the reiteration of official exegesis, thus making us more susceptible to the learning of standardized and widely shared interpretive meanings. In some traditions, the guardians of doctrinal orthodoxy may despair of the laity's apparent sloth and ignorance in matters of exegesis and try to prod them into thinking more deeply about such matters (perhaps coercing out of the hapless mouths of participants 'off-the-cuff' responses that, more often than not, may be ridiculed or dismissed).

A very different pattern of exegetical thinking tends to accompany rituals that are rarely performed. For reasons we must put aside here,[44] low-frequency rituals typically involve comparatively high levels of emotional arousal. In many cases, such as initiation rites and the climactic ceremonies of millenarian cults, a person undergoes the rituals only once in a lifetime (although they may subsequently help to orchestrate such rites for others) and the experience is likely to be highly traumatic. For instance, we know from ethnographic research in regions like Melanesia, Amazonia, Aboriginal Australia, and Africa that traditional forms of initiation may involve terrifying ordeals (including beatings, bodily mutilation or scarification, burning, and coerced participation in acts that would normally be considered immoral, unacceptable and disgusting, such as cannibalism, ritualized homicide, and so on).[45] For most or all peoples, not only are these kinds of experiences intrinsically shocking, but sometimes the element of sadism is greatly emphasized and the tortures exacerbated through the use of trickery, blindfolding, threatening, and scapegoating. Participation in such rituals is capable of triggering long-term rumination on questions of meaning in a way that participation in more humdrum, routinized rituals is not. Initiates assume that there must be good reason for having to endure such ordeals but the meanings of the ritual tortures and privations are tantalizingly opaque. Somewhere in the details of what occurs and the cryptic murmurings of the initiators, clues must be buried. The initiate thus embarks on a lifetime of potentially irresolveable ruminations, a process of exegetical reflection that may unfold in fits and spurts but never entirely fades.

Ritual ordeals can thus provide a stimulus for spontaneous exegetical reflection. And there are undoubtedly other routes to such an outcome. In some cases, the analogue of participation in a highly arousing, shocking, and personally consequential collective ritual may be found in a more personal and solitary experiences.

A state of delirium, a brain seizure, a close shave with death or an apparently miraculous intervention or visitation, for instance, might well have similar effects. These are the kinds of episodes that one tends to remember and reflect upon. Like rituals, they may have puzzling components that trigger a search for intentional meaning – why did this happen to me, at that particular time and place, with such-and-such a set of consequences? The sensation that there must be an agent behind it all is a natural consequence of our 'mindreading' minds. But it is also the kind of question to which doctrinal systems may supply ready-made answers. Often, they provide a schematized framework for the interpretation of such experiences, which may by turns enfold our experience and give it meaning or fail to deliver a satisfactory solution and drive us on to further acts of doctrinal creativity.

The two routes to religious innovation just outlined also generate distinct modes of storage and transmission. The reiteration of a creed, through repetitive sermonizing and the continual re-reading of sacred texts, leads to the storage of standardized narratives, dogmas, and exegetical commentaries in *semantic memory*.[46] Information of this kind, codified in language, is ideally suited to efficient transmission across wide areas by potentially quite small numbers of proselytizing individuals (e.g. priests, missionaries, prophets, gurus, and messianic leaders). As long as the Word is subject to frequent reiteration in the far-flung locations to which it spreads, people will readily notice when unauthorized versions are proposed. And if mechanisms for policing the orthodoxy can be introduced, heretical innovation can be punished and suppressed. In general, determined innovators can only succeed by setting up rival organizations of their own, often via processes of schism and splintering. By contrast, the kinds of revelations generated by traumatic rituals are much more costly and difficult to spread or to regulate. They are hard to spread because they arise out of forms of collective action rather than individual oratory or the written word. Transmission across populations generally requires either contiguous contagion or wholesale migration and carries great risk of mutation of both the practices and their meanings as the tradition spreads. And because the mysteries behind the rituals can only be divined through personal reflection and revelation, creative outputs tend to be diverse and idiosyncratic. If there is no forum for public rehearsal or inscription of these outputs, they remain esoteric (as personal or localized mystical exegesis and cosmology). The best chance of preserving such knowledge is to convert it into a more routinized orthodoxy, and so there is often a dynamic interaction between these two modes of religious innovation and transmission.

The above features form aspects of two distinctive 'modes of religiosity' which I refer to as 'doctrinal' and 'imagistic' respectively.[47]

Both independently and jointly these modes of religiosity facilitate the creative elaboration of our most exotic and cumulatively intricate religious ideas. Our exceptional capacities as a species for cross-domain analogical thinking and inductive reasoning provide the motor driving innovation, given appropriate triggering mechanisms, while our capacity for semantic memory provides the principal means of storing those innovations, given the necessary conditions of doctrinal reiteration and institutional routinization.

The evolution and history of religion

So how are we to connect the *universal religious repertoire*, deriving from our evolutionary heritage, and the great *diversity of religious thinking and behaviour*, that derives from distinctive histories of innovation and transmission?

A simple but powerful way of envisaging the role of evolution and history in religion is to think of the entire process as a sort of 'ratchet effect'.[48] A ratchet does two things: it *turns* a bolt so that it moves progressively into its thread but it also *holds* the bolt in place so that the tool remains connected to it. The holding function is the equivalent of our evolutionary heritage, which remains constant across the world's cultural environments. Regardless of local histories of cultural innovation and transmission, our fixed, generic cognitive capacities churn out more or less the same kinds of religious outputs in all places and at all times (the 'universal religious repertoire'). Insofar as this is a creative process, it is only minimally so, in much the same way that small variations in birdsong or in tool use among chimpanzees might be seen as an outcome of creativity. To say that we are always 'reinventing the wheel' is to understate the situation, since the universal religious repertoire is certainly more ancient than the wheel and has probably been reinvented many more times. By contrast, the turning of the bolt is equivalent to the cumulative effects of history through which more rarified religious ideas are created, stored, and passed on. Such ideas are more 'rarified' in the sense that they are relatively hard to cognize and thus require special care and attention (e.g. techniques of public reiteration or codification in sacred texts) if they are to endure. Notions of the Christian Holy Trinity or the Noble Truths of Buddhist scholarship, for instance, are too distant from our intuitive ways of thinking to stand much chance of independent invention or indeed to survive in the absence of pedagogic support or external mnemonics.[49]

The universal religious repertoire may have emerged around the time of the cultural explosion about 50,000 years ago,[50] though some writers attribute concepts of supernatural agency to archaic *homo sapiens* and even to some earlier hominid species.[51] The emergence of the *imagistic mode* is probably rather more recent, though it certainly pre-dates the first appearance of the doctrinal mode and by a very substantial margin. Some evidence of imagistic practices can be found as far back as the Upper Paleolithic,[52] whereas the doctrinal mode appears probably no less recently than 6,000 years ago.[53] Thus, whereas *intuitive* religious thinking is at least as old as our fully-modern species, imagistic and (subsequently) doctrinal modalities of transmission, seem to have emerged during *historical* rather than *evolutionary* time. Nowadays, all three ways of acquiring and transmitting religion are widely distributed in the world's religious traditions. And these three modalities of transmission inevitably influence each other.

Consider the following example. All religious traditions dominated by the doctrinal mode by definition incorporate highly repetitive forms of ritual and oratory. Under certain conditions, this kind of routinization can give rise to boredom and lowered motivation (what's become known as the 'Tedium Effect').[54] In conditions of demoralization, techniques of policing the orthodoxy typically become less effective, resulting in the emergence and spread of more intuitive ideas and practices. Whenever this drift towards the universal religious repertoire becomes sufficiently entrenched within a doctrinal tradition we tend to find a backlash in the form of movements of doctrinal reform. Often these entail high levels of religious excitement, triggering imagistic-type revelations and a rejuvenation of doctrinal authority. Once the religious police are back in power, we see a return to routinization. Many aspects of this pattern were famously described by Max Weber and a variety of other distinguished scholars.[55] What we now have in prospect, though, is a cognitive explanation for these phenomena.

Conclusions

Marett and his colleagues recognized that the causes of religious continuities and differences around the world and over time were to be explained in terms of a combination of evolved psychological universals and historically contingent ecological contexts. The extent to which we will be able to demonstrate this in detail, and thereby truly to *explain* religion (and other cultural phenomena), will depend in part on how successfully anthropologists can connect their empirical and theoretical activities and ambitions to those of neighbouring sciences. Concerted efforts are also needed *within* our discipline. In Marett's day, highly erudite and learned scholars could very nearly master *all* the information available on patterns of variation in a field such as religion (the extraordinary accomplishments of Sir James Frazer, for instance, spring to mind). Nowadays, however, this is unthinkable. It is difficult enough for anthropologists to keep abreast of findings in their own specialist areas of regional and topical interest, let alone to command expert knowledge of the ethnographic record as a whole. Consequently, comparative anthropology must increasingly become a collaborative enterprise.

An example of the direction in which I believe we need to go is provided by recent projects designed to test and refine the 'modes of religiosity' theory. This work[56] has generated startling new discoveries about the way doctrinal and imagistic modes affect each other, and are in turn affected by more cognitively optimal religious practices.[57] Because of the explanatory potential of these sorts of theories, the cognitive science of religion has become a rapidly expanding field over the last fifteen years. There is now a growing demand for postgraduate training in this area and funding bodies are increasingly supporting this kind of research. Publishers are rapidly establishing new journals and textbooks on cognition and culture,[58] and there is also scope for the creation of new projects and centres for the scientific study of cultural phenomena.[59] I think Robert Ranulph Marett would have approved of at least some of these developments. The question is whether *contemporary* anthropologists will see the potential that lies before us – and join the revolution.

Notes

1. This chapter is based on the Marett Lecture presented at the University of Oxford on 16 September 2005, as part of the Oxford Anthropology Centenary Celebrations and while I was at the time Director of The Institute of Cognition and Culture, Queen's University, Belfast. I thank Exeter College and the Institute of Social and Cultural Anthropology, at the University of Oxford, for inviting me to present the lecture.
2. Hirshfeld 1996.
3. Although any such potential would need to be offset against the moral arguments for disposing of the material in a manner commensurate with the wishes of those who originally provided it.
4. According to Tooby and Cosmides, our fate is already sealed: 'mainstream sociocultural anthropology has arrived at a situation resembling some nightmarish short story Borges might have written, where scientists are condemned by their unexamined assumptions to study the nature of mirrors only by cataloguing and investigating everything that mirrors can reflect. It is an endless process that never makes progress, that never reaches closure, that generates endless debate between those who have seen different reflected images, and whose enduring product is voluminous descriptions of particular phenomena' 1992: 42.

5. A sentiment echoed by Morphy, this volume.
6. Marrett 1917, 1920, 1929.
7. Baillargeon 1987; Baillargeon and Hanko-Summers 1990; Spelke 1991.
8. Keil 1986, Atran 1990.
9. Barkow, Cosmides, and Tooby 1992; Mithen 1996.
10. Baillargeon 1987; Gelman 1988; Massey & Gelman 1988; Mandler, Bauer, and McDonough 1991; Gopnik, Meltzov, and Kuhl 1999.
11. Farah and Wallace 1992, Hillis and Caramazza 1991.
12. For a discussion, see Hirshfeld 1996.
13. Stewart 2005.
14. Boyer 2001a.
15. Boyer 1990, 1992, 1993, 1994a, 1994b, 1996, 2001a, 2001b.
16. Boyer and Ramble 2001.
17. Boyer 2001a.
18. Carey 1985, Wellman 1990, Leslie 1994, Bloom 2000.
19. Dunbar 1998.
20. Williams, Whiten, Suddendorf and Perrett 2000.
21. Baron-Cohen, Tager-Flusberg and Cohen 2000.
22. Baron-Cohen 1995.
23. Some anthropologists (e.g. Lutz 1985) and psychologists (e.g. Miller 1984) have argued that ToM is significantly influenced by cultural differences but we require very much more rigorous and systematic research on the topic before much on the subject can be said with any confidence.
24. Bering, McLeod and Shackelford (in press); Bering, Hernández-Blasi and Bjorklund (in press); Bering and Johnson (1994).
25. Boyer 2001; Barrett 2004.
26. Stewart 2005.
27. Meltzoff 1995; Johnson 2000.
28. Guthrie 1993.
29. See for instance Barrett 2004.
30. Turiel 1983.
31. Nichols 2004.
32. Nucci 1986.
33. A primate analogy would be the presentation of status and rank.
34. Mayr 1976; see also Tooby and Cosmides 1992.
35. Catchpole and Slater 1995.
36. Povinelli 2000.
37. Early attempts to demonstrate this, for instance in the form of the 'Sapir-Whorf Hypothesis' did not provide strong evidence for the shaping effects of varying cultural/linguistic (or, more broadly, ecological) contexts on cognition (D'Andrade 1995: 182–83). Subsequent assertions in support of cognitive relativism, for instance in relation to the development of emotions (Harré 1986, Heelas 1986), theory of mind (Lutz 1985, Miller 1984), the learning of embodied skills (Toren 2001) and other core areas of psychology have so far lacked precise and rigorous substantiation. Much more research is needed on this topic before any firm conclusions can be reached.
38. These differences in the creative process have their analogue in other kinds of human endeavour (Eysenck 1995).
39. Humprey and Laidlaw 1994.
40. Bloch 1974, 2004.
41. On the connections between personality and creativity, see Eysenck 1993; for a general consideration of this issue in relation to religious thinking, see Berner 2004.
42. Whitehouse 2004.

43. Some preliminary experimental support for this claim has been gathered (Whitehouse 2004: 83, fn.11) although the main basis for this claim is based on ethnographic observation (Whitehouse 1995).
44. Whitehouse 2005.
45. For ethnographic examples, see Lowie 1924, Turnbull 1962, Meggitt 1962, Allen 1967, Strehlow 1970, Barth 1975, 1987, Tuzin 1980, Herdt 1981, 1982, Verswijver 1992.
46. The distinction between semantic and episodic memory was first advanced by Tulving (1972) and has subsequently given rise to a very substantial body of research (for an overview, see Baddeley 1997: Chapter 20).
47. Whitehouse 1995, 2000, 2004
48. A phrase I adapt from Tomascello (1999) for rather different purposes here.
49. Recent experiments suggest that levels of repetition necessary for successful transmission of the Four Noble Truths of Buddhism to naïve adults (non-Buddhist undergraduate students) are remarkably high (Whitehouse 2004: 84, fn.21).
50. Mithen 1996.
51. Mania and Mania 1988.
52. Whitehouse 2000; see also: Lewis-Williams 1997 and Pfeiffer 1982.
53. Whitehouse 2000.
54. Whitehouse 2004.
55. Max Weber (1930, 1947); see also Benedict 1935; Gellner 1969; Goody 1968, 1986, 2004; Turner 1974; Lewis 1971; Werbner 1977; Barth 1990, 2002.
56. Sponsored in the UK by the British Academy, the University of Cambridge, and Queen's University Belfast and in the USA by the Templeton Foundation, Emory University, and the University of Vermont (for further details, see http: //www.qub.ac.uk/fhum/banp).
57. See in particular Whitehouse and Laidlaw 2004, Whitehouse and Martin 2004, Whitehouse and McCauley 2005.
58. For details of the Cognitive Science of Religion book series at AltaMira Press, see: http://www.altamirapress.com/series/; for details of the *Journal of Cognition and Culture*, see: http://www.ingentaconnect.com/content/brill/jocc.
59. These include the Institute of Cognition and Culture at Queen's University Belfast (http: //www.qub.ac.uk/icc/), the Centre for Religion and Cognition at the University of Groningen http://religionandcognition.com/crc/), The International Association for the Cognitive Science of Religion (http://www.iacsr.com/), The Mind and Society in the Transmission of Religion Project at the Academy of Finland (http://www.mv.helsinki.fi/home/ipyysiai/Project%20second_page_1.htm), and the Religion, Cognition, and Culture Project at Aarhus University (http: //www.teo.au.dk/en/research/current/cognition).

Chapter 10

THE VISCERAL IN THE SOCIAL: THE CROWD AS PARADIGMATIC TYPE

David Parkin

Two developments in anthropology occurring in the late twentieth and early twenty first centuries affected the relationship between the social and the biological. First, there was a resurgence in kinship studies, prompted both by Schneider's early ideas (1984) and by later anthropological scrutiny of the new reproductive and stem cell technologies (e.g. Strathern 1991; Franklin 1997; Edwards 2000; Franklin and McKinnon 2001). Strathern actually refers to this as the 'new kinship' (1991: Acknowledgements). As in Carsten (2000; 2003), it can be summarised as to do with how physical ties are seen by a people to develop after birth and over time through the sharing of food, shelter, and practices, and, I would add, objects, rather than just through descent or blood ties. This relatedness incurred through sharing rather than descent is said nevertheless to create a kind of consubstantiality – a physical entity. So, while genealogy is largely discarded, corporeal physical density is substituted. It is not, however, claimed that this is in any way an approach from biological anthropology nor indeed that it is in some sense a biological phenomenon. Carsten's edited volume of 2000 is entitled *Cultures of relatedness*, and, like other studies of this time (e.g. Bamford 2004; Howell 2003; Storrie 2003; Bestard 2004), in fact wishes to dissolve any distinction between biological and socio-cultural, however much they may vary in their understanding of cultures of relatedness.

A second development is a reconsideration of ideas formerly dismissed as deterministic socio-biology. In part, Darwinian evolutionary theory in the last two decades of the twentieth century was presented as a way of understanding social behaviour, in two forms. One is evolutionary anthropology, which looks at foraging strategies, mate choices, marriage practices, parental investment patterns, strategic use of energy and how to maximise genetic representation in future generations. The other is the use of a kind of evolutionary psychology with, as an example, Pascal Boyer looking at human cognition as a way of explaining, for instance, the cognitive 'naturalness' of religious ideas (1994b), and Harvey Whitehouse explaining religiosity as based on divergent cognitive modes (2000; 2004) . A key background text is the 1999 volume edited by Knight, Dunbar and Power, entitled *The Evolution of Culture*, which also wants to explain within a general evolutionary approach such anthropological phenomena as the emergence of language, symbolism, ritual, gender ideologies, magico-religious myths, totemism and taboo.

Alongside these two developments, Ingold, in 2004a, emphasises the epistemological priority of relationality over genealogy as explaining not only social interaction but also social and human evolution itself. His idea of relationality does not follow straight genealogical lines but 'is to be envisaged as a dense and tangled cluster of interlaced threads or filaments, any point in which can be connected to any other ... [It] allows us to conceive of a world in movement, wherein every part or region enfolds, in its growth, its relations with all the others' (Ingold 2004a: 140).'

So, how might these different perspectives on the social, biological and psychological be linked? Are there concepts which, through such interlinking, give us the opportunity to rethink anthropology? My starting point is in fact the idea of there being non-genealogical cultures of relatedness based on consubstantial physicality. But I want to push this idea of relatedness further, by focusing on a population's moments of concentrated density in which bodily physicality and emotion temporarily transcend and sometimes destroy relatedness, despite being drawn from it. Biological and psychological insights become relevant, though we may need new vocabulary to describe them. One adjective that usefully describes all these features is 'visceral', both in its primary sense of referring to internal bodily organs and in its extended sense of physically felt emotion.

I wish to develop this sense of the visceral. It may first be approached through two key ideas: density of interaction and effervescence, the latter as made famous by Durkheim. They are not the same: density of interaction can in principle be measured, being either light or heavy. But it may, of course, be experienced differently in other cultures: in

Tokyo, in the vast crush of people on the main streets going to work, I never saw anyone making eye contact nor bumping into another person, nor talking. In London's main streets, people eye others, talk loudly, bump into each other and complain about the crowdedness. We cannot, in other words, assume a common response to a particular density. That is to say, a particular ratio of people to place does not by itself determine anything. Its effect is mediated by socio-cultural attitudes and responses to different levels of interactional density. Some of this variable effect is contained in Durkheim's notion of effervescence, which he also called *sur-excitation* and which sometimes took the form of an immense collective enthusiasm, presupposing the experience of what the people concerned regard as a high density of interaction.

But whereas interactional density can by itself be subject to some kind of 'objective' measure of relationships devoid of affect (i.e. there are in principle a limited number of relationships in a group of five people which we can count without worrying about their content), effervescence clearly denotes bodily or physical pressure and high emotional pitch, the experience of which is subject to particular socio-cultural understandings or interpretations . Let me deal with each notion in turn.

Density of interaction

In the apparent revival of interest in kinship as comprised by broad cultures of relatedness rather than as based on blood connectedness, the key feature for me is that of 'substance', rather than that of 'code' (cf. Schneider 1984). If we accept that substance comes from sharing (food, residence, relationships, objects), then sharing as a concept touches on that of 'participation' in the sense proposed by Lévy-Bruhl, whom I invoke in order to recapture something of an era in which the social was made up of what we would nowadays call overlapping psychological, cognitive and physiological assumptions. For Lévy-Bruhl, persons and objects are connected in a seamless way in the 'prelogical' mind through what he calls mystic relations. Yet, it is also clear that this connectedness concerns more than mental and mystic representations for it is made manifest in physical 'contact, transference, sympathy, telekinesis', force and struggle, as when a sleeping man is possessed by a combative or toiling spirit and wakes up 'stiff, unrefreshed, or with limbs aching from muscular rheumatism ...', or when his soul leaves him and he is left 'cold, pulseless, and apparently lifeless.' (Lévy-Bruhl 1926: 73–84). Tylor had talked of two 'biological problems' deeply impressing early humans, which they resolved through their belief in animism: namely how to reconcile life with death and how to explain the appearance in dreams of apparently autonomous humans (Tylor 1903: 428). While Lévy-Bruhl rejected Tylor's theory of animism, he clearly retained not only a psychological but also essentially a physical, bodily and hence biological idiom in his description of examples of participation. 'Participation', animism and cultures of relatedness thus all draw on notions of shared, physical substance in their collective representations. Substance is in this sense material, and indeed each concept presupposes the material coming together of parts that make the whole. Relatedness is, here, about materiality.

We can, moreover, talk of a high density of social relationships that takes on the experience of a materiality, which we might in English call pressure, oppressiveness, and heaviness (Parkin 1999). High density social interaction is of course a relative concept, for what is regarded as dense for one society or person is not necessarily for another, but situationally it has effect. It is akin to the feeling of something substantial, a kind of materiality. Sharing objects or resources adds to people's personae and so prosthetically reinforces their interaction. We can feel, and indeed be literally, weighed down, or shorn of space, by the objects and equipment shared by those close to us but which we cannot forsake and may depend on. In other words, substance, participation or sharing, and social density reinforce each other and point to an area of enquiry which transcends the concern with cultures of relatedness alone.

We might say that no phenomenon is entirely material, being always through the very fact of its recognition caught up in semantic webs. For Ardener, however, the two are conjoined and make up a semantic materiality, of varying densities (1982: 3–13). The cue was Whorf's famous examples of category confusion. Gasoline drums marked 'empty' (i.e. of liquid) are in fact full of explosive fumes, but people feel unthreatened (since 'empty' connotes absence of danger) and smoke cigarettes near them, resulting in accidents. This simple semantic confusion is literally explosive and clearly very much of the material world and not only a matter of mistaken verbal reference.

Speaking over a generation ago, Ardener also shows how the statistical is part of this semantic materiality and can be used to show differing density. A 'hand' in English hand-shaking stops at the wrist, but in Ibo the term to translate hand (*aka*) also includes the rest of the arm up to the shoulder and any part of it can be extended in handshaking. Mistakes between members of the two communities can occur. An Englishmen would interpret his upper arm or elbow being gripped in greeting as having a different meaning from if it was his hand. Statistically, you can say that English 'handshakes' are concentrated in the area of the hand while, for Ibo, they are dispersed along the arm (ibid). The example may be dated if it can be shown that more English greetings are nowadays of the Ibo type, which is also of course a statistical change (from concentrated to dispersed tactility).

If we can apply this notion of statistically measurable semantic materiality to hand-shaking, then we can certainly also do so with regard to densities of human interaction. Wahabi Muslim reformists object to the way Sufi commonly interlink arms, sing and dance or at least move their bodies together rhythmically at 'forbidden' celebrations of the Prophet's birthday, insisting instead that bodily distance and still posture should prevail at religious gatherings. Sociometry was once popular in 1950s American sociology and was intended to show how interaction developed along certain, ultimately predictable, paths. It can, however, be seen as semantically measurable, with differences and shifts occurring in people's understanding of their physical proximity and bodily engagement in interaction with each other. Kapferer's early study of factory workers in Zambia (1972) was called 'transactionalist', as befitted the prevailing theoretical direction, but could easily be rethought as illustrating measurable semantic materiality.

This is not to say that statistical measurement of interactions needs actually to be carried out by anthropologists nor that it provides an underlying truth upon which ideas and words are built. That would be to fall into the old trap of privileging the material and measurable as determining the social and linguistic. The social and material go together, and are in fact semantic materiality as defined above. In this going-together, persistent arcs and concentrations of transactions and interactions of the kind meticulously analysed by Kapferer, and technically measurable, are always likely to be interpreted within terms that confirm or confront existing convention. They are never socially and semantically neutral.

The point of this and many other instances of variations in people's understanding of interactional density is that it extends the notion of substance with regard to cultures of relatedness. The substance shared is not just food and residence but includes the interactional space, speed, angle, and direction of bodies relating to each other through identified spatial co-ordinates. It is biological to the extent that it refers to the shaping, posturing and directional course not just of individual but of mutually interrelated human bodies, which, as life-forms, are affected by their shared density. Consider, for instance, the well-known instance of gradual conformity to a shared menstrual cycle by fecund co-resident, interacting women, which may have had radical implications even for human cultural evolution, as well as immediate social organisation (Knight 1991; Power 1999). Or, inversely, the different understandings of and responses to 'crowding', and thence riots and violence (Tambiah 1996), which I will be addressing, or, again, the frequency and nature of communal rituals as providing rationed sources of protein through feasting on animals (Rappaport 1968; but see also 1984). How much communal conformity and conflict arise from different interactional densities, and what are the effects, if any, on conception and reproduction, and how are these noticed and talked about? The fact that humans may interpret such densities through language, gesture and representation, as well as through physical response, does not detract from the biological quality of such ecology of interaction, which is to that extent both social and biological.

A conventional view of biology as sharing blood (kinship) or exchanging it (reproduction and affinity) in the interests of social and species perpetuity is not, however, to be dismissed. It is, after all, the aspect of biology which, through modern technology, continues to be, and is increasingly privileged as, the basis of parental rights in Euro-America, if not always elsewhere. Social definitions of 'kinship' used to be an awkward entry-point into this aspect of biological understanding, for anthropologists could not be sure that the *pater* was the *genitor*, nor sometimes the *pater* himself. They might then say the distinction was irrelevant if the society itself did not make it. In fact, even when social rather than physical fatherhood was the formally recognised principle, the 'horror' entailed in incest in some societies (Goody 1956) suggests that rights in women's reproduction were a greater matter of concern than was always recognised. In principle, DNA testing can nowadays clarify who begets whom, a right now accorded to males in Britain who have doubts or curiosity about their own fatherhood, and with some mind-boggling social implications that will extend the debates arising from the new reproductive technologies.

Such DNA testing may also make more interesting the finding that certain primates, including humans, can through smell identify close kin and so, though it has not been demonstrated, avoid mating with them (Porter and Moore 1981; Dunbar 1994: 773–74). Logically, tracing such trails of smells, along with DNA testing, could amount to a new kind of genealogical reckoning behind which false, manipulated or mistaken spoken or written genealogies could not always hide. The biological would comprise the social.

However, the effect on us and our lives through different interactional densities may be regarded as also a part of biology. It is not always to do with ecologically and nutritionally influenced human procreation nor staged growth. But it is to do with bodily responses and developments that may sometimes have life-altering consequences, extending to evolution itself. Thus, to what extent does a shared menstrual cycle create or express female solidarity in opposition to men and affect modes and rates of reproduction? How much does claustrophobic stress exacerbate disease, or repeated communal violence shape somatic responses to the possibility of death or injury? In some parts of the world children die because their parents are both unknowing carriers of the gene (for haemoglobin S) sometimes leading to sickle-cell anaemia. Compared with groups lacking the gene, does this genetic proclivity significantly reinforce fears and beliefs in the culturally illicit mixing of blood-lines between prohibited members of a group, or what we translate as incest? Conversely, does repeated and prolonged religious enthusiasm elevate endorphins and aid health, in the same way that well-being occurs through laughing, running, swimming, cycling, eating and breastfeeding, or among males whose testosterone levels increase when successfully competing against other males?

These questions are about endocrine systems under neurological control but are also about interactional densities detracting from or, sometimes, helping health and fecundity, and hence are questions about life, death, and social continuity. They are also about cognition, for people develop concepts to deal with them. They may encompass but go beyond bare questions of energy inputs and expenditure. Even the field of energetics itself in biological anthropology, while concerned with the measurable inputs of nutrition and energy expenditure (Ulijaszek 1995), reveals unexpected responses to crisis. For instance, in a large group with high interaction among its members, the energy costs of sexual reproduction are not just a matter of women producing gametes, gestation, lactation and childcare, and of men providing gametes, courtship, childcare, and triumphing over other males. Dilemmas enter. A woman who takes reproductive advantage of a genetically well-endowed male who will move on to other females may jeopardize her chances of settling with another male seeking a long-term union and helping with childcare. For his part, the long-term male strategist has to balance his strategy of offering long-term care against the chances of being cuckolded by a male offering better genes and sex, which can easily happen in large groups of men and women (Key and Aiello 1999: 22–27). Again, energetics can indicate how low intake of food among groups of children, as in famines or through denial, may diminish their propensity and inclination for robust and prolonged play, apparently in the interest of conserving nutrition for body growth. But, conversely, severely enforced activity, such as intensive child labour, uses up the energy and reduces body growth. This is, then, not just a case of low input mechanically resulting in either reduced activity or impaired bodily development, but of relational densities and speed of interaction (such as frequency and intensity of labour or play) being brought into the equation in ways that we would otherwise define as social, ecological and, given the grief and distress of famines and enforced labour, emotional. Indeed, Key and Aiello suggest with regard to their analysis of male and female strategies of reproduction 'that emotions such as love and guilt may play a very important role in maintaining cooperative bonds between males and females by constraining the temptation to give in to the benefits of short-term matings' (Key and Aiello 1999: 27).

Effervescence and the visceral

In these senses, it becomes difficult and irrelevant to separate the biological from the social, with the result that 'socio-biological' becomes the compromise if clumsy term. It is because the socio-biological is in fact caught up in webs of emotion and semantic materiality, that I prefer to call it the visceral (Parkin 1999; see also Taussig 2003).

In meaning both the insides of the physical body and the 'inner states' of emotional expression, 'visceral' transcends the distinction between biological and social. Let me add a third sense of referring to what goes on between as well as within bodies. This enables the term also to denote connections between people. According to this definition, the visceral then treats the emotional as a physical rather than bodily disconnected mental condition, and, through its third sense, as extended to and shared by others. With echoes here of Marriott's famous co-resident Brahmins as similarly joined up through shared physical and moral particles (1976), we can here consider Durkheim's concept of 'effervescence'.

Durkheim brought physical and bodily explanations into his use of this notion to account for sentiments of religion and morality much more than has been acknowledged. This neglect is probably because two other strands of the argument have been emphasised instead: the moral and the emotional. First is the standard view that such social effervescence as collective religious enthusiasm induces adepts to think of themselves as a discrete moral grouping through their recurrent worship of and identification with a totemic emblem of divinity, culminating in what Chau calls an 'intense sociality' (Chau 2006: 158). The second is that, although Durkheim was allegedly 'anti-psychologistic' in explaining the social only in terms of the social (e.g. suicide corresponding with such social status as widowhood, bachelorhood, or religious persuasion and not with the suicide's state of mind), effervescence presupposes the emotional condition of collective sacred identification, even though Durkheim hardly ever used the term emotion itself (Pickering forthcoming). While his Cartesian stance separates the physicality of the human body from its emotions, a non-Cartesian review of his data indicates that emotional, socio-religious and moral factors merge with those of the body and physicality to explain effervescence. Let us go back to Durkheim himself to see the role of physicality in his ideas (see especially 1957 [1915]: 188–223).

His notion of effervescence is informed by what he sees as a human belief in an immanent, impersonal life force or vital principle (*mana*) which pervades men, their totemic animals and images, and inspires sentiments of fear, respect, attachment and morality, which in turn reinforce such belief. The force is not, however, an abstract idea but is an energy which is imagined as the material form of a vegetable or animal species. 'When we say that these principles are forces, we do not take the word in a metaphorical sense; they act just like veritable forces. In one sense, they are even material forces which engender physical effects. ... But in addition to this physical aspect, they also have a moral character' (Durkheim 1915: 190). The life-force is then variously 'energy', 'physical' and 'biological' (ibid: 224) as well as moral and emotion-laden. Mauss also emphasised the materiality of the principles in early humans: 'A l'origine, l'homme se représente non comme un principe immortel, mais comme une chose éminemment permissible et mobile ... dont dépend la vie du peuple et celle de la nature' (Mauss 1968: 130). Nor is this generative, vital force confined to totemism, for its ambiguous and transformable physical and moral ordering also informs the so-called 'advanced religions', and charges a high God with the task of being both cosmic guardian and judge of human conduct (Durkheim 1915: 190). Human experience of the force, which is sometimes likened by Durkheim to electricity, is not only religious. 'There are periods in history when, under the influence of some great collective shock, social interactions have become much more frequent and active. Men look for each other and assemble together more often than ever. That general effervescence results which is characteristic of revolutionary or creative epochs' (ibid: 210–11). Effervescence, whether religious or otherwise, 'often reaches such a point that it causes unheard-of actions. The passions released are of such an impetuosity that they can be restrained by nothing' (ibid: 216).

In his monumental study of Durkheim, Lukes gives limited attention to the notions of effervescence and the life-force with which it associated. Lukes is content with Durkheim's partial description of effervescence as those 'periods of creation and renewal' (when) 'men are brought into more intimate relations with one another, when meetings and assemblies are more frequent, relationships more solid and the exchange of ideas more active' (Lukes 1973: 422; and cf. Turner 1969: 95–96 on 'communitas'). In selecting these relational aspects of Durkheim's definition, Lukes reflects the explanatory language of 'social determination', prevalent in the 1970s when his book was published. We might nowadays question what the very idea of the 'social' really means beyond being a convenient, short-hand notation for people in institutionally bounded sets of relationships. 'Social determination' suggests the social as an engine which pushes the non-social, whatever that is, into shape. It has continuing value in countering theories of individualism which ignore history and the pressure of events. But another view of the social is that it is also irreducible ideas and motivations, which are not to be regarded as epiphenomena of the social. The concept conveys, moreover, nothing of the ideas of passion and physical force as also used by Durkheim in his descriptions, which indicate a biological and material element in his view of social interaction. Interestingly, various commentators on Durkheim writing between 1937 and 1948 are castigated by Lukes for having interpreted Durkheim's *The division of labour* as a 'biologistic' rather than sociological explanation of change through differentiation. And while Lukes is right to reject any view of demographic change as a 'purely "biological" process' (Lukes 1973: 168, including footnote 47), the factors of increasing relational density through the growth, migration and concentration of populations in cities, identified by Durkheim as concomitant with increasing moral density, inevitably have visceral, or biological and emotional repercussions, some deemed negative for life and health and some positive.

This sets up two possible directions. One is to explore the bodily relatedness of crowds and other examples of effervescence, and the other is to pursue the course of emotional expression associated with effervescence. As well as subsuming what was once distinguished as the social and biological, this should allow the idea of the visceral to emerge as an autonomous process and hence field of enquiry.

The crowd as paradigmatic type

A recent substantial anthropological study of crowds is that of Tambiah (1996) on ethnic and nationalist conflicts and violence in South Asia. This study of nearly four hundred pages stands out among many other anthropological studies of ethnicity for its preparedness to grapple with the graphically and visually unpalatable side of ethno-nationalism. By contrast, many studies of ethnicity place such analytical emphasis on ethnic quests for identity, competition for resources, cultural misunderstanding and intolerance, and colonial or nationalist marginalisation, that we forget that the associated violence is sometimes of the most horrendous and brutal kind. It may need to be explained as, at some point, autonomously self-perpetuating, however much precipitated by ethnic or, say, religious tensions. And lest Tambiah might be accused of seeming to indicate that violent crowd riots are a predominantly South Asian feature, he makes clear that what he is describing is found over time everywhere, including the French Revolution and, when he was writing, Northern Ireland, and other examples from Europe.

As Tambiah's use of the English term 'crowd' indicates, its meaning tends towards the negative and connotes destructiveness, as in riot crowd, though, not, as he says, necessarily a lack of purposiveness, for even during the course of riots many people are systematic about what they loot, which categories of people or property they attack, and generally when to stop in the face of superior opposition. He recognises also that, following Durkheim's characterisation of effervescence, we can talk of the euphoria of crowds as well as their destructiveness . Le Bon's earlier study of 1895 viewed them quite differently, as only ever destructive, though Durkheim may not have known it since he does not cite it. While Tambiah does not share Le Bon's right-wing distrust of democracy and socialism, he does incline to the perspective on crowds (*les foules*) as tending towards the destructive.

The term *crowd* in English, derived from the old German *kruden* (to press or hasten), commonly refers to a wide range of positive and negative instances of effervescence and is at best an odd-job word, for which an equivalent in many non-European languages is not always easily found. An impression is that many non-European terms for crowd in fact denote excitable but essentially benign assemblies. Chau refers to the Chinese terms *hunguo, renao,* and *lauziat* as of this kind, and, citing other anthropologists, other non-Chinese words as similarly positive, including the Sherpa *hlermu,* the Balinese *ramé,* and other Indonesian terms (2006: 149–51. To these we might add the African Bantu concept of *ngoma,* which, while conventionally translated as drum, in fact commonly refers to groups of people enthusiastically and/or excitedly gathered for dance, song and healing and other rituals (Janzen 1992). Other Bantu terms denote assemblies whose positive or negative nature has to be defined situationally.

While mindful of all these inevitable variations, the English term *crowd* can be taken as paradigmatically suggesting a collective entity standing between enduring forms of assembly on the one hand, and very *ad hoc* gatherings on the other, i.e. between formally constituted social organisations and loosely brought together masses of people. This intermediary idea of the crowd is reinforced by an observation that Tambiah makes with regard to his South Asian examples. He notes that riot crowds tend to recur, being part of wider solidarities, divisions and conflicts, but that 'they are also mercifully short-lived, not only because after an initial period of chaos and paralysis, the police and army can assert their dominance, but also because as human outbursts these riots have a short life cycle of orgasmic violence and spent energies' (Tambiah 1996: 215), after which people normally return to the routine of their daily lives. The visceral idiom is further supported by a citation (unreferenced) from Marx, who asks why conflicts between ethnic and nationalist groups 'should culminate in brutal contradiction, the shock of body against body. ...' (Tambiah 1996: 220). Canetti (1984) and Buford (1992) are also cited for indicating how in the density of the crowd people overcome their fear of being bodily touched by strangers, and how at a tense football match for instance, the physical pressure of bodies against each other is emotionally constitutive of the occasion. Chau (2006: 148–56) describes the benign Chinese concept of *honghuo* (or *renao*) as 'social heat', which is generated as crowds gather at special events, to be likened, he says, to the compressed molecular creation of physical heat, and becoming also emotional, passionate and feverish. As Tambiah puts it pithily, 'a physically dense crowd also produces a psychic density' (1996: 274).

In formal assemblies, body-persons occupy their allocated spaces and obey the regulations imposed on them. Does adherence to such regulations preclude collective effervescence? One of the most impressive sights is that of hundreds and in some cases thousands of Muslim males assembled for prayer in or at some of the world's great mosques. Despite the large numbers, there are interludes of absolute silence between prayers, and also overall bodily co-ordination, symmetry and set distance in the various movements that prescribe the *salat*, which include the requirement that each worshipper periodically bows and greets the companion on either side of him (Parkin 2000: 142). This regulated structure hardly seems to conform to Durkheim's idea of vibrant effervescence. And yet, the emotional tension and believed spiritual power of such vast and regulated worship suggest that such communal prayer is, so to speak, the alter-ego of effervescence, held in check and yet capable of switching to a much more viscerally charged gathering. This we can observe in my earlier example of the bodily interlinking of arms, the up-and-down bobbing of celebrants, their fingers pointed up to God, and the chanting and singing, such as occur at a Sufi *maulidi* festival commemorating the Prophet's or a saint's birthday, much condemned by radical Muslim opponents for being, among other reasons, false mortal rather than divine worship and so 'undisciplined' and out of control. In fact, the question of the control over people's bodily emotionalism in worship is really what is at issue, with the Sufi wishing to retain it and their opponents wishing to wrest it from them. Non-religious occasions are also sometimes contested in the same way. European soccer crowds are for the most part relatively benign, considering the conditions under which they come together, but their evident capacity to tilt over into violence, even when involving a tiny minority of perpetrators, characterises them as always likely to get out of control. While for Durkheim effervescence describes how human assemblies build or re-enact communally experienced religious affirmation through belief in the power of a common symbol, we can also note its cyclical ambivalence as sometimes controlling but as sometimes controlled by those undergoing its effects.

Crowds can be thought of similarly, as at one point alternating between fear and aggressive panic and perpetrating 'orgasmic and agonistic violence', as Tambiah puts it (1996: 215, 223, and *passim*), and at another, experiencing moments of excited and enthusiastic communion by reference to, say, a common icon or theme believed to represent them.

Ethnic, national and religious communities become essentialised through the polarisation of conflicts between them, so that their many day-to-day internal differences, and even the autonomy of individuals, are put aside during the passion and violence of actual conflict. We need not resort here to explanation in terms of 'primordial' ties. It is rather that the short-lived enthusiasms, hatreds and violence are borne along by a visceral charge that condenses the otherwise distinct pattern of relatedness that constitutes the community, suspending the specificity of obligations and turning interaction into mutual detraction.

In regard to the violence of riot crowds, Tambiah poignantly invokes the psychological explanation of social dissociation (ibid: 293–94). Persons merge their individual selfhoods with others in the crowd, depersonalise and reduce their victims to an ethnic or sectarian enemy stereotype, and in this altered state commit aggressive acts which would not happen in everyday life and from which, after the short duration of the attacks, they distance themselves, treating the event as not needing to be remembered nor brought into their sense of their core lives. It is a kind of partial, collective amnesia, in contrast to the often indelible trauma suffered by the victims. This is not a culture of relatedness but its antithesis, a bodily and emotional transcendence and even destruction of such a culture. And yet it relies upon an icon of relatedness beckoning attack. The psychological gloss is in fact partial, for the origins of violent impulse do not rest only in the perpetrators, as Tambiah acknowledges (1996: 236–39), for there will be wider, exacerbating socio-political conditions, those who manipulate existing and historical sensitivities, and those who put out false rumours which feed into burgeoning resentments. Perpetrators may blame or even justify their violence on ethno-nationalist opposition, which is in turn blamed on the perpetrators of violence, the personalised embodiments of opposition.

The crowd, at its negative extreme of riotous violence, is then bodies impacting on and through each other, expressed emotionally as fear, panic, resentment, anger and hatred, and perhaps later as guilt and remorse. While recognising the possible emergence of such antagonism, Durkheim has a generally more positive rendering of the sentiments in effervescence as the basis of religious conviction. It is a view of the benign crowd that we can sometimes extend to politics: in November 1989 I experienced the extraordinary euphoria and physical closeness that accompanied the fall of communism and the wall dividing East and West Berlin, as we clambered from the western side onto the wall, hands reaching out to help up complete strangers, others digging chunks out of it with picks, and the East German guards standing at ease, hands behind backs, smiling in response to the happy greetings of West Germans – the same guards who had previously been instructed to shoot anyone attempting to escape over the wall, and some of whose faces I remembered from the eastern side of the wall a couple of years earlier as grim icons of severity.

Durkheim had in mind more regular, alternating and hence differentiated assemblies based on relatedness (membership of a clan) expressed through representative totems and giving rise to the development of religious sentiment. To that extent he had in mind the beginnings of social institutions through repeated effervescence, which presupposes total institutions. The effervescence of crowds, as I have been understanding them, is less institutionally poised than this. Being only a refraction of wider social relatedness, it can be that of *ad hoc* gatherings with no institutional consequences or, if repeated in similar circumstances involving the same people, form a rudimentary institutional basis, even moving from antagonism to incorporation.

In fact, collective religious enthusiasm is as much agonistic as harmonious, as adepts alternately contest and reconcile emerging beliefs or compete to possess or control sacred objects. In other words, effervescence, like the crowd, is inherently ambivalent emotionally, able to switch moods through a combination of internal and external dynamism. Inscribed within the bodily constitution of the crowd, then, we have in effervescence the potential for schismogenesis, expressed as either bodily embrace or violence and always sheer physical energy. Tambiah again (1996: 304–5), points to the effect on athletes of their home crowd passionately urging them on to ever greater effort, sometimes successfully but sometimes meeting with failure, at which point the crowd's adulation can turn to venomous hostility. It is a process of inter-subjective stimulation, familiar in the to-and-fro rhetoric of preacher and congregation, which for Durkheim dialectically generates a 'real force' which may unite them or, we may add, split them in the face of disappointment.

Crowds, like effervescence, comprise bodily interaction (hands reaching out, shoulders pressed) and emotional ambivalence (alternately fear/anger and adoration). They are the fuzz and buzz around our more conventional ideas of relatedness as recognised paths of rights, duties, reciprocities and exactions. Crowds are not-yet or suspended culture and society, inconsistent or unclear as to whether they draw on existing social conventions and conflicts.

Discussion: the crowd as evolutionary turning point?

I have moved from the initial idea of a culture of relatedness through that of interactional density, to effervescence and to the crowd as a particular instance of visceral charge. Density of social interaction presupposes bodily and semantic materiality, the weight or indeed lightness of which are experienced physically and emotionally. Viscerally charged assemblies such as crowds may obscure as much as reaffirm relatedness, and, as riot crowds, deny it. The physical energy, force and passion that allows for religious transcendence is also that which eventuates in violence, political and religious.

The idioms of body, materiality, energy, force, and passion return us to Tylor's, Lévy-Bruhl's and Durkheim's invocation of biology, which, with psychology and physics, clearly influenced the language and thinking of these and other scholars at the end of the nineteenth and beginning of the twentieth century, even when, as in the case of Durkheim, sociological prevailed over psychological explanation. Psychology, biology and physics were the template for the developing sociology, especially that of the *Année sociologique*.

This seems nowadays again to be the case. Cognitive anthropology, and the cognitive sciences generally, draw on psychology, and sometimes neurology and biology (Deeley 2004), and analogies with physics are not uncommon. Tambiah himself apologetically but interestingly devotes a few pages on parallels 'pilfered from physics', such as the Doppler effect, and the theories known as catastrophy, chaos, and turbulence (Tambiah 1996: 291–96).

It might be argued that ideas borrowed analogically from another discipline remain only metaphorical explanatory aids and are not the 'real' thing, i.e. the original concept. But this is to assume a line of unambiguous closure between one discipline and another. Physics uses laboratory experiments and anthropology does not, and perhaps here the demarcation is clearest. Even so, a borrowed concept like chaos theory, while bereft of its application in physics, feeds into the borrowing epistemology, as in Spencer's explanation of change among pastoralists (Spencer 1974). The incorporation and abridgement of psychological concepts in anthropology is commonplace and, while not undermining its disciplinary distinctiveness (cf. Gluckman 1964), has clearly reshaped its methodological scope.

Taking this development further, I would see an anti-Cartesian position as treating psychology as part of biology (the mind and body understood as part of each other), and cognition as inextricably linked to emotions, especially nowadays when the production and operation of emotions are understood either in terms of functions of the social as well as physical brain (Dunbar 2003; Kringelbach 2005) or, as with smell, in terms of genetically influenced choices of mates. So, when anthropologists study emotions, even those collectively expressed as effervescence, they can acknowledge the possible route into physiological and neurological brain research, where psychologists and biologists also meet.

In his critical review of anthropological approaches to the study of emotions, Beatty (2005) advances the view of them as neither set in lexicon nor consistently derived from an understanding of human experience and nature, including inner states. Different cultures may cluster them in distinctive ways but, whatever the vocabulary denoting them, emotional expression and description come out of the pressures and persuasions that people are subject to in particular situations. Indeed, our own first experience of them among the peoples we study is during our fieldwork among them, rather than as based on pre-learned theoretical models applied in the field. Nor do emotions emanate from transcendental ideas unanchored in action. It is in the field that we observe the pressurised shaping of emotions through interaction, and yet we later convert such overt practices into the comparative cultural study of inner feelings and the words describing them, taking either a universalist, relativist or other theoretical stance. Beatty argues 'that we should remain agnostic about the subjective element of emotions and look closer at varying pragmatic contexts. This would entail a shift away from worrying about affect, and from inner/outer quandaries, to what I have called emotional practices', which include '... the patterned intimacies of kinship, the contagious, collective sentiments of ethnic and political violence, the cultural psychology of religion and ritual (from Durkheimian "effervescence" to Clifford Gertz's "moods and motivations")' (2005: 34). Beatty further refers to work on the cultivation of emotional states in religion as a basis of piety and to Tambiah on crowd fury (ibid: 35. footnote). This is consistent with a visceral understanding of relatedness, with its extended sense of the effect on each other of people's different bodily emotions and actions, and of undulating and alternating physical and psychic densities.

As an example, let me draw attention here to the strong links that biologists note between the emotions, the nose and its capacity to smell, and other aspects of human physiology, as instanced in potential mate arousal and selection. This illustrates well that a culture of relatedness, which will include on-going, socially prescribed marriage and sexual preferences and prohibitions, cannot help but engage, however fleetingly, with the genetically endowed odour elements of people in interaction: do you marry or have sex with persons that your nose tells you are genetically preferable or with the ones that society dictates? The socio-cultural may here sometimes reinforce the biological. But it may sometimes struggle with it, as when the use of perfumes, deodorants or women's contraceptive pill thwart and even reverse (as with contraceptive pills) the otherwise 'natural' emotional and physical response to scent-producing glands (which is for women to prefer men who are not close kin, that is to say, of a dissimilar genotype or MHC (major histocompatibility complex) to themselves (Wedekind et al 1995; Wedekind and Penn 2000)). Societies use different personal perfumes, to different extents and on different occasions, and in some cases hardly at all. Different uses of congruent and incongruent scents thus produce different emotional and social responses, which might at first be glossed as the biological and social trying to determine each other, but which in fact makes up the visceral charge between people. Like percussion, smell marks transition between events (Needham 1967; Howse 1991) and has its greatest effect when of concentrated, short-lived duration, paradoxically fixing and periodically retriggering the event in memory and relived emotion.

At certain kinds of effervescent occasion the visceral charge of the crowd is heightened through the use, not only of body (and other) odours, but also the display of vivid colour in dress and banners, and through percussion, chanting, singing, music and dancing. Such performances and display typify all shades of political persuasion. Altered states of consciousness resulting from these activities need not always have an enemy figure in mind, but may create well-being and be used in healing treatments. Lüdtke (2005: 50–53) describes the *pizzica* healing dance in Salento, Italy, in which some dancers become ecstatic and refer afterwards to their experiences as 'orgasmic', 'magic', 'out-of-body', and 'trance' , these being some of the descriptions used to refer to crowd behaviour (see Tambiah above).

These experiences can occur in what are otherwise enduring, regulated occasions, say a festival, carnival, or dance or therapy group. Allen (2000: 86), citing Reynolds (1967: 106–7), suggests that the roots of 'carnival' are pre-human and occur among primates such as chimpanzees, and that it was with human assemblies of enthusiasm during periods of seasonal concentration that religion and socio-kinship structures develop out of them . This is the evolutionary view of assembly in which relatedness is acknowledged and creates ordered structure. What, however, are the conditions under which relatedness is not recognised and so does not regulate behaviour? When do assemblies become unruly crowds and persecute those judged to be minorities or minors? Percussion, for instance, may also mark the transition not just between events or moods but between passivity and violence. The repetitive single stroke of the marching drum may aim at settling nerves before engagement in war, but speeded up it increases the adrenalin necessary for the act. More eerily, a crowd's bio-rhythmic, staccato chanting, especially of a repeated single word, can express adulation for the hero-figure but can be the baying cry for a brutal scapegoating or lynching of an individual or minority. Ardener (1989: 93; based on 1970: 147–48) describes a howling mob outside the well-roofed house of a cowering old man who, being wealthy, would in more prosperous times be honoured but, now in times of poverty, is thought to be a witch killing others for his gain. Chau talks of the masses' enthusiasm in China for the collective effervescence of *honghuo* in political rallies turning to overzealous intimidation, especially during the periods of the Great Leap Forward and the Cultural Revolution (Chau 2006: 167). A transition to intimidation and violence may characterise any collective and concentrated, sensation-inducing activities, from march and percussion to dancing and chanting, which may well begin as planned but which contain within themselves the potential, especially if subject to manipulation or perturbation, for allowing a shift in crowd mood from coordinated display to uncoordinated scramble. It would be unwarranted to read intrinsic meaning into collective displays of dress, banners, drums, music, dancing and singing. But, as Cohen (1993) and others have shown in the study of carnival, they are there to be taken up by political and religious causes which may claim them as having been their own symbolic property in the first place.

But in order for this idea of symbolic appropriation to develop, there must surely be some consistency of aims among those in the collectivity who make claim to it. And indeed it is on effervescent occasions of the kind that Durkheim focused on, that objects or totems, activities and images would take on symbolic value, so contributing to the clan or other group's emerging culture of relatedness and identity. But this possibility is precluded when the grouping or crowd drifts away from such possible consolidation and turns towards uncontrolled violence. Does this fact have implications for our understanding, then, of the conditions of relatedness and crowd dynamics under which symbolic investment occurs?

Let me begin to answer by considering the proposal that the development of the 'social brain' among humans, including its capacity for symbolic representation, derived from their increasing ability to outwit each other through deception in the pursuit of desired resources and objectives and yet to restore trust through communal symbols and ritual (Knight et al 1999: 6). Such social skills need more than a balance of co-operation and competition. Timing and visibility are important. When should you indicate who your allies are, and how open should you be in doing so? When and how openly should you signal warnings to your rivals? In other words, when do you need to be secretive and deceitful in communicating your intentions to the best advantage, and at what point should conciliatory ritual symbolism be invoked? These questions, reminiscent of earlier transactionalists, ask how collective display can both hide and communicate, or how, as symbols, their ambivalence can invite either interpretation.

During emotionally heightened occasions, the banners, dress and performances may encourage crowd euphoria and yet can also, at the triggering of a disagreeable incident, be regarded as provocative. We can instance the contestable use in the 1980s of the Union Jack as for some indicating the unity of the British as one people and for others the right-wing fascist movement aimed at dividing them. Of course such sudden dissension can be engineered and is to that extent the result of rational calculation, as might be the response of the opposition. But the resultant conflicts, whether or not they are regarded as rational reactions, take on the characteristic features of the riot crowd in which the push and pressure of impacting bodies precludes rational consideration, in the sense that the activities are no longer the most efficient means to intended ends, and that intentions themselves are no longer clear. People caught up in such crowds afterwards tell of the loss of control they experienced over themselves, their companions and any collective orientation.

This is the antithesis of the conditions under which social skills and symbolic behaviour can be deployed and developed. The development of the social brain would be impeded by such antithetical conditions. It may be that, given its limited duration, the unruly crowd would not anyway be a significant threat to the social brain's development. Much depends on how frequently collective effervescence attains this state, a question that is not posed in the Durkheimian literature. Too much negative effervescence precludes a settled state of symbolic or totemic identification and would surely prevent people from consolidating the social skills that they might otherwise acquire through incremental strategising.

Overpopulation, a very high density of interaction, and internecine relatedness are the context in which modern crowds occur. Perhaps, therefore, the crowd was not a phenomenon of early humankind. It is difficult to imagine small bands of hunter–gatherers losing sight of their relatedness (however unmarked or loosely marked by kinship terms of address), even when faced by the fiercest threats, in most cases predatory animals. Even competition with other human groups over resources might be avoided by the simple expedient of moving away to other resources. This is not to say that anger, rage, frustration, resentment and hatred were absent from their emotional repertoire. But we can legitimately ask whether such sentiments played a lesser role in their lives than is the case for modern humanity. Conversely, given the counterpart to such passions as those of intense adulation, love and loyalty which we also associate with modern humans, we can further ask whether these, too, played a lesser role. Could it be that early humans were more 'rational' than modern ones, in that they could usually make decisions about where to hunt, gather and reside, and with whom to marry, relatively unaffected by the fear of high density interaction reversing their intentions?

Against this speculation, it may be that the emotional quotient, so to speak, is constant whatever the interactional density: i.e. that a small group grappling with wild beasts or rivals experienced as much visceral charge as a large riot crowd butchering opponents. This raises the further question of whether the biological or neurological faculty for emotional expression has changed significantly from early to modern humankind, in terms of its range and role in socio-ecological response and decision-making. In recent times, the moving evidence of the earliest cave art suggests no change since then in the brain's capacity for emotional expression, though not necessarily in the types and amounts of particular emotions and the social contexts of their occurrence. For evidence of neurological change, we would presumably need to go back much further.

Dunbar points to an exponential increase in hominid and subsequent human social group size from some 1 million years ago, settling on about 150 persons in a group, alongside an increase in brain size and later a kind of social language to service these many relationships (Dunbar 2003: 173; Hurford in Knight et al 1999: 181–82). Does an even greater increase in group size then create the conditions in which a sense of close relatedness among core members could simply be overwhelmed at times of collective effervescence by large numbers in the group who did not see themselves as relationally bound to each other to the same extent? Or can this only happen when large groups compete and aggregate as in transhumance or in land settlement? If full language only developed with tool-making about 40–50,000 years ago (the Upper Paleolithic Revolution), do we then have the further situation in which the crowd and its attendant features became lexically identified as such, thereby entering explicit human consciousness, and entailing in turn not just the deployment of emotions on such viscerally charged occasions, but also the linguistic means to refer to them? Kringelbach notes that emotions have scientifically been viewed on two levels: 'the *emotional state* that can be measured through physiological changes such as visceral and endocrine responses, and *feelings*, seen as the subjective experience of emotion' (2005). The distinction presupposes that between, first, the physical production of emotions in evolution and, later, conscious reflection on them through language, and in due course through various cultural classifications of emotion.

It is common in anthropology to see in such taxonomies evidence of increasing cultural complexity. The systematic and often hierarchical naming of emotions or inner states feeds into other cultural taxonomies and areas, both the literary and the scientific. And yet the viscerally charged, passionate crowd can for a short period reject this, repeating slogans or dispensing with language altogether in its violence, sometimes thereafter acknowledging with remorse this temporary loss of the cognitive ordering of the emotional, but sometimes, as Tambiah notes (above), disavowing its occurrence. Is the crowd in these respects an increasing feature of modern ever-urbanizing, demographically explosive society? Atran and others (2004) make the interesting observation with regard to animal and plant classification that, while many so-called small, indigenous peoples have rich and extensive folk biology taxonomies, most people living in modern, industrialised, urban societies have an impoverished and naïve knowledge by comparison, being therefore less 'scientific' in these respects than, say, ordinary Amazonians. If crowds, especially riot crowds, are becoming a more frequent and influential global phenomenon in the conduct of human affairs and in challenging emerging cultures of relatedness, they can be regarded as part of the same phenomenon of increasing cognitive, emotional and physical estrangement of human from human, and human from non-human entities. Tracing changes in the density and effervescence of human relatedness or, to use it as a paradigmatic type, in the emergence and development of the crowd, straddles traditional disciplinary boundaries and so helps define the new anthropological holism.

Acknowledgement

I thank Richard Fardon for copious and penetrating comments on an earlier version of this paper.

BIBLIOGRAPHY

Allen, J. 2000. From Beach to Beach: The Development of Maritime Economies in Prehistoric Melanesia, in S. O'Connor and P. Veth (eds), *East of Wallace's Line: Studies of Past and Present Maritime Cultures of the Indo-Pacific Region*, Modern Quaternary Research in Southeast Asia, volume 16. Rotterdam: A. A. Balkema, 139–76.

Allen, M.R. 1967. *Male Cults and Secret Initiations in Melanesia*. Melbourne: Melbourne University Press.

Allen, N.J. 2000. *Categories and Classifications: Maussian Reflections on the Social*. Oxford and New York: Berghahn.

Annual Report on British New Guinea, From 1 July, 1889 to 30 June, 1890. 1891. Queensland: Government Press.

Annual Report on British New Guinea, from 1 July, 1892 to 30 June, 1893. 1894. Queensland Government Press.

Annual Report on British New Guinea, From 1 July, 1893 to 30 June, 1894. 1895. Queensland: Government Press.

Annual Report on British New Guinea for 1902–03. 1904. Queensland: Government Press.

Appadurai, A. (ed.) 1986. *The Social Life of Things*. Cambridge: Cambridge University Press.

Arce, A. and E. Fisher. 1999. The Accountability of Commodities in a Global Market Place: the Cases of Bolivian Coca and Tanzanian Honey, in R. Fardon, W. van Bimsbergen, and R. van Dijk (eds), *Modernity on a Shoestring*. Leiden and London: Eidos.

Ardener, E. 1970. Witchcraft, Economics and the Continuity of Belief, in M.Douglas (ed.), *Witchcraft Confessions and Accusations*. London: Tavistock.

——— 1982. Social anthropology, language and reality, in D. Parkin (ed.), *Semantic Anthropology*. London and New York: Academic Press.

——— 1989. *The Voice of Prophecy and Other Essays*, ed. M. Chapman. Oxford: Blackwell.

Astington, J.W. 1993. *The Child's Discovery of the Mind*. Cambridge: Cambridge University Press.

Atran, S. 1990. *Cognitive Foundations of Natural History: Towards an Anthropology of Science*. Cambridge: Cambridge University Press.

Atran, S., D. Medin, and N. Roos. 2004. Evolution and Devolution of Knowledge: A Tale of Two Biologies. *Journal of The Royal Anthropological Institute* 10(2): 395–420.

——— 2005. The Cultural Mind: Environmental Decision Making and Cultural Modeling Within and Across Populations. *Psychological Review* 112(4): 744–76.

Axelrod, R. 1997. *The Complexity of Cooperation: Agent-based Models of Competition and Collaboration.* Princeton: Princeton University Press.

Baddeley, A. (ed.) 1997. *Human Memory: Theory and Practice.* Hove: Psychology Press.

Bahuchet, S.D., D. Mckey, and I. de Garine. 1991. Wild Yams Revisited: Is Independence from Agriculture Possible for Rain Forest Hunter-Gatherers? *Human Ecology* 19: 213–43.

Baillargeon, R. 1987. Young Infants' Reasoning About the Physical and Spatial Characteristics of a Hidden Object. *Cognitive Development* 2: 179–200.

Baillargeon, R.and S. Hanko-Summers. 1990. Is the Top Object Adequately Supported by the Bottom Object? Young Infants' Understanding of Support Relations. *Cognitive Development* 5: 29–53.

Baker, P.T. 1965. Multidisciplinary Studies of Human Adaptability: Theoretical Justification and Method, in J.S. Weiner (ed.), *International Biological Programme: Guide to the Human Adaptability Proposals.* London: Special Committee for the International Biological Programme, International Council of Scientific Unions. 63–72.

Balée, W. 1993. Indigenous Transformations of Amazonian Forests: An Example from Maranhão, Brazil. *L' Homme* 126–28: 231–54.

Barkow, J., L. Cosmides, and J. Tooby, (eds). 1992. *The Adapted Mind.* New York: Oxford University Press.

Bamford, S. 2004. Conceiving Relatedness: Non-substantial Relations Among the Kamea of Papua New Guinea. *Journal of The Royal Anthropological Institute* 10(2): 297–306.

Baron-Cohen, S. 1995. *Mindblindness: An Essay on Autism and Theory of Mind.* Cambridge, MA: MIT Press.

Baron-Cohen, S., H. Tager-Flusberg, and D.J. Cohen (eds). 2000. *Understanding Other Minds: Perspectives from Developmental Cognitive Neuroscience.* Oxford: Oxford University Press.

Barrett, J.L. 2004. *Why Would Anyone Believe in God?.* Walnut Creek, CA: AltaMira Press.

Barrett, L., R.I.M. Dunbar, and J.E. Lycett. 2002. *Human Evolutionary Psychology.* Basingstoke: Palgrave-Macmillan, and Princeton: Princeton University Press.

Barth, Fredrik. 1975. *Ritual and Knowledge Among the Baktaman of New Guinea.* New Haven, CT: Yale University Press.

——— 1987. *Cosmologies in the Making: A Generative Approach to Cultural Variation in Inner New Guinea.* Cambridge: Cambridge University Press.

——— 1990. The Guru and the Conjurer: Transactions in Knowledge and the Shaping of Culture in Southeast Asia and Melanesia. *Man* 25: 640–53.

——— 2002. Review of *Arguments and Icons. Journal of Ritual Studies* 16: 14–17.

Barton, F.R. 1910. The Annual Trading Expedition to the Papuan Gulf, in C.G. Seligmann, *The Melanesians of British New Guinea*, Cambridge: Cambridge University Press. 96–120.

Bates, D. forthcoming: *The Soul of Science*.

Bauman, Z. 1999. *Culture as Practice* (new edition). London: Sage.

Beatty, A. 2005. Emotions in the Field. What are we Talking About? *Journal of the Royal Anthropological Institute* 11(1): 17–37.

Beaulieu, D.L. 1984. Curly Hair and Big Feet: Physical Anthropology and the Implementation of Land Allotment on the White Earth Chippewa Reservation, *American Indian Fall Quarterly*, Fall 1984: 281–314.

Bellwood, P. 2005. *First Farmers: The Origins of Agricultural Societies*. Oxford: Blackwell.

Benedict, R. 1935. *Patterns of Culture*. London: Routledge and Kegan Paul.

Bereczkei, T. and R.I.M. Dunbar. 1997. Female-biased Reproductive Stratgeies in a Hungarian Gypsy Population. *Proceedings of the Royal Society of London* 264B: 7–22.

Bergson, H. 1911. *Creative Evolution*, trans. A. Mitchell. London: Macmillan.

Bering, J.M., K.A. McLeod, and T.K. Shackelford (in press). Reasoning about Dead Agents Reveals Possible Adaptive Trends. *Human Nature*.

Bering, J.M., C. Hernández-Blasi, D.F. Bjorklund (in press). The Development of 'Afterlife' Beliefs in Secularly and Religiously Schooled Children. *British Journal of Developmental Psychology*.

Bering, J.M., and D.D.P. Johnson. 2005. 'O Lord ... You Perceive my Thoughts from Afar': Recursiveness and the Evolution of Supernatural Agency. *Journal of Cognition and Culture* 5: 118–42.

Berndt, R.M. 1966. The Wuradilagu Song Cycle of Northeast Arnhem Land. *Journal of American Folklore* 79(311): 195–243.

Berner, U. 2004. Modes of Religiosity and Types of Conversion in Medieval Europe and Modern Africa, in H. Whitehouse and L.H. Martin (eds), *Theorizing Religions Past: Archaeology, History, and Cognition*. Walnut Creek, CA: AltaMira Press.

Bestard, J. 2004. Kinship and the New Genetics. The Changing Meaning of Biogenetic Substance. *Social Anthropology* 12(3): 25–263.

Beuchat, H. and M. Mauss. 1979 (1906). *Seasonal Variations of the Eskimo: A Study in Social Morphology*, trans. J. Fox. London: Routledge and Kegan Paul.

Blackwood, B. 1927. A Study of Mental Testing in Relation to Anthropology, *Mental Measurement Monographs*. Serial no. 4, December 1927. Baltimore.

———— 1930. Racial Differences in Skin-colour as Recorded by the Colour Top, *Journal of the Royal Anthropological Institute* 60: 137–68.

———— Drawings and Hair Samples Collected by Miss Blackwood/NORTH AMERICA. Blackwood Papers. 1994.15/. Manuscripts and Photographs Department, Pitt Rivers Museum.

———— Fieldnotes. BB.A3.46–75. Blackwood Related Documents File A3 Plains. Manuscripts and Photographs Department, Pitt Rivers Museum.

———— 1924–1927. Diary. Blackwood Papers Box 12. Manuscripts and Photographs Department, Pitt Rivers Museum.

Bloch, M. 1974. Symbols, Song, Dance and Features of Articulation or is Religion an Extreme Form of Traditional Authority? *Archives Europeenes de Sociologie* 15: 55–81.

———— 2004. Ritual and Deference, in H. Whitehouse and J. Laidlaw (eds), *Ritual and Memory: Toward a Comparative Anthropology of Religion.* Walnut Creek, CA: AltaMira Press.

Bloom, P. 2000. *How Children Learn the Meanings of Words.* Cambridge, MA: MIT Press.

Bogin, B. 1999. Evolutionary Perspective on Human Growth. *Annual Reviews in Anthropology* 28: 109–53.

Bogin, B. and J. Loucky. 1997. Plasticity, Political Economy, and Physical Growth Status of Guatemala Maya Children Living in the United States. *American Journal of Physical Anthropology* 102: 17–32.

Bohm, D. 1980. *Wholeness and the Implicate Order.* London and Boston: Routledge and Kegan Paul.

Bourdieu, P. 1984 (1979). *Distinction. A Social Critique of the Judgement of Taste.* London: Routledge and Kegan Paul.

Boyer, P. 1990. *Tradition as Truth and Communication.* Cambridge: Cambridge University Press.

———— 1992. Explaining Religious Ideas: Outline of a Cognitive Approach. *Numen* 39: 27–57.

———— 1993. Pseudo-natural Kinds, in P. Boyer (ed.), *Cognitive Aspects of Religious Symbolism.* Cambridge: Cambridge University Press.

———— 1994a. Cognitive Constraints on Cultural Representations: Natural Ontologies and Religious Ideas, in L. Hirschfeld and S. Gellman (eds), *Mapping the Mind: Domain-specificity in Cognition and Culture.* Cambridge: Cambridge University Press.

———— 1994b. *The Naturalness of Religious Ideas: A Cognitive Theory of Religion.* Berkeley/Los Angeles: University of California Press.

———— 1996. What Makes Anthropomorphism Natural: Intuitive Ontology and Cultural Representations. *Journal of The Royal Anthropological Institute* 2: 1–15.

———— 2000. Evolution of the Modern Mind and the Origins of Culture: Religious Concepts as a Limiting Case, in P.C. Carruthers and A. Chamberlain. (eds), *Evolution and the Human Mind: Modularity, Language and Meta-cognition.* Cambridge: Cambridge University Press.

———— 2001a. *Religion Explained: The Evolutionary Origins of Religious Thought.* New York: Basic Books.

———— 2001b. Cultural Inheritance Tracks and Cognitive Predispositions: The Example of Religious Concepts, in H. Whitehouse (ed.), *The Debated Mind: Evolutionary Psychology versus Ethnography.* Oxford: Berg.

———— 2003. Religious Thought and Behaviour as By-products of Brain Function. *Trends in Cognitive Sciences* 7(3): 110–24.

Boyer, P. and C. Ramble. 2001. Cognitive Templates for Religious Concepts: Cross-cultural Evidence for Recall of Counter-intuitive Representations. *Cognitive Science* 25: 535–64.

Breinl, A. 1914. *Port Moresby to Daru. An Account of a Journey on Foot and by Canoe.* Townsville: Australian Institute of Medicine.

Brown, A.K., Laura Peers, and members of the Kainai Nation. 2006. *Pictures Bring Us Memories/Sinaakssiiksi aohtsimaahpihkookiyaawa, Photographs and Histories from the Kainai Nation.* Toronto: University of Toronto Press.

Brumann, C. 1999. Why a Successful Concept Should not be Discarded. *Current Anthropology* (special issue), 40: S1–S14.

Buford, B. 1992. *Among the Thugs: The Experience and the Seduction of Crowd Violence.* New York: Norton.

Burbank, V. 1985. The *Mirriri* as Ritualized Aggression. *Oceania* 56: 47–55.

Canetti, E. 1984. *Crowds and Power.* New York: Farrar, Strauss and Giroux.

Canguilhem, G. 1975. *La Connaissance de la Vie.* Paris: Librairie J. Vrin.

Carey, S. 1985. *Conceptual Change in Childhood.* Cambridge, MA: MIT Press.

Carruthers, P. 2002. The Cognitive Functions of Language. *Brain and Behavioral Sciences* 25: 657–726.

Carsten, J. (ed.) 2000. *Cultures of Relatedness.* Cambridge: Cambridge University Press.

——— 2003. *After Kinship.* Cambridge. Cambridge University Press.

Catchpole, C.K. and P.J.B. Slater. 1995. *Bird Song: Biological Themes and Variations.* Cambridge: Cambridge University Press.

Certeau, M. de. 1984. *The Practice of Everyday Life.* Berkeley: University of California Press.

Chalmers, J. 1895. *Pioneer Life and Work in New Guinea, 1877–1894.* London: Religious Tract Society.

Chau, A.Y. 2006. *Miraculous Response: Doing Popular Religion in Contemporary China.* Stanford: Stanford University Press.

Chen, L., X. Yang, H. Jiao and B. Zhao. 2004. Effect of Tea Catechins on the Change of Glutathione Levels caused by Pb(++) in PC12 cells. *Chemical Research and Toxicology* 17: 922–28.

Cheng, M.L.,H.Y. Ho, H.C. Teng, C.H. Lee, L.Y. Shih, and D.T. Chiu. 2005. Antioxidant Deficit and Enhanced Susceptibility to Oxidative Damage in Individuals with Different Forms of Alpha-thalassaemia. *British Journal of Haematology* 128: 119–27.

Cheng Shide (ed.) 1984. *Neijing jiangyi* 內經講義 *(Interpretation of the Inner Canon).* Shanghai: Shanghai kexue jishu chubanshe.

Child, B. 1998. *Boarding School Seasons: American Indian Families, 1900–1940.* Lincoln: University of Nebraska Press.

Clark, A. 1997. *Being There. Putting Brain, Body and World Together Again.* Cambridge, MA: The MIT Press.

Clark, J and K. Kelly. 1993. Human Genetics, Palaeoenvironments and Malaria: Relationships and Implications for the Settlement of Oceania. *American Anthropologist* 95: 612–30.

Clarke, D. 1978. *Analytical Archaeology.* 2nd edn. London: Methuen.

Clement, C. 1999. 1492 and the Loss of Amazonian Crop Genetic Resources. I (The Relation Between Domestication and Human Population Decline) and II (Crop Biogeography at Contact). *Economic Botany* 53(2): 177–216.

Clifford, J. and G. Marcus (eds). 1986. *Writing Culture: The Poetics and Politics of Ethnography.* Berkeley and London: University of California Press.

Cohen, A. 1993. *Masquerade Politics: Explorations in the Structure of Urban Cultural Movements.* Oxford and Providence: Berg.

Collins, K.J and J.S. Weiner. 1977. *Human Adaptability: A History and Compendium of Research.* London: Taylor and Francis.

Coluzzi, M. 1999. Malaria Genetics. The Clay Feet of the Malaria Giant and its African Roots: Hypotheses and Inferences about Origin, Spread and Control of Plasmodium falciparum. *Parassitologia* 41: 277–83.

Coluzzi, M., A. Sabatini, A. della-Torre, M.A. Di Deco, and V. Petrarca. 2000. A Polytene Chromosome Analysis of the *Anopheles gambiae* Species Complex. *Science* 298: 1415–8.

Conrad, W.L. and L.A. Bridgland. 1950. Native Agriculture in Papua-New Guinea, in E.H. Hipsley and F.W. Clements (eds), *Report of the New Guinea Nutrition Survey Expedition, 1947,* Sydney: Government Printer, 72–91.

Conway, D.J. 2003. Tracing the Dawn of *Plasmodium falciparum* with Mitochondrial Genome Sequences. *Trends in Genetics* 19: 671–74.

Coombes, A.E. 1994. *Reinventing Africa: Museums, Material Culture and Popular Imagination in Late Victorian and Edwardian England.* London and New Haven: Yale University Press.

Cooper, D.E. 1996. *World Philosophies: An Historical Introduction.* Oxford and Cambridge MA: Blackwell.

Crosby, E. 1976. Sago in Melanesia. *Archaeology and Physical Anthropology in Oceania* 11: 138–55.

Damasio, A. 2000. *The Feeling of What Happens. Body, Emotion and the Making of Consciousness.* London: Vintage.

D'Andrade, R. 1995. *The Development of Cognitive Anthropology.* Cambridge: Cambridge University Press.

Darwin C. 1859. The Origin of Species by Means of Natural Selection. London: John Murray.

———— 1874. *The Descent of Man, and Selection in Relation to Sex.* London: John Murray.

———— 1950. *On the Origin of Species by Means of Natural Selection, or, the Preservation of Favoured Races in the Struggle for Life.* London: Watts [reprint of First Edition of 1859].

Dawkins, R. 1976. *The Selfish Gene.* Oxford: Oxford University Press.

Deeley, P.Q. 2004. The Religious Brain: Turning Ideas into Convictions. *Anthropology and Medicine* 11(3): 245–67.

Deetz, J. 1977. *In Small Things Forgotten. The Archaeology of Early American Life.* New York: Anchor Books.

Deetz, J and E. Dethlefsen. 1966. Death's Heads, Cherubs, and Willow Trees: Experimental Archaeology in Colonial Cemeteries. *American Antiquity* 31: 502–10.

Deleuze, G. and F. Guattari. 1983. *On the Line,* trans. J. Johnston. New York: Semiotext(e).

Demeer, K., R. Bergman, J.S. Kusner, and H.W.A. Voorhoeve. 1993. Differences in Physical Growth of Aymara and Quechua Children Living at High-altitude in Peru. *American Journal of Physical Anthropology* 90: 59–75.

Denevan, W. 1996. A Bluff Model of Riverine Settlement in Prehistoric Amazonia. *Annals of the Association of American Geographers* 86: 654–81.

———— 2001. *Cultivated Landscapes of Native Amazonia and the Andes.* New York: Oxford University Press.

Denoon, D. 1989. *Public Health in Papua New Guinea. Medical Possibility and Social Constraint, 1884–1984*. Cambridge: Cambridge University Press.

Densmore, F. 1979 (1929). *Chippewa Customs*. St. Paul: Minnesota Historical Society Press.

Department of Culture, Media and Sport (DCMS). 2005. *Guidance for the Care of Human Remains in Museums*. Available at: www.culture.gov.uk/global/publications/archive_2005/guidance_chr.htm (accessed 30 December 2005).

Derrida, J. 1976. *Of Grammatology* (trans. G.C. Spivak). Baltimore: Johns Hopkins University Press.

Descola, Ph. 1993. Les Affinités Sélectives. Alliance, Guerre et Prédation dans l'Ensemble Jivaro, *L' Homme* 126–28: 171–90.

——— 1994. *In the Society of Nature*. Cambridge: Cambridge University Press.

——— 1996. Constructing Natures: Symbolic Ecology and Social Practice, in Ph. Descola and G. Pálsson (eds), *Nature and Society: Anthropological Perspectives*. London: Routledge. 82–102.

Despeux, C. 1996. Le Corps, Champ Spatio-temporel, Souche d'Identité. *L'Homme* 137: 87–118.

——— 2001. The System of the Five Circulatory Phases and the Six Seasonal Influences (*wuyun liuqi*), a Source of Innovation in Medicine under the Song, in E. Hsu (ed.), *Innovation in Chinese Medicine*. Cambridge: Cambridge University Press. 121–65.

Dewey, K.G., G. Beaton, C. Fjeld, B. Lonnerdal, and P. Reeds. 1996. Protein Requirements of Infants and Children. *European Journal of Clinical Nutrition* 50: S119–S150.

Diamond, J. 1997. *Guns, Germs and Steel. A Short History of Everybody for the last 13,000 Years*. London: Vintage.

Diamond, J. and P. Bellwood. 2003. Farmers and their Languages: The First Expansions. *Science* 300 (25 April): 597–603.

Dobzhansky, T. 1972. Natural Selection in Mankind, in G.A. Harrison and A.J. Boyce (eds), *The Structure of Human Populations*. Oxford: Clarendon Press.

Donovan, K.O., D.E. Shaw, and D. Amato. 1976. Sago and Haemolysis. *Papua New Guinea Medical Journal* 20: 167–74.

Douglas, M. 1973. *Natural Symbols: Explorations in Cosmology*. London: Pelican.

Douglas, M. and B. Isherwood. 1979. *The World of Goods: Towards an Anthropology of Consumption*. London and New York: Routledge.

Dressler, W.W. 1995 Modeling Biocultural Interactions: Examples from Studies of Stress and Cardiovascular Disease. *Yearbook of Physical Anthropology* 38: 27–56.

Dufour, D.L. (in press) Biocultural Approaches in Human Biology. *American Journal of Human Biology*.

Dunbar, R.I.M. 1992. Neocortex Size as a Constraint on Group Size in Primates. *Journal of Human Evolution* 22: 469–93.

——— 1993. Coevolution of Neocortex Size, Group Size and Language in Humans. *Behavioral and Brain Sciences* 16: 681–735.

—— 1993. Behavioural Adaptation in G.A. Harrison (ed.), *Human Adaptation*, Oxford: Oxford University Press. 73–98.

—— 1994. Sociality among Humans and Non-human Animals, in T. Ingold, (ed.) *Companion Encyclopaedia of Anthropology: Humanity, Culture and Social Life*. London and New York: Routledge, 756–82.

—— 1995. *The Trouble With Science*. London: Faber and Faber, and Cambridge, MA: Harvard University Press.

—— 1996. *Grooming, Gossip and the Evolution of Language*. London: Faber and Faber and Cambridge, MA: Harvard University Press.

—— 1998. The Social Brain Hypothesis. *Evolutionary Anthropology* 6: 178–90.

—— 2003. The Social Brain: Mind, Language, and Society in Evolutionary Perspective. *Annual Review of Anthropology* 32: 163–81.

Dunbar, R.I.M., L. Barrett, and J.E. Lycett. 2005. *Introduction to Evolutionary Psychology*. Oxford: One World Books.

Dunbar, R.I.M., A. Clark, and N.L. Hurst. 1995. Conflict and Cooperation Among the Vikings: Contingent Behavioural Decisions. *Ethology and Sociobiology* 16: 233–46.

Dunlop. I. 1986. *One Man's Response*. Sydney: Film Australia.

Durkheim, E. 1957 (1915). *The Elementary Forms of the Religious Life*, trans. J.W. Swain. London: George Allen and Unwin.

Dwyer, P.D. and M. Minnegal. 1994. Sago Palms and Variable Garden Yields: A Case Study from Papua New Guinea. *Man and Culture in Oceania* 10: 81–102.

Eaton, J.W., J.R. Eckman, E. Berger, and H.S. Jacob. 1976. Suppression of Malaria Infection by Oxidant Sensitive Host Erythrocytes. *Nature* 264: 758–60.

Edwards, E. (ed.) 1992. *Anthropology and Photography, 1860–1920*. New Haven and London: Yale University Press in association with The Royal Anthropological Institute.

—— 2001. *Raw Histories: Photographs, Anthropology and Museums*. Oxford: Berg.

Edwards, J. 2000. *Born and Bred: Idioms of Kinship and New Reproductive Technologies in England*. Oxford and New York: Oxford University Press.

Ehara, H., S. Kosaka, N. Shimura, D. Matoyama, O. Morita, C. Mizota, H. Naito, S. Susanto, M.H. Bintotr, and Y. Yamamoto. 2002. Genetic Variation of Sago Palm (*Metroxylon sagu Rottb.*) in the Malay Archipelago, in K. Kainuma, M. Okazaki, Y. Toyoda and J.E. Cecil (eds), *New Frontiers of Sago Palm Studies*. Tokyo: Universal Academy Press. 93–100.

Elias, M., L. Rival and D. McKey. 2000. Perception and Management of Cassava (*Manihot esculenta Crantz*) Diversity among Makushi Amerindians of Guyana (South America). *The Journal of Ethnobiology* 20(2): 239–65.

Ellen, R. 1982. *Environment Subsistence and System*. Cambridge: Cambridge University Press.

Ellen, R. (ed.) 2006. *Ethnobiology and the Science of Humankind*. Special Issue of the *Journal of the Royal Anthropological Institute*.

Ellison, P.T. 2003. Energetics and Reproductive Effort. *American Journal of Human Biology* 15: 342–51.

Erikson, C. 2000. An Artificial Landscape Fishery in the Bolivian Amazon. *Nature* 408: 190–93.

Erikson, Ph. 1984. De l'Apprivoisement à l'Approvisionnement: Chasse, Alliance, et Familiarisation en Amazonie Amérindienne. *Techniques et Cultures* 9: 105–40.

Evans-Pritchard, E.E. 1940. *The Nuer*. Oxford: Clarendon Press.

Eveleth, P.B and J.M. Tanner. 1976. *Worldwide Variation in Human Growth*. Cambridge: Cambridge University Press. First edition.

—— 1990. World*wide Variation in Human Growth*. 2nd edn. Cambridge: Cambridge University Press.

Eysenck, H.J. 1993. Creativity and Personality: Suggestions for a Theory. *Psychological Inquiry* 4: 147–78.

—— 1995. *Genius: the Natural History of Human Creativity*. New York: Cambridge University Press.

Farah, M.J. and M.A. Wallace. 1992. Semantically-bounded Anomia: Implications for the Neural Implementation of Naming. *Neuropsychologia* 30: 609–21.

Fardon, R. (ed). 1990. *Localizing Strategies. Regional Traditions in Ethnographic Writing*. Edinburgh: Scottish Academic Press; and Washington: Smithsonian Institution Press.

Fardon, R., W. van Bimsbergen, and R. van Dijk (eds). 1999. *Modernity on a Shoestring*. Leiden and London: Eidos.

Farmer, S., J.B. Henderson and M. Witzel. 2000. Neurobiology, Layered Texts, and Correlative Cosmologies: A Cross-Cultural Framework for Premodern History. *Bulletin of the Museum of Far Eastern Antiquities* 72: 48–90.

Farquhar, J. 1994. *Knowing Practice: the Clinical Encounter of Chinese Medicine*. Boulder: Westview Press.

—— 1999. Technologies of Everyday Life: the Economy of Impotence in Reform China. *Cultural Anthropology* 14 (2): 155–79.

Fausto, C. 2001. *Inimigos fiéis. História, Guerra e Xamanismo na Amazônia*. Sao Paulo: EDUSP.

Feng C.D. 2003. Les Cinq Cycles et les Six Soufflés: La Cosmologie de la Medicine Chinoise Selon les Sept Grands Traités du *Suwen*. Thèse de Doctorat en Sciences Religieuses, Ecole Pratique des Hautes Etudes, Paris.

Fforde, C., J. Hubert, and P. Turnball, (eds). 2001. *The Dead and Their Possessions: Repatriation in Principle, Policy and Practice*. London: Routledge.

Flach, M. 1994. Sago Palm, Metroxylon sagu Rott. Promoting the Conservation and Use of Underutilized and Neglected Crops, 15. Rome: International Plant Genetic Resources Institute.

Flatz, G. 1987. Genetics of Lactose Digestion in Humans. *Advances in Human Genetics* 16: 1–77.

Flinn, M. 2005. Temper Tantrums: Display or Dysfunction? *American Journal of Human Biology* 17: 265.

Flintt, J., A.V. Hill, D.K. Bowden, S.J. Oppenheimer, P.R. Sill, S.W. Serjeantson, J. Bana-Koiri, K. Bhatia, M.P. Alpers, A.J. Boyce, et.al. 1986. High Frequencies of Alpha-thalassaemia are the Result of Natural Selection by Malaria. *Nature* 321: 744–50.

Floud, R. 1983. A Tall Story? The Standard of Living Debate. *History Today* 33: 36–40.

Flynn, T. 1994. Foucault's Mapping of History, in G. Gutting (ed.), *The Cambridge Companion to Foucault*. Cambridge: Cambridge University Press. 28–46.

Food and Agriculture Organization. 1998. Committee on World Food Security, Twenty–fourth session. Guidelines for National Food Insecurity and Vulnerability Information and Mapping Systems (FIVIMS): Background and Principles. Rome: Food and Agriculture Organization of the United Nations.

Foucault, M. [1971] 1991. Nietzsche, Genealogy, History, in P. Rabinow (ed.), *The Foucault Reader: an Introduction to Foucault's Thought*. Harmondsworth: Penguin. 76–100.

——— [1975] 1979. *Discipline and Punish: the Birth of the Prison*. Harmondsworth: Penguin.

——— [1976] 1990. *The History of Sexuality*. Harmondsworth: Penguin.

Franklin, S. 1997. *Embodied Progress: A Cultural Account of Assisted Conception*. London and New York: Routledge.

Franklin, S. and S. McKinnon (eds). 2001. Relative Values: Reconfiguring Kinship Studies. Durham, N.C.: Duke University Press.

Frisancho, A.R. 1993. *Human Adaptation and Accommodation*. Ann Arbor: University of Michigan Press.

Furth C. 1999. *A Flourishing Yin: Gender in China's Medical History, 960–1665*. Berkeley: University of California Press.

Geertz, C. 1975. *The Interpretation of Cultures*. London: Hutchinson.

Gell, A. 1998. *Art and Agency: An Anthropological Theory*. Oxford: Clarendon Press.

Gellner, E. 1969. A Pendulum Swing Theory of Islam, in R. Robertson (ed.), *Sociology of Religion: Selected Readings*. Harmondsworth: Penguin Education.

Gelman, S. 1988. The Development of Induction within Natural Kind and Artefact Categories. *Cognitive Psychology* 20: 65–95.

Gibson, J.J. 1989. *The Ecological Approach to Visual Perception*. Boston: Houghton Mifflin.

Gibson, J. 2001. Food Demand in the Rural and Urban Sectors of PNG, in R.M. Bourke, M.G. Allen and J.G. Salisbury (eds), *Food Security for PNG*. Canberra: Australian Centre for International Agricultural Research. 45–53.

Gibson, R.S. 1990. *Nutritional Assessment*. Oxford: Oxford University Press.

Gillies E. 1976. Causal Criteria in African Classifications of Disease, in J.B. Loudon (ed.), *Social Anthropology and Medicine*. London: Academic Press. 358–95.

Ginker, R. 1994. *Houses in the Rainforest: Ethnicity and Inequality among Farmers and Foragers in Central Africa*. Berkeley: University of California Press.

Glei, M., M. Matuschek, C. Steiner, V. Bohm, C. Persin, and B.L. Pool-Zobel. 2003. Initial *in vitro* Toxicity Testing of Functional Foods Rich in Catechins and Anthocyanins in Human Cells. *Toxicology in Vitro* 17: 723–29.

Gluckman, M. (ed.) 1964. *Closed Systems and Open Minds: The Limits of Naivety in Social Anthropology.* Edinburgh: Oliver and Boyd.

Golden, M.H. 1988. The Role of Individual Nutrient Deficiencies in Growth Retardation of Children as Exemplified by Zinc and Protein, in J.C. Waterlow. (ed.), *Linear Growth Retardation in Less Developed Countries,* New York: Raven Press. 143–63.

Goodman, A.H. 1998. The Biological Consequences of Inequality in Antiquity, in A.H. Goodman and T.L. Leatherman (eds), *Building a New Biocultural Synthesis. Political-economic Perspectives on Human Biology.* Ann Arbor: University of Michigan Press. 147–69.

Goodman, A. and T.L. Leatherman. (eds), 1998a. *Building a New Biocultural Synthesis: Political-economic Perspectives on Human Biology.* Ann Arbor: University of Michigan Press.

—— 1998b. Traversing the Chasm Between Biology and Culture: An Introduction, in A.H. Goodman and T.L. Leatherman (eds), *Building a New Biocultural Synthesis. Political-economic Perspectives on Human Biology.* Ann Arbor: University of Michigan Press. 3–41.

Goody, E. (ed.) 1995. *Social Intelligence and Interaction.* Cambridge and New York: Cambridge University Press.

Goody, J. 1956. A Comparative Approach to Incest and Adultery. *British Journal of Sociology.* 7: 286–305.

—— 1968. Introduction, in J. Goody (ed.), *Literacy in Traditional Societies.* Cambridge: Cambridge University Press.

—— 1986. *The Logic of Writing and the Organization of Society.* Cambridge: Cambridge University Press.

—— 2004. Is Image to Doctrine as Speech to Writing? Modes of Communication and the Origins of Religion, in H. Whitehouse and J. Laidlaw (eds), *Ritual and Memory: Toward a Comparative Anthropology of Religion.* Walnut Creek, CA: AltaMira Press.

Gopnik, A., A.N. Meltzov and P. Kuhl. 1999. *The Scientist in the Crib: Minds, Brains, and How Children Learn.* New York: William Morrow.

Gosden, C. and C. Knowles. 2001. *Collecting Colonialism: Material Culture and Colonial Change.* Oxford: Berg.

Graham A.C. 1986. *Yin-yang and the Nature of Correlative Thinking.* Singapore: Institute of East Asian Philosophies.

—— 1989. *Disputers of the Tao: Philosophical Argument in Ancient China.* La Salle, IL: Open Court.

Granet, M. 1934. *La Pensée Chinoise.* Paris: La Renaissance du Livre.

Grantham-McGregor, S., C. Powell, P. Fletcher. 1989. Stunting, Severe Malnutrition and Mental Development in Young Children. *European Journal of Clinical Nutrition* 43: 403–9.

Griffiths, T. 2001. Finding One's Body: Relationships Between Cosmology and Work in North-West Amazonia, in L. Rival, and N. Whitehead (eds), *Beyond the Visible and the Material: the Amerindianization of Society in the Work of Peter Rivière.* Oxford: Oxford University Press. 247–62.

Grinberg, L.N., H. Newmark, N. Kitrossky, E. Rahamim, M. Chevion and E.A. Rachmilewitz. 1997. Protective Effects of Tea Polyphenols against Oxidative Damage to Red Blood Cells. *Biochemical Pharmacology* 54: 973–78.

Groube, L. 1993. Contradictions and Malaria in Melanesian and Australian Prehistory, in M. Spriggs, D. Yen, W. Ambrose, R. Jones, A. Thorne and A. Andrews (eds), *A Community of Culture: the People and Prehistory of the Pacific*. Canberra: Department of Prehistory, Research School of Pacific Studies, Australian National University. 164–86.

Groves, M. 1972. The Hiri, in *Encyclopaedia of Papua New Guinea*, volume 1. Melbourne: University of Melbourne Press. 523–27.

Guthrie, S. 1993. *Faces in the Clouds: A New Theory of Religion*. New York: Oxford University Press.

Guzmán Gallegos, M.A. 1997. *Para Que la Yucca Beba Nuestra Sangre. Trabajo, Género y Parentesco en una Comunidad Quechua de la Amazonia Ecuatoriana*. Quito: Abya Yala y Cedime.

Haberle, S.G. 1996. Palaeoenvironmental Changes in the Eastern Highlands of Papua New Guinea. *Archaeology in Oceania* 31: 1–11.

Haberle, S.G., G.S. Hope and S. van der Kaars. 2001. Biomass Burning in Indonesia and Papua New Guinea: Natural and Human Induced Fire Events in the Fossil Record. *Palaeogeography, Palaeoclimatology and Palaeoecology* 171: 259–68.

Hacking I. 1986. The Archaeology of Foucault, in P. Rabinow (ed.), *Foucault: a Critical Reader*. Oxford: Basil Blackwell. 27–40.

Hall, A.J. 1983. Health and Diseases of the People of the Upper and Lower Purari, in T. Petr (ed.), *The Purari – Tropical Environment of a High Rainfall River Basin*. The Hague: Dr. W. Junk Publications. 493–507.

Hallpike, C.R. 1969. Social Hair. *Man* (New Series) 4(2): 256–64.

Hancock, J.F. 1992. *Plant Evolution and the Origin of Crop Species*. Englewood Cliffs, NJ: Prentice Hall.

Hanna, J.M. and Baker, P.T. 1979. Biocultural Correlates to the Blood Pressure of Samoan Migrants in Hawaii. *Human Biology* 51: 481–97.

Hardenbergh, S.H.B. 1996. Behavioral Quality and Caloric Intake in Malagasy Children Relative to International Growth References. *American Journal of Human Biology* 8: 207–23.

Harper D. 1998. *Early Chinese Medical Literature: the Mawangdui Medical Manuscripts*. London: Kegan Paul.

——— 2001. Iatromancy, Diagnosis and Prognosis in Early Chinese Medicine, in E. Hsu (ed.), *Innovation in Chinese medicine*. Cambridge: Cambridge University Press.

Harré, R. 1986. The Social Constructionist Viewpoint, in R. Harré (ed.), *The Social Construction of Emotions*. Oxford: Blackwell.

Harrison, F. 1995. The Persistent Power of 'Race' in the Cultural and Political Economy of Racism. *Annual Review of Anthropology* 24: 47–74.

Harrison, G.A. 1988. Part II, in *Human Biology: An Introduction to Human Evolution, Variation, Growth and Adaptability*, by G.A. Harrison, J.M. Tanner, D.R. Pilbeam and P.T. Baker. Oxford: Oxford University Press.

——— 1993. Physiological Adaptation, in G.A. Harrison (ed). *Human adaptation*. Oxford: Oxford University Press. 55–72.

―――― 1997. The Role of the Human Adaptability International Biological Programme in the Development of Human Population Biology, in S.J. Ulijaszek and R.A. Huss–Ashmore (eds), *Human Adaptability: Past, Present and Future.* Oxford: Oxford University Press. 17–25.

Harrison, S. 2004. Emotional Climates: Ritual, Seasonality and Affective Disorders. *The Journal of the Royal Anthropological Institute* 10(3): 583–602.

Heelas, P. 1986. Emotion Talk Across Cultures, in R. Harré (ed.), *The Social Construction of Emotions.* Oxford: Blackwell. 99–120.

Henderson, J.B. 1984. *The Development and Decline of Chinese Cosmology.* New York: Columbia University Press.

Herdt, G.H. 1981. *Guardians of the Flutes: Idioms of Masculinity.* New York: Columbia University Press.

―――― (ed.) 1982. *Rituals of Manhood: Male Initiation in Papua New Guinea.* Berkeley: University of California Press.

Hilger, M.I. 1998 (1939). *Chippewa Families: A Social Study of White Earth Reservation, 1938.* St. Paul: Minnesota Historical Society Press.

―――― 1992 (1951). *Chippewa Child Life and its Cultural Background.* St. Paul: Minnesota Historical Society Press.

Hill, J. 1993. *Keepers of the Sacred Chants: The Poetics of Ritual Power in an Amazonian Society.* Tucson: University of Arizona Press.

Hill, J. and F. Santos Granero (eds), 2002. *Comparative Arawakan Histories: Rethinking Language Family and Culture Area in Amazonia.* Urbana: University of Illinois Press.

Hillis, A.E. and Caramazza, A. 1991. Category-specific Naming and Comprehension Impairment: A Double Dissociation. *Brain* 114: 2081–94.

Hipsley, E.H. and Clements, F.W. 1950. *Report of the New Guinea Nutrition Survey Expedition, 1947.* Sydney: Government Printer.

Hirschfeld, L.A. 1996. *Race in the Making: Cognition, Culture, and the Child's Construction of Human Kinds.* Cambridge, MA: MIT Press.

Hitchcock, N.E. and N.D. Oram. 1967. *Rabia Camp: A Port Moresby Migrant Settlement.* New Guinea Research Bulletin Number 14. Canberra: New Guinea Research Unit, Australian National University.

Hladik, A. and E. Dounias. 1993. Wild Yams of the African Forest as Potential Food Resources, in C.M. Hladik, A. Hladik, O.F. Linares, H. Pagezy, A. Semple and M. Hadley (eds), *Tropical Forests, People and Food.* Paris: UNESCO and Parthenon Publ. 163–76.

Hodges, H. 1964. *Artifacts. An Introduction to Early Materials and Technology.* London: John Baker.

Hope, G.S. and J. Golson. 1995. Late Quaternary Change in the Mountains of New Guinea, in J. Allen and J.F. O'Connell (eds), *Transitions. Antiquity,* 69(265): 818–30.

Hornborg, A. 2005. Ethnogenesis, Regional Integration, and Ecology in Prehistoric Amazonia: Toward a System Perspective. *Current Anthropology* 46(4): 589–620.

Hoskins, J. 1998. *Biographical Objects.* New York and London: Routledge.

Howell, S. 2003. Kinning: The Creation of Life Trajectories in Transnational Adoptive Families. *Journal of the Royal Anthropological Institute* 9(3): 465–84.

Howse, D. 1991, Olfaction and Transition, in D. Howse (ed.), *The Varieties of Sensory Experience: A Sourcebook for the Anthropology of the Senses.* Toronto: University of Toronto Press.

Howse, D. (ed.) 1996. *The Varieties of Sensory Experience.* Toronto and London: University of Toronto Press.

—— 2003. *Sensual Relations.* Ann Arbor. University of Michigan Press.

Hsu, E. 1994. Change in Chinese Medicine: *bian* and *hua*: an Anthropologist's Approach, in V. Alleton and A. Volkov (eds) *Notions et Perceptions de Changement en Chine.* Paris: Institut des Hautes Etudes Chinoises, Collège de France, 41–58.

—— 1999. *The Transmission of Chinese Medicine.* Cambridge: Cambridge University Press.

—— 2000a. *Zangxiang* in the *Canon of Categories* and Tendencies towards a Body-centred Traditional Chinese Medicine. *Ziran kexueshi yanjiu* 自然科學史研究 (*Studies in the History of Natural Sciences*) 19(2): 165–87.

—— 2000b. Towards a Science of Touch, Part I: Chinese Pulse Diagnostics in Early Modern Europe. *Anthropology and Medicine* 7(2): 251–68.

—— 2001a. *The Telling Touch: Pulse Diagnostics in Early Chinese Medicine, with Translation and Interpretation of Ten Medical Case Histories of Shi ji 105.2 (ca 90 BC).* Habilitationsschrift in Sinologie, Fakultät fuer Orientalistik und Altertumswissenschaft, Universität Heidelberg.

—— 2001b. Pulse Diagnostics in the Western Han: how *mai* and *qi* determine *bing*, in E. Hsu (ed.), *Innovation in Chinese Medicine.* Cambridge: Cambridge University Press. 51–91.

—— 2001c. Die drei Körper – oder sind es vier? *Curare* 24: 57–64.

—— 2003. 'Die drei Körper – oder sind es vier?' Medizinethnologische Perspektiven auf den Körper, in T. Lux (ed.), *Kulturelle Dimensionen der Medizin.* Berlin: Reimer. 177–91. (Revised and expanded version of 2001c.)

—— 2005. Tactility and the Body in Early Chinese Medicine. *Science in Context* 18(1): 7–34.

—— forthcoming. *The Telling Touch: Pulse Diagnosis in Early Chinese Medicine, with Translation and Interpretation of the Entire Memoir of Chunyu Yi and his Twenty-five Medical Case Histories in Shi ji 105 (ca 90 BC).* Cambridge: Cambridge University Press.

Huangdi neijing 黃帝內經 (*Yellow Emperor's Inner Canon*). Eastern Han, 1st – 2nd Century CE. Anon. References to Ren Yingqiu 任應秋 (ed.), *Huangdi Neijing Zhangju Suoyin* 黃帝內經章句索引 Beijing: Renmin Weisheng Chubanshe, 1986.

Hugh-Jones, C. and S. Hugh-Jones. 1996. La Conservation du Manioc Chez les Indiens Tukano: Technique et Symbôlique, in C.M. Hladik, A. Hladik, H. Pagezy, O. Linares, G. Koppert, and A. Froment (eds), *L'alimentation en Forêt Tropicale. Interactions Bioculturelles et Perspectives de Développement.* Vol. II, Paris: UNESCO. 897–902.

Human Tissue Act. 2004. Available at: www.opsi.gov.uk/acts/acts2004/20040030.htm

Hume, J.C.C., E.J. Lyons and K.P. Day. 2003. Malaria in Antiquity: A Genetics Perspective. *World Archaeology* 35: 180–92.

Humphrey, C. and J. Laidlaw. 1994. *The Archetypal Actions of Ritual: A Theory of Ritual Illustrated by the Jain Rite of Worship.* Oxford: Oxford University Press.

Hundhausen, C., C. Bosch-Saadatmandi, K. Augustin, R. Blank, S. Wolffram and G. Rimbach. 2005. Effect of Vitamin E and Polyphenols on Ochratoxin A-induced Cytotoxicity in Liver (HepG2) Cells. *Journal of Plant Physiology* 162: 818–22.

Huss-Ashmore, R.A. and R.B. Thomas. 1988. A Framework for Analyzing Uncertainty in Highland Areas, in I. de Garine and G.A. Harrison (eds), *Coping with Uncertainty in Food Supply.* Oxford: Clarendon Press. 452–68.

Hvalkof, S and A. Escobar. 1998. Nature, Political Ecology, and Social Practice: Toward an Academic and Political Agenda, in A.H. Goodman and T.L. Leatherman (eds), *Building and New Biocultural Synthesis. Political–Economic Perspectives on Human Biology.* Ann Arbor: University of Michigan Press. 425–50.

Ingold, T. 1986. *Evolution and Social Life.* Cambridge: Cambridge University Press.

—— 1993. The Art of Translation in a Continuous World, in G. Pálsson. (ed). *Beyond Boundaries: Understanding, Translation and Anthropological Discourse.* Oxford: Berg. 210–30.

—— 1996. Why Four Why's? A Response to Dunbar. *Cultural Dynamics* 8: 375–84.

—— 1999. 'Tools for the Hand, Language for the Face': An Appreciation of Leroi-Gourhan's Gesture and Speech. *Studies in the History and Philosophy of Biological and Biomedical Science* 30: 411–53.

—— 2000a. *The Perception of the Environment: Essays on Livelihood, Dwelling and Skill.* London: Routledge.

—— 2000b. Evolving Skills, in H. Rose and S. Rose (eds), *Alas Poor Darwin: Arguments against Evolutionary Psychology.* London: Jonathan Cape and New York: Random House. 225–46.

—— 2001a. From Complementarity to Obviation: On Dissolving the Boundaries Between Social and Biological Anthropology, Archaeology and Psychology, in S. Oyama, P.E. Griffiths and R.D. Gray (eds), *Cycles of Contingency: Developmental Systems and Evolution.* Cambridge, MA: MIT Press. 255–79.

—— 2001b. From the Transmission of Representations to the Education of Attention, in H. Whitehouse (ed.), *The Debated Mind: Evolutionary Psychology versus Ethnography.* Oxford: Berg. 113–53.

—— 2002. Between Evolution and History: Biology, Culture, and the Myth of Human Origins. *Proceedings of the British Academy* 112: 43–66.

—— 2002. Between Evolution and History: Biology, Culture and the Myth of Human Origins, in M. Wheeler, J. Ziman and M. A. Boden (eds), *The Evolution of Cultural Entities.* Oxford: Oxford University Press. 43–66.

—— 2003a. Three in One: How an Ecological Approach can Obviate the Distinctions between Mind, Body and Culture, in A. Roepstorff, N. Bubandt and K. Kull. (eds), *Imagining Nature: Practices of Cosmology and Identity.* Aarhus: Aarhus University Press. 40–55.

——— 2003b. Two Reflections on Ecological Knowledge, in G. Sanga and G. Ortalli. (eds), *Nature Knowledge: Ethnoscience, Cognition, Identity*. New York: Berghahn. 301–11.

——— 2004a. Beyond Biology and Culture: The Meaning of Evolution in a Relational World. *Social Anthropology* 12(2): 209–21.

——— 2004b. Culture on the Ground: The World Perceived through the Feet. *Journal of Material Culture* 9(3): 315–40.

——— 2004c. Leroi-Gourhan and the Evolution of Writing, in F. Audouze and N. Schlanger. (eds), *Autour de L'homme: Contexte et Actualité d'André Leroi-Gourhan*. Quetigny: Libraire Archéologique. 109–23.

——— 2007. *Lines: A Brief History*. London: Routledge.

Jackson, J. 1983. *The Fish People: Linguistic Exogamy and Tukanoan Identity in Northwest Amazonia*. Cambridge: Cambridge University Press.

Janzen, J.M. 1992. *Ngoma: Discourses of Healing in Central and Southern Africa*. Berkeley, Los Angeles and London: University of California Press.

Jelliffe, D.B. 1966. *Assessment of Nutritional Status of the Community*. Geneva: World Health Organization.

Jenkins, T. 2003. Burying the Evidence. *spiked online* 24 November 2003. Available at: www.spiked-online.com/Articles/00000006DFDE.htm.

Jenks, A.E. 1916. Indian–White Amalgamation: an Anthropometric Study. *Studies in the Social Sciences*. University of Minnesota. March 1916, IV/6.

Johnson, S. 2000. The Recognition of Mentalistic Agents in Infants. *Trends in Cognitive Sciences* 4: 22–28.

Journet, N. 1995. *La Paix des Jardins. Structures Sociales des Indiens Curripaco du Haut Rio Negro (Colombie)*. Paris: Musée de l'Homme.

Kahn, J. 1995. *Culture, Multiculture, Postculture*. London: Sage.

Kalinowski, M. 1991. *Cosmologie et Divination dans la Chine Ancienne. Le Compenium des Cinq Agents (*Wuxing dayi, *vie Siècle)*. Paris: Ecole Française d'Extrême-Orient.

——— 2003. *Divination et Société dans la Chine Médiévale*. Paris: Bibliothèque Nationale de France.

Kandinski, W. 1982. Point and Line to Plane [1926], in K.C. Lindsay and P. Vergo. (eds), *Kandinsky: Complete Writings on Art, vol. 2: 1922–1943*. London: Faber and Faber. 617–36.

Kapferer, B. 1972. *Strategy and Transaction in an African Factory*. Manchester: Manchester University Press.

Katz, S.H. and J. Schall. 1979. Fava Bean Consumption and Biocultural Evolution. *Medical Anthropology* 3: 459–76.

Keegan, D.J. 1988: *The 'Huang-ti Nei-Ching': the Structure of the Compilation; the Significance of the Structure*. Ph.D. Thesis in History, University of California, Berkeley.

Keen, I. 2000. A Bundle of Sticks: The Debate over Yolngu Clans. *Journal of the Royal Anthropological Institute* 6(3): 419–36.

Keil, F.C. 1986. 'The Acquisition of Natural Kind and Artefact Terms, in A. W.D. Marrar (ed.), *Conceptual Change*. Norwaood, NJ: Ablex.

Key, A.C. and L.C. Aiello. 1999. The Evolution of Social Organization, in C. Knight, R. Dunbar, and C. Power (eds), *The Evolution of Culture: An Interdisciplinary View*. Edinburgh: Edinburgh University Press. 15–33.

Keyeux, G., C. Rodas, N. Gelvez, and D. Carter. 2002. Possible Migration Routes into South America Deduced from DNA Studies of Colombian Amerindian Populations. *Human Biology* 74: 211–33.

Keys, A., J. Brozek, A. Henschel, O. Mickelson and H.L. Taylor. 1950. *The Biology of Human Starvation*. Minneapolis: University of Minnesota Press.

Kjaer, A., A.S. Barfod, C. Asmussen and O. Seberg. 2002. Genetic and Morphological Variation in the Sago Palm (*Metroxylon sagu Rottb.*) (Arecaceae) in Papua New Guinea, in K. Kainuma, M. Okazaki, Y. Toyoda and J.E. Cecil (eds), *New Frontiers of Sago Palm Studies*. Tokyo: Universal Academy Press. 101–10.

Klee, P. 1961. *Notebooks, Volume 1: The Thinking Eye*, ed. Jürg Spiller. London: Lund Humphries.

Komlos, J. 2003. Editor's Introduction. *Economics and Human Biology* 1: v–vii.

Knauft, B.M. 1993. *South Coast New Guinea Cultures*. Cambridge: Cambridge University Press.

Knight, C.D. 1991. *Blood Relations. Menstruation and the Origin of Culture*. New Haven, CT: Yale University Press.

Knight, C., R. Dunbar and C. Power. 1999. An Evolutionary Approach to Human Culture, in R. Dunbar, C. Knight and C. Power (eds), *The Evolution of Culture: An Interdisciplinary View*. Edinburgh.: Edinburgh University Press. 1–11.

Knowles, C. 2000. Reverse Trajectories: Beatrice Blackwood as Collector and Anthropologist, in M. O'Hanlon and R. Welsch (eds), *Hunting the Gatherers: Ethnographic Collectors, Agents and Agency in Melanesia, 1870s–1930s*. Methodology and History in Anthropology, vol. 6. Oxford: Berghahn Books.

—— 2004. Beatrice Blackwood (1889–1975), in *New Dictionary of National Biography*. Oxford: Oxford University Press.

Koselleck, R. 1989. Linguistic Change and the History of Events. *The Journal of Modern History* 61(4): 649–66.

—— 2002. Social History and Conceptual History, in *The Practice of Conceptual History: Timing History, Spacing Concepts*. Stanford: Stanford University Press. 20–37.

Kramer, M.S. 1987. Determinants of Intrauterine Growth and Gestational Duration: A Critical Assessment and Meta-analysis. *Bulletin of the World Health Organization* 65: 663–737.

Kringelbach, M.L. 2005. The Human Orbitofrontal Cortex: Linking Reward to Hedonoic Experience. *Nature Reviews Neuroscience* 6: 691–702.

Kuriyama, S. 1993. Concepts of Disease in East Asia, in K.F. Kiple (ed.), *The Cambridge World History of Human Disease*. Cambridge University Press, Cambridge. 52–59.

Kuper, A. 1999. *Culture: The Anthropologists' Account*. Cambridge, MA: Harvard University Press.

Kwiatkowski, D.P. 2005. How Malaria has Affected the Human Genome and What Human Genetics can Teach us about Malaria. *American Journal of Human Genetics* 77: 171–92.

Laland, K., J. Odling-Smee and M. Feldman. 2000. Niche Construction, Biological Evolution and Cultural Change. *Behavioral and Brain Sciences* 23: 131–46.

Lasker, G.W. 1969. Human Biological Adaptability. *Science,* 166: 1480–86.
—— 1994. The Place of Anthropometry in Human Biology, in S.J. Ulijaszek and C.G.N. Mascie–Taylor (eds), *Anthropometry: The Individual and the Population.* Cambridge: Cambridge University Press. 1–6.
Lathrap, D.W. 1970. *The Upper Amazon.* New York: Praeger.
Lawes, W.G. 1876–85. Diary. Sydney: Manuscript, Mitchell Library.
Leach, E.R. 1954. *Political Systems of Highland Burma. A Study of Kachin Social Structure.* London: The Athlone Press.
—— 1958. Magical Hair. *Journal of the Royal Anthropological Institute of Great Britain and Ireland* 88(2): 147–64.
—— 1968. Virgin Birth (letter). *Man* (N.S.) 3: 655–66.
Leatherman, T.L. 1994. Health Implications of Changing Agrarian Economics in the Southern Andes. *Human Organization* 53: 371–80.
Leatherman, T.L and A. Goodman. 2005. Coca-colonization of Diets in the Yucatan. *Social Science and Medicine* 61: 833–46.
Le Bon, G. 1960 (1897). *The Crowd: A Study of the Popular Mind.* (1895. Trans. From *La Psychologie des Foules.*) New York: Viking Press.
Ledoux, J. 2003. *The Synaptic Self: How Our Brains Become Who We Are.* Harmondsworth: Penguin Books.
Lehman, J., D. Kern, B. Glaser and W. Woods, eds. 2003. *Amazonian Dark Earths. Origins, Properties, and Management.* Dordrecht: Kluwer Academic Publisher.
Leijing 類經 (Canon of Categories). Qing, 1624. Zhang Jiebin 張介賓. Beijing: Renmin Weisheng Chubanshe, (1965) 1985.
Leroi-Gourhan, A. 1993. *Gesture and Speech* (trans. A. Bostock Berger). Cambridge, MA: MIT Press.
Leslie, A.M. 1994. Pretending and Believing: Issues in the Theory of ToMM. *Cognition* 50: 211–38.
Levinson, S. 1995. Interactional Biases in Human Thinking, in E. Goody (ed.), *Social Intelligence and Interaction.* Cambridge: Cambridge University Press.
Lévi-Strauss, C. 1943. Guerre et Commerce Chez les Indiens d'Amérique du Sud. *Renaissance* 1: 122–39.
—— 1950. The Use of Wild Plants inTropical South America, in J.H. Steward (ed.), *Handbook of South American Indians. Vol. 6: Physical Anthropology, Linguistics and Cultural Geography of South American Indians.* Smithsonian Institution, Bureau of American Ethnology. Washington, DC: US Government Printing Office. 465–86.
Lévy-Bruhl, L. 1926. *How Natives Think.* (Trans L.A. Clare from *Les Functions Mentales des Sociétés Inférieures*). London: George Allen and Unwin.
Lewis, I.M. 1971. *Ecstatic Religion: A Study of Shamanism and Spirit Possession.* London: Routledge.
Lewis-Williams, J.D. 1997. Agency, Art, and Altered Consciousness: A Motif in French (Quercy) Upper Paleolithic Parietal Art. *Antiquity* 71: 810–30.
Lewontin, R. 1972. The Apportionment of Human Diversity. *Evolutionary Biology* 6: 381–98.
Lindman, J.M. and L.T. Michele, eds. 2001. *A Centre of Wonders: The Body in Early America.* Ithaca: Cornell University Press.

Little, M.A. 1982. The Development of Ideas on Human Ecology and Adaptation, in F. Spencer (ed.), *A History of American Physical Anthropology, 1930–80*. New York: Academic Press. 405–33.

—— 1991. Multidisciplinary Studies of Human Adaptability: Twenty-five Years of Research. *Journal of the Indian Anthropological Society* 26: 9–29.

Livingstone, F.B. 1958. Anthropological Implications of Sickle Cell Gene Distribution in West Africa. *American Anthropologist* 60: 533–62.

Lloyd G.E.R. [1950] 1983. Introduction, in *Hippocratic Writings*. Harmondsworth: Penguin.

—— 2004. *Ancient Worlds, Modern Reflections: Philosophical Perspectives on Greek and Chinese Science and Culture*. Oxford: Clarendon Press.

Long, R. 2002. *Walking the Line*. London: Thames and Hudson.

Low, H. 1848. *Sarawak: Its Inhabitants and Productions*. London: Richard Bentley.

Lowie, R. 1924. *Primitive Religion*. New York: Boni and Liveright.

Lüdtke, K. 2005. Dancing Towards Well-being: Reflections on the *Pizzica* in Contemporary Salento, Italy, in L.D. Giudice and N. van Deusen (eds), *Performing Ecstasies: Music, Dance and Ritual in the Mediterranean*. Ottawa: Institute of Mediaeval Music.

Lukes, S. 1973. *Emile Durkheim, His Life and Work: A Historical and Critical Study*. London: Allen Lane.

Lü shi chun qiu 呂氏春秋 (*The Annals by Mister Lü*). Warring States, ca. 239 BCE. Lü Buwei 呂不韋. *Si bu bei yao* 四部備要.

Lutz, C.A. 1985. Ethnopsychology Compared to What? Explaining Behaviour and Consciousness Among the Ifaluk, in G. White and J. Kirkpatrick (eds), *Person, Self, and Experience: Exploring Pacific Ethnopscyhologies*. Berkeley: University of California Press.

Ma Jixing 馬繼興 1990. *Zhongyi wenxianxue* 中醫文獻學. (*Study of Chinese Medical Texts*). Shanghai kexue jishu chubanshe, Shanghai.

Macknight, C.C. 1978. *The Voyage to Marege, Macassan Trepangers in Northern Australia*. Melbourne: Melbourne University Press.

Magowan, F. 2001. Waves of Knowing: Polymorphism and Co-substantive Essences in Yolngu Sea Cosmology. *The Australian Journal of Indigenous Education* 29(1): 22–35.

Maher, R.F. 1961. *New Men of Papua*. Madison: University of Wisconsin Press.

—— 1984. The Purari River Delta Societies, Papua New Guinea, After the Tommy Kabu Movement. *Ethnology* 23: 217–7.

Major J.S. 1993. *Heaven and Earth in Early Han Thought. Chapters Three, Four and Five of the* Huainanzi. Albany: State University of New York Press.

Mandler, J., P. Bauer and L. McDonough. 1991. Separating the Sheep from the Goats: Differentiating Global Categories. *Cognitive Psychology* 23: 263–98.

Mania, D. and U. Mania. 1988. Deliberate Engravings on Bone Artefacts of Homo Erectus. *Rock Art Research* 5(2): 91–107.

Marett, R.R. 1917. Presidential Address: The Psychology of Culture-contact. *Folk-Lore* 28: 13–35.

—— 1920. *Psychology and Folk-lore*. London: Methuen.

—— 1929. *The Threshold of Religion, 4th Edition*. London: Methuen.

Marriott, M. 1976. Hindu Transactions: Diversity Without Dualism, in B. Kapferer (ed.), *Transaction and Meaning*. Philadelphia: Institute for the Study of Human Issues. 109–42.

Martin, D.L. 1998. Owning the Sins of the Past: Historical Trends, Missed Opportunities, and New Directions in the Study of Human Remains, in A.H. Goodman and T.L. Leatherman, (eds), *Building a New Biocultural Synthesis. Political-economic Perspectives on Human Biology*. Ann Arbor: University of Michigan Press. 171–90.

Massey, C. and R. Gelman. 1988. 'Preschoolers' Ability to Decide Whether Pictured Unfamiliar Objects can Move Themselves. *Developmental Psychology* 24: 307–17.

Mauss, M. 1968. *Oeuvres. 1. Les Functions Sociales du Sacré*. Paris: Les Editions de Minuit.

—— 1979. *Sociology and Psychology*. London: Routledge and Kegan Paul.

Mawangdui Hanmu boshu zhengli xiaozu 馬王堆漢墓帛書整理小組 (eds), 1985.

Mawangdui Hanmu boshu 馬王堆漢墓帛書 (*The Silk Documents from a Han Tomb at Mawangdui*). Vol 4. Beijing: Wenwu Chubanshe.

Mayr, E. 1976. Behavior Programs and Evolutionary Strategies, in E. Mayr (ed.), *Evolution and the Diversity of Life: Selected Essays*. Cambridge, MA: Harvard University Press.

McCracken, G. 1997. *Big Hair: A Journey into the Transformation of Self*. London: Indigo.

McElroy, A. and P.K. Townsend. 2004, *Medical Anthropology in Ecological Perspective*. Boulder: Westview Press.

McMullen D. 1988. *State and Scholars in T'ang China*. Cambridge: Cambridge University Press.

Meggitt, M.J. 1962. *Desert People: A Study of the Walbiri Aborigines of Central Australia*. Sydney: Angus and Robertson.

Meltzoff, A. 1995. Understanding the Intentions of Others: Re-enactment of Intended Acts by 18-month old Children. *Developmental Psychology* 31: 838–50.

Métailié, G. 2001. The *Bencao gangmu* of Li Shizhen: an Innovation in Natural History? in E. Hsu (ed.), *Innovation in Chinese Medicine*. Cambridge: Cambridge University Press, 221–61.

Meyer, M. 1994. *The White Earth Tragedy*. Lincoln: University of Nebraska.

Miller, B.D. 2005. Culture, Nature and Unbalanced Secondary Sex Ratios in India: Continuity and Change from the 1872 Census to the Era of HIV/AIDS. *American Journal of Human Biology* 17: 265.

Miller, D. 1987. *Material Culture and Mass Consumption*. Oxford: Basil Blackwell.

Miller, D. 1994. *Modernity: An Ethnographic Approach*. Oxford and Providence: Berg.

Miller, J.R. 1996. *Shingwauk's Vision: A History of Native Residential Schools*. Toronto: University of Toronto Press.

Miller, J. 1984. Culture and the Development of Everyday Social Explanation. *Journal of Personality and Social Psychology* 46: 961–78.

Mithen, S. 1996. *The Prehistory of the Mind: A Search for the Origins of Art, Religion and Science*. London: Thames and Hudson. 1998. London: Phoenix.

────── 2006. Ethnobiology and the Evolution of the Human Mind, in R. Ellen (ed.), *Ethnobiology and the Science of Humankind.* Special Issue of the *JOURNAL OF THE ROYAL ANTHROPOLOGICAL INSTITUTE.*

────── 2006. Ethnobiology and the Evolution of the Human Mind, in R. Ellen (ed). *Ethnobiology and the Science of Humankind: A Retrospective and a Prospective.* Special issue of *JRAI.* S45–S62.

Moore, H. and M. Vaughan. 1994. *Cutting Down Trees: Gender, Nutrition and Agricultural Change in the Northern Province of Zambia, 1890–1990.* Oxford: James Currey.

Morphy, H. 1984. *Journey to the Crocodile's Nest.* Canberra: Australian Institute of Aboriginal Studies.

────── 1991. *Ancestral Connections: Art and an Aboriginal System of Knowledge.* Chicago: University of Chicago Press.

────── 1993 Cultural Adaptation, in G.A. Harrson. (ed.). *Human Adaptation,* Oxford: Oxford University Press. 99–150.

────── 1995. Landscape and the Reproduction of Yolngu Society, in E. Hirsch and M. O'Hanlon (eds), *The Anthropology of Landscape: Between Place and Space.* Oxford: Clarendon Press. 184–209.

────── 1999. Death, Exchange, and the Reproduction of Yolngu Society, in F. Merlan, J. Morton and A. Rumsey (eds), *Scholar and Sceptic: Australian Aboriginal Studies in Honour of L.R. Hiatt.* Canberra: Aboriginal Studies Press. 123–50.

────── 2005. Seeing Indigenous Australian Art, in M. Westerman (ed.), *Anthropologies of Art.* Williamstown: Sterling and Francine Clark Art Institute. 124–42.

────── in press. Sites of Persuasion – *Yingapungapu* at the National Museum of Australia, in I. Karp, C.A. Kratz, L. Szwaza and T. Ybarra-Frausto (eds), *Museum Frictions: Public Cultures/Global Transformations.* Durham: Duke University Press.

Morphy, H., P. Deveson and K. Hayne. 2005. *The Art of Narritjin Maymuru* (CD-ROM) Canberra: ANU E Press.

Morris B. 1990. Thoughts on Chinese Medicine. *Eastern Anthropologist* 42: 1–33.

Morris, H.S. 1953. *Report on a Melenau Sago Producing Community in Sarawak.* Colonial Research Studies No. 9. London: Colonial Office.

Murphy, S. 2005. *Securing Enough to Eat.* Winnipeg, Manitoba: International Institute for Sustainable Development.

Napier, J. 1967. The Antiquity of Human Walking, in *Human Variations and Origins: Readings from the Scientific American.* San Francisco: Freeman. 116–26.

Needham, J. 1956. *Science and Civilisation in China. Vol. 2: History of Scientific Thought.* Cambridge: Cambridge University Press.

Needham, R. 1967. Percussion and Transition. *Man* (N.S.) 2: 606–14.

────── 1981. Inner States as Universals, in R. Needham, *Circumstantial Deliveries.* Berkeley: University of California Press. 53–71.

Nichols, S. 2004. *Sentimental Rules: On the Natural Foundations of Moral Judgment.* Oxford: Oxford University Press.

Nucci, L. 1986. Children's Conceptions of Morality, Social Conventions, and Religious Prescription, in C. Harding (ed.), *Moral Dilemmas: Philosophical and Psychological Reconsiderations of the Development of Moral Reasoning.* Chicago: President Press.

Ohtsuka, R. 1983. Oriomo Papuans. Ecology of Sago-eaters in Lowland Papua. Tokyo: University of Tokyo Press.

Okamoto, A., T. Ozawa, H. Imagawa and Y. Arai. 1985. Polyphenolic Compounds Related to Browning of Sago Starch. *Nippon Nogeikagaku Kaishi* 59, 1257–62.

Oram, N. 1982. Pots for Sago: the Hiri Trading Network, in N. Oram, (ed.), *The Hiri in History. Further Aspects of Long Distance Motu Trade in Central Papua,* Canberra: The Australian National University Pacific Research Monograph Number Eight. 1–33.

——— 1992. Tommy Kabu. What Kind of Movement? *Canberra Anthropology* 15: 89–105.

Ots, T. 1987. *Medizin und Heilung in China: Annäherungen an die Traditionelle Chinesische Medizin.* Berlin: Reimer.

——— 1990. The Angry Liver, the Anxious Heart and the Melancholy Spleen: the Phenomenology of Perceptions in Chinese Culture. *Culture, Medicine, and Psychiatry* 14: 21–58.

Ozawa, T., A. Okamoto, H. Imagawa and Y. Arai. 1991. Oxidases for Phenolic Compounds Contained in Sago Palm Pith, in N. Thai-Tsiung, T. Yiu-Liong and K. Hong-Siong (eds), *Proceedings of the Fourth International Sago Symposium, Kuching, Sarawak, Malaysia.* Sarawak: Ministry of Agriculture and Community Development, and Department of Agriculture. 173–87.

Pandya, V. 1993. *Above the Forest: A Study of Andamanese Ethnoanemology, Cosmology, and the Power of Ritual.* Oxford: Oxford University Press.

Panter-Brick, C., A.W. Wardak, M. Eggerman and R. Crowther. 2005. Bio-psychosocial Markers of Mental Health: Research with Refugee, Street, and Non-displaced Afghan Youth in the Wake of War. *American Journal of Human Biology* 17: 266.

Parkin, D. 1985. Reason, Emotion and the Embodiment of Power, in J. Overing (ed.), *Reason and Morality.* London: Tavistock. 135–51.

——— 1991. *Sacred Void: Spatial Images of Work and Ritual among the Giriama of Kenya.* Cambridge: Cambridge University Press.

——— 1999. Conclusion: Suffer Many Healers, in J. Hinnells and R. Porter (eds), *Religion, Health and Suffering.* London and New York: Kegan Paul International. 433–58.

——— 2000. Invocation: *Salaa, Dua, Sadaka* and the Question of Self-determination, in D. Parkin and S.C. Headley (eds), *Islamic Prayer Across the Indian Ocean: Inside and Outside the Mosque.* Richmond, Surrey: Curzon.

Passi, S., M. Picardo, C. Zompetta, C. De-Luca, A.S. Breathnach and M. Nazzaro-Porro. 1991. The Oxyradical-scavenging Activity of Azelaic Acid in Biological Systems. *Free Radical Research Communications* 15: 17–28.

Pasveer, J. 2003. The Djief Hunters: 26,000 Years of Lowland Rainforest Exploitation on the Bird's Head of Papua, Indonesia. PhD thesis. Groningen, Rijksuniversiteit:

Pearse, A . 1901. Letter to Warlow Thompson. 24/3/–LMS Letters M1353. Canberra: National Library of Australia.

Peers, L. 1994. *The Ojibwa of Western Canada, 1780–1870*. Winnipeg and St. Paul: University of Manitoba and Minnesota Historical Society Presses.

—— 2003. Strands which Refuse to be Braided: Hair Samples from Beatrice Blackwood's Collection at the Pitt Rivers Museum. *Journal of Material Culture* 8(1): 75–96.

—— 2004. Repatriation: A Gain for Science? *Anthropology Today*, 20(6): 3–4.

Penniman, T.K. 1976. Obituary: Beatrice Mary Blackwood, 1889–1975. *American Anthropologist* 78(2): 321–22.

Petersen, J., E. Neves and M. Heckenberger. 2001. Gift from the Past: *terra preta* and Prehistoric Amerindian Occupation in Amazonia, in C. McEwan, C. Barreto and E. Neves (eds), *Unknown Amazon: Culture in Nature in Ancient Brazil*. London: British Museum Press. 50–85.

Petr, T. 1983. Aquatic Pollution in the Purari Basin, in T. Petr (ed.), *The Purari. Tropical Environment of a High Rainfall River Basin*. The Hague: Dr W. Junk Publishers. 325–39.

Petr, T. and J. Lucero. 1979. Sago Palm Salinity Tolerance in the Purari River Delta, in *Ecology of the Purari River Catchment*. Purari River (Wabo) Hydroelectric Scheme Environmental Studies, Volume 10. Waigani and Konedobu, Port Moresby: Office of Environment and Conservation and Department of Minerals and Energy.

Pfeiffer, J. E. 1982. *The Creative Explosion: An Inquiry into the Origins of Art and Religion*. New York: Harper and Row.

Pickering, W.S.F. Forthcoming. The Place of Emotion in the Religious Thought of Emile Durkheim (1858–1917).

Piña-Cabral, J. 2005. The Future of Social Anthropology. *Social Anthropology* 13(2): 119–28.

Piperno, D. and D. Persall. 1998. *The Origins of Agriculture in the Lowland Neotropics*. San Diego: Academic Press.

Platt, J.R. 1964. Strong Inference. *Science* 146: 347–53.

Pollard, T.M., N. Unwin, C. Fischbacher and J.K. Chamley. 2005. Reproductive Function in Women of South Asian Origin in the UK: A Biocultural Perspective. *American Journal of Human Biology* 17: 264.

Porkert, P. 1974. *The Foundations of Chinese Medicine: Systems of Correspondence*. Cambridge, MA: MIT Press.

Porter, R.H. and J.D. Moore. 1981. Human Kin Recognition by Olfactory Cues. *Physiology and Behavior* 27: 493–95.

Povinelli, D.J. 2000. *Folk Physics for Apes: The Chimpanzee's Theory of How the World Works*. Oxford: Oxford University Press.

Power, C. 1999. 'Beauty magic': the Origins of Art, in Knight, C., R. Dunbar and C. Power. (eds), *The Evolution of Culture: An Interdisciplinary View*. Edinburgh: Edinburgh University Press. 15–33.

Prentice, A.M., R.G. Whitehead, S.B. Roberts and A.A. Paul. 1981. Long-term Energy Balance in Child-bearing Gambian Women. *American Journal of Clinical Nutrition* 34: 2790–99.

Qiu Maoliang (ed.) 1985. *Zhenjiuxue (Acupuncture and Moxibustion)*. Shanghai: Shanghai Kexue Jishu Chubanshe.

Queen S. 1996. *From Chronicle to Canon: the Hermeneutics of the Spring and Autumn, According to Tong Chung-shu.* Cambridge: Cambridge University Press.

Rabinow P. [1984] 1991. *The Foucault Reader: An Introduction to Foucault's Thought.* Harmondsworth: Penguin.

Radcliffe-Brown, A.R. 1952. *Structure and Function in Primitive Society: Essays and Addresses.* London: Cohen and West.

Ramos, A. 1980. *Hierarquia e Simbiose: Relações Intertribais no Brasil.* São Paulo: Editora Hucitei.

Rappaport, R.A. 1968 (1984 a new enl. ed.). *Pigs for the Ancestors: Ritual in the Ecology of a New Guinea People.* New Haven and London: Yale University Press.

—— 1999. *Ritual and Religion in the Making of Humanity.* Cambridge: Cambridge University Press.

Rauwerdink, J.B. 1986. An Essay on Metroxylon, the Sago Palm. *Principes* 30: 165–80.

Rayner, A. 1997. *Degrees of Freedom: Living in Dynamic Boundaries.* London: Imperial College Press.

Ren. 1986. (see under *Huangdi neijing* References to Ren Yinqiu).

Renard-Casevitz, F.M. 2002. Social Forms and Regressive History: From the Campa Cluster to the Mojos and From the Mojos to the Landscaping Terrace-builders of the Bolivian Savanna, in J.D. Hill and F. Santos Granero (eds), *Comparative Arawakan Histories. Rethinking Language Family and Culture Area in Amazonia.* Urbana: University of Illinois Press. 123–46.

Reynolds, V. 1967. *The Apes, the Gorilla, Chimpanzee, Orangutan and Gibbon: Their History and Their World.* London.

Rhoads, J. 1982. Sago Palm Management in Melanesia: An Alternative Perspective. *Archaeology in Oceania* 17: 20–27.

Richards, A.I. 1932. *Hunger and Work in a Savage Tribe: A Functional Study in Nutrition Among the Southern Bantu.* London: Routledge.

Riley, I.A., D. Lehmann and M.P. Alpers. 1992. Acute Respiratory Infections, in R.D. Attenborough and M.P. Alpers (eds), *Human Biology in Papua New Guinea. The Small Cosmos,* Oxford: Oxford University Press. 281–88.

Rindos, D. 1984. *The Origins of Agriculture: An Evolutionary Perspective.* Orlando: Academic Press, and London: Routledge and Kegan Paul.

Rival, L. 1999. Introductory Essay on South American Hunters-and-Gatherers, in R. Lee and R. Daly (eds), *The Cambridge Encyclopedia of Hunters and Gatherers.* Cambridge and New York: Cambridge University Press. 77–85.

—— 2001. Seed and Clone. A Preliminary Note on Manioc Domestication, and its Implication for Symbolic and Social Analysis, in L. Rival and N. Whitehead (eds), *Beyond the Visible and the Material: the Amerindianization of Society in the Work of Peter Rivière.* Oxford: Oxford University Press. 57–80.

—— 2002. *Trekking Through History. The Huaorani of Amazonian Ecuador.* New York: Columbia University Press.

—— 2006. Amazonian Historical Ecologies, in R. Ellen (ed.), *Ethnobiology and the Science of Humankind: A Retrospective and a Prospective.* Special issue of JRAI. S79–S94.

———— 2006. *Huaorani Ways of Naming Trees.* Unpublished manuscript.

Rivière, P.G. 1985. Unscrambling Parenthood: The Warnock Report. *Anthropology Today* 1(4): 2–7.

Roosevelt, A. 1998. Ancient and Modern Hunter-gatherers of Lowland South America: An Evolutionary Problem, in W. Balée (ed.), *Advances in Historical Ecology.* New York: Columbia University Press. 190–212.

Rowlands, M. 2003. *Externalism.* Acumen Publisher Ltd.

Sagli, S. 2003. Acupuncture Recontextualized: The Reception of Chinese Medical Concepts among Practitioners in Norway. Ph.D. thesis, Department of General Practice and Community Health, University of Oslo.

Sahlins, M. 1977 (1976). *The Use and Abuse of Biology: An Anthropological Critique of Socio-biology.* London: Tavistock.

Salick, J. 1995. Toward an Integration of Evolutionary Ecology and Economic Botany: Personal Perspectives on Plant/People Interactions. *Ann. Missouri Bot. Garden* 82: 25–33.

Sauer, C.O. 1936. American Agricultural Origins: A Consideration of Nature and Agriculture, in R.H. Lowie (ed.), *Essays in Anthropology in Honor of A.L. Kroeber.* Berkeley: University of California Press. 279–98.

———— 1947. Early Relations of Man to Plants. *Geogr. Rev.* 37: 1–25.

Schell, L.M. 1991a. Effects of Pollutants on Human Prenatal and Postnatal Growth: Noise, Lead, Polychlorobiphenyl Compounds, and Toxic Wastes. *Yearbook of Physical Anthropology* 34: 157–88.

———— 1991b. Risk Focusing: An Example of Biocultural Interaction, in R. Huss-Ashmore, J. Schall and M. Hediger (eds), *Health and Lifestyle Change.* Philadelphia: MASCA Research Papers in Science and Archaeology Number 9. 137–44.

Schell, L., J. Ravenscroft, M. Gallo, M. Denham and M. Schneeberger. 2005. Advancing Biocultural Models by Working with Communities. *American Journal of Human Biology* 17: 266.

Scheid, P. 2002. *Chinese Medicine in Contemporary China.* Durham, NC and London: Duke University Press.

Scheper-Hughes, N. and M. Lock. 1987. The Mindful Body: a Prolegomenon to Future Work in Medical Anthropology. *Medical Anthropological Quarterly* 1(1): 6–41.

Schneider, D.M. 1984. *A Critique of the Study of Kinship.* Ann Arbor: University of Michigan Press.

Schurr, T.G. 2004. The Peopling of the New World: Perspectives from Molecular Anthropology. *Annual Review of Anthropology* 33: 551–83.

Seligmann, C.G. 1910. *The Melanesians of British New Guinea.* Cambridge: Cambridge University Press.

Serjeantson, S.W., P.G. Board and K.K. Bhatia. 1992. Population Genetics in Papua New Guinea: A Perspective on Human Evolution, in R.D. Attenborough and M.P. Alpers (eds), *Human Biology in Papua New Guinea. The Small Cosmos.* Oxford: Oxford University Press. 198–233.

Shiji 史記 (*Records of the Historian*). Han, c. 90 BC. (1959) 1975. Sima Qian 司馬遷. Beijing: Zhonghua shuju.

Silverman, S. 2005. The United States, in F. Barth, A. Gingrich, R. Parkin, and S. Silverman (eds), *One Discipline, Four Ways: British, German, French, and American Anthropology.* The Halle Lectures. Chicago and London: University of Chicago Press.

Singer, M. 1998. The Development of Critical Medical Anthropology: Implications for Miological Anthropology, in A.H. Goodman and T.L. Leatherman (eds), *Building a New Biocultural Synthesis. Political-economic Perspectives on Human Biology,* Ann Arbor: University of Michigan Press. 93–123.

Sivin, N. 1987. *Traditional Medicine in Contemporary China. A Partial Translation of* Revised Outline of Chinese Medicine (1972) *with an Introductory Study on Change in Present-day and Early Medicine.* Ann Arbor: Center for Chinese Studies, University of Michigan.

—— 1993. *Huang ti nei ching,* in M. Loewe (ed.), *Early Chinese Texts: a Bibliographical Guide.* Berkeley: Society for the Study of Early China and the Institute of East Asian Studies, University of California.

—— 1995a. State, Cosmos, and Body in the Last Three Centuries B.C. *Harvard Journal of Asiatic Studies* 55 (1): 5–37.

—— 1995b. IV: The Myth of the Naturalists, in *Medicine, Philosophy and Religion in Ancient China. Researches and Reflections.* Aldershot: Variorum. 1–33.

Skov, L. and B. Moeran (eds), 1995. *Women, Media and Consumption in Japan.* Richmond, Surrey: Curzon.

Smith, M.T. 1993. Genetic Adaptation, in G.A. Harrison (ed.), *Human Adaptation,* Oxford: Oxford University Press. 1–54.

Sober, E. 1980. Evolution, Population Thinking and Essentialism. *Philosophy of Science* 47: 350–83.

Southwold, M. 1979. Religious Belief. *Man* 14: 628–44.

Spelke, E.S. 1990. Principles of Object Perception. *Cognitive Science* 14: 29–56.

—— 1991. Psysical Knowledge in Infancy: Reflections on Piaget's Theory, in S. Carey and R. Gelman (eds), *Epigenesis of the Mind: Essays in Biology and Knowledge.* Hillsdale, NJ: Lawrence Erlbaum.

Spencer, P. 1974. Drought and the Commitment to Growth. *African Affairs* 73: 419–27.

Steward, J. and L. Faron. 1959. *Native Peoples of South America.* New York: McGraw-Hill.

Stewart, E. 2005. The Cognitive Foundations of Spirit Possession in an Afro-Brazilian Religious Tradition. Phd Dissertation, Queen's University Belfast.

Stiller, J., D. Nettle and R.I.M. Dunbar. 2004. The Small World of Shakespeare's Plays. *Human Nature* 14: 397–408.

Stinson, S., B. Bogin, R. Huss-Ashmore and D. O'Rourke. 2000. *Human Biology. An Evolutionary and Biocultural Perspective,* London: Wiley-Liss.

Storrie, R. 2003. Equivalence, Personhood and Relationality: Processes of Relatedness Among the Hoti of Venezuelan Guiana. *The Journal of the Royal Anthropological Institute* 9(3): 407–28.

Strathern, M. 1988. *The Gender of the Gift: [roblems with Women and [roblems with Society in Melanesia.* Berkeley and London: University of California.

—— 1991. Acknowledgements. *Reproducing the Future.* Manchester. Manchester University Press.

Strehlow, T.G.H. 1965. Culture, Social Structure, and Environment in Aboriginal Central Australia, in R.M. and C.H. Berndt (eds), *Aboriginal Man in Australia: Essays in Honour of Emeritus Professor A.P. Elkin.* Sydney: Angus and Robertson.

Stringer, C. Bones of Contentio. *Telegraph.* 12 November 2003.

Swadling, P., N. Araho and B. Ivuyo. 1991. Settlements Associated with the Inland Sepik-Ramu Sea. *Indo-Pacific Prehistory Association Bulletin* 11: 92–112.

Swedlund, A. and H. Ball. 1998. Nature, Nurture, and the Determinants of Infant Mortality: A Case Study from Massachusetts, 1830–1920, in A.H. Goodman and T.L. Leatherman, (eds), *Building a New Biocultural Synthesis. Political-economic Perspectives on Human Biology,* Ann Arbor: University of Michigan Press. 191–228.

Tambiah, S. 1996. *Leveling Crowds: Ethnonationalist Conflicts and Collective Violence in South Asia.* Berkeley and London: University of California Press.

Tanner, J.M. 1981. *A History of the Study of Human Growth.* Cambridge: Cambridge University Press.

Taussig, M. 2003. Viscerality, Faith and Scepticism: Another Theory of Magic, in B. Mayer and P. Pels (eds), *Magic and Modernity: Interfaces of Revelation and Concealment.* Stanford: Stanford University Press.

Taylor, K. 2005. *Chinese Medicine in Early Communist China 1945–1963: A Medicine of Revolution.* London: Routledge/Curzon.

Thomas, N. 1991. *Entangled Objects.* Cambridge, MA, and London: Harvard University Press.

Thomas, R.B. 1997. Wandering toward the Edge of Adaptability: Adjustments of Andean People to Change, in S.J. Ulijaszek and R.A. Huss-Ashmore (eds), *Human Adaptability: Past, Present and Future.* Oxford: Oxford University Press. 183–232.

——— 1998. The Evolution of Human Adaptability Paradigms: Toward a Biology of Poverty, in A.H. Goodman and T.L. Leatherman (eds), *Building a New Biocultural Synthesis. Political-economic Perspectives on Human Biology,* Ann Arbor: University of Michigan Press. 43–73.

Tomasello, M. 1999. *The Cultural Origins of Human Cognition,* Cambridge MA: Harvard University Press.

Tooby, J. and L. Cosmides. 1992. The Psychological Foundations of Culture, in J. Barkow, L. Cosmides, and J. Tooby (eds), *The Adapted Mind.* New York: Oxford University Press.

Toren, C. 2001. The Child in Mind, in H. Whitehouse (ed.), *The Debated Mind: Evolutionary Psychology versus Ethnography.* Oxford: Berg.

Torres, A.M., K.E. Peterson, A.C.T. de Souza, E.J. Orav, M. Hughes and L.C. Chen. 2000. Association of Diarrhoea and Upper Respiratory Infections with Weight and Height Gains in Bangladeshi Children aged 5 to 11 years. *Bulletin of the World Health Organization* 78: 1316–23.

Torun, B., P.S.W. Davies, M.B.E. Livingstone, M. Paolisso, R. Sackett and G.B. Spurr. 1996. Energy Requirements and Dietary Energy Recommendations for Children and Adolescents 1 to 18 years old. *European Journal of Clinical Nutrition* 50, S37–S81.

Townsend, P.K. 1974. Sago Production in a New Guinea Economy. *Human Ecology* 2: 217–36.

————— 2003. Resource Management in Asia-Pacific Working Paper No. 49 *Palm Sago: Further Thoughts on a Tropical Starch from Marginal Lands.* Resource Management in Asia-Pacific Working Paper No. 49. Canberra: Australian National University.

Trivers, R.L. and D. Willard. 1973. Natural Selection of Parental Ability to Vary the Sex Ratio. *Science* 179: 90–92.

Tulving, E. 1972. Episodic and Semantic Memory, in E. Tulving and W. Donaldson (eds), *Organization of Memory*. New York: Academic Press.

Turiel, E.1983. *The Development of Social Knowledge: Morality and Convention*. Cambridge: Cambridge University Press.

Turnbull, C. 1962. *The Forest People: A Study of the Pygmies of the Congo*. New York: Simon and Schuster.

Turner, V.W. 1969. *The Drums of Affliction*. Oxford: Clarendon Press.

————— 1974. *Dramas, Fields, and Metaphors: Symbolic Action in Human Society*. Ithaca, N.Y.: Cornell University Press.

Tuzin, D.F. 1980. *The Voice of the Tambaran: Truth and Illusion in Ilahita Arapesh Religion*. Berkeley: University of California Press.

Tylor, E.B. 1871. *Primitive Culture: Researches into the Development of Mythology, Philosophy, Religion, Art, and Custom*. London

————— 1903. (4th edition). *Primitive Culture*. Volume 1. John Murray. London.

Ulijaszek, S.J. 1983. Palm Sago (Metroxylon Species) as a Subsistence Crop. *Journal of Plant Foods* 5: 115–34.

————— 1990. Nutritional Status and Susceptibility to Infectious Disease, in G.A. Harrison and J.C. Waterlow (eds), *Diet and Disease*, Cambridge: Cambridge University Press. 137–54.

————— 1991. Traditional Methods of Sago Palm Management in the Purari Delta of Papua New Guinea, in N. Thai-Tsiung, T. Yiu-Liong and K. Hong-Siong (EDS) *Proceedings of the Fourth International Sago Symposium, Kuching, Sarawak, Malaysia*. Sarawak: Ministry of Agriculture and Community Development, and Department of Agriculture. 122–26.

————— 1993. Evidence for a Secular Trend in Heights and Weights of Adults in Papua New Guinea. *Annals of Human Biology* 20: 349–55.

————— 1995. *Human Energetics in Biological Society*. Cambridge: Cambridge University Press.

————— 1996. Long-term Consequences of Environmental Influences on Human Growth and Development: Toward a Theoretical Framework, in C.J.K. Henry and S.J. Ulijaszek (eds), *Long-term Consequences of Early Environment*, Cambridge: Cambridge University Press. 1–6.

————— 1996. Energetics, Adaptation and Adaptability. *American Journal of Human Biology* 8: 169–82.

————— 1997a. Human Adaptation and Adaptability, in S.J. Ulijaszek and R.A. Huss-Ashmore (eds), *Human Adaptability: Past, Present and Future*, Oxford: Oxford University Press. 7–16.

————— 1997b. Human Adaptability Research Methodology, in S.J. Ulijaszek and R.A. Huss-Ashmore (eds), *Human Adaptability: Past, Present and Future*. Oxford: Oxford University Press. 261–80.

———— 1998. Hypertension among Adults of the Purari Delta of the Gulf Province, Papua New Guinea Population. *Papua New Guinea Medical Journal* 41: 65–71.

———— 2001. Socioeconomic Status, Body Size and Physical Activity of Adults on Rarotonga, the Cook Islands. *Annals of Human Biology* 28: 554–63.

———— 2002. Sago, Economic Change and Nutrition in Papua New Guinea, in K. Kainuma, M. Okazaki, Y. Toyoda and J. Cecil (eds), *New Frontiers of Sago Palm Studies*, Tokyo: Universal Academy Press. 219–26.

———— 2003. Socioeconomic Factors Associated with Physique of Adults of the Purari Delta of the Gulf Province, Papua New Guinea. *Annals of Human Biology* 30: 316–28.

———— 2005a. Biocultural Perspectives on Food Security in Papua New Guinea. *American Journal of Human Biology* 17: 266–67.

———— 2005b. Purari Population Decline and Resurgence Across the Twentieth Century, in S.J. Ulijaszek (ed.). *Population, Reproduction and Fertility in Melanesia*, Oxford: Berghahn Books.

———— and J.A. Lourie 1994. Anthropometric Measurement Error, in S.J. Ulijaszek and C.G.N. Mascie-Taylor (eds), *Anthropometry: The Individual and the Population*, Cambridge: Cambridge University Press. 30–55.

———— and S.P. Poraituk. 1983. Subsistence Patterns and Sago Cultivation in the Purari Delta, in T. Petr, (ed). *The Purari – Tropical Environment of a High Rainfall River Basin.* The Hague: Dr. W. Junk Publications. 577–88.

———— and S.P. Poraituk. 1993. Making Sago: Is it Worth the Effort? in C.M. Hladik, A. Hladik, O.F. Linares, H. Pagezy, A. Semple and M. Hadley (eds), *Tropical Forests, People and Food. Biocultural Interactions and Applications to Development.* Paris: UNESCO Publications. 271–80.

———— and S.S. Strickland. 1993a. *Nutritional Anthropology. Prospects and Perspectives.* London: Smith Gordon.

———— and S.S. Strickland, eds. 1993b. *Seasonality and Human Ecology.* Cambridge: Cambridge University Press.

Unschuld, P.U. 1980. *Medizin in China. Eine Ideengeschichte.* München: Beck.

———— 1988. Culture and Pharmaceutics: Some Epistemological Observations on Pharmacological Systems in Ancient Europe and Medieval China, in S. Van der Geest and S. R. Whyte (eds), *The Context of Medicines in Developing Countries.* Dordrecht: Kluwer Academic Publishers. 179–97.

———— 2003. *Huang Di nei jing su wen: Nature, Knowledge, Imagery in an Ancient Chinese Medical Text.* Berkeley: University of California Press.

Unschuld P.U., J.S. Zheng and H. Tessenow. 2003. The Doctrine of the Five Periods and Six Qi in the *Huang Di nei jing su wen*, in P.U. Unschuld (ed.), *Huang Di nei jing su wen: Nature, Knowledge, Imagery in an Ancient Chinese Medical Text.* Berkeley: University of California Press. 385–488.

Valussi, E. 2003. Beheading the Red Dragon: a History of Female Inner Alchemy. Ph.D. thesis in History, School of Oriental and African Studies, University of London.

Verswijver, G. 1992. *The Club-fighters of the Amazon: Warfare Among the Kaiapo Indians of Central Brazil.* Gent: Rijksuniversiteit te Gent.

Viveiros de Castro, E. 1998. Cosmological Deixis and Amerindian
    Perpectivism. *Journal of the Royal Anthropological Institute* 4(3): 469–88.
de Walt, B.R. 1998. The Political Ecology of Population Increase and
    Malnutrition in Southern Honduras, in A.H. Goodman and T.L.
    Leatherman (eds), *Building a New Biocultural Synthesis. Political-economic
    Perspectives on Human Biology,* Ann Arbor: University of Michigan Press.
    295–316.
Wang A. 2000. *Cosmology and Political Culture in Early China.* Cambridge:
    Cambridge University Press.
Warry, W. 1998. *Unfinished Dreams: Community Healing and the Reality of
    Aboriginal Self-government.* Toronto: University of Toronto Press.
Watanabe, H. 1971. Running, Creeping and Climbing: A New Ecological and
    Evolutionary Perspective on Human Evolution. *Mankind* 8: 1–13.
Waterlow, J.C. 1992. *Protein Energy Malnutrition.* London: Edward Arnold.
Weber, M. [1921] 1980. *Wirtschaft und Gesellschaft. Grundriss der
    Verstehenden Soziologie.* 5. Auflage. Tübingen: Mohr.
———— 1930. *The Protestant Ethic and the Spirit of Capitalism.* London: George
    Allen and Unwin.
———— 1947. *The Theory of Social and Economic Organization.* Oxford: Oxford
    University Press.
Wedekind, C., T. Seebeck, F. Bettens and A.J. Paepke. 1995. MHC-dependent
    Mate Preferences in Humans. *Proc R Soc Lond B.* 260: 245–49.
Wedekind, C. and D. Penn. 2000. MHC Genes, Body Odours, and Odour
    Preferences. *Nephrol dial transplant.* 15: 1269–71.
Weiner, J.S. 1966. Major Problems in Human Population Biology, in P.T.
    Baker and J.S. Weiner (eds), *The Biology of Human Adaptability,* Oxford:
    Clarendon Press. 1–24.
Weiner, J.S and J.A. Lourie. 1969. *Human Biology. A Guide to Field Methods.*
    Oxford: Blackwell Scientific Publications.
———— 1981. *Practical Human Biology.* London: Academic Press.
Weismantel, M. 1995. Making Kin: Kinship Theory and Zumbagua
    Adoptions. *American ethnologist* 22: 685–704.
Wellman, H. 1990. *The Child's Theory of Mind.* Cambridge MA: MIT Press.
Werbner, R.P., ed. 1977. *Regional Cults.* London: Academic Press.
Wheeler, M. 2005. *Reconstructing the Cognitive World: The Next Step.*
    Cambridge, MA: MIT Press.
Whitehouse, H. 1995. *Inside the Cult: Religious Innovation and Transmission in
    Papua New Guinea.* Oxford: Oxford University Press.
———— 2000. *Arguments and Icons: Divergent Modes of Religiosity.* Oxford:
    Oxford University Press.
———— 2004. *Modes of Religiosity: A Cognitive Theory of Religious
    Transmission.* Walnut Creek, CA: AltaMira Press.
———— 2005. Emotion, Memory, and Religious Rituals: An Assessment of Two
    Theories, in K. Milton and M. Svasek (eds), *Mixed Emotions.* Oxford: Berg.
Whitehouse, H. and J.A. Laidlaw (eds). 2004. *Ritual and Memory: Toward a
    Comparative Anthropology of Religion.* Walnut Creek, CA: AltaMira Press.
Whitehouse, H. and L.H. Martin (eds). 2004. *Theorizing Religions Past:
    Archaeology, History and Cognition.* Walnut Creek, CA: AltaMira Press.

Whitehouse, H. and R.N. McCauley. 2005. *Mind and Religion: Psychological and Cognitive Foundations of Religiosity*. Walnut Creek, CA: AltaMira Press.

WHO, Health Education Unit .1986. Life-Styles and Health. *Social Science and*  *Medicine* 22(2): 117–24.

Wilbert, J. (ed.) 1961. *The Evolution of Horticultural Systems in Native South America. Causes and consequences*. Carracas, Venezuela: Antropológica Supplement 2.

Wiley, A.S. 1992. Adaptation and the Biocultural Paradigm in Medical Anthropology: A Critical Review. *Medical Anthropology Quarterly* 6: 216–36.

——— 2004. *An Ecology of High-altitude Infancy*. Cambridge: Cambridge University Press.

Williams, F.E. 1924. *The Natives of the Purari Delta*. Anthropological Report No. 5. Port Moresby: The Government Printer.

——— (1940) *Drama of Orokolo: The Social and Ceremonial Life of the Elema*. Oxford: Clarendon Press.

Williams, J.H.G., A. Whiten, T. Suddendorf and D.I. Perrett. 2000. Imitation, Mirror Neurons, and Autism, in *Neuroscience and Biobehavioural Reviews* 25: 287–95.

Wilson, E.O. 1975. *Sociobiology: The New Synthesis*. Cambridge, MA: Belknap Press of Harvard University Press.

Wilson, D.S. 2002. *Darwin's Cathedral*. Chicago: University of Chicago Press.

Winterhalder, B. 1981. Optimal Foraging Strategies and Hunter Gatherer Research in Anthropology: Theories and Models, in B. Winterhalder and E.A. Smith (eds), *Hunter-Gatherer Foraging Strategies*. Chicago: University of Chicago Press. 13–35.

Winterhalder, B. and C. Goland. 1993. On Population, Foraging Efficiency and Plant Domestication. *Current Anthropology* 34: 710–15.

Winthrop, K. 2001. Historical Ecology: Landscapes of Change in the Pacific Northwest, in C. Crumley (ed.), *New Directions in Anthropology and Environment*. Walnut Creek: Altamira Press. 203–22.

Wolf, E. 1961. Concluding Comments, in J. Wilbert (ed.), *The Evolution of Horticultural Systems in Native South America. Causes and Consequences*. Caracas: Editorial Sucre. 111–16.

Working Group on Human Remains. 2003. Report. Department of Culture, Media and Sport. Available at: www.culture.gov.uk/cultural_property/ wg_human_remains/default.htm

Wrangham, R.W. (in press). The Cooking Enigma, in P. Ungar. (ed). *Early Hominin Diets: The Known, the Unknown, and the Unknowable*. Oxford: Oxford University Press.

Wrangham, R.W. and N.L. Conklin-Brittain. 2003. The Biological Significance of Cooking in Human Evolution. *Comparative Biochemistry and Physiology, Part A* 136: 35–46.

Yin Huihe 印會河 (ed.), 1984. *Zhongyi jichu lilun* 中醫基礎理論 (*TCM Fundamentals*). Shanghai: Shanghai keji chubanshe.

Young, A. 1976. Internalizing and Externalizing Medical Belief Systems: An Ethiopian Example. *Social Science and Medicine* 10: 147–56.

Zhou, W-X., D. Sornette, R.A. Hill and R.I.M. Dunbar. (2005). Discrete
    Hierarchical Organization of Social Group Sizes. *Proceedings of the Royal
    Society of London* 272B: 439–44.
Zimmermann, F. 1987. *The Jungle and the Aroma of Meats: an Ecological Theme
    in Hindu Medicine.* Berkeley: University of California Press.

INDEX